A Concise History of France

This is the most up-to-date and comprehensive study of French history available, ranging from the early Middle Ages to the present. Among its central themes are the relationships between state and society, the impact of war, competition for power and the ways in which power has been used. While taking full account of major figures such as Philip Augustus, Henri IV, Louis XIV, Napoleon and de Gaulle, it sets their activities within the broader context of changing economic and social structures and beliefs, and offers rich insights into the lives of ordinary men and women. This third edition has been substantially revised and includes a new chapter on contemporary France – a society and political system in crisis as a result of globalisation, rising unemployment, a failing educational system, growing social and racial tensions, corruption, the rise of the extreme right and a widespread loss of confidence in political leaders.

ROGER PRICE is Emeritus Professor of History at Aberystwyth University. He has written extensively on French history; his more recent publications include *The French Second Empire: An Anatomy of Political Power* (2001) and *People and Politics in France, 1848–1870* (2004).

D0162076

CAMBRIDGE CONCISE HISTORIES

This is a series of illustrated 'concise histories' of selected individual countries, intended both as university and college textbooks and as general historical introductions for general readers, travellers, and members of the business community.

For a list of titles in the series, see end of book.

A Concise History of France

THIRD EDITION

ROGER PRICE

CAMBRIDGE
UNIVERSITY PRESS

CAMBRIDGE
UNIVERSITY PRESS

University Printing House, Cambridge CB2 8BS, United Kingdom

One Liberty Plaza, 20th Floor, New York, NY 10006, USA

477 Williamstown Road, Port Melbourne, VIC 3207, Australia

4843/24, 2nd Floor, Ansari Road, Daryaganj, Delhi - 110002, India

79 Anson Road, #06-04/06, Singapore 079906

Cambridge University Press is part of the University of Cambridge.

It furthers the University's mission by disseminating knowledge in the pursuit of education, learning and research at the highest international levels of excellence.

www.cambridge.org
Information on this title: www.cambridge.org/9781107603431

© Cambridge University Press 1993, 2005, 2014

First published 1993
Reprinted 1993, 1994, 1995, 1999, 2001, 2004
Second edition 2005
Third edition 2014

A catalogue record for this publication is available from the British Library

ISBN 978-1-107-01782-5 Hardback
ISBN 978-1-107-60343-1 Paperback

CONTENTS

PLATES

The author and publishers acknowledge the following sources of copyright material and are grateful for the permissions granted. While every effort has been made, it has not always been possible to identify the sources of all material used, or to trace all copyright holders. If any omissions are brought to our notice, we will be happy to include the appropriate acknowledgements on reprinting.

FIGURES

TABLES

ACKNOWLEDGEMENTS

The author of a general work of this kind owes a great deal to many people, including the students taking my courses at the University of East Anglia between 1968 and 1993 and subsequently at Aberystwyth, colleagues past and present, and the library staff at both institutions, as well as those at the National Library of Wales. I am especially grateful to William Davies of Cambridge University Press for setting me the challenge in the first place and subsequently for encouraging other projects. His successor, Michael Watson, together with Isabelle Dambricourt and Chloe Dawson, provided valuable assistance in the preparation of subsequent editions, as did Elizabeth Friend-Smith, Fleur Jones and Abigail Jones. The following friends read and commented on the original manuscript: Malcolm Crook, Colin Heywood, Oliver Logan and the greatly missed Peter Morris. Heather Price has made an enormous contribution. Richard Johnson at the University of East Anglia drew some of the maps, and Mary Richards, Jean Field and Mike Richardson, copy-editors for Cambridge University Press, made extremely helpful suggestions.

For their constructive criticism, for their patience, for their love and for laughter, I remain profoundly grateful to Richard, Luisa, Luca and Charlotte; to Siân, Andy, Molly and Lilly; to Emily, Dafydd and Eleri; to Hannah and Simon; and to my dearest Heather.

Introduction

The entity we know as France is the product of a centuries-long evolution, during which a complex of regional societies was welded together by political action, by the desire for territorial aggrandisement of a succession of monarchs, ministers and soldiers. There was nothing inevitable about the outcome. It was far from being a linear development, and we must try to avoid a teleological approach to explaining its course. The central feature was the emergence of a relatively strong state in the Ile-de-France and the expansion of its authority. Our task is to explain how and why this occurred.

The invitation to write a book covering such an extensive chronological period raises prospects both attractive and daunting. It represents an opportunity to set the normally more restricted concerns of the professional historian within a broad historical context, but also creates major problems of perspective and of approach. Questions will always be asked concerning 'the extent to which it is possible to reconstruct the past from the remains it has left behind' (R. J. Evans). The evidence historians have to deal with is made up of fragments, often chance survivals, which need to be contextualised in an effort to reconstruct their meaning. Every history is selective, but none more so than a work covering so many centuries. The problem is what to select, how best to make sense of the chaos of events, of the succession of generations that is at the heart of history, and how to define historical time and the shifting boundaries between continuity and change. A descriptive, chronologically organised political history would be possible, but would run the risk of turning into a meaningless catalogue of great men and their acts.

The emergence of social history from the 1920s, often associated with Marc Bloch and Lucien Febvre, founders of the so-called *Annales* school, required even the political historian to set great men and the evolving institutions of the state within the context of changing social systems. As historians continued their self-critical dialogue with the past and debated the relative importance of economic, cultural and ideological factors in the process of social formation and change, a proliferation of approaches developed. The appealing simplicities of a structuralist, class-based and neo-Marxist approach, associated in the 1960s and 1970s with Fernand Braudel and Ernest Labrousse, were rejected as over-deterministic and leading to a reductionist neglect of the 'historical actors', of 'culture' and of community. A determination to integrate the 'poor' into the historical record was followed by a desire to recognise the significance of gender and ethnicity as keys to the explanation of choice and behaviour. The insights of social anthropology have also been deployed to create an awareness of the importance of language, images and symbolic action in the construction of social identity and of a 'cultural' history that assumes that ideology, rather than society and the economy, is central to the human experience.

In the absence of general laws of historical development and as a result of a greater awareness of the sheer complexity of human interaction, a crisis of confidence developed amongst historians. This deepened in the face of a challenge from a 'post-structuralist' and 'postmodernist' philosophy associated with Michel Foucault, Jacques Derrida and others, which, at its most extreme, emphasises that every perception of 'reality' is mediated by language, that every text has a range of possible meanings and that historical research itself is nothing more than a reflection on discourse. If the past has no reality outside the historians' representation of it, it follows that 'reality' cannot be distinguished from its representation. History thus becomes merely one literary genre amongst others, little different from the novel.

Valuable in encouraging historians to question their assumptions, a post-structuralism that challenges the bases on which the social sciences have been constructed, including the belief in a verifiable knowledge and the value of empirical research, has ultimately to be dismissed as an intellectual dead end: as little more than the rehashing of ancient philosophical arguments concerning the nature of reality. Jargon-ridden and increasingly self-referential, postmodernism became a caricature of itself, an arrogant and élitist linguistic game. Whilst it is important to acknowledge the need to develop more complex and inclusive models of causation, it is also vital to approach 'culture and identity, ...language and consciousness, as changing phenomena to be explained rather than as the ultimate explanation of all other social phenomena' (Tilly). Individuals develop a social awareness within the multiplicity of complex situations experienced in daily life. Identity is not a constant. The construction of a meaningful explanatory context by the historian requires acknowledgement of the large- as well as the small-scale structures that impinge on the individual and provide the bases for social interaction.

The real crisis facing history is probably its fragmentation. Typically the professional historian engages in research leading to the publication of monographs designed to advance knowledge and analysis, in teaching intended to develop critical and questioning attitudes amongst students and in what the French refer to as 'vulgarisation' – a most unfortunate term to describe the essential task of communicating with the widest possible audience. The challenge this imposes is to reconcile professional credibility with the commercial demands of the media. Both in print and on television, demands for accessibility threaten to result in simplifying distortions of complex historical situations and a return to the worst kind of descriptive history, together with accounts of the deeds of the great that, by downplaying context, ignore the revolution in historical method inaugurated almost a century ago by Bloch and Febvre.

The central theme of this book is thus the continuing process of interaction between state and society. The state has been defined by the historical sociologist Theda Skocpol (in *States and Social Revolution*, 1979) as 'a set of administrative, policing and military organisations headed, and more or less well coordinated, by an executive authority'. The maintenance of these administrative and coercive organisations of course requires the extraction of resources from society – demands that are magnified in the case of war, which has in consequence served as a major stimulus to the evolution of state institutions. At least since John Locke, liberal writers have tended to concentrate on the state as a morally neutral force, enforcing law and order and defending its citizens against external threats. This ignores the question of the social origins of legislators and law enforcers, the ways in which they perceived their roles, and their attitudes towards those over whom they ruled. The alternative tradition is represented by Karl Marx and the Italian sociologists Vilfredo Pareto and Gaetano Mosca, who saw the state as the instrument of a ruling minority, and by Antonio Gramsci, who insisted upon the significance not only of coercive state institutions but of the cultural predominance achieved by social élites as means of maintaining social control and limiting the impact of otherwise competing value systems.

This is not to argue that the state somehow automatically represents the interests of a socially dominant class. It is certainly not to argue that the state is ever a unified entity. Its capacity for intervention in society varies over time and between places. The state's engagement in institutional, political and military competition and efforts to strengthen its own institutions might well lead to conflict over the appropriation of resources. Nevertheless, the recruitment of senior state officials overwhelmingly from amongst members of social élites, and the superior capacity of these to influence the representatives of the state, strongly suggest a predominating influence. Even if this is accepted, however, competition *within* the élites to influence or control state activities remains a potent source of conflict.

The central questions posed are about political power. Why is it so important? Who possesses it? How is it used? In whose interests, and with what consequences? How do *subjects* react to the activities of *rulers*? The likelihood of collective resistance appears to have been determined by established perceptions of rights and justice, capacity for organisation, opportunities for protest, and perceptions of the likelihood of success or the prospects of repression, and thus to have been influenced by changes both in social structures and relationships and in institutional arrangements. Why does political change occur?

It should be evident that these are questions about social systems as well as political structures and behaviour. Indeed, it should be obvious that social order is maintained not simply, or even primarily, through state activity but by means of a wide range of social institutions, including the family and local community, religious, educational and charitable bodies, and tenurial and workplace relationships – not according to some carefully conceived overall plan but because the processes of socialisation, and day-to-day contacts, serve to legitimise and enforce a wide range of dependencies. The forms of control exercised are largely determined by the attitudes created in daily life – in short, by the rationale of the age, and of the group – as well as by the social structure and resources employed by both the state and social élites. The sense of powerlessness so common amongst the poor and their need to be prudent suggest that the absence of overt conflict does not necessarily mean the non-existence of social and political tension.

Some social groups have been privileged as subjects for historical study, others marginalised. Fashions change, however, as the development of 'history from below' and of less condescending attitudes towards the urban and rural populations has made clear. Predominantly male historians, employing documentary sources largely produced by men, have also been accused – and with reason – of gender blindness. This is not the place to argue the merits of community or class as opposed to gender as analytical categories, nor to consider the practical difficulties of introducing gender as a concept into a history of France. Suffice it to say what has become and always should have been obvious, namely that men and women have unique as well as shared experiences and that gendered perceptions affect the formation of social identity and the whole range of economic, social and political discourse and activity. The historian's objective ought to be 'to integrate any experience that was defined by gender into the wider social and economic framework' (Hufton), whilst acknowledging that gender too is culturally and historically conditioned.

Another dimension that we would ignore at our peril is the spatial – a theme that Fernand Braudel, reflecting the French tradition of close association between history and geography, made so much his own. The crucial importance of communications networks in limiting or facilitating the scope of both economic and political activity, and the diffusion of ideas, will become obvious in the course of this book. The main purpose of this brief introduction, however, is to set the scene by considering some of the continuities in French history.

An obvious feature of France (within its modern boundaries) is its geographical diversity. The geographer Philippe Pinchemel distinguishes five natural regions: an oceanic and temperate zone in the *north-west*, extending from the Vendée to Champagne, which is a lowland region, covered with a thick layer of fertile soil with abundant rainfall; the *north-east*, an area of plateaux and limestone cuestas with, apart from isolated fertile areas, poor soils, and suffering from severe continental climatic conditions; the *south-west*, with its plains, hills and plateaux, is greener, more fertile and less rock-strewn than the *south-east*, which is a region stretching from the Limousin to the plains of Provence, from Roussillon to the plains of the Saône, which he describes as a 'mosaic...full of natural contrasts', with infertile limestone plateaux, and steep hillsides interspersed with small, discontinuous, and fertile areas of plain and valley enjoying a Mediterranean climate; and, finally, the *mountains* – the Massif Central, Jura, Alps and Pyrenees – which are inhospitable to settlement because of their thin soils and short growing season, and obstacles to the movement of people and goods. If in general terms the north belongs to the temperate climatic zone, and the south with its dry summers and high temperatures to the Mediterranean, the mountains complicate the picture, in particular pushing northern climatic traits towards the south. Furthermore, as one moves inland, oceanic climatic traits give way to continental tendencies. In climatic terms, then, France is characterised by important local variations, by a high degree of irregularity and seasonal anomalies in temperature and rainfall. Since time immemorial, and well into the nineteenth century – for as long as low-productivity agricultural systems and isolation persisted – the menace posed to staple cereal harvests by adverse climatic conditions, most notably in the north by wet summers and in the south by drought, represented the threat of malnutrition or worse for the poor. At no other time was the pivotal question of the control of scarce resources, of access to land and food supplies, presented with such acuity. By intensifying social tension, poor harvests created major political problems.

Nevertheless, societies subjected to climatic stress were capable of adaptation. The development of the French landscape is indeed evidence of continuous human adjustment, not only to geographical imperatives but also to changing population densities and to

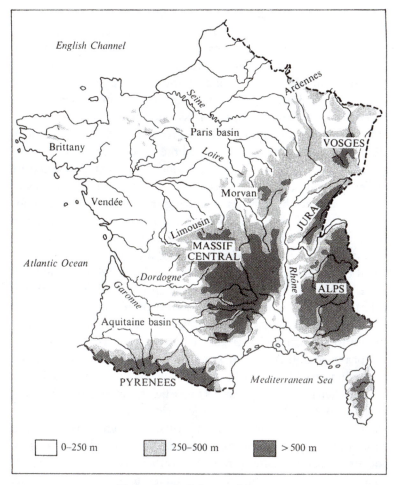

Figure I.1 Relief map of France

socio-political pressures. Rural and urban landscapes alike are the product of a complex interaction between natural conditions and technological and demographic change, and of the complicated overlap between phases of development. The twentieth century, and especially the post-Second-World-War years with mechanisation, the use of chemical weedkillers and fertilisers and the amalgamation of farms, saw more thoroughgoing changes than any other, but the contrasts between areas of enclosed and open field, often created in the Middle Ages as settlement spread along the river valleys and plains and lower slopes, still affect the landscape. In Picardy, the Ile-de-France, Nord and Champagne, and much of eastern France in particular, wide open spaces with few trees are associated with nucleated villages and the concentration of population, although the customary practices associated with the communal grazing and collective rotation of the three-field system began to disappear from the early nineteenth century. The Mediterranean region, even though the transport revolution transformed the agriculture of its plains by giving access to mass markets for wine, also remains marked by earlier structures, with its concentrated habitat and the remains of terraces cut into the hillsides, signifying the continuing struggle for subsistence. Only from the late nineteenth century, as population densities in the countryside declined, as autarky became unnecessary with access to reliable external supplies, did the long extension of cereal cultivation come to an end. Throughout the west, the landscape is still marked by enclosure and dispersed settlement patterns, indicating a gradual process of colonisation of the land in the Middle Ages. Although changes in scale have obviously occurred, the basic structure of settlement has remained remarkably permanent since the end of the Middle Ages. Thick hedges or granite walls mark boundaries and provide shelter for animals, whilst complex networks of often sunken lanes provide access to the fields. Lower Normandy and Brittany, Anjou, Maine and the Vendée provide other distinctive types, where arable farming in the valley bottoms was combined with the exploitation of forest resources and upland pastures. Soil structures and natural resources rather than farming methods affected the capacity of local economies to sustain population. Densities therefore varied considerably as did living standards. Traditional building styles, often disguised by modern additions, provide further reminders of past regional distinctiveness. The railway, motor transport and declines in transport costs have led to the mass production of building materials and greater uniformity in construction in both town and country as brick, and later concrete, replaced worked stone or wood.

In the traditional social system prevailing until the nineteenth century – overwhelmingly rural – the major stimulus to increased agricultural production was population growth, and the means

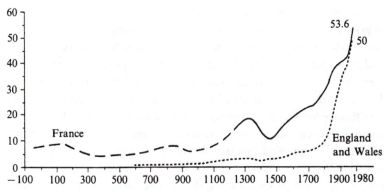

Figure I.2 Comparative evolution of population (in millions). France, and England and Wales.

employed to secure more food involved primarily the cultivation of previously unused land, and the more frequent cropping of the existing arable land, with slow improvements in crop rotation. Overuse and the farming of marginal land reduced productivity and increased the likelihood of harvest failure, undernourishment, the spread of disease, and the high mortality associated with a generally impoverished environment. This largely explains the obsessive popular concern with subsistence. In modern society the main stimulus to increasing agricultural production is urbanisation, and the changes in diet made possible by industrialisation and greater prosperity. Food supplies are secure because of the possibility of importation, and productivity increased by means primarily of technical change – fodder crops, increased specialisation and, most recently, motorisation, fertilisers, weedkillers, artificial insemination, and selective animal and plant breeding accompanied by the amalgamation of farms. Capital has increasingly replaced land and labour as the major factor of production. Cheap bulk transport and the more rapid diffusion of information have brought new opportunities for farmers, but within far more competitive markets.

The evolution of the population also had a major impact on the environment, promoting successive waves of land clearance and the cutting down of forests until the later nineteenth century, and then, through urbanisation, the extension of towns and cities into the surrounding rural areas, and the reconstruction of the cities themselves, as

railway lines and broad boulevards permitted the easier penetration
of goods and people, and eliminated the picturesque confusion of the
late medieval to early modern structures, which survived until the
middle of the nineteenth century. Again, the post-1945 years have
seen far more extensive destruction and building than ever before.
The centuries-long creation of an urban network has been of crucial
significance for the overall development of French society. In so many
respects, market villages and towns of varying sizes were the essential
dynamic element within society. Growing as they did on crossroads in
the communications systems, their demands served to stimulate the
rural production of foodstuffs and manufactures, whilst additionally
they exercised growing administrative and political control over their
hinterlands.

Constructing a typology is difficult. Slow and expensive communications promoted the development of a network of often small
market centres. Most small towns achieved only local or regional
significance. The larger centres were, even before the coming of the
railway, served by high-capacity water- or seaborne links and by the
circulation of thousands of little barges or ships. Paris, benefiting
from the Seine and its tributaries, which brought food, fuel and
timber for construction, played a central historical role, as did
major regional centres such as Lyon, and ports such as Marseille,
Bordeaux and Rouen. Their location and activities and those of
their hinterlands clearly affected the regional distribution of wealth.
They exercised considerable administrative and cultural influence
and served as residential centres for local élites and a complex
mixture of professional and craftsmen. They also attracted large
numbers of the poor and destitute in hope of work or charity.
Industrialisation promoted a process of selective and accelerated
growth within this essentially medieval urban network. In order to
meet the needs of growing populations for housing, work, services,
education and hygiene, and to ease the movement of goods and
people, the fabric of towns underwent a drastic transformation.
Here again, it was population growth, improved communications
and market integration that encouraged technological innovation.
The structure and technology of manufacturing activity had remained
fundamentally unchanged since the Middle Ages. The late eighteenth
and nineteenth centuries saw the application of mechanical power in

the factory system, competing with traditional dispersed urban and rural workshops. This heralded an era of continued and accelerating technological innovation, with especially rapid phases of growth in the 1840s and 1890s, and after 1945.

The stress upon communications is surely not misplaced. The quality of links by land and water determined not just the possibilities for trade, the structure of demand for food and manufactures and the capacity of city populations to grow, but also the ability of governments to inform themselves, to pass on instructions and to impose their authority. Before the nineteenth-century transport revolution, the sheer size of France and its continental structure made the problems of communication and control far more acute than in Britain, an island easily penetrated by water.

The unity initially imposed by political activity and military power was reinforced by means of an increasingly pervasive communications revolution, a process beginning in the eighteenth century with the improvement of roads and waterways and proceeding by means of the introduction of fundamentally new technologies – railways, telegraphy, telephones and, most recently, information technology, with their impact reinforced through universal education and the mass media. These innovations have provided previously undreamed-of facilities for the movement of people and products, and for the means of entertainment, of education and, ultimately, of social control. Through them was created a more highly developed sense of belonging to a particular political community, and eventually of national identity in the contemporary meaning. Economic, social, cultural and political integration are thus all fundamentally dependent upon the development of the means of communication and, with a genuine circularity, upon the demand for better communications inspired by changing perceptions of a society's economic, cultural and political needs.

The structure of this book is dictated by its length and by its main objective, which is to provide the reader with an understanding of contemporary France. It is impossible to understand the present without considering the past, but it might be argued that the impact of the past declines with time, so the recent past receives more detailed consideration than periods less close to our own. Each of the chapters focuses on a more or less lengthy period identified by the predominance of continuity over change in the evolution of economic and social structures and political problems. The long medieval and early modern period was characterised by the struggle of kings anxious to assert themselves against the claims of territorial magnates and an unruly nobility, within the context of a population system in which growth was kept in check by low agricultural productivity and repeated Malthusian crises, and the economy was characterised by the slow penetration of rural society by capitalism and urban initiative. The Revolution and Empire were consequences of the failure to establish a coherent and effective political system and resulted in the rise of a mass politics within the context of a society already experiencing the first stages of a transition to modern capitalism. The period from 1815 to 1914 saw the acceleration of economic, social and political change, and a long struggle between the proponents of political reform (of *mouvement*) and those of *résistance*, the latter supported usually by the state. This was followed by a period of economic and social stagnation and devastating war from 1914 to 1945, and then the unprecedently prosperous decades of reconstruction and economic growth, and of massive social change, that followed the Second World War. The final chapter focuses on the emergence since the 1970s of a post-industrial society, and on the opportunities and costs of continuing European integration and of a wider globalisation. Inevitably, given the delay between writing and publication, this book will tend to be out of date in some respects as far as the present is concerned. If it assists in the understanding of events it has not even contemplated, however, it can be counted a success.

MEDIEVAL AND EARLY MODERN FRANCE

INTRODUCTION

The purpose of this section is to consider the making and evolution of the social and political systems that developed in France during the Middle Ages and early modern period until 1789 – the emergence of what German historians have labelled the *Lehnstaat*, or feudal monarchy, and of its successor *Ständestaat*, or state of the society of orders. This was a world ruled by kings and princes with a dominant aristocratic and noble social élite, and which, in spite of its burgeoning towns, remained overwhelmingly rural and agricultural. Power depended both upon wealth and the control of scarce resources, and especially access to land, and upon status, defined as a 'social estimation of honour' by the German sociologist Max Weber, and accorded in particular to the priests, who prayed for human salvation, and to the warriors, who defended society. These concepts, sanctified by the Church, legitimised social relationships and served to justify a complex of contemporary modes of social control. In the last resort, however, the ability to squeeze taxes, rents, feudal dues and tithes out of the population depended upon the use of armed force.

When might France be said to have come into existence? As we shall see, the process of state construction was gradual, uneven and interrupted. In the aftermath of the collapse of the Roman Empire and of the Frankish kingdoms that replaced it, this involved the creation of political organisations capable of assuming control over broader territories, and of mobilising their economic and human resources. It took the form of a struggle between competing territorial magnates for local, regional and, finally, national supremacy. In this process some political units grew in size at the expense of their competitors. To a large extent this is a history of war, but military prowess was closely linked to processes of commercialisation, improved communications and urban growth. These were developments that had positive appeal to territorial magnates. The growth of bureaucratic and military power increased their ability both to subordinate subjects and to wage external war. The development of the state thus involved a reinforcement of the means of social control but also served as a cause of conflict, the latter due to competition within élites internally and to resistance by non-élites to efforts to control and exploit them, as well as to rivalry with external competitors. For the subject peoples there was nothing like a modern sense of nationalism. By the late Middle Ages a vague sense of loyalty to a particular dynasty might have been created, and, derived from the Hundred Years War, a sense of being different from other peoples. Even then, local solidarities and the strength of custom and culture make it extremely difficult to generalise about either social or political developments. A process of socialisation within the family and small face-to-face community determined the outlook of most of the population. This established norms of behaviour and provided an essentially self-regulating mechanism of control, within which respect for the priest and seigneur was usually an unquestioning response to the desire for security and sustenance in this world and salvation in the world hereafter. Of course, this is not to deny that relationships habitually based upon deference and cooperation could not, in certain circumstances, breed hostility and conflict.

I

Population and resources
in pre-industrial France

Historians have too often allowed their interest in dramatic political events to obscure more fundamental historical realities – the continuities in the economic and social structures that so profoundly shaped political systems. France remained an overwhelmingly agrarian society for centuries, with rural inhabitants continuing to account for around 85 per cent of the total population even in the eighteenth century. The pace of change was slow and subject to regression, with farmers barely able to produce sufficient food to support themselves, let alone the élites and town dwellers who depended upon them. Throughout the centuries considered in this chapter, although productive techniques in both agriculture and industry improved and the organisation of communications and trade became more efficient, there were no fundamental structural changes in the mode of production and distribution of commodities. The process of capital accumulation was inevitably limited by mass poverty. The repeated cycles in which population growth first stimulated increased production, but was then brought to an end by shortages of food and demographic crisis, are proof of this. Only towards the end of this long period, in the eighteenth century, can signs of fundamental change and the emergence of a new, far more productive economic and social system be detected.

Societies employing relatively simple technologies tend to experience slow change. Lack of information renders judgements concerning the pace of this change hazardous, with such key indicators as the yields of arable crops clearly varying considerably between places and from year to year. Recent research suggests that between the ninth and thirteenth centuries cereal yields might have doubled from around 2.5 to 4 plants per seed, reflecting the stimuli of population growth and increasing trade. Water power and, from the twelfth century, windmills were increasingly employed to ease the task of milling. Food supply was generally adequate, and its nutritional quality probably improving. Instability and uncertainty were constant characteristics of traditional society, however. With such low ratios of seed to yield, a reduction in the harvest of, say, a third below 'normal' meant that the available food supply had been halved, since half the remaining corn had to be retained as seed. For the longer term, these centuries of relatively secure subsistence encouraged earlier marriage and population growth, so that pressure on food resources was evident again by the late thirteenth century and certainly in the fourteenth century. Wheat yields varying between 2.5 per seed in the Alps and an exceptional 8 to 9 on the fertile plains north of Paris were characteristic of the early fourteenth century. Productivity was stagnant, reflecting an inability to improve technology to the degree necessary to produce a lasting increase in per capita output or to protect food supply. Traditional agricultural systems were certainly more flexible than is often assumed. That they were able to respond to the growing population and enlarged market opportunities is evinced by an accumulation of minor changes and the spread of market gardening, orchards and dairy farming around major towns, by the vineyards on slopes around Paris, the provision of industrial raw materials such as wool, flax and woad and the cultivation of cereals on large market-orientated farms belonging to the crown, nobles and – increasingly – the urban bourgeoisie. There were major regional differences in population densities and levels of socio-economic development, however. In most places poor communications meant that there was little stimulus to produce for markets outside the local community and strong pressures to ensure its own supply of food.

Characteristic of most areas was the *petite culture* typical of impoverished people making the best of local natural resources in response to an essentially short-term perspective. Peasant farmers sought greater security and status through the purchase or rent of land. They remained poorly clothed, ill-housed and badly fed, and

Plate 1.1 Peasant ploughing, end twelfth century. Note the wheels and metal ploughshare. Horses tended to remain a luxury for centuries longer and oxen or cows were used as draught animals.

were motivated by risk avoidance rather than profit – a rational pattern of behaviour when markets were fragmented by poor communications and food supply remained insecure. The peasant concentrated upon the production of cereals, keeping only those livestock required for milk, meat or wool, or as draught animals. His essential aim was to provide for the subsistence needs of the household. Innovations in terms of new plants or work practices were accepted only when they did not threaten the existing equilibrium. The constant problem was how to maintain the fertility of the soil. The small numbers of livestock limited the supply of precious fertilising manure, and forced farmers to leave one-third – or, on poor soils, as much one-half – of the land fallow each year in order to rest it and to provide pasture. Caring for the soil was essential if disastrous long-term consequences were to be avoided. In the shorter term removing land from cultivation was an often intolerable burden for the poor, and had to be imposed by collective pressure. The shortage of draught animals and prevalence of light ploughs meant that successful farming depended on back-breaking human activity, using hand tools. Only in Flanders, on account of the close presence of urban markets, the use of town waste as fertiliser, and relatively high crop yields, were farmers able, during the Middle Ages, to break out of this unproductive system, to suppress the fallow and cultivate root crops as feed for higher densities of livestock. The process required more oxen and horses, ploughs, harnesses, harrows and rakes, scythes and sickles, wagons and barrels, stimulating demand for the services of agricultural labourers and rural artisans, and for iron for tools. Although the slow replacement of oxen and human labour by horses together with the use of iron plough tips, especially in the larger farms and in northern France from the later twelfth century, allowed more rapid, deeper and repeated ploughing, which resulted in increased yields, the horse was costly, its health was fragile and it required far more feed than the ox. Not until the eighteenth and early nineteenth centuries were these processes to become generalised.

The great period of land clearance that had begun around the year 1000 reached its apogee in the thirteenth century. The landscape was transformed as forests contracted under the axe and flame – and in spite of their value as a source of building materials, fuel and sustenance for animals and humans – as marshes were drained and as terraces were cut into the hillsides. This represented the continuing struggle to maintain a balance between population and food supply. It was then that most of the network of some 35,000 communities that exist today was created. These developments were the result of population growth, but they were also stimulated by favourable – that is, relatively dry and mild – climatic conditions and the slow growth of trade in the conditions of greater security that followed the end of the Viking incursions in the north and those of the Saracens in the south. The sense of greater security was further reinforced by the growth of royal authority over warring barons. A limited commercialisation of the economy occurred. From as early as the tenth century, but especially in the middle of the eleventh century, traders in luxuries such as spices, ivories and rugs from the East, or in wine – an eminently commercial crop wherever waterborne transport existed (as around Paris and Bordeaux) – as well as in more bulky foodstuffs, created increasingly well trodden earthen trackways between the various little towns. These developed, as fortified settlements, in privileged geographical positions at crossroads or bridging points. They included Marseille, Rouen, Arras, Orléans and Paris – the sites of Roman cities, which had declined from the fourth century. More generally, it would become increasingly impossible to live in complete autarky, not only because there were products such as salt and iron that needed to be purchased but also because of the demands of seigneurs, the Church and especially the state, for the payment of dues and taxes. The peasant was forced into the monetary economy. The process was gradual, varied in form over space and time and far from linear. In general, local markets multiplied, serving trade between towns and their hinterlands, whilst from the eleventh and twelfth centuries fairs increasingly provided foci for long-distance trade in relatively high-value and portable commodities. The great fairs at Troyes, Provins, Bar-sur-Aube and Lagny in Champagne, and the networks of middlemen who connected the north-west with the south, developed under the protection of local counts for as long as they were able to offer effective protection and a sound and abundant local currency. From the late thirteenth century new routes would develop as a result of the growth of seaborne trade. Coinage, the essential means of payment, circulated increasingly widely, although, from our perspective, slowly. It also remained in short supply, because of the limited production of bullion and the tendency of those who obtained it to hoard such a scarce and useful commodity.

The crucial intermediary role of the towns as markets for locally produced foodstuffs and as centres for consumption and production needs to be stressed, but so too does the minuscule size of most of these towns by our own standards. To contemporaries, Paris in 1320 – its population estimated at somewhere between 80,000 and 200,000 – appeared monstrous. It had doubled its size in two generations as the centre of royal government, and because of its river network it was the major regional commercial centre. The growth of towns was most evident in the north between the basins of the rivers Maine and Escaut and that of the Seine, and linked to the maritime trades in wine, salt and wool. Lille, Douai and Arras – expanding centres of cloth production – and such other stages in maritime trade as Rouen, La Rochelle, Bordeaux, Bayonne and Marseille all had between 15,000 and 40,000 inhabitants. Increased agricultural productivity favoured the growth of trade, and a widening in the range of activities, as well as the development of urban social hierarchies based upon wealth. Merchants, organised in guilds that sought to establish a monopoly by restraining competition, were distinguished from the small shopkeepers and artisans, as well as from the often turbulent journeymen and labourers. Relatively prosperous periods, such as the twelfth century, saw the widespread construction – using local materials – of solid housing and improvements in diet.

On the basis of very incomplete data, demographic historians have estimated that the population (within the boundaries of modern France) grew from around 5 million in 1000 to perhaps 15/19 million by the middle of the thirteenth century, with population densities (at their highest in the north, in Normandy, Picardy and the Ile-de-France) probably quadrupling from around 10 to 40 inhabitants per square kilometre – levels that would not be surpassed until the technological revolution of the late eighteenth and nineteenth centuries. This growth was associated with fundamental continuities signified above all by a demographic regime characterised by high rates of birth and mortality, low celibacy, relatively late marriage, low illegitimacy and low pre-marital conception, and by the dominance of the nuclear family. Most of the population subsisted on a cereal-based diet, supplemented with vegetables and occasionally meat. Perhaps 15 to 20 per cent of the population endured chronic undernourishment and lacked the stamina necessary for sustained labour. Chronic pain caused by toothache, broken bones, rheumatism and respiratory difficulties could be eased only by folkloric remedies. Although spectacles can be found in fourteenth-century illustrations, for most people nothing could be done to correct failing eyesight. Harvest failure intensified the problem of endemic poverty. With their immune systems further weakened, the starving – particularly the very young and the old – were all too likely to fall victim to dysentery, diarrhoea, respiratory complaints and all manner of common illnesses. Epidemic crises were also frequent: smallpox, plague, influenza, typhoid, typhus and malaria. Mortality rates were particularly high in the pathogenic environment created in communities polluted by garbage and human waste and growing only through constant immigration. The depredations of war have to be added to those of famine and disease, as soldiers not only murdered civilians but also consumed their food stocks and spread infection. The frequency of these crises, the suffering and fear they engendered and the limits they imposed upon population growth made them fundamental features of traditional civilisation.

The recurrence of subsistence crises, reflecting a complicated mix of economic, social and political factors, was repeated proof of an inability to ensure that food production kept pace with growing population. The diversification of crops in a subsistence polyculture remained for most farmers the essential means of safeguarding their families from the impact of climatically induced famine, but as population densities grew the risk of harvest failure increased as more and more arable land had to be devoted to the cultivation of basic cereals, further reducing the density of livestock and supply of manure, and, crucially, productivity per head. At the same time a fragmentation of farms and a growth in the numbers of landless occurred, increasing the vulnerability of much of the population. Prosperity or misery, life or death, remained fundamentally dependent on a good harvest. The impact of harvest failure varied considerably. It was likely to be especially severe in its effects when population densities were already high, and in the absence of alternative food resources, or if stocks had been depleted by two or three successive poor harvests, by deterioration and by the feeding habits of rats and insects. Wet summers were a particular threat to the cereal harvests; cold springs to the vine; drought at any time to pasture. Mortality increased and birth rates fell as people adjusted to changing economic prospects and marriages were postponed.

Dependence on the harvest promoted a sense of submissiveness to nature and to the Divine Will. Most adults had experienced severe *mortalités* during which family and friends had been decimated by famine or disease. After two or three relatively benign centuries, by the late thirteenth century there were already signs of extreme population pressure on resources in many regions, as prices, rents and land values rose, as wages fell and debt increased and as manufacture, attracted by cheap labour, spread into the countryside. It is possible that a general cooling of the Earth's surface reduced levels of productivity, and certainly there were devastating famines in 1309–11 and especially 1315–17, when cereal production fell by around one-third, fruit rotted in damp conditions and livestock

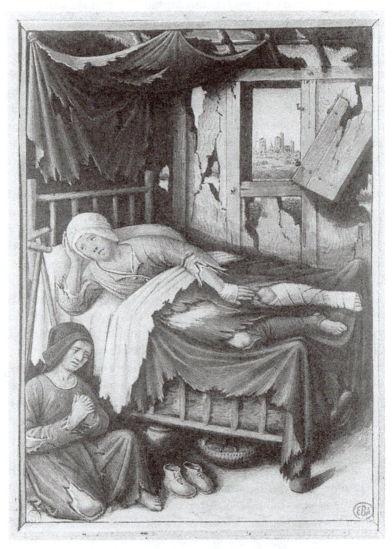

Plate 1.2 Misery: the wars, famines and epidemics of the period of the Hundred Years War reduced the population by around 40 per cent. Miniature attributed to Jean Bourdichon.

numbers were sharply reduced by rinderpest and anthrax. The impact of poor harvests was magnified by the effect of speculation and panic buying on prices in societies in which reserves were limited by low yields and the lack of storage facilities, and in which transport difficulties meant that it was slow and costly to move foodstuffs from one region to another. Impoverishment constantly threatened much of the population. Not only was starvation a prospect, but in addition undernourished people were exposed to the impact of disease and, in cold winters, to hypothermia. Debility, psychological misery and premature ageing were common. Repeated high mortalities were proof of the precariousness of human life. The solidarities of the family and community were often vital to survival but subsistence crises were also a major cause of disorder. Resentment was thus expressed against those – landowners, seigneurs and merchants – with surpluses to sell, or whoever – lords, priests or officials – failed in their duty to protect the poor.

The arrival of the Black Death in 1347/8 massively increased mortality. Its repeated visitations were the main cause of a catastrophic collapse of the population, in many communities by between a third and a half. It spread along the trade routes, with especially lethal consequences in crowded urban centres. The emotional impact of such a massive mortality in so brief a time is difficult to imagine. Of those infected, between 60 and 80 per cent could expect a hideous death. The successive visitations of the plague (with twenty-two epidemics in Paris down to 1596) can be associated with hot and humid springs and summers, when fleas multiplied and contagion was more likely. Panic spread, as those who could afford to do so escaped from the cities. They left behind empty and silent streets, shops boarded up and the all-pervading stench from rotting corpses. This could only be divine punishment for human sin. Processions of penitents begged for forgiveness. Many sought oblivion in alcohol. Others searched for scapegoats, generally Jews or individuals suspected of witchcraft. Over time the plague bacterium appears to have become less virulent. Perhaps populations developed some immunity. *Cordons sanitaires*, established by the authorities in an effort to prevent the spread of the disease, also had an impact. Nevertheless, during the seventeenth century around 35 per cent of the population (*c.* 2.4 million people) would succumb, and during the last great outbreak of bubonic plague, in southern France in 1720, half the population of Marseille, some 50,000 people, would die.

The devastating combination of subsistence crises, plague and war in the fourteenth and fifteenth centuries substantially reversed previous trends towards population growth and had a profound impact on settlement and the rural landscape, on crop systems, on property ownership and on social relationships. Only with the restoration of peace and a reduction in the virulence of the plague would gradual demographic recovery occur. The reduction in population pressure itself brought easier access to resources, better living standards and greater independence for the poor. Surviving peasants were able to increase the size of their landholdings and to abandon marginal land. It was possible to renegotiate feudal exactions. Tenants were able to secure rent reductions, and labourers higher wages. Although nobles and the urban bourgeoisie subsequently reconstituted their property, particularly in the more fertile and commercially inclined areas, a substantial part of the countryside would remain in the hands of peasant farmers. Demographic recovery was to be slow. Earlier marriage resulted in more births, but the impact was reduced by high infant mortality. Population growth, continuing in spite of the famine and epidemic of 1480–2, was thus only clearly visible from the 1450s. It was also patchy, and most evident on the rich cereal-growing plains of the north – the areas most integrated into commercial networks. The population within the present borders of France reached about 20 million by 1515 (16 to 17 million within the then existing frontiers), and fluctuated around that level for the next two centuries. This phase of recuperation from the successive disasters of the fifteenth century lasted until the 1560s. Population growth, underemployment and declining productivity gradually intensified the impact of poor harvests, however, whilst deteriorating climatic conditions with the onset of the 'Little Ice Age' contributed to the creation of famine conditions in 1618, 1630/1, 1649, 1661/2, 1693/4, 1709/10 and 1712/13. The brutality of the soldiery during the Hundred Years War with England, and subsequently the wars of religion and the Fronde, further aggravated the situation.

Although most regions enjoyed some recovery from about 1600 to the 1640s, and many until the 1670s, during the Thirty Years

War the north-east would again be devastated. In addition, the seventeenth century would see endemic popular revolts against the growing burden of taxation levied to meet the costs of war. The reign of Louis XIV would thus end with two very difficult decades, marked especially by the disastrous harvests and intensely cold years of 1693/4 – when perhaps 2 million people died – and 1709/10, with stagnation prolonged in most areas into the 1730s. These proved to be the last major famines, however.

From around 1730 to 1750 France entered into a period of sustained population growth and of demographic transition. The population grew rapidly from a maximum of 22 million in 1715 to 28 million in 1789. The chronology and rate of change varied considerably between regions. Dearth continued to afflict the poor with an often severe impact on diet and resistance to disease, most notably in 1739–41, at the end of the 1760s, again in 1787/8 and repeatedly during the first part of the following century. Such *crises de subsistence*, when cereal price rises of the order of 50 to 150 per cent occurred, rather than the tripling of earlier periods, were sufficient to cause considerable misery and unrest but not major mortalities. Moreover, wars were to be fought largely beyond the frontiers and, in the absence of religious motives, were far less barbaric than previously.

The reasons for population growth were complex but included the improvement of food supply resulting from the slow, albeit cumulative, increase in agricultural productivity favoured by relatively good climatic conditions, improved communications and the more efficient distribution of foodstuffs, together with administrative assistance to the poor to provide them with subsidised bread or work relief, and the spread of rural manufacture and with it the ability to supplement incomes gained from the land. Epidemic mortality was reduced by marginal improvements in diet and nursing rather than by improved medical care, as well as by the official establishment of *cordons sanitaires* to prevent the transmission of disease and especially by changes in the virulence of the diseases themselves. Improved living conditions and demographic expansion were particularly evident in the north, east and south-east, whilst in contrast high mortality and a recrudescence of violent demographic crisis occurred from the 1770s in Brittany and parts of the centre

(Orléanais, Berry and Touraine). In an intermediary region made up of Normandy, much of the Paris basin and parts of the centre and south-west, there is evidence that rates of population growth were already being affected by the voluntary restriction of births.

Everywhere, however, frequent undernourishment meant continued susceptibility to murderous nutritional disorders, whilst the crises that occurred with growing frequency in the last three decades of the century, if not as spectacular as those of the previous century, were still evidence of widespread poverty and physiological misery, of renewed population pressure on resources and a resultant degradation of living standards and of the continued vulnerability of a low-productivity agricultural system to climatic fluctuations. The fundamental factor in the economic cycle remained the state of the harvest. Moreover, in a predominantly rural society, rising population densities meant a plentiful supply of potential tenants and labourers, which implied growing subdivision of the land, pressure on wages and impoverishment. The development of rural manufacture and of seasonal migration can be seen as evidence of a desperate struggle to make ends meet. In such a situation, those who controlled scarce resources, and especially access to land, were in a very strong position. Demographic conditions thus had a vital impact on the distribution of resources as well as on the division of income between social groups.

In spite of the continued burden of poverty, a long period of economic transformation had nevertheless commenced that, if it did not initially involve significant technological innovation, might be seen as a prelude to the structural change in the economy that was to take place in the nineteenth century. As in developing countries today, economic growth would offer escape from hunger, disease and early death. The major stimuli to change were to be population growth, rising prices and growing internal trade, facilitated by the improvement of communications and the increased supply and more rapid circulation of money. Reductions in the cost of transport of a product had the effect of reducing its price to the consumer and enlarging its market. Increased external commerce also played its part, with the triangular trade in slaves and colonial products enriching the mercantile bourgeoisie in Bordeaux, Marseille, Nantes, Rouen and Le Havre and stimulating shipbuilding, fishing, agriculture and textiles in the hinterlands of these cities.

As so often in the past, in the aftermath of the demographic crisis that had marked the late seventeenth and early eighteenth centuries, and the restoration of the balance between population and food supply, economic expansion (initially recovery) could begin once again. What distinguishes this period, in France as elsewhere in western Europe, from its predecessors is that the increase in activity was to be relatively rapid and that it was to be sustained. There was to be no repetition of the crises, so effectively described by the English clergyman Thomas Malthus, in which the growth of the population and of production in agriculture and industry was decisively reversed by harvest failure, epidemic and war. There were certainly periodic food shortages but their impact would be less severe. Famine had given way to dearth. Although much continuity with earlier periods survived, rising productivity and urbanisation would identify the eighteenth century as the beginning of a new epoch with the onset of a period (*c.* 1730 to *c.* 1840) of slow, interrupted but gradually accelerating transition to an industrial society, which would eventually result in a transformation of the human condition.

In agriculture, still by far the predominant source of employment and income, change took the form of land clearance, the slow spread of buckwheat in the poor soils of the Massif Central and Brittany, of maize in the south-west and of the potato and of agricultural fodder, and the reduction of fallow, particularly in the north. The most optimistic estimates are of an increase of 60 per cent in agricultural production between 1701–10 and 1781–90, though there must be some doubt about this, given the shortcomings of the sources of information and the continued technical stagnation of most farms well into the next century. Moreover, communication difficulties continued to restrict commercial incentives largely to the river valleys and plains. Geographical conditions were the basis of major regional disparities. Besides a small minority of large landowners and wealthy peasants found particularly in the relatively urbanised north and the Paris region, there was a mass of small-scale peasant farmers whose essential objective remained family subsistence, and who frequently found themselves in debt as part of the daily struggle to achieve this and to pay taxes, rents and seigneurial dues. In spite of a fashionable interest in agronomy, large landowners in general had little incentive to invest in agriculture. As the population grew, peasants competed to rent farms and hire out their labour. A process of piecemeal, unspectacular change was nevertheless taking place. The growing population and enhanced commercial opportunities, together with rising prices, stimulated efforts to increase production.

The rural population also was becoming more than ever reliant upon supplementary activities, including temporary migration, carting and the manufacture at piece rates for urban merchants of a variety of products including cloth, nails and cutlery. This growing diversification of employment provided additional resources and helped make possible the continuing rise in population. Economic historians have linked this process of 'proto-industrialisation' to industrialisation proper in some areas, as urban merchants, initially taking advantage of cheap sources of rural labour, were able to accumulate capital and begin very slowly, from the 1780s, to adopt British techniques and to mechanise production. Although, according to one estimate, the production of manufactured goods increased by 4.5 times between 1701–10 (a period of depression) and 1781–90, it is clear, however, that this occurred almost entirely on the basis of traditional modes of production. These were either applied in small urban workshops, loosely dependent in the large towns on self-regulating guilds, certainly anxious to protect their privileges and monopolies but responding to an expanding market by intensified specialisation and division of labour, or else dispersed through the countryside. Everywhere production depended overwhelmingly on human or animal power, supplemented exceptionally by wind or water. The key figure in this expansion was the merchant, organising the distribution of raw materials and the finished product. Properly speaking, this was a period of commercial rather than industrial capitalism, and its prosperity remained closely dependent upon that of agriculture. The expansion of manufacture had similarly taken place in previous periods of population growth. That in this case it was to be sustained and transformed is what needs explanation.

Although towns remained essentially commercial and administrative centres, some of them experienced considerable population growth due to immigration. By 1789 just under 20 per cent of the total population, some 5,400,000 people, might be classified as urban. The rather diffuse network of large towns together with a mass of smaller centres provided a framework not only for economic activity but also for increasingly close administrative control. Paris, which by the sixteenth century had between 200,000 and 250,000 inhabitants (about 1.5 per cent of the total French population), by the middle of the seventeenth century had a population of *c.* 550,000, and by the end of the following century this had grown to 650,000 (2 to 2.5 per cent of the population), reflecting the absence of major demographic crises in the eighteenth century and a process of accelerating urbanisation, accompanied by the embellishment of the nation's major cities. The destruction of medieval walls and the construction of new *quartiers*, of wide boulevards, broad squares and handsome aristocratic town houses, was evidence of the accumulation of wealth and growing demand for luxury goods.

During the eighteenth century France became the world's foremost economic power. In manufacturing the rate of growth – at around 1.9 per cent per annum – was probably higher than that for Britain (*c.* 1.2 per cent). In terms of agricultural productivity, however, Britain appeared to be in the lead, and this was reflected in superior living standards. More effective communications, more developed markets, higher agricultural productivity and higher per capita demand for manufactures had already created production bottlenecks in textiles and in metallurgy that had stimulated technical innovation and the diffusion of new technology. Britain had begun a transition away from a civilisation based on water and wood as sources of energy and heat towards one based upon coal and the steam engine. If British technology was already becoming more advanced, it would be during the Revolutionary–Imperial period that a major gulf developed, however, ensuring that if French entrepreneurs were to be impelled by similar competitive technological imperatives they would remain behind for much of the following century.

The distinction between economic and social structures and political institutions is of course to some degree an arbitrary one, with the latter embedded within, rather then distinct from, the former. Nevertheless, this is the background against which state building occurred, against which we must write our political history. These are the factors and conditions that largely determined the resources of men and money that were to be available at any particular time to those who controlled the state, or else were contenders for power.

2

Society and politics in medieval France

The Kingdom of France emerged slowly out of the ruins of the Carolingian Empire. The Treaty of Verdun in 843 divided the empire between the sons of Louis le Débonnaire and established a western kingdom, which would gradually reserve for itself the name 'France'. In describing these and subsequent events, historians are dependent on the patchy survival of evidence largely produced by ecclesiastics and generally ambiguous in character; on chronicles, whose authors exaggerated and distorted for political, ideological or rhetorical effect; on royal charters, which projected an idealised image of kingship; and on legal documents presenting abstract principles of justice. Around 1000 chroniclers such as the monk Aimoin, at Fleury-sur-Loire, created a tradition identifying this *Francia* with Roman Gaul and described it as the rampart of Christianity. The subsequent creation of modern France, the work of centuries, would be inspired by the dream of a reconstruction of the kingdom of Charlemagne. There were many obstacles to the survival, let alone the enlargement, of any political unit. Initially poor communications and lack of information, low population densities, small revenues and the absence of salaried officials made it impossible to bind together large territorial units. Inevitably, government was decentralised. A period of political and territorial fragmentation ensued that lasted into the twelfth century. To a very substantial extent the evolution of the various lordships and principalities was determined by the results of war and the social structures shaped by organisation for war. People looked for security to local lords, and they themselves to regional princes, often – as in the case of Flanders, Burgundy and Aquitaine – the heirs of territorial commanders established by the Carolingian Charles the Bold. This fragmentation, clearly evident in the ninth century, was taken a stage further from around 900 as former royal administrators, the local counts and subsequently the *castellans* who had served as their deputies took advantage of rivalries between their nominal superiors to carve out for themselves increasingly autonomous power bases. At every level in society men sought protection from their more powerful neighbours, sometimes hoping to play one off against another and creating an intermixture of often conflicting obligations destructive of any sense of political hierarchy. Thus, to take an extreme example, around 1150 the Count of Champagne was the vassal of ten different seigneurs (including the King of France, Duke of Burgundy and Archbishop of Reims). For centuries great nobles would continue to affirm their autonomy and seek allies to help them to maintain it. Forms of contractual relationship, of clientage, were created, especially in the north, in which the weaker became the vassal of the more powerful. They agreed to perform military service and offer counsel, and to provide financial aid in return for protection and justice. In this process, kings, princes and counts sought to reinforce their own power by binding warriors, and particularly the mounted knights who formed the core of any army, to themselves. Landownership and the wealth it conferred on its possessors allowed for lavish hospitality.

Thus, 'great' men might be attracted to the royal household. This enhanced the king's role as warlord, whilst promoting support for the Church and the ceremonial assertion of monarchical authority. The award of a fief, with land and its revenues, occurred at a ceremony whose rituals and religious nature, with oaths often sworn over holy relics, was intended both to reinforce the sense of obligation between the contracting parties – the seigneur and his man – and to publicise its existence. Nevertheless, the proliferating number of castles, initially wooden towers on a mound for shelter surrounded by a palisade and ditch (motte and bailey) and, from the eleventh century, stone keeps, was indicative of a continuing fragmentation of power, of widespread insecurity and of mounting anarchy. Castles might serve as permanent bases for mounted troops and nodes of

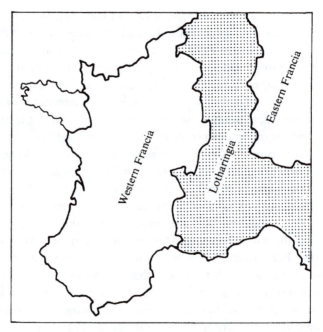

Figure 2.1 The creation of France, I: the Treaty of Verdun, 843. (Source: Revel, *L'espace français*.)

monarchical control or as centres for the assertion of an independent authority as the fief and its surrounding lands came to be regarded by those controlling it as a hereditary possession. Fortresses both served to protect and to ensure control over local populations. They were also key elements in the incessant struggles between seigneurs for control over territory, which often degenerated into brigandage or vendetta. To curb this disorder the Church sought to encourage the ideals of Christian knighthood; at the same time a sense of belonging to a distinctive social order developed amongst those mounted warriors able to control land and resources and to equip themselves properly for the wars that were their *raison d'être*. A shared code of conduct evolved, celebrated in a rich vernacular culture of epic and romance. War was perceived to be a heroic enterprise, the source of glory and reputation and, in the age of crusades, of securing eternal salvation. To regulate the slaughter, the rules of chivalry defined honourable conduct between gentlefolk, whilst doing little to protect common soldiers or civilians – members of servile classes, who were generally regarded with contempt. Further signs of a growing group cohesion can be seen in the development of marriage strategy as a means of avoiding the subdivision of fiefs and of creating networks of solidarity, and of a sense of pride in lineage. By the middle of the twelfth century to the early thirteenth a largely hereditary privileged order of nobles existed. In spite of the ability – particularly in periods of economic expansion – of wealthy non-nobles to purchase fiefs and develop a noble lifestyle, and of the king to create nobles, the nobility increasingly became a relatively closed caste, which survived until the night of 4 August 1789. It included both heirs of the Carolingian aristocracy and those *châtelain* families that through vassalage and war had acquired the hereditary right to a fief.

In contrast, peasants settled on these lands were subject to the disciplinary procedures imposed by the lord's court and suffered a range of exactions, the burden of which varied considerably between places and over time. In return for 'protection' they owed a *cens* in money or produce, were obliged to make use of the lord's oven, mill or wine press and were required to serve as soldiers and to construct fortifications, in addition to working the land directly farmed by the lord. They gained access to plots of land by providing their lords with the resources to guarantee their safety. The lord and peasant accepted binding obligations but on a very unequal basis. By the eleventh century most peasants were reduced to the status of serfs by their need for security and protection. Although in the less densely settled south the power of lords over their land was less complete, in the north it was presumed that all land was held in fief. The accepted custom was that of 'No land without seigneur'. Serfs suffered from restrictions on their rights of movement outside the community, and depended on their lord's permission (obtained on payment of a tax) to marry or pass on their possessions to their children. These measures were designed to preserve the economic integrity of the *seigneurie*.

Exploitation by the lord was restrained primarily by his self-interest in the continuing capacity of his serfs to fulfil their various obligations in cash and kind, together with the Christian commitment to protect the weak. The conditions of the rural masses clearly improved during periods of prosperity or when, following demographic disaster, land was in plentiful supply whilst the supply of labour to work it had diminished. In these situations lords were prepared to make concessions. A process of emancipating serfs was clearly under way as early as the twelfth century, and was largely completed after the Black Death, although the obligation to pay seigneurial dues was to survive until 1789. In the meantime, the economic, social and cultural subordination of the peasantry was punctuated by minor incidents of violent resistance in the dark of night, about which the historical documents are largely silent. A repertoire of actions existed, reflecting the strength of community traditions and organisation, and an appreciation of the opportunities for verbal or violent protest. There were also occasional mass uprisings or *jacquerie*. The brutality displayed by both the insurgents and those who suppressed these risings revealed the force of pent-up tension and perhaps also, in some periods, the emotional instability of populations subject to the terrors of famine, plague and war.

The relationships contracted during this period of 'feudalism' lasted from the ninth century into the twelfth and clearly corresponded to the weakness of the state and of its capacity to offer protection and justice. They represented forms both of economic exploitation and of political control, as the lord levied tolls, and fees at markets and fairs, enjoyed the profits and power of justice and generally extended his authority over formerly free peasants. Many of the forms of social obligation created were to survive until 1789, although their significance was to alter with changing social and political structures. For a mass of humble folk, the payment of dues to seigneurs and tithes to the clergy continued to be justified by the need to maintain the warriors and priests who provided protection in this world and, in the case of the clergy, hope everlasting.

Even in this period of fragmentation of state power, however, the ideal of monarchy survived, inspired by the legend of Charlemagne and by the concept of Christian kingship, of the monarch as the defender of his people, the fount of justice and protector of the Church. In 987 on the death of Louis V, the last Carolingian, assemblies of nobles and bishops held at Compiègne and Senlis had offered the crown to Hugh Capet, a powerful magnate, Count of Paris, Senlis, Dreux and Orléans. He quickly began to turn elective kingship into hereditary monarchy by persuading his peers to accept his son, Robert, as his heir. The adoption of primogeniture further reduced the likelihood of disputed successions. It had not been intended that the Capetians should gain much more than symbolic authority, however. The decline of royal influence continued. The lords of Brittany, the Massif Central and southern France largely ignored the king's existence, their sense of independence reinforced by the ethnic and cultural distinctiveness of the populations they sought to control. Centrifugal forces remained dominant, with the king enjoying little more status than any other territorial prince and engaging in constant wars for land and power. Frontiers were fluid, reflecting changing rivalries and alliances. The strength of the Capetians in northern France was based essentially upon the lands held or dominated by the king and his ability to secure vassalage both within the Ile-de-France and its immediate surrounding area (for example, from the Counts of Anjou, Blois and Soissons). It depended too on possession of the castles, which served as vital power bases. Even within his own *demesne,* in the eleventh century the king's rights were challenged frequently by the ambitions of local *castellan* families such as the Montlhéry and Montmorency, as well as by neighbouring territorial princes such as the Counts of Anjou and Blois-Champagne or the Dukes of Normandy and Flanders. Territorial magnates had to be handled with care. The last two were especially threatening, because through strenuous efforts within their own territories they enjoyed much greater success than the Capetians in maintaining feudal hierarchy and central authority. They insisted upon the performance of homage and military service and maintained close control over high justice and the Church. As always, however, much depended upon the strength and personality of individual counts or dukes. In Normandy the death of William the Conqueror in 1087 was followed by a period of political confusion and breakdown of central authority as Robert Curthose and William Rufus disputed the inheritance. In these circumstances, appeals for arbitration might be made to the king, and advantage taken of such disputes. Nevertheless, strengthened by their position as kings of England, the dukes refused to do homage to the French king until well into the twelfth century, and periods of serious hostilities occurred between 1109 and 1113 and 1116 and 1120. The survival of Capetian authority came to depend upon carefully constructed systems of alliance.

Plate 2.1 Coronation of a king of France. Anointment with Holy Oil distinguished the Capetians from other territorial lords, giving their claims added legitimacy. Miniature from the middle of the eleventh century. Bibliothèque nationale.

In this situation the one distinguishing feature of the Capetian king was his sacred character. By the eleventh century he alone was anointed during his coronation at Reims with holy oil, with the chrism sent from Heaven in the mouth of a dove for the fifth-century coronation of Clovis, the first Christian King of France. Kingship could thus be represented as a form of priesthood. Following his coronation, the king was even capable of working miracles by curing scrofula through the touch of his hand and the sign of the cross. Nonetheless, it was to be centuries before the Capetian monarchs were to achieve even a fragile political hegemony. This depended upon the establishment of a real military and political dominance over the princes and nobles, who remained, at least nominally, royal vassals. It required the development of the administrative, financial, judicial and military systems necessary initially to assert, and subsequently to maintain, royal power. The beginnings of this process are evident from the late eleventh century. Inevitably it was slow, given both the practical difficulties and the countervailing efforts of local magnates to use similar methods to affirm their own rival territorial power. Conflict was likely, especially in frontier zones in which authority was uncertain. In its essence this period – the second feudal age, as the great French medievalist Marc Bloch has labelled it – was characterised by the growing ability of the Crown to use feudal institutions in its own interests. Anarchy was replaced by growing institutional order, although, whenever royal authority weakened, magnates were likely to seek to reinterpret their relationship with the king. Fidelity was an elastic concept.

The growth of population and of economic activity was of crucial importance to the accumulation of royal power during such key periods as the late eleventh to early twelfth centuries and the early fourteenth century, during the reign of Philip Augustus (1180–1223), Saint Louis (1226–70) and Philip the Fair (1285–1314). When the king's men were finally installed in Lyon in 1312 population densities were higher then they would be again before the eighteenth century. Moreover, the Capetians benefited from the location of their territories in a fertile region crossed by waterways and roads. The development of state institutions can be associated closely with the growth of an exchange economy. Both depended upon the improvement of communications, the revival of towns as foci of power and commerce, the more rapid circulation of money and enhanced productive capacity. A long-term process of increased economic activity resulted in the growth of revenue from the royal domain, feudal dues and the administration of justice, tolls and taxes. Relationships throughout society were being monetised. This permitted the development of a salaried and dependent bureaucracy and larger, more effective armies. To some degree, princes were able to replace aristocrats with more dependent officials and household knights drawn from the lesser nobility, to hire mercenaries to supplement the feudal levy and to build increasingly complex and expensive stone fortresses able to withstand battering rams and catapults. First referred to at the siege of Metz in 1324, cannons must initially have represented a frightening spectacle of fire and smoke rather than an effective weapon.

Practically, the main causes of administrative reform were the needs of war. The old principle that the king should live off the income of his own domain failed to provide the resources for political expansion or for the creation of a permanent armed force to supplement the feudal levy. Such measures as the confiscation of Jewish property in 1306 or that of the Knights of the Temple in 1307 were only a temporary palliative. Philip Augustus and Saint Louis were able to levy extraordinary taxes to finance the crusades, which were such a powerful representation of Christian piety. Other wars justified new impositions. Conquest was a means of increasing resources. Moreover, the growth of bureaucracy meant increasing peacetime expenses. From the reign of Philip the Fair both direct taxation (especially the *taille*, which in some areas fell on property, in others on persons) and indirect taxation (for example, drink, livestock and salt) were tolerated as a quasi-permanent means of financing the long wars against the English. On occasion, especially in the violent fourteenth century, the pill was sweetened by the summoning of an Estates-General representing nobles, urban bourgeois and clergy, who might be persuaded of the need to levy taxes. The principle of permanent taxation remained unacceptable, however, and royal attempts to introduce new taxes were a potent cause of discord. Additionally, the practical problems remained of estimating the scale of the resources that might be taxed and, for the taxpayer, of obtaining cash – a scarce resource. Nevertheless, the main features of state development were control over a growing territory; the development of central administrative and judicial systems; and enhanced influence over, and the ability to make use of, the institutions of the Church resulting from the victory of Gallicanism (the theory of the temporal independence of the state and the liberties of the Church of France) over the ideal of papal theocracy.

The area under Capetian control thus gradually expanded from its original territorial base in the Ile-de-France. Within these domains the king and his entourage had traditionally sought to maintain their authority by travelling between castles and manors, directly supervising their administration and holding court. The royal *demesne* was the principal source of revenue and military manpower, its value enhanced by the development of accounting systems based on survey and inquest, and on the maintenance of records such as exchequer rolls. From the middle of the eleventh century administrative units, *prévôtés*, were created, each administered by *prévôts* as the agents of royal power. The administration of justice – a source of authority, respect and revenue – might be reinforced, employing persuasion or pressure, according to the social standing of those involved. The period between the twelfth and fifteenth centuries was one of transition, during which a feudal-seigneurial governmental system began to transform itself through the development of its legislative functions and the accretion of bureaucratic forms of administration into a monarchical system, which survived in its essentials until the Revolution. The reign of Louis VI (1108–37) saw the further development of the royal court from the king's entourage into a more effective organ of government. The court remained the centre of political activity, attracting the able and powerful and, through its culture, influencing the lifestyle of the upper classes. Nevertheless, Louis VI and his advisers, Abbot Suger of St Denis and Raoul de Vermandois, made an effort to restrict the hereditary claims of noble families to particular offices and sought to define their bureaucratic functions. In spite of this affirmation of public power and development of administrative organisation, it remained impossible and would have been unwise to exclude powerful territorial lords from the Council, the supreme organ of government. Personal relationships continued to be of fundamental significance. The obvious danger was that, especially during a royal minority, or when the king was weak, rival groups would develop within the Council and paralyse the administration.

Other twelfth-century innovations included the creation of *baillis*, despatched into the provinces as roving inspectors and judges, and the growing use of written documents, allowing the more effective recording and transmission of information and instructions. Nobles as well as clerks needed to acquire literacy. A gradual osmosis resulted between the culture of the schools and that of the court and with it the emergence of a civilisation based on classical values and those of chivalry. Rather than following the court in its perambulations, a permanent central organisation of professional administrators dependent upon the monarch, composed of clergy and minor nobles with some legal training, was gradually created. Paris owed to its geographical location its already considerable commercial and strategic significance. With its growing governmental functions, and its massive cathedral, increasingly well fortified during the reign of Philip Augustus, provided with paved streets, new government buildings and aristocratic residences, equipped with a university that trained theologians and canon and civil lawyers, with an increasingly literate merchant class able to communicate along the trade routes, it assumed increasingly the functions of a capital city. Furthermore, by 1210, as a result of a major programme of repair and construction, 113 fortresses protected the royal *demesne*.

From the middle of the thirteenth century under St Louis, a king inspired by the religious ideals of the 'royal lawmaker' (*roi justicier*), and especially in the early fourteenth century, specialised institutions born within the royal court began to achieve a more independent existence, as the volume and complexity of their activities increased. The parlement established by St Louis next to the Sainte-Chapelle – constructed in 1246–8 as a reliquary for the thorns with which Jesus had been crowned at his crucifixion – assumed the role of the sovereign court of appeal presiding over a hierarchical system of royal courts. During the fourteenth century it would acquire responsibility for remonstrating against royal ordinances that its members felt did not 'conform to reason'. Together with the Chambre des comptes to supervise financial administration, these were signs of the further professionalisation of legal and administrative personnel. They were to be supplemented from the fifteenth century by additional parlements created largely in peripheral provinces acquired during and in the aftermath of the Hundred Years War. Their creation both recognised the particular susceptibilities of newcomers and served as a means of integrating them more effectively within

France. In these various ways the activities and influence of the royal administration became increasingly pervasive. This was combined with insistence upon the better organisation and procedure, as well as the essential fairness and superiority, of royal justice in comparison with that offered in the seigneurial and ecclesiastical courts. From the thirteenth century the king as suzerain took advantage of growing political strength to insist upon the right of appeal from the seigneurial to royal courts, and from the fifteenth century upon the crown's duty to abolish seigneurial courts guilty of abusing their powers. This was resented bitterly, as a threat to the dignity and status of the seigneur, to his authority over subordinates and to his income. The ecclesiastical courts claimed jurisdiction in cases involving clerics, in crimes against religion, in marital affairs and in many disputes over property. The effort to reduce their competence was closely linked to the Gallican struggle against the claims of the papacy to enjoy political supremacy over kings.

In spite of the growing royal power, basic economic and social structures ensured that government remained decentralised. The primary function of the monarchy was the administration of justice as the essential means of preserving public order. Noble violence, peasant protest and the widespread criminality of desperately poor people created immense difficulties. With a small central bureaucracy, in an era of poor communications, government remained inescapably dependent upon the cooperation of local élites, and particularly municipal magistrates and rural seigneurs. Communes received privileges, ensuring greater autonomy, in return for accepting responsibility for their own administration, for the enforcement of the law, the collection of taxes and the raising of a militia. Supervision was difficult. As late as 1535 there were only around 7,000 to 8,000 royal officials (including those in minor positions: one official for every 2,000 inhabitants). Most poor people in any case avoided the judicial system, and continued to do so well into the nineteenth century. They preferred to regulate their affairs within the community and to avoid the costs, waste of time, and risks of interference by an external authority ill-equipped by its culture and language, experience and sympathies to understand the concerns of ordinary people. Local hierarchies and networks of obligation remained important determinants of interaction between the royal administration and communities. Effective government depended on achieving a degree of consensus and on respect for local customs and élites.

The personal element remained central to government. Strong and effective monarchs such as Louis VI or Philip Augustus, supported by a small number of influential counsellors, were able to tighten the ties of vassalage and reaffirm its hierarchical character. They were willing to take judicial and, if need be, military action against insubordinate or disloyal officials or territorial lords. Many *castellans* lacked the military means to resist this royal centralisation, and reconciled themselves to acting as the king's agents in the administration of justice, the collection of taxes and the raising of soldiers, and as the protectors of the Church. In comparison with kings and princes, who were able to avoid the subdivision of their property by inheritance, lesser nobles were weakened by the passing of each generation. In a period of economic expansion many minor nobles were impoverished by their growing taste for luxury, and as a result their dependence on their feudal superior increased. The crusades, a continuous movement spread over three centuries, represented a massive investment of men and resources. They were a brutal expression of faith, which reduced internal violence by means of the removal – and, indeed, premature death – of many young warriors. In contrast to earlier trends, a process of a concentration of power, in the hands of territorial princes as well as the king, was under way. The doctrine of monarchical superiority was clearly enunciated by Louis VI's advisor, Suger, the abbot of St Denis, who insisted that vassals of the king's vassals owed primary allegiance to the monarch, placed at the summit of the feudal hierarchy, rather than to their direct seigneurs (as was the Anglo-Norman practice). This ran contrary to established custom, according to which 'the vassal of my vassal is not my vassal', and took well into the thirteenth century to win acceptance. In 1202, however, Philip Augustus felt able to use his rights as feudal seigneur to require homage from King John for his territories – Normandy and Aquitaine – in so doing weakening the authority of the English king over his vassals in those provinces. Any apparent increase in the power and prestige of the king made it more likely that vassals engaged in disputes would appeal to the monarch as the feudal arbiter, rather than taking matters into their own hands. Such appeals could be used to justify military expeditions into regions formerly outside royal control, such as the Mâconnais in 1160. In these cases war was the means of implementing judicial decisions, and it was by use of the law that the king was able to impose his authority on, and even confiscate the lands of, major, princely, vassals. In a changing social and political context, kings were able to use the feudal system, which had emerged originally out of the weakness of the central power, in order to restore their authority. Their growing success could be seen in the response of vassals to the call for troops to defend the kingdom against the Holy Roman Emperor Henry V in 1124. Increased attendance at the king's court was another sign. For much of the eleventh century the great nobles and bishops had deserted the royal court, leaving it to the turbulent minor nobles of the Ile-de-France. This situation clearly began to change with the reaffirmation of royal authority by Louis VI. There was a growing concern to give advice to the king, an interest in acquiring office and a desire to share power. Increasingly, status came to be determined by the crown.

The reign of Philip Augustus represented a decisive stage in the development of the French state in terms of its territorial expansion and ability to subdue powerful rivals. The king was able to exploit his position as feudal overlord and protector of the Church in order to intervene in the affairs of such powerful vassals as the English King Henry II, who by 1165 controlled more than a half of France, including territory within 60 kilometres of Paris. The destruction of this Angevin empire was made easier as a result of the vicious quarrels between Henry II and his sons, which in themselves encouraged and also represented complex feudal divisions within the dispersed Plantagenet domains. Although defeated by Richard (died 1199), subsequently Philip enjoyed major successes against the indecisive and unpopular John and his various allies. A period of probing in frontier regions and efforts to win over local lords, often by posing a greater threat to their survival than could be mounted by the English kings, was followed by the conquest of Normandy and, in 1214, by triumphant victories over the English king at La Roche-aux-Moines, followed by the defeat at Bouvines of Otto IV, Holy Roman emperor, and his Flemish and English allies. These victories ensured a major shift in the European balance of power and a massive reduction in the power of the English king.

Plate 2.2 Return of Philip Augustus to Paris after his victory at Bouvines. Fifteenth-century miniature. Bibliothèque royale Albert I, Brussels.

In contrast, the conquered territory substantially enhanced the financial and manpower resources of the French monarchy. The revenue of the Crown increased by 160 per cent between 1180 and 1203 – a development that itself required the enlargement of the central administration. As his title and the eagle on his seal suggested, Philip represented an 'imperial' image of monarchy. As king he owed homage to God alone, whilst royal authority was clearly set above noble power.

Louis VIII (1223–6) was able to complete the conquest of Poitou and additionally to extend royal power into Languedoc, justifying the latter by the Church's condemnation of the Cathar 'heresy' and the Crown's duty, as defender of the faith, to slaughter the offenders. Marriages and their accompanying dowries were another means by which the Crown acquired territory. For example, in 1180 Philip

Augustus obtained the Boulenois and Artois on his marriage to the niece of the Count of Flanders. The failure of the marriage of a brother of St Louis and the heiress to the Count of Toulouse (in 1229) to produce issue led to Toulouse becoming part of the royal domain in 1271; it was by marriage, too, that Philip the Fair acquired Champagne and Brittany in 1291. The Dauphiné, in contrast, was acquired in 1349 by purchase. This continuous growth in the royal domain represented an accumulation of resources and of power.

Ideologically, a Church anxious to secure social order, and insisting upon the sacred rights and responsibilities of the monarch, supported the enhancement of royal powers. Foremost amongst these was protection of the Church itself and the punishment of 'heretics' and non-believers, particularly those of the Jewish faith. From the late tenth century the Church had used the threat of excommunication in a largely vain effort to secure respect for 'the Peace of God' and had supported the king in his role as guardian of peace. In a period of monarchical weakness it had preserved the traditions of bureaucratic administration and provided an alternative institutional structure. It shared also in the benefits of the return to order and prosperity that made possible the reconstruction of the great cathedrals of Paris, Reims and Chartres and numerous parish churches – structures that, through their scale and the emotional impact of their statues, stained glass and murals, exercised great symbolic power. Through its network of parishes and its involvement in the daily life of the population, the Church provided an explanation of the universe and norms of behaviour for rich and poor, and justified the social system in terms that continued to be used throughout the *ancien régime*, namely that God had divided mankind into three groups: those who prayed, those who fought and those who laboured. The interdependence of these groups was the basis of social and political order. Those who worked were required to serve and maintain the others in return for prayers and protection. Salvation was the reward for fulfilling one's obligations. The role of the monarch as a military leader likely to be called upon to wage 'just' wars and to punish 'evil' in God's name, and the sacred nature of his functions, moreover, ensured that the Church would insist upon the masculine character of monarchy. Women were regarded as physically and emotionally unsuitable to hold power.

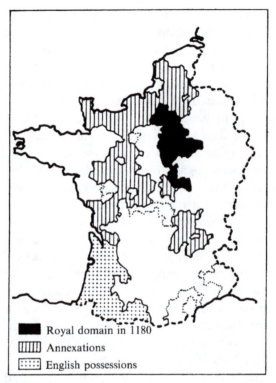

Figure 2.2 The creation of France, II: the reign of Philip Augustus, 1180–1223. (Source: Revel, *L'espace français*.)

The relationship between state and Church, although essentially based upon interdependence, with many churchmen (initially because of their virtual monopoly of writing) occupying positions in the royal court, was also plagued by conflict of interest. The Church resented the use by kings of rights of appointment to monasteries and bishoprics as a form of patronage and their efforts to control the land and resources belonging to these institutions. Kings were suspicious of the papacy's claim to exercise supreme authority on earth, as the representative of God, *le Seigneur*. The reforms introduced by Pope Gregory VII and his successors in the second half of the eleventh century had sought to establish a church in every community and to stimulate the evangelical zeal of the clergy by insisting on celibacy, amongst other virtues, as a means of eliminating the corruption caused by worldly interests. Another objective had been to secure greater independence from secular interference and to affirm the Pope's spiritual and political supremacy through the right to excommunicate and depose kings. Better communications had helped to make closer papal control over the provinces of the Church possible. The rise of royal power made this intolerable, however, leading in particular to a bitter conflict between Philip the Fair and Pope Boniface VIII over the taxation of the clergy, and the right of the king to discipline clerics. This dispute, in which a prominent role was played by the new university-trained lawyers, well versed in Roman law, saw the emergence of Gallicanism as a counter to theocratic ideals. Philip the Fair insisted that he held his throne directly from God, and was supported by a meeting of the three orders (Estates-General) convoked at Notre-Dame de Paris in 1302. The weakness of the papacy in the fourteenth century, including the period of 'Babylonian captivity' in Avignon (1309–77), and the existence of rival popes between 1373 and 1418, allowed the further affirmation of these Gallican liberties. This culminated in the Pragmatic Sanction of Bourges in 1438: an agreement by an assembly of the clergy substantially to restrict papal authority and fiscal exactions in France.

Thus, over a period of three centuries, the kings of France had succeeded in asserting themselves militarily and ideologically. There remained substantial threats to the survival of their power, however. Even when the various principalities had been brought under closer royal control they retained their own customs and laws – rights confirmed at the time of their accession to the royal domain. Until the Revolution, geographical variations in legal custom would reflect the political divisions of the eleventh and twelfth centuries and earlier. The legal traditions of the south, where written law and Roman usages were dominant, differed significantly from those of the north, where custom remained uppermost. Particularly significant were differences in inheritance practices between areas where equal division of property between heirs occurred, and fragmentation was more likely, and those, especially in the south, in which a father could advantage one child in order to keep the family's property intact. In general, nobles enjoyed the considerable advantage, when it came to the accumulation of property, of being able to leave at least two-thirds of their possessions to their eldest son. These differences were reinforced by linguistic variations, with the *langue d'oc* of southern France being far closer to Latin than the *langue d'oïl* of the north. Moreover, and in spite of the development of the administrative power and resources of the monarchy, distance, slowness of communication and the small size of the royal bureaucracy restricted effective central control. The possibility remained of resistance to the royal authority from over-mighty vassals, and urban or rural communities. Especially when combined with English interference, this threatened anarchy in a militarised society in which the government was far from achieving a monopoly of armed force. Thus, in 1314, leagues of nobles were organised in Brittany, Picardy, Burgundy and Champagne to demand respect for provincial customs and to protest against taxes. The political danger was increased when delegates from these areas met together, but, fortunately for the Crown, they were unable to agree upon a common strategy. On an altogether different scale was the series of events known as the Hundred Years War.

For some 130 years, from around 1335, a succession of famines, plagues and wars plunged four successive generations into misery and despair and threatened the very existence of both dynasty and state. Rising population densities meant that problems of food supply were inevitable. The arrival of bubonic plague in western Europe in 1347 carried off perhaps a third of its inhabitants, and other waves followed the first murderous epidemic at intervals of about fifteen years. Although, during the Hundred Years War, there were relatively few major battles, long periods of low-intensity warfare caused severe economic and social disruption as soldiers plundered and raped, destroyed homes, livestock and crops, spread disease and brutalised populations, whilst trying to avoid serious conflict. Thus, guerrilla warfare and widespread brigandage were accompanied by the collapse of ordered government. A previously well-ordered society appeared to be in danger of collapsing.

In these circumstances, just as in the eleventh century, the search for security encouraged renewed fortification and intensified localism. Forms of 'bastard' feudalism, of clientelism, developed, with the towns to a far greater extent than previously playing a key role as military centres, places of refuge and sources of money. The weak attached themselves to patrons more powerful than themselves. The inevitable immediate result was a weakening of royal authority. In the longer term the wars were again a powerful force in stimulating improvement in the royal administration. Although medieval armies were small compared with those of later periods – with, for example, perhaps 12,000 to 15,000 French deployed against 8,000 English and Welsh at Agincourt in October 1415 – they were substantial in relation to the resources available. Attempts to raise taxation were always dangerous, however, and likely to provoke discontent amongst those nobles who were not part of the growing bureaucracy and who continued to insist that the monarch should live off the revenues of his domain. Between 1356 and 1358, during the captivity of John II and reflecting the weakness of a government discredited by defeat at Crécy and Poitiers, the dauphin, the future Charles V, was faced with dissent not only from the nobles but also from the merchants of Paris, led by their *prévôt* Etienne Marcel, and with the complaints of the provincial estates meeting at Paris and Toulouse. In periods of monarchical weakness and crisis such bodies were inevitably more assertive. Efforts to conciliate élites (noble, urban bourgeois and clergy) through provincial estates and Estates-General, such as those of 1343 and 1355/6, ran the risk of giving a platform to critics determined to limit the arbitrariness of royal officers. They felt able to demand regular meetings, the right of consent to taxation or the summoning of the feudal levy, and a role in the selection of royal officers – claims that the dauphin Charles finally proved unwilling to accept. These developments coincided with peasant uprisings (*jacqueries*) that threatened much of the Paris region, as the rural population protested against both royal taxation and the exactions of a nobility that had proved itself incapable of protecting its dependents against marauding bands of soldiers. The divergent interests of these groups, and the widespread desire for strong government and social order, helped to promote a temporary recovery. Nevertheless, the minority of Charles VI in the 1380s, and his subsequent insanity at a time of profound Europe-wide demographic and economic crisis, provoked another round of war, revolt and massacre, and, following a truce in 1388, renewed English intervention in 1412.

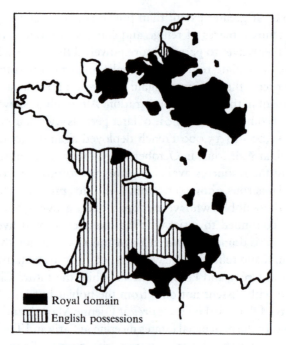

Figure 2.3 The creation of France, III: the Treaty of Brétigny, 1360. (Source: Revel, *L'espace français*.)

The wars themselves were caused by problems of suzerainty and conflicting claims to the throne of France. Between 1293 and 1297 Philip the Fair had sought to crush his most dangerous vassals, the King of England as Duc de Guienne, and the Count of Flanders, whose power was based on the commercial and industrial prosperity of the Flemish cities. Edward I had managed to retain Guienne, but had felt obliged to render homage for it. Flanders had been punished severely, militarily and financially.

Philip died in 1314. By 1328 his three sons were also dead, and the direct line of Capetian succession extinguished. The alternative claimants in this situation were Philip's daughter, Isabelle, whose son Edward III had succeeded to the English crown recently, and her cousin Philip, Count of Valois. His claim, as Philip VI, was recognised by an assembly of leading nobles and clergy meeting at Vincennes, because he was an adult male, and as a means of excluding the King of England. At this stage Edward III's primary concerns were restoring order in England itself and retaining what was left of Guienne. In 1329, at Amiens, he paid homage. His laying claim to the throne of France in 1337 was probably conceived of as a potentially lucrative military adventure and a means of securing the English wool trade with Flanders, of protecting what remained of the Plantagenet heritage in the south-west and of diverting the energies of the warlike English barons onto the Continent.

At Crécy (1346) and Poitiers (1356), poorly organised and ineptly commanded French armies suffered major defeats by English armies, which effectively employed heavily armed men-at-arms with archers on their flanks. These disasters must have appeared as God's judgement. At Poitiers the French king, John the Good (II), was taken prisoner. Although Edward III did not demand the French Crown, in the ensuing negotiations for his release he forced John to abandon half his kingdom, including Normandy. The dauphin, the future Charles V, refused to recognise this agreement, however, and war-weariness on both sides led to a compromise treaty signed at Brétigny in 1360, which left the English king, in return for freeing John II, with much of the south-west and a massive amount of gold, but neither Anjou nor Normandy. The peace was short-lived. In 1368 Charles V was able to take advantage of resentment amongst the barons of Aquitaine at efforts by the English to impose a centralised administration and increase taxation, and of their appeal to him as suzerain to adjudicate. Ten bitter years of war followed during which the English territories in Aquitaine were gradually reduced to a small area in Gascony around the ports of Bordeaux and Bayonne, tied to England by the wine trade. Only in 1388, as a result of sheer exhaustion, was a lengthy truce agreed, lasting until 1412, when an English expeditionary force ravaged parts of Normandy and Anjou. This was followed in 1415 by the much more serious efforts of Henry V. He took advantage of the intermittent madness of Charles VI and the rivalry this encouraged between the princes of the blood. Henry V's first campaign culminated in the slaughter of the French nobility at Agincourt and was followed by a further invasion in 1417. At Troyes in 1420 a treaty was signed by which Henry V married Catherine, daughter of Charles VI, and was recognised as heir to the French Crown. In 1422 his youthful successor, Henry VI, became king of both England and France.

Plate 2.3 The siege of Orléans. Joan of Arc was to play a major role in the liberation of the city, one of the wealthiest and most strongly fortified in France. Artillery was used by both sides. Late fifteenth-century miniature. Bibliothèque nationale.

The bases for this dual monarchy were weak, however. The French dauphin, calling himself Charles VII, who controlled the west, centre and Midi, not unnaturally rejected the settlement. For the English, maintaining armies in the field was expensive and effective control of conquered areas difficult. Continued success was to a large degree dependent upon the support of a French party associated with the Duke of Burgundy. In 1429, inspired by the initial successes of Joan of Arc, the French recovery gathered pace. Duke Philip the Good, anxious about the impact of war on Burgundy, made a separate peace in 1435, and, in the fifteen years that followed, the English cause met growing resistance and suffered defeat after defeat, losing Paris itself in 1436. Areas formerly under English rule were encouraged to accept the restoration of French sovereignty by relatively moderate treatment. Along with other areas recently incorporated into the kingdom, they were allowed to retain their provincial estates with the right of consent to direct taxes, or else received parlements with important administrative and judicial functions, on the model of that of Paris.

The dramatic succession of famines, plagues and wars over a period of at least 130 years had reduced the population from between 16 and 17 million to about 12 million. If the social structures of an overwhelmingly rural society remained substantially unaltered, the process of adjustment to such an intense and prolonged series of crises ensured that the economy was more commercialised and that the state became more bureaucratic. The economic and political importance of the towns grew. The wars themselves did much to enhance both dynastic loyalty and, as a result of the monarchy's calls for support against the English, the development of a diffuse sense of French identity. From the 1450s, during a century in which, despite harvest failures, the masses enjoyed relatively favourable conditions, order was restored, the population grew once again, trade flourished and the resources were provided for a strengthening of state institutions. The result would be the creation, out of feudalism, of a dynastic state, an *état royal*, the central elements of which – monarchy, religion, aristocratic honour and clientage – would, however, continue to be subject to considerable strains.

3

Society and politics
in early modern France

The misery caused by the long wars against the English and wide-spread internal disorder encouraged the construction of an ideal of good government – a vision of a state strong enough to impose order. The glorification of monarchy by historians, artists and architects, given public expression in ritual, ceremony, the law and religion, established the image of *la douce France* ruled over by the 'most Christian king' – warrior, protector of the Church, saviour of his people. Renewed efforts were made to subdue the military nobility by offering them employment in the royal service. Although bitter disputes over taxation continued, royal impositions were gradually accepted in principle and for the 'common good'. The closing years of the reign of Charles VII (1435–61), together with that of Louis XI (1461–83), constituted a major phase of political reconstruction, when growing economic activity facilitated a major increase in the revenue of the state, with tax income increasing from some 1.7 million *livres tournois* in 1439 to 2.3 million in 1449 and 5.1 million in 1482. The necessities of war and the establishment of a secure income would, from 1439, allow the creation of a permanent army of between 12,000 and 15,000 men, equipped with artillery, and reduce dependence on the feudal levy (which was finally abolished only in 1697). This constituted a first step towards the emergence of a state monopoly of armed force. The provision of military support for increasing numbers of administrative and judicial officials was a central feature of greater political centralisation. By 1515 the 16 million inhabitants of the kingdom were governed through an

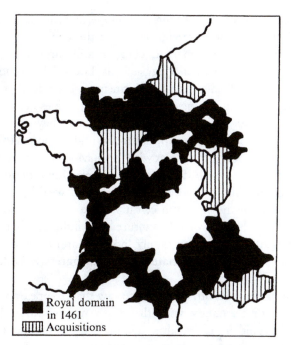

Figure 3.1 The creation of France, IV: the reign of Louis XI, 1461–83. (Source: Revel, *L'espace français*.)

administrative structure that, including soldiers and dependents, gave sustenance to some 600,000 people – about 4 per cent of the total population. Nobles nevertheless continued to play a central role in the preservation of law and order. The basic administrative unit was the *châtellainerie*, royal or seigneurial – typically a castle, dependent lands and rights, and a single 'custom'. In 1500 that of Pontoise included forty-three parishes. *Châtelains*, as well as town councils, were responsible for courts, which enforced high (capital offences), middle or low justice (property disputes, minor injuries), with communities themselves enforcing decisions. In what remained a lightly policed society, however, in which the number of agents of the king remained relatively small, 'self-help' was habitual and violence common.

Effective government depended on strong monarchical leadership and, in particular, the ability to restrain aristocratic rivalry and contain centrifugal forces. The recovery of royal power was marked

also by the notion that the king was 'emperor in his kingdom', by
the reassertion of the sovereign rights of the courts, by an effort
to make justice more coherent, cheaper and more popular and
by the determination of a king such as Louis XI to choose his
own dependent officials. The appointment of provincial governors
initially drawn from amongst middle-ranking nobles aroused bitter
resentment amongst the greater nobility, until they succeeded in
securing for themselves these appointments and the access to patronage and military power that went with them. Much of the old nobility
had disappeared anyway during the wars, providing opportunities
for upward mobility by successful soldiers and wealthy bourgeois.
By the middle of the sixteenth century there were around 25,000
noblemen, divided by wealth, culture and influence but sharing
perceptions of personal and family 'honour' and a sense of social
superiority still closely associated with the aggressive code of the
warrior.

The end of the fifteenth century also saw the disappearance of the
principality of Burgundy with the death without male heirs of
Charles the Bold in 1477, although the settlement that followed
resulted in the definitive loss of most of Flanders. In 1491 the
marriage of Anne of Brittany to Charles VIII finally extinguished
the last autonomous princely state, no longer able to preserve its
independence by taking advantage of the quarrels between England
and France. It was all in marked contrast to the political fragmentation of the year 1000, or the threatened dissolution of the kingdom
during the Hundred Years War. The impact of geography and of
provincial particularism, and the defence of noble privilege, of course
remained firm restraints on the affirmation of royal power. During
the minority of Charles VIII, however, the regent, Anne de Beaujeu,
felt confident enough to convoke the first truly national and representative Estates at Tours in 1484, with one deputy from each order
and each *bailliage*, establishing a form of election not dissimilar to
that of 1789. The right of these delegates to present their *cahiers
de doléances* (lists of grievances) and to discuss government policy
was also established. Although deputies docilely voted taxes,
however, the promise to recall them in the following years was not
kept. Whilst accepting its responsibilities before God, the monarchy
remained unwilling to justify its actions before men.

The long reign of Francis I (1515–47), like those of his illustrious successors Henri IV and particularly Louis XIV, was to be marked by the determination of a strong and confident personality, advised by a small council, to impose his will. Whilst rehabilitating Paris as his capital, Francis, like Louis XI, was attracted to the Loire valley. At Chambord he created a palace that served as a carefully constructed symbol of royal glory, a fit setting for courtly life and for an endless round of ritual and ceremony, interspersed with hunting, as well as a vital centre for the distribution of patronage. The royal household continued to play a central role in the exercise of power, providing a focus for loyalty and attracting those in search of financial reward and appointments in the army and bureaucracy. Although the ideal of fidelity remained influential, feudal relationships had largely collapsed during the long wars and were being replaced by less formal patron–client relationships. The monarchy offered its noble clients a share in power, which allowed them to safeguard their private interests and to construct their own armed client networks and to use office holding as a means of supplementing the income from their estates. Moreover, life at a peripatetic court, the pre-eminent cultural centre, facilitated the continuing redefinition of noble manners and taste. For the ambitious and those who could afford the costs of appearance, this was the place to be. The ordinance of Villers-Cotterêts in 1539, through its insistence on the use of French in place of Latin in official documents, accelerated the process by which it became the daily language of local élites, the lingua franca of trade and, slowly (in a centuries-long process of diffusion, completed only by compulsory education towards the end of the nineteenth century), the language of the masses.

In establishing the administrative state the kings of France were in effect creating the nation. During the reign of Francis I scholars appealed to the precedents set by Roman emperors and by Charlemagne and to the Bible to reinforce the monarch's claim to be 'emperor' in his kingdom and 'supreme guardian' of both state and Church. Nevertheless, a distinction was made between his absolute authority and despotism. Thus, Claude de Seyssel in 1515 insisted on the limits imposed on the monarch by divine law, the rules of natural justice and the accumulated legislation of the kingdom, as interpreted by the parlements. The evident optimism of humanistic writers in the early sixteenth century, their pride in the rediscovery of antiquity and rejection of the barbarism of the more immediate past, and the apparent prosperity and material well-being of much of the population, moreover, should not blind us to the fragility of an equilibrium threatened by population growth, war and religious dissent.

War represented an opportunity for a monarch to enhance his reputation and honour and to achieve dynastic territorial objectives. It was assumed simply that subjects would welcome the opportunity for glory. Brilliant military successes and appalling disasters succeeded each other. The dream of European hegemony and the rivalry that developed between Francis and the Habsburg Charles V were to embroil the country in a succession of external wars and closely related internal disorder, lasting until 1661. Frontier regions were devastated, whilst the permanent gains were limited. In the east, Metz, Toul and Verdun were acquired. Calais was taken from the English. More significantly, the size of armies, and the cost of their supplies and equipment, of muskets, artillery and fortifications, increased substantially, and with this the monarchy's financial problems. Furthermore, a royal minority or a weak king (and the sons of Henri III and Catherine de Medici, ruling between 1559 and 1584, were all inexperienced and ineffective) encouraged factionalism at court and throughout the royal administration as private ambitions competed with official responsibilities. It was evident that powerful territorial magnates remained capable of mounting a military challenge to the monarch.

The situation was envenomed by religious dissent. The continued vitality of the Roman Catholic Church was evident from the high levels of expenditure on the construction and restoration of religious edifices, in the popular piety manifesting itself in processions, pilgrimages and confraternities, and through the veneration of holy relics and the appeals to intercessory saints, in particular to the Virgin Mary. There was also widespread support for the regeneration of the Church and the improvement of pastoral care. Amongst the better educated a humanist interest in biblical studies developed, as well as criticism of clerical 'abuses'. To a large degree, Protestantism emerged from this movement for reform. In an era when almost every aspect of life was influenced by religious belief, and when the Roman Catholic Church was the repository of so much influence, religious disputes were a matter of passionate concern, and inevitably became entangled with existing social and political divisions. Francis I was a sceptic in religious matters. His successor, Henri II (1547–59), was a man of faith. For both, however, the Church was a major political instrument and source of revenue, and as such had to be protected. There was also the obvious danger that religious disputes would encourage or serve as a pretext for political disaffection. Factional divisions at the centre were reflected in struggles between the clients of great men in the provinces, which, whatever the apparent political and religious justification, often degenerated into little more than banditry.

Protestantism involved the demand for a religion based upon the Bible and deliverance from an oppressive clerical institution. For conservatives, the defence of social order inevitably required the protection of religious and moral orthodoxy, and was the primary responsibility of the king as the Lord's anointed. Failure would render him unworthy of his high office. The nightmare prospect of the eventual accession to the throne of the Protestant Henri of Navarre would in 1576 serve as the justification for the establishment by the Guise family and their clients of a Holy League, committed to a crusade against heresy. The geography of adherence to Protestantism is not easy to explain. In part it reflects the regional influence of major magnates such as the Montmorency-Châtillon and the Bourbon families, their kin and clients, and the impact of religious disputes upon conflict for political power within the nobility. The Royal Council itself was divided by bitter factional rivalry. Initially, most Protestant churches were to be found in rural Languedoc, Picardy, Normandy, around Paris and in the east in Champagne and Burgundy. Protestantism appealed to perhaps a fifth or a quarter of the population at some time or other and in particular to relatively literate urban communities of professional men and artisans. The poorer classes appeared indifferent. Rural areas remained overwhelmingly loyal to the Catholic Church, with rare exceptions such as the Cévennes, where the adherents of reform were motivated in part by the desire to abolish the tithe. Initially divided by schism, Protestants were encouraged by John Calvin, and forced by persecution, to organise themselves more effectively. A synod assembled in Paris in 1559 drafted a confession of faith and provided for regular local, regional and national assemblies. Evangelical propaganda took on an uncompromising tone, encouraged by the profound belief that God's saving grace was preordained. Protestants insisted that the rituals of the Catholic Church were mere human inventions, offensive to the Lord, and should be replaced by simple religious services organised around sermons, prayers and psalms. Their hatred of 'idolatry' resulted in widespread iconoclasm.

The eventual north–south divide, with Protestants increasingly restricted to the region around Montauban, Nîmes and La Rochelle, would result from military failure and subsequent persecution. A complex of factors combined to explain this defeat of Protestantism. They include the opposition of the monarchy, which through its Concordat with the papacy in 1516 had gained supremacy over the Church already and was able to control the appointment of bishops and abbots and strictly limit papal financial exactions. Protestantism was a threat to the secular and religious bases of the French monarchy. Furthermore, it challenged religious 'truth', and, in comparison with parts of Germany, the press and universities appear to have exercised a less dynamic role in the diffusion of new ideas. Perhaps, too, clerical corruption was less scandalous, whilst Calvinism failed to appeal to popular religious sensibilities. Indeed, the Protestant challenge reinvigorated the Catholic Church, an institution that was uniquely well placed to mobilise those for whom the parish retained its central cultural role – the place for baptism, marriage and burial, with its priest offering the keys to eternal salvation through confession and penance and participation in the Eucharist. In sermons, pamphlets and murals depicting a frightening vision of the Last Judgement, heresy was associated with the Devil. A widespread fear of divine wrath was engendered. A duty of intolerance was imposed on all those who feared God's judgement and sought to assuage the divine anger so evident from the famine and plague of 1586/7. By the 1560s the Protestants were already too weak to achieve dominance but as yet too strong to be eliminated. The wars of religion that ensued would represent a massive crisis of monarchical authority.

Under these pressures royal government would undergo a process of disintegration, particularly following the death of Henri II in

1559. This left a minority succession and a situation that encouraged faction rivalry, and the formation of rival armies, by the great magnates, each of whom sought to justify his actions in religious terms. Intense faith combined with personal ambition and loyalty to kin. During the wars fought between 1562 and 1598 both sides rejected the possibility of compromise. Even tyrannicide could be justified on religious grounds. In these circumstances central control over the increasingly faction-ridden administrative and judicial systems largely collapsed. The violence and the apocalyptic fears generated by civil war were symbolised by the St Bartholomew's Night massacre, beginning on 27 August 1572. During the festivities celebrating the marriage of Prince Henri of Navarre to Marguerite of Valois it appears that Charles IX ordered the murder of leading Protestants. Events rapidly ran out of control, and in four days some 10,000 people were slaughtered in Paris and twelve provincial cities. This served only to prolong the conflict in spite of the already clearly inferior military position of the Protestants. Murder, rape, torture and looting exemplified how completely civilised values were forgotten in these wars of religion, in a struggle between rival belief systems. In the regions worst affected by conflict, particularly in the east, where Spanish forces intervened in support of the Holy League, the likelihood of food shortage and epidemic was increased greatly by the constant movement of troops. The opinions of the anonymous author of the *Vindications of Liberty against Tyrants* (1579), who sought to justify resistance to rulers who had violated their covenant with their subjects, might be contrasted with those of Jean Bodin, who, in the *Six Books of the Commonwealth* (1576), insisted that there ought to be a single source of authority in both the family and the state. He utterly condemned contrary views, which could lead only to 'a licentious anarchy...worse than the harshest tyranny in the world'.

The crisis deepened. The collapse of revenue made it difficult to maintain a royal army in the field. Those who claimed that he had failed to combat heresy challenged the authority of Henri III. He lost control of Paris after a 'day of barricades' (12 May 1588), and, in the course of an Estates-General convoked at Blois, the delegates of the capital demanded regular meetings of this body. They insisted that it should assume the right of consent to taxation and

Plate 3.1 The sacking of a farm: a classic image of the misfortunes of war. The soldiers break down the door, murder the men, rape the women and carry off whatever takes their fancy. Musée Bargoin, Clermont-Ferrand. Photo: Giraudon/the Bridgeman Art Library.

war, and even the duty of deposing monarchs who failed to respect the 'fundamental' laws of the kingdom and to protect the Church. The king's response to this challenge was to order the murder of the leaders of the Holy League – the Duke and the Cardinal of Guise. Subsequently, denounced as a 'wicked Herod', he was himself assassinated by a Dominican friar. The legitimate heir was his cousin, the Protestant military leader, Henri of Navarre, who claimed the throne as Henri IV. The new king faced enormous difficulty in securing recognition of his rights and in restoring the financial situation, military strength and authority of the Crown. Catholic nobles were conscious both of the threat to their faith and to the privileges they had derived previously from the monarchy. Henri, a master of compromise, sought to conciliate his opponents, however. He was greatly assisted by a widespread desire for the restoration of order. A strong current of opinion favoured support for the legitimate king and resented Spanish intervention in support of the Catholic League. This sentiment was reinforced amongst both nobles and urban élites by the apparent threat of anarchy represented by the radicalisation of the League in some northern cities and by peasant violence. The political situation improved to a significant degree following the decision of Henri IV (in 1593) to accept the Catholic faith. The surrender of Paris, a stronghold of the Holy League, in March 1594 was followed by an ostentatious display of religious devotion by the new king. Nonetheless, the Edict of Nantes (1598) offered Protestants a compromise peace, with politico-military guarantees of their freedom to worship provided in the form of nearly 200 towns, mainly in the south, that they were to control.

Another major innovation, with far-reaching consequences, was the *paulette* (1604), which provided for the payment of a fee in return for which office holders were allowed to bequeath or even sell their positions. The sale of office, as a revenue-raising device, had begun in the fourteenth century and had become increasingly frequent during the reign of Francis I. To the purchaser it offered a financial return, tax exemptions, social status and, in some cases, eventual ennoblement. Thus the investment was a rational use of capital, as well as 'providing an important channel for social mobility, administrative personnel for the state and an important source of crown revenue' (Doyle). In the short term the sale of office served to reduce magnate influence on the bureaucracy, restricting the ability of great lords to construct dependent clienteles. In the longer term private ownership of state office and the creation of a largely self-perpetuating élite were to become major obstacles to judicial and fiscal reform. It was difficult for the state to control or dismiss its own officials. The problem would be compounded by the multiplication of the number of such 'venal' offices, on a scale unsurpassed in Europe, to meet the costs of war in the seventeenth century. There were *c.* 5,000 venal officers early in the fifteenth century, but by the mid-1660s there would be 45,000, and by 1789 70,000. The system, which allowed the ennoblement of successful bourgeois families, diverted them from trade into the legal or administrative professions. Although their presence was resented bitterly by established nobles, it did allow for continuous upward mobility, for a constant renewal of the élite and for the creation of a certain sense of common interest within the propertied classes.

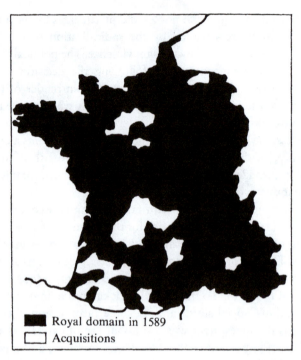

Figure 3.2 The creation of France, V: expansion of the royal domain during the reign of Henri IV, 1589–1610. (Source: Revel, *L'espace français*.)

The assassination of Henri IV in 1610 removed a strong and effective ruler. Concerned by the prospect of another period of internal disorder, the deputies of the Third Estate summoned to an Estates-General in 1614 declared it to be a fundamental law that the king 'is sovereign in his state, holding his crown from God alone'. Their worst fears appeared to be confirmed when – during the regency of Marie de Medici, and then, once he had come of age, during the rule of Louis XIII (1610–43) – faction rivalry initiated a return to anarchy, only gradually brought to an end between 1625 and 1642 when Cardinals Richelieu and then Mazarin sought to restore effective central leadership. Concerned by the continued ability of Protestant nobles such as the Duc de Rohan and his brother Soubise to muster military forces, by rebellion in the south-west in 1621/2 and following the successful siege of La Rochelle in 1626, Richelieu was able to strip the Protestants of their political and military privileges and finally bring the wars of religion to an end. At the same time, and as part of the continuing effort to build up client networks entirely dependent on the Crown, the powers of the provincial governors were reduced through the appointment of royal *commissaires*, the forerunners of the later *intendants*. At this stage, these functionaries, provided with considerable supervisory and remedial powers as agents of the Royal Council, were merely detached on temporary missions. They held non-venal commissions and were dependent upon the Crown in a way that the mass of royal *officiers* were not. They were required to cooperate with the governors and to establish good relationships with local élites, and were given particular responsibility for justice, police and finance. Rapidly becoming a normal feature of provincial government, they proved able to virtually double tax income in the decade after 1635. This enabled the monarchy to raise a permanent army and to engage in campaigns on an unprecedented scale, largely in central Europe during the Thirty Years War (1618–48), to prevent encirclement by the Spanish and Austrian Habsburgs. It reduced dependence on the military support of the great nobles and urban militias, and by enhancing opportunities for service in the royal army considerably increased the Crown's powers of patronage. On the downside, massive tax increases provoked a renewal of popular protest, made all the more dangerous in the case of the Fronde (1648–52) by the simultaneous expression of grievances by elements of the great nobility and magistrature irritated by the aggressive methods of the two cardinals and the obvious accumulation of great fortunes by their families.

The Fronde – a confused mixture of conflicts – prolonged the devastation caused by the Thirty Years War, particularly northeast of Paris. It revealed the continued ability of feudal grandees such as the Orléans, Condé, Conti and Longueville to challenge the authority of the Crown, weakened again by a minority on the accession of the five-year-old Louis XIV in 1643. Faction rivalry led the great aristocrats to act as regional warlords, mobilising kin, clients and dependants. At least initially, they enjoyed the support of many office holders, including the magistrates of the Paris parlement, irritated by the devaluation of existing offices through continued sales, as well as by rising taxation. The 'tyrannical' excesses of royal power were denounced and calls were heard for the summoning of an Estates-General. In August 1648 barricades appeared once again in the streets of Paris, and the following January the young king was forced to flee from his capital – an experience that marked him for life. Eventually this fragmented assault petered out, on account of the mutual hostilities of its leading proponents and the appalled reaction of disaffected officials to the arrogance of the grandees and their willingness to call on Spanish support. Lesser nobles and magistrates alike had taken advantage of popular grievances but soon were afraid that protest might get out of hand. Chronic and endemic poverty and widespread brutality were characteristics of seventeenth-century society. Vagabonds and undisciplined troops increased the sense of insecurity. Poor harvests intensified popular misery and the likelihood of violent resistance to the financial exactions of seigneurs and clerics, and especially the demands of government. When royal *officiers* were interested parties, the lack, or else excessive cost, of legal redress often seemed to leave little alternative. The expression of discontent took various forms. The 'exploiters' could be punished by stone throwing, the destruction of their property or, in extreme cases, by mutilation and death. Animals might be maimed, hayricks set on fire, seigneurial or royal agents beaten up, or contempt expressed for the offender in various ways, such as ribald songs, the more structured use of 'rough music' (*charivari*) or through burning an effigy at carnival. The latter was a customary means of expressing a grievance, part of a recognised litany of protest – a useful means of letting off steam, and thus less likely to meet with official repression. In the absence of an effective local policing system and backed by a sense of communal solidarity, such actions might at least ensure that landlords, seigneurs and the collectors of tithes and taxes behaved with prudence, torn as they were between their duty to the Crown and the need to retain respect within their particular communities.

Even so, following a poor harvest, the pressures on wide sections of the community could become intolerable. The well-being of normally prosperous peasants and artisans might seem to be menaced by the tax collector. The very survival of the poor was threatened. The anxiety and bitterness and the emotional instability that resulted could overcome any lingering fear of official retribution and provoke brutal protest, leading occasionally to major revolts. These were likely to involve mostly peasants with a leavening of urban artisans, tradesmen and impecunious minor nobles and professional men. They developed especially when there was no local garrison, or when, because of war, troops had been transferred to the frontiers. The most notable risings occurred in Guienne and other south-western provinces in 1548, in Dauphiné in the late 1570s, in Normandy and Brittany and again in the south-west in the 1590s, in the south-west once more in 1624 (Quercy) and, in 1636-7, the most serious of all, the *Croquant* revolts affecting a wide area between the rivers Loire and Garonne, followed in 1639 by the revolt of the *Nu-Pieds* in Normandy. There were an estimated 282 popular risings between 1635 and 1660. The rebels used community structures and economic networks as a basis for organisation, and employed custom and religion as justificatory beliefs. Certainly, the general climate of opposition to authority encouraged such action, particularly against tax collectors. New taxes, or rumours of such, were enough to cause church bells to be rung, emissaries from various communities to meet and crowds to march. The strength of popular feeling can be explained by the pressure imposed by a monetary tax on a predominantly subsistence rural economy. It forced peasants to search desperately for something to sell or for remunerative employment, often depriving them of foodstuffs upon which they depended, or forcing them into debt. Revolt was most likely in wartime, when taxes, which anyway had been more or less arbitrarily imposed on a community by outsiders for purposes they rarely understood, were increased. Although a serious menace to social order, these revolts rarely posed a threat to the social system. They represented a demand for the easing of burdens and for 'justice'. Most seigneurs shared the anti-fiscalism of the protesters, themselves viewing taxes as a threat to the payment of rents and feudal dues. Peasants were unable to escape from a profound sense of dependence on land-owners and the clergy. They lacked a vision of an alternative society. In the end, the localism and limited objectives of these rebellions meant that they were easily suppressed once sufficient military force had been gathered and local élites, frightened that the turbulent crowds might turn on them, were willing once again to cooperate with royal officials.

The coronation of Louis XIV in 1654 represented a symbolic celebration of the end of this time of troubles. In spite of these

Plate 3.2 Louis XIV in 1660, aged twenty-two, already marked by a sense of his personal dignity. Engraving by P. van Schuppen, after a painting by W. Vaillant. © Roger-Viollet/TopFoto.

disorders, the administrative machine had survived and, however inadequately, continued to function. It could serve as the basis for an eventual restoration of the Crown's authority. Indeed, the wars, which had increased the state's financial needs, had intensified governmental impatience with such intermediary bodies as the provincial Estates and municipalities and encouraged authoritarianism on the part of its officers. The later seventeenth century was to see the virtual disappearance of large-scale armed revolts, and reinforcement of the repressive apparatus of the state. This was associated with less onerous fiscal demands, a reduction in religious tension and the development of a better-disciplined society, due to the spread of education and especially the more effective religious socialisation associated with the Catholic Counter-Reformation. Subsequently the most serious cause of popular protest was to be high food prices, leading to riots in market places, and attacks on food transports and on merchants suspected of speculation. The numbers of such incidents increased into the eighteenth century as growing commercialisation and the intensification of the profit motive came into conflict with the subsistence needs of the poor and traditional conceptions of economic morality. Disorder remained common until improved communications, modernised marketing systems and greater security in food supply were established in the middle of the nineteenth century.

To a greater extent even than that of Henri IV, the reign of Louis XIV (1643–1715) is obscured by myth. It is safe to characterise it, however, as a further attempt to bring to an end the political fragmentation and social anarchy symbolised by the Fronde. The king's greatest success was to be the internal pacification achieved in the early years of his reign. On assuming personal control of government in 1661, Louis appeared to be immensely energetic but also dangerously avid for glory. In the continuing struggle for European hegemony with the Habsburgs the French would enjoy the advantage of a relatively homogeneous kingdom, with interior lines of communication as well as the capacity to mobilise resources more effectively. Initial success, resulting in the annexation of the Franche-Comté and strategic towns in Flanders (1678) and of Strasbourg (1681), and the threat of French hegemony, only alarmed the rest of Europe, however. Eventually permanent mobilisation for war would bring disaster, but, in the meantime at least, foreign armies were largely excluded from French soil, the French army itself was more regularly paid and better disciplined, and the nobility were employed more fully in the service of the state – both in the army and at court – than ever before. The disarmament of noble châteaux and of the towns, commenced by Richelieu and Mazarin, also continued. For the first time an effective royal monopoly of armed force was achieved.

In many respects Louis XIV was operating a system of government created by his predecessors, in which the role of the monarch, as the Lord's anointed, was to serve as the symbol and source of unity. The upper nobility (*haute noblesse*) was compensated for the loss of its provincial power by means of substantial pensions and employment in honorific positions at court, as well as in the provincial governorships and the higher military commands and episcopal appointments that they saw as their due, whilst the bellicose energies of the lower nobility were channelled into the king's service in an army that had grown to around 360,000 by the beginning of the eighteenth century and that was now more effectively royal and less an instrument of the great nobility. The constant waging of war would satisfy the nobility's medieval perception of themselves as the warrior caste. The careful control of patronage systems and of the army allowed the king to purchase the loyalty of members of the élite or, if necessary, to use coercion. Architecture and the decorative arts were employed at Versailles to provide a splendid setting for the rituals, ceremonies, ballets and masques, which added to the spectacle of court life. Bishop Bossuet prayed that 'the glorious dignity and the majesty of the palace might blaze out, for all to see, the splendid grandeur of royal power'. More widely, statues and engravings, pamphlets and histories, and the clergy preaching from their pulpits all contributed to the construction of an iconography of power, a cult of monarchy, associated with the image of an all-powerful Sun King. Besides symbolising royal power and glory, Versailles provided a focal point for an aristocratic civilisation and for the diffusion throughout society of more restrained behaviour, of a new civility, politeness and good taste. Attendance on the king at court was the means of affirming rank and obtaining high office and pensions, of sharing in the royal bounty. From the point of view of the monarchy, the enormous cost of constructing the palace was money well spent. It increased the dependence of the upper nobility, meant that they could be more closely supervised, and weakened their ties with the lesser provincial nobles. The members of such up-and-coming families as the Colbert, Le Tellier and

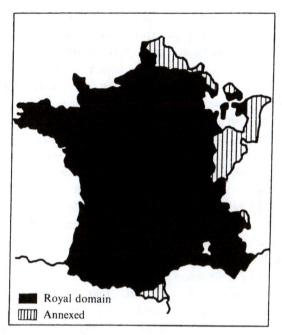

Figure 3.3 The creation of France, VI: the reign of Louis XIV, 1643–1715.
(Source: Revel, *L'espace français*.)

Phélypeaux were willing to devote themselves to their master's objectives, whilst enriching themselves in the process. This enhanced regality also ensured that kings, treated with exaggerated respect and deference, confident in their God-given authority and more than ever isolated from alternative forms of reality, were to remain obsessively committed to the achievement of personal glory and dynastic aggrandisement.

Another major act, of both direct political and symbolic significance, was the renewed assault on Protestantism, culminating in the revocation of the Edict of Nantes in 1685. This was probably inevitable. Catholics were appalled by the toleration of heresy. Already, the military provisions of the edict had been substantially whittled away. The existence of an armed state within the state was clearly intolerable. After 1622 only La Rochelle and Montauban remained under Protestant control. Whilst it confirmed the Edict of Nantes, the Peace of Alès in 1629 suppressed the right to maintain even these towns as places of safety. By then too the Protestant party had been weakened by many desertions, most significantly by noble leaders afraid of losing access to royal patronage. The Catholic Counter-Reformation, which really began to make its impact on France only from the first decade of the seventeenth century, was also beginning to have profound effects, imposing a new order and a crusading spirit on a Church that by now had recovered most of the resources usurped or lost during the Wars of Religion. During the decades of tense coexistence that followed, special taxes were imposed on Protestant congregations, and over three-quarters of their churches were closed. Efforts were also made to encourage conversions by billeting troops on families (*dragonnades*). In 1685 Louis XIV, convinced of the validity of the principle 'One faith, one king, one law', was able to revoke the edict with little risk of serious resistance. Protestants faced the alternatives of conversion, going underground or emigration. Some 140,000 to 160,000 chose the last option. Undoubtedly, the fact that these included many merchants and manufacturers (although partly compensated for by the influx of refugee Irish Catholics) had damaging economic consequences. The subsequent assault on Jansenism, whose supporters attacked corruption within the Church and called for the achievement of spiritual perfection, would be motivated similarly by hostility towards 'heresy' and in response to what the king judged to be a challenge to his authority. In 1713 the refusal of the Paris parlement to register the condemnatory papal bull *Unigenitus* heralded an ongoing dispute over authority in state and Church.

That Louis XIV could make effective use of the political system reflected not just his own considerable ability but also the heartfelt desire of the better-off to avoid a renewal of internal anarchy and the king's determination to exclude potentially troublesome magnates from his council in favour of dependent members of a relatively new bureaucratic nobility. King and nobles alike were imbued with a more clearly defined sense of social hierarchy and mutual dependence, in which the king stood indisputably at the summit and could appeal to the honour and loyalty of his nobles. A king-centred patriotism developed, as service to the monarch was idealised, taking priority over all other relationships. A carefully constructed etiquette increased the social distance between Louis and his nobles.

Although disputes still occurred, their significance was limited both by the superior power of the monarchy and the involvement of most noble families, whether of the old 'sword' nobility or of the substantially new judicial-cum-bureaucratic 'robe' nobility, in the state service. The nobility developed a growing confidence that their needs were served best within rather than against the state. This compact would survive for as long as the élites remained sure that the monarchy was protecting their vital interests.

Certainly, Louis XIV thought of himself as absolute, and many popular historians have taken him at his own estimation. The development of absolutism (a late eighteenth-century label), a crucially important stage in the process of state building, involved an increase in the interventionist capacity of the central power, by means of the further development of bureaucratic administration, although Louis XIV and his successors would continue to face many of the same obstacles, including those of distance, poor communications and inadequate resources, as their predecessors. They had to work within the limits set by established institutions and extremely varied and heterogeneous laws and customs, and by the bounds of a pre-industrial society. The implementation of the policies of the central government in the provinces depended especially upon the *intendants*, recruited amongst aspiring young noble members of the Privy Council. Each was responsible for one of the thirty-three major administrative units (*généralités*), with subordinate officials (*subdélégués*), usually local nobles, under their orders, each administering an *élection*. They supervised all aspects of general and increasingly of municipal administration, including justice and the assessment and collection of taxes. These few agents of the central administration depended upon the willing cooperation of local notables, both nobles and commoners – men who owed their influence to their personal wealth, ownership of property, and influence within their communities as much as to their offices. At the base of the judicial hierarchy were the privileged urban oligarchies and in particular 70,000 seigneurial courts. Thus, in most circumstances, the representatives of the central government were local men still and behaved as such. Family connections and local solidarities provided permanent obstacles to the development of bureaucratic government. Conflicts over jurisdiction and rivalries between governmental institutions abounded, exacerbated by the successive creation of new, and often venal, offices, which increased the cost greatly and slowed the processes of administration and justice. Covert disobedience and the failure to implement instructions replaced open defiance. The situation of the *intendants* was made all the more difficult by the inadequate numbers of police. For example, Lyon, with 150,000 inhabitants, employed only eighty-four. The countryside was secured by a royal corps of mounted constabulary (the *maréchaussée*) with a national strength of only 4,000. Community self-regulation was the ideal. When substantial disorder threatened, there was no alternative to calling in the army, but this could take time and was resisted by military commanders. For all these reasons, the *intendants* were forced to adapt to local circumstances. By the 1780s they were experiencing a gradual decline in their authority as a consequence of weakness at the centre, due to the renewed assertiveness of the nobility and the combativeness of the institutions within which noble interests were represented best.

The shortcomings of the system were obvious, especially in the frequent partiality and cruelty displayed in the administration of justice. Moreover, reform was extremely difficult. The purchase of office only reinforced the sense of independence of the mass of office holders (*officiers*). Governments did not dare suppress venal office, nor could they afford to buy out office holders. At best a strong king, such as Louis XIV, could use patronage to control such key institutions as the few remaining provincial Estates and the parlements, which were the highest courts of law in their particular regions but also responsible for the registration of government edicts, which was necessary before they acquired the force of law. The failure of kings to summon an Estates-General between 1615 and 1789, however, and the absence of a representative and consultative institution at the national level seriously weakened relationships between the monarchy and its leading subjects.

In this situation internal administration remained 'a dialogue between the Crown and a series of local élites, institutions and social groups, each one jealously guarding its traditions and undeniably legal privileges' (Mettam). In the towns various groups (*officiers*, corporations, and so on) were accorded privileges in return for payment and service as part of the royal administration. In the countryside the key role remained that of the noble seigneur. The exercise of power at local and regional levels continued to depend upon relationships within the noble élites and those between nobles and the social groups they sought to dominate. What was willed at the centre was not necessarily implemented in the locality. This was evident especially in the crucially important administration of finance. War and preparation for war were constant features of the *ancien régime* state and central to its institutional development. Its costs were the main charge on the budget – rarely below one-third, often over one-half, reaching 70 per cent during wars. During the reign of Louis XIV the army grew in size from some 80,000 to 340,000 by 1696. Its equipment, training and tactics were improved, it was better supplied, and the field army was supported by a state-of-the-art network of frontier fortresses designed by the brilliant military engineer the Marquis de Vauban. The prolonged wars of attrition that characterised the period imposed a crushing fiscal burden on the population, however, and represented a warning about the difficulty of disengagement from military commitments. Because of the fiscal exemptions enjoyed by the nobles and clergy, the burden of taxation was borne primarily by the peasants, those least able to bear it. The situation was made even worse by the high cost of levying taxes, which depended upon the holders of venal office or, in the case of indirect taxes, on tax farmers – consortia of businessmen under contract to the Crown – both operating through thousands of personal agents. These groups were at least as interested in personal profit as in serving the state. The efforts to encourage manufacture and colonial trade associated with Jean-Baptiste Colbert were part of a drive to increase tax revenue as the means of achieving military supremacy; their impact on state revenues was at best marginal, and on economic structures it was negligible. Increasingly, recourse to loans raised on the Paris capital market was necessary, leading to an accumulation of debt and to a growing dependence of the Crown upon its financiers. The cost of servicing these mounting debts absorbed 15 to 20 per cent of the budget for most of the eighteenth century, but an unsustainable 49 per cent by 1788. The mutual interest of (mainly recently ennobled) financiers and the leading noble families who provided most of their capital in preserving such a profitable system was to prove a constant obstacle to reform.

Plate 3.3 Construction of a road. The movement of people and goods was made easier by the *corvée* (1738), the establishment of the *Corps des Ponts et Chaussées* (1750) and substantial government investment. Painting by J. Vernet (1774). Musée du Louvre, Paris. Photo: Giraudon/the Bridgeman Art Library.

The reign of the Sun King came to an end with an intense social crisis caused by the burden of taxation at a time when, as in 1694, harsh weather and repeated harvest failure, or between 1708 and 1710 an accumulation of military and natural disasters, would in any case have had a devastating demographic impact. A state of mutual exhaustion brought twenty-five years of war to an end with the Treaties of Utrecht and Rastadt in 1713/14. In August 1715 a depressed and dying monarch warned his infant successor that

all your happiness will depend on your submitting yourself to God and on the care that you take in bringing relief to your people. This means that you should avoid, as far as possible, making war. It is the ruin of the people. Do not follow the bad example that I have set you. I have often gone to war too lightly and pursued it for vanity's sake. Do not imitate me but be a prince of peace.

The political order had survived nevertheless. Moreover, in contrast with these calamitous decades, the remainder of the eighteenth century, and in particular the years between 1745 and 1770, were to be characterised by economic and demographic recovery, and long periods of internal peace and order. Greater prosperity was evident in the rapid expansion of internal trade, in the greater intrusion of market forces throughout society, and particularly in the emergence of a leisured, middle-class consumer category. Overseas commerce expanded rapidly. The colonial trade in slaves, sugar, indigo, tobacco and coffee brought wealth to the merchants of Bordeaux, Marseille, Nantes, Rouen and Le Havre. The Caribbean colonies were a source of great prosperity but, additionally, a potent cause of rivalry with Britain. The disruptive impact of war and the frequent prospect of poor harvests causing a generalised economic crisis were symptomatic of the continued fragility of the socio-political system. Although there were signs of technical innovation in both farming and manufacture, and in spite of the fact that easier climatic conditions, improved communications and the better distribution of foodstuffs limited the intensity of subsistence crises, the basic economic and social structures of a pre-industrial society survived. France remained a predominantly agrarian society, with manufacturing dispersed in small workshops in town and country alike, and the entire economy dominated by the harvest. The legal hierarchy of a society of orders remained intact, justified as it had been around the year 1000 by the distinction between those who prayed, those who fought and those who laboured. Status was thus based upon notions of honour, codified by law. Wealth both reinforced and cut across these distinctions. The growing monetisation of society ensured that, increasingly, status was perceived to be for sale. In a strictly hierarchical – though not entirely immobile – society, the poor were kept in their place by the need to gain a living, by dependence, by fear, by a sense of inferiority and by the pressing need to display outward respect. Similarly the political institutions of the *ancien régime* changed only very slowly, with precedent being used to considerable effect by the defenders of vested interest. Nevertheless, and in spite of the slow pace of social change, these formal structures were coming to be seen as increasingly anachronistic.

In recent years it has become unfashionable to emphasise the social causes of the Revolution of 1789. In place of the once familiar Marxist view of a struggle between a declining nobility and a rising bourgeoisie, increasingly historians have come to stress the interests nobles and bourgeois had in common, as well as the divisions of interest within each of these groups. They have quoted Anne-Robert-Jacques Turgot's observation in 1776 that '[t]he cause of privilege is no longer the cause of distinguished families against commoners, but the cause of the rich against the poor' and have described the emergence of an élite of *notables* of which nobles were only a part. Prosperity promoted a proliferation of social élites. In a society that defined itself in terms of orders, there were groups at the summit of each order, which tended to distinguish themselves by their wealth, status and power from the rest of their order. Nobles and wealthy non-nobles had shared interests in landownership, a common life-style and the enjoyment of privilege. The bourgeoisie remained an essentially pre-industrial class, being composed mainly of land-owners, professional men, financiers and merchants, and, far from being hostile to nobility, wealthy commoners were engaged in the process of acquiring noble status as the ultimate mark of their personal success. Many members of this class enjoyed a recognised status and shared in privileges recognised by law, including the right of self-regulation, the protection of specific interests, and tax exemptions accorded to members of the liberal professions, manufacturing guilds and municipalities. If this was the case, the problem will be to explain why the lines of conflict as they were drawn in 1789 would largely separate nobles and bourgeois. The rapid collapse of the regime, paralleled perhaps only by the events of 1989/90 in eastern Europe, is surely inexplicable without consideration of the underlying social tensions.

Certainly, the French nobility did not comprise a declining social group. Although land remained by far the main source of income, and most families restricted themselves to traditional investments in property and in office and enjoyed the benefits of rising prices from about 1730, many nobles were at the forefront of innovation in textiles, mining and metallurgy, as well as in agriculture. Moreover, successful business and professional men still sought nobility as the ultimate symbol of achievement. Whilst impoverished families of ancient lineage often resented these nouveau riche newcomers, the nobility constituted a relatively open élite, which continued to renew itself. Like any other social group, the nobility were divided – between wealthy and impoverished nobles, court nobles and provincial gentry, old and new, and political clienteles and family clans – into groups that had differing perceptions of their vital interests. The mass of provincial nobles resented the power and ostentation of the great court families (some 4,000 people), who monopolised pensions, favours and senior positions in the army and bureaucracy. Due to their privileged access to the king, these families were able to enhance their status as power brokers, and, in terms of culture and manners, set the tone for all those with social pretensions. Of course, families of old lineage poured scorn on the affectations of the recently ennobled, many of whom would nevertheless succeed in fully integrating themselves within the course of two or three generations – an achievement frequently symbolised by the move from judicial office (robe nobility) to military service. The need to 'appear' encouraged conspicuous consumption: the possession of both a landed estate and a town house, the adoption of the latest fashions in furnishings and dress. Many noble families could barely make ends meet, however. Some were unable to afford the education or the investment necessary to acquire office, or the equipment essential to a military career. Only their pride, the cult of honour, the sense of belonging to a race apart (given a semblance of historical credibility in such books as the Comte de Boulainvilliers'

1732 *Essai sur la noblesse de France*), the right to wear a sword, and the family pew in the village church allowed them to maintain a 'social distance' between themselves and the peasantry. Poor nobles faced the eventual prospect of being forced to take on degrading manual or moneymaking activities, which might well lead to *dérogeance* or the loss of noble status and privilege, including the tax exemptions made all the more important by their possessors' impecunious position. The great majority came somewhere in between these extremes. For them, a decent income, education and culture were the means of keeping up appearances. They might choose to avoid the expense and stress of court life, dividing their time between château and town house, supervising their estates, playing a role in local administration, distributing charity, 'protecting' their people and engaging in the daily symbolic relationships between superior and inferior denoted by language – the use by the superior of the familiar *tu* (you) and by the inferior, in response, of the formal *vous*, or by the deference associated with the removal of one's hat. A carefully planned marriage strategy was the crucial means of keeping the family patrimony intact. This might involve the division of inheritance to favour the eldest son and even the dispatch of unmarriageable daughters to a nunnery. In terms of a family's capacity to appear *comme il faut*, women clearly had a central role to play. In spite of sexual double standards and the fact that females were defined socially by their relationships with men, in practice the formal division between the public, male-dominated, and the private spheres of life was weakened by informal influences and female dominance over the household.

The number of nobles by 1789 has been estimated variously at between 110,000 and 350,000 (0.5 to 1.5 per cent of the population), owning between one-quarter and one-third of the land. In France, unlike Britain, titles and noble status descended from the father to all his children. Acceptance of the lower figure would suggest that one in four noble families had acquired nobility during the eighteenth century, a relatively high rate of upward mobility, but if the higher estimate is accurate only around one in twelve families had been recently ennobled, which would support a more plausible view of the second order as a relatively self-contained, though far from closed, caste. Compared with other social groups, the nobility's privileges and distinctive values gave them a greater sense of corporate unity and of moral superiority. Their traditional commitment had been to military service, but with improved education increasingly nobles had become bureaucrats as well as warriors. The latter was regarded as the most honourable of its functions, through which its members sacrificed their lives and justified their fiscal and seigneurial privileges. As had been the case from time immemorial, nobles occupied all the important offices of Church and state; of sixty-five ministers in office between 1718 and 1789, only three were non-nobles, although others came from recently ennobled families. Nobles were thus both the agents of a centralising royal power and, in the provinces, its most determined opponents. It would take the Revolution to impose a greater sense of unity.

The 'bourgeoisie' also constituted an extremely diverse group. In current usage the term (when it was not used in the technical sense to designate an enfranchised citizen of a city) was applied to the property owner or *rentier*. To *vivre bourgeoisement* meant to live primarily from unearned income, and to share the disdain aristocrats felt for those who devoted themselves to 'dishonourable' money-grubbing activities, or who demeaned themselves by serving others, as shopkeepers did, or were engaged in degrading manual labour. Often such people belonged to the charmed circle of holders of ennobling office, admission to which required the wherewithal to purchase, but also useful contacts and family connections. Similarly, a legal practice required an expensive education but also offered the prospect of a comfortable lifestyle, leisure for the cultivation of the intellect, and a degree of independence.

Although the structure of the bourgeoisie varied with the range of economic and administrative functions of a particular town, wealthier members of the class were inevitably few in number and formed a relatively coherent group, living in close proximity in newly constructed mansions, furnished in the latest style, meeting socially and intermarrying. Below them in status came the less successful *négociants* (men of commerce), *marchands* (traders, manufacturers and retailers) and professionals and the lower middle class of shop-keepers and self-employed artisans. There could be little sense of solidarity amongst such diverse groups. The artisans took pride in their 'art', in skills acquired through a long apprenticeship. Both they and the journeymen they employed shared a sense of moral community that limited the tensions between master and man and distinguished them from the members of other trades and especially from the mass of servants and unskilled labourers, the unemployed and the sick, who were desperately striving to make ends meet, often by resort to petty crime and prostitution. In a town such as Orléans in 1789, *négociants, marchands,* officials, professional men and shopkeepers made up 7 per cent of the active inhabitants and master-artisans 30.8 per cent. Although only 16 per cent of the population lived in towns, most of which were small and essentially medieval in appearance, the dynamic impact of these places as economic, administrative, political and cultural centres should not be underestimated.

If the nobility frequently represented a goal and a model to aspiring members of the middle classes, they might also often resent its arrogance. The most common path to nobility was through the purchase of ennobling office. Jacques Necker calculated that there were some 4,000 of these. It was also necessary to withdraw from 'degrading' moneymaking activities and to adopt the lifestyle of a landed gentleman. Even then the process of assimilation could take two or three generations. Moreover, in spite of a substantial increase in the cost, economic prosperity and growing wealth intensified competition for ennobling office, which, after all, promised enhanced status, profit and tax exemptions. Nevertheless, demand for office was growing at the same time as institutions such as the parlements were becoming more exclusive. The result was a perceived reduction in the opportunities for social promotion and increased hostility towards the established nobility, particularly at the local level, at which noble *hauteur* was more likely to be experienced. This does not mean that, before 1789, the bourgeoisie were becoming class-conscious. Certainly, however, some of the better-educated and more self-aware landowners, merchants, *rentiers* and professional men were attracted by meritocratic and egalitarian ideas, and were increasingly resentful of noble privilege.

In spite of the emergence of something akin to class structures based upon income and socio-professional origins, the old concepts of 'honour' and 'dignity' continued to influence social relationships. Aristocratic pretensions and insistence upon legal and social distinctions were a cause of tension. Inevitably, these affectations were resented both by the newly ennobled en route to assimilation and, especially, by those commoners aware of aristocratic disdain. The path to social promotion and final respectability was in practice obstructed by all manner of pitfalls. The number of ennobling offices was always relatively small. Economic depression might spoil the best-laid plans. Lawyers, landowners, *officiers*, large merchants (*négociants*) and *rentiers* were essentially conservative in their outlook, however, and their resentment was only beginning to find political expression before the pre-revolutionary crisis. In part this was a response to the so-called 'noble reaction', an effort to preserve noble predominance in appointments to civil office and senior positions in the army. Nobles felt that they, and they alone, were the natural counsellors of the monarchy, and that they had a right – indeed, a duty – to serve. Thus their privileges were a just reward for service. In many respects the label 'reaction' is a misnomer. It did not take the form of a deliberate offensive on the part of the privileged. Nobles were behaving much as they always had. The term does convey accurately a growing disquiet about their behaviour amongst other social groups, however. The loi Ségur of 1781 (largely a codification of earlier measures) restricted direct entry into certain commissioned ranks in the army to men belonging to families that had been noble for at least four generations, with the aim of creating an officer corps imbued with traditional martial values. The law had little practical consequence. Even before the decree about 95 per cent of officers were nobles. Nevertheless, it served as proof of growing noble exclusivism to non-nobles, and, indeed, to the recently ennobled, against whom it was primarily directed. Other features of this 'noble reaction' had an impact on rural life.

Towards the end of the eighteenth century it is estimated that the nobility owned around 25 per cent of the land, the clergy 6 to 10 per cent, the bourgeoisie around 30 per cent and peasants 40 to 45 per cent. In a period of rising prices, land was an attractive investment, the possession of which, moreover, secured social status. Much of the noble and clerical property was concentrated on the fertile northern plains, whilst the proportion owned by peasants tended to increase towards the south. To the north-east of a line from Caen to Lyon nobles owned about 30 per cent of the agricultural land, whilst to the south-west their share rarely exceeded 20 per cent. In some localities, particularly closer to large towns, the proportions were much higher. For many landowners there was little incentive to invest capital in agricultural improvement, especially when rental income was rising and might be supplemented with income from seigneurial dues or office holding. By these various means the relatively small number of noble families were able to appropriate perhaps one-quarter of the revenue from agriculture. This economic power was reinforced by the social and political power conferred by seigneurial justice and the support these families enjoyed in case of dispute from an administration itself consisting of nobles determined to defend the social order. The conditions of peasant life varied considerably from region to region according both to ecology and to the division of property. They made up about three-quarters of the population but, following the payment of rents, seigneurial dues, tithes and taxes, were left with little more than one-third of the income from the land. The survival of seigneurial obligations was a reminder of the peasants' 'servile' status, as was the seigneurs' right to judge disputes. Peasants were obliged to perform labour services for both lord and state. They were required to offer up a portion of the harvest to the seigneur and the Church and to make use of the lord's mill and winepress. Even their ownership of land was subject to restrictions. When it was sold a fee had to be paid to the seigneur, who also enjoyed a prior right of purchase and much-prized hunting rights. The increasingly common practice by which professional *feudistes* combed through charters in a search for lapsed obligations could either be viewed as a form of business rationalisation or as intensified exploitation, depending on one's point of view.

Other key factors influencing the situation of the rural population included tenurial arrangements, habitat structures, communal practices and cultural traditions, and legal status, with around 1 million classified as serfs in the Franche-Comté and Nivernais whilst other peasants were free agents. Significantly, however, only a minority, perhaps one-third, had access to sufficient land to maintain their families. The remainder were forced to rent land or seek employment as agricultural labourers or in the rapidly expanding rural manufactures in order to subsist. Population pressure and the continuous parcellation of smallholdings drove many peasants into destitution, allowing landlords to increase the size of their estates, whilst at the same time further subdividing holdings to increase the number of tenants on short leases. As in previous periods of demographic recovery, the intensification of commercial relationships and the move towards production for sale enhanced the value of the basic economic resources, and intensified the competition to control them. Some landowners were encouraged to develop more remunerative means of exploiting their economic resources, through improved farming methods, greater commercialisation of the product, investment in the exploitation of raw materials on and under the land (particularly water, wood and coal) and attempts to increase the returns from rentals and seigneurial dues (assisted by better surveying, mapping and accounting techniques). In a period of growing population pressure on resources, the rise in rents and prices led to a deterioration in the situation of the growing numbers of poor, struggling to obtain access to land, employment or at least charity. Inevitably, such conditions increased the hostility of the mass of the population towards those – whether nobles, bourgeois, clerics or the better-off peasants – who appeared to be accumulating land and to be exploiting the scarce resources they controlled at the expense of the rural community. As always, such pressures stimulated peasant resistance, though this inevitably came from a position of weakness in the face of seigneurial justice and noble domination of the judicial and administrative systems.

Seigneurialism raised complex economic and legal issues and caused endless friction. Resistance by communities took various forms, including lawsuits over such matters as the enclosure of common land and the restriction of customary rights of usage in forests, and increasing criminality in what remained a harsh and brutal world, in spite of growing literacy and the Church's efforts to encourage greater self-control. Both provide evidence of a more combative spirit and of resistance on the part of the rural poor to the development of a capitalistic agriculture. This was evident especially when, after a poor harvest, the rise in food prices caused by panic buying and speculation made the burden of rents, seigneurial dues, tithes and taxes, which even in a good year extracted anywhere between one-third and one-half of the peasants' gross revenue, all the more intolerable. Certainly, there was nothing new in this, nor in the tendency of the poor to explain their misery by personalising their problems and in particular blaming the parasitic activities of merchants, seigneurs and the clergy. The seigneurial presence, with its courts of law (so important in the resolution of land disputes), the right to levy dues and labour service, and its irritating monopolies, hunting privileges and pomp, was particularly strong in the north, east and centre-east, but much less so in the Massif Central and the south. It must all have seemed increasingly redundant when the seigneur no longer offered protection against marauders and when most of his judicial functions had been rented out to local lawyers or taken over by the monarchy. Although frequently commoners owned these rights, the system nonetheless remained closely identified with the nobility. It was in those areas in which the seigneurial system was most burdensome that the capitalistic pressures to acquire land and to maximise returns were also most intense. In contrast, the tithe payable to the Church was particularly high, at around 10 to 12.5 per cent of the crop in the south-west, whilst averaging 7 to 8 per cent for France as a whole. Taxation was another burden borne primarily by the peasants, who were additionally required to perform labour service on the roads, billet and transport troops and serve in the militia. If there were no major anti-taxation revolts in the eighteenth century, there was certainly bitter resentment, especially of indirect taxes such as the *gabelle* on salt. Nevertheless, the burden of protest had shifted clearly from resistance to the demands of the state to defence of communal interests against the increasingly capitalistic practices of landlords and seigneurs, of merchants and farmers.

It was the financial problems of the state, however, that were to cause the final crisis of the *ancien régime*. The demise of Louis XIV had been followed by the regency of Philippe d'Orléans (1715–23), during which the Scottish adventurer John Law was encouraged to develop his grand plans for the eventual repurchase of venal offices. In 1716 Law established a private bank with the right to issue banknotes, and which assumed responsibility for the state debt in return for the granting of monopoly trading privileges and responsibility for the collection of indirect taxes. The outcome was disastrous. Law's efforts to keep his complex enterprises afloat generated a speculative frenzy as more and more banknotes and shares were issued. When the bubble finally burst, in May 1720, those who had held on in the hope of further gain lost heavily. Speculators who had sold already made enormous fortunes. The state itself was able to repay loans with devalued banknotes. Subsequently, from 1726 to 1743, Cardinal de Fleury served as Louis XV's (1715–74) leading minister. The king has been portrayed both as the idle embodiment of vice and as a ruler who sponsored reforms towards the end of his long reign that might have saved the monarchy. The essential characteristic of this period was its relative freedom from external war. These were years of administrative reorganisation, of declining expenditure and taxation. They were an interlude between the wars of the Sun King and a new series of conflicts. Typically historians have neglected these relatively peaceful years.

Even so, Louis XV proved to be too weak and Cardinal de Fleury too old (at ninety) to resist the pressure from courtiers to enter the War of the Austrian Succession (1741–8) on the side of Prussia against the hereditary Habsburg enemy. In 1756 a reversal of alliances astounded opinion as France engaged in a conflict (the Seven Years War) over colonial possessions with Britain, in alliance with Austria. The results were catastrophic. Led by court favourites of doubtful competence, the army experienced a series of defeats in Germany, whilst prized colonies were lost, and commerce disrupted due to neglect of the navy and British maritime supremacy. The Treaty of Paris, which brought hostilities to an end, was especially humiliating. Moreover, by 1763 the national debt stood at an enormous 2,200 million *livres*, and every effort to improve the state's financial position through increased taxation met with opposition from the privileged classes. This was voiced by the parlements, and most notably by that of Paris, whose jurisdiction covered one-third of the kingdom. In all, there were thirteen of these 'sovereign' courts of law that served as final courts of appeal, together with twenty-five other more specialised sovereign courts, generally dealing with fiscal matters. Once having purchased their offices, the members of these courts were irremovable, and had a long tradition of opposition to the monarchy, expressed in the form of *remonstrances* or criticisms of various legislative proposals, and by refusals to register laws, without which they were inoperable within a court's jurisdiction.

Plate 3.4 The battle of Fontenoy during the War of Austrian Succession, 11 May 1745. Marshal de Saxe presents captured flags to Louis XV. Painting by H. Vernet. © RMN-Grand Palais (Château de Versailles)/ Christian Jean.

Although the king could force registration (by means of a procedure known as a *lit de justice*), parlements could thus delay the implementation of legislation and publicise their grievances. Parlements also had extensive administrative responsibilities in their localities, and these could bring them into conflict with the royal bureaucracy. Historically their members were usually divided, and unable to stand up to a determined government. From the 1750s, however, they appear to have voiced increasing criticism of government policy. In part this resulted from renewed conflict over Jansenism. The Archbishop of Paris, Christophe de Beaumont, believed that it was his duty to extirpate finally a philosophy that he believed was Calvinism in disguise and that represented a threat to the unity of the Church. In denouncing such extreme measures as the refusal of priests to administer the last rites to supporters of Jansenism, the Parlement of Paris was able to pose once again as the guardian of the fundamental laws of the kingdom. Its magistrates were to serve as a focal point for the development of political dissent, serving above all to express noble dissatisfaction. Most members of the parlements had inherited their offices and were already nobles (for the period 1775–90 this was true of 97 per cent in Toulouse, 90 per cent in Grenoble and 82 per cent in Paris, with much smaller proportions elsewhere), whilst membership conferred nobility upon the remainder. As nobles they were determined to safeguard their liberties, privileges and property, but in addition they were imbued with vague ideals concerning their duty to protect the nation against royal 'despotism'. This mixture of liberal principles and the defence of privilege attracted considerable public support. The Parlement of Paris claimed the right to verify taxation in 1763/4. Subsequently provincial parlements protested against government policy and even went on strike.

By the end of 1769 the budget deficit had reached 63 million *livres*, and the following two years' revenue had been spent in advance. In this desperate situation, and in order to circumvent opposition, for once, Louis XV acted with determination, provoking widespread accusations of 'despotism'. In February 1771 his energetic and ruthless chancellor René Maupeou exiled the Parlement of Paris to the provinces and determined to replace the venal magistrates with salaried officials dependent upon the state. The Abbé Terray began the work of tax reform, and by 1774 the budget was almost in balance, and the state's credit restored. This was the moment at which Louis XV died of smallpox. His young successor, a weaker man, dominated by his courtiers and anxious to avoid unpopularity, abandoned Maupeou's reforms just at the moment they were beginning to take effect. Until his death in 1781, the primary concern of his first minister, the Comte de Maurepas, was to conciliate the nobility by restoring the 'natural' partnership between the Crown and the sovereign courts. Thus the monarchy lost the political initiative. Although, following the chastening experience of Maupeou's reforms, for many years the parlements were to be more circumspect in their opposition, they were simply biding their time. Frequent requests continued to be made for an Estates-General, or at least provincial Estates, to consent to taxation. This helped to feed the growing current of criticism evident from the middle of the century, most notably in the thirty-five volumes of the *Encyclopédie* published between 1751 and 1772. This was a collective work edited by Denis Diderot and Jean d'Alembert. Its 150 contributors, inspired by the belief that progress was possible through the development of human reason, rejected appeals to the traditional authority of custom or religion, and insisted upon rational criticism of established institutions and behaviour. Typically, the Abbé Coyer in his *La Noblesse commerçante* (1756) ridiculed justifications of seigneurial privilege based upon the age-old military role of the nobility. All this contributed to the development of a complex intellectual climate that served to justify all manner of discontents. Thus Voltaire, who had initially praised the English parliament as a check on royal power, came to see the best hope of reform in the enlightened exercise of that power. More widely, the classical learning shared by every educated man, and so evident throughout literature and the arts, encouraged interest in conceptions of citizenship and patriotism associated with the Roman Republic, inspiring Jacques-Louis David's sensational pictorial depiction of the 'Oath of the Horatii'. In the *Social Contract*, Jean-Jacques Rousseau went so far as to propose the renunciation of individual rights and privileges in favour of a collective general will. These writers, the so-called *philosophes*, lacked a precise political programme. They favoured monarchy because of its supposed social utility, but many nobles and professional bourgeois desired a wider participation in government. This resulted in the development of a doctrine, based very much upon Montesquieu's *Esprit des Lois*, which demanded both the enlargement of the parlement's own constitutional role to include the approval of legislation and of taxation and the protection of the 'fundamental laws' of the kingdom, and at the same time condemned 'despotism', a debased form of monarchical government. In effect, a new political culture seems to have begun to emerge from the 1750s. Certainly, its proponents did not see themselves as revolutionaries but played the dangerous game of expressing contempt for established values, and presented new ideas on such matters as the duties of government and the role of the propertied classes, with little thought for the possible practical implications of their views. Meritocratic rather than egalitarian, nevertheless they supported greater civil liberty and freedom from the constraints of administrative regulation and from the restrictive effects of corporative organisation on economic activity, with 'happiness' as the objective and 'reason' as the means. As a practical matter, reform of the legal system was supported widely. It was assumed that the abolition of conflicting jurisdictions and complex judicial procedures would make justice available to all. They were particularly bitter critics of the Church, which seemed to exemplify the irrational and super-stitious, and to serve as the enemy of reason.

The impact of this 'Enlightenment' is not easy to assess. Undoubtedly, it proved to be fashionable in educated circles – noble and non-noble – particularly amongst the younger generations, gathering in provincial academies, in upper-class *salons* and the socially more diverse Masonic lodges, in reading rooms and cafés. It faced little in the way of structured, intellectual opposition. The spread of literacy, and the existence of a relatively well educated professional bourgeoisie, had created a wider audience for new ideas than ever before. The number of books published annually had risen from fewer than 1,000 in 1715 to over 4,000 by 1789; whilst in 1700 only three newspapers existed, all of them published by the government, by 1785 there were over eighty, including some published abroad. Even so, it is difficult to determine how far down the social hierarchy new ideas percolated. In intention at least, the Enlightenment was not directed at the mass of the population. Its proponents were suspicious, and indeed frightened, of popular unrest. The use of the apparently universalistic language of rights and justice encouraged the popularisation of new ideas amongst an increasingly literate middle-class and artisan audience, however, in simplified and often distorted form, through pamphlets and by word of mouth. A more scurrilous, satirical and often pornographic literary underworld also developed, which forcefully employed the language of the Enlightenment to attack privilege and corruption in high places. Censorship, although an irritation, proved largely inef-fective. It is worth remembering, though, that most of the population was untouched by new ideas, and that even in the educated classes many, especially amongst the older generations, and away from intel-lectual circles, were left indifferent or hostile. Traditional and religious ideas continued to hold sway. Although declining in significance, religious works retained their predominant place amongst the output of the printing press, merely hinting at the weight of conservatism in this 'age of enlightenment' in which most of the population remained totally or functionally illiterate. Amongst the 130,000 ecclesiastics active in the 1780s, some 50,000 parish priests and curates, recruited from amongst the better-off and literate sections of the rural population, middle classes and artisanate, offered religious, moral and – additionally – political guidance. Better educated than ever before, and assisted by monks and nuns engaged in good works, their increasingly Christocentric spirituality won them widespread love and respect. Paradoxically, there was also growing resentment of their condescending, and often arrogant, obsession with moral and especially sexual misdemeanours. The decline in religious vocations and in bequests to secure prayer for souls in Purgatory suggests that all was not well. Furthermore, priests themselves were often dissatisfied with a situation in which nobles monopolised high office (only 1 per cent of bishops appointed between 1774 and 1793 were non-noble) and were able to appropriate much of the income from the tithe. This inner tension would have significant consequences in 1789.

In the meantime, however, the political conservatism of the clergy ensured that the message from the pulpit – still the most efficacious means of transmitting news and views – continued to focus on the image of the 'good king' (*roi-père*). If anything went wrong, and especially when food prices rose, the fault was not the king's but that of his incompetent or evil-intentioned ministers. Thus the efforts of Turgot in the 1770s to reduce the regulatory powers of the corporations, to establish freedom of internal trade in cereals and more generally to create a framework that would encourage economic activity and thereby increase government tax revenue met with considerable opposition from bureaucrats and the parlements, afraid that deregulation would lead to increased popular disorder, and themselves subscribing to popular fears of a speculative 'famine plot'. In the very imperfect market conditions that prevailed, because of poor communications, it was perhaps inevitable that the poor harvest of 1775 and rising prices, together with suspicion of Turgot's intentions, should provoke widespread protest, the so-called 'flour war', which contributed to his subsequent dismissal and the restoration of market regulation.

Enlightenment ideals were not without their influence in governing circles, however, as can be seen from the abolition of the last vestiges of serfdom in the royal domains in 1779, the ending of judicial torture and the extension of civil rights to Protestants. Many of the major reforms of the legal system that were implemented after 1789 were already under discussion. Criticism itself achieved respectability, and many of the leading critics were integrated into the establishment. In spite of this, contemporaries were left with an overwhelming sense of governmental inflexibility in the face of the mounting wave of criticism that characterised the 1780s – a movement encouraged, paradoxically, by the self-interested criticism of monarchical 'despotism' voiced by such privileged noble institutions as the parlements. This itself was largely a response to the opportunities provided by the state's deteriorating financial situation and its increasingly desperate search for remedies.

There were three major financial problems: tax exemptions, the inefficiency and corruption of tax collection, and the lack of a stable system of public credit. Reform plans came and went. In 1775 Turgot proposed the establishment of local and provincial assemblies, elected by property owners, which would assume responsibility for tax collection, particularly of the land tax, which he proposed should become the main source of government revenue. Together with his plans to reform the guilds as well as the *corvée* (labour service on the roads), this was denounced by powerful vested interests, and his position in the king's government was fatally weakened as a result of his criticism of military expenditure. Subsequently, Jacques Necker, a Swiss banker, was appointed director-general of finance (1777–81) because of the expertise he displayed in raising the loans necessary to finance French participation in the American War of Independence. He succeeded in establishing two, nominated, provincial assemblies, as an experiment, and in these instituted the precedent of voting by head (rather than by estate) as well as a doubling of the representation of the Third Estate. His successors – Jean-François Joly de Fleury, Henri Ormesson and Charles Calonne – reversed these attacks on venality but managed to arouse bitter opposition by attempting to reduce the tax exemptions enjoyed by the privileged classes.

Although all the figures are very approximate because of the absence of central budgetary control, it has been estimated that by 1788, in a year of peace, 26.3 per cent of government spending was

military in character, and 23.2 per cent civil, whilst a massive
49.3 per cent was absorbed in funding government debt (against a
more 'normal' 15 to 20 per cent). Frequently, public opinion blamed
the growing debt upon the extravagance of Queen Marie-Antoinette
and the court, and this indeed made up over 5 per cent of total
expenditure. The primary cause of the financial crisis was the cost
of war and of preparation for war, however. The future stability of
the French kingdom had required the avoidance of military commitments, but Louis XVI had ardently desired French participation
in the American War of Independence as a means of gaining revenge
for the defeats of the Seven Years War. The successes of French
arms were financed by Necker mainly through loans, which were
to weigh heavily upon the financial system. At the same time, proposals to increase the taxation of the privileged classes were blocked
by the parlements. The government's reluctance to proceed with
these was increased, moreover, by the fact that most of the projected
reforms would have resulted in a short-term loss of revenue. Even as
awareness of the problem grew in ministerial circles, a tendency
remained for the king and his ministers of war and the navy to
spend without counting the cost. Nevertheless, by the summer of
1788 the government was effectively bankrupt, and in August the
financial controller-general, Charles Lambert, was obliged to sus-
pend interest payments on the debt. It was evident that consideration
of the need to adapt an archaic system of financial management and
tax collection to the needs of a modern state could not be postponed
for much longer. It had long been clear that tax revenue could be
increased significantly only by reducing the exemptions on direct
taxation enjoyed by the clergy, nobility, various urban corporations,
and so on, and by bringing the collection of indirect taxes, hitherto
farmed out to private companies, under direct state control. The
taille, the major direct tax, was levied almost exclusively on the
peasantry, and had effects counter to the policy of encouraging
increased productivity as an alternative means of increasing tax
income. The obstacles to reform were both technical and social.
Although France was probably less heavily burdened by taxes than
the Netherlands or Britain, public opinion was convinced of the
contrary, in part because of the complexity, diversity and regional
variations in the type and scale of taxation, all of which contributed

to a sense of arbitrariness. The Netherlands and Britain also had the advantage of more effective credit institutions and governments, which, enjoying greater public confidence, were able to mobilise loans at a lower rate of interest. Socially, the major obstacle to reform was the nobility. Certainly, many nobles were prepared to contemplate change in return for a greater share in political power, but in practice whatever course of action ministers took seemed to face opposition from some segment of a social élite whose intransigence might seem to mark a growing sense of insecurity regarding its own status. The last desperate effort to overcome this resistance was to lead directly to revolution.

PART II

THE DUAL REVOLUTION: MODERN AND CONTEMPORARY FRANCE

INTRODUCTION

The causes of the French Revolution have been debated endlessly. During the twentieth century this led to the adoption of two successive orthodoxies. First came that associated with Georges Lefebvre and historians of a Marxist persuasion. They claimed that the Revolution was the achievement of a rising 'bourgeoisie' determined to challenge the social pretensions and political dominance of the nobility. It represented a 'turning point' in history, a 'decisive' moment, bringing about the final, and much-delayed, ending of the feudal system. The way was open for the development of capitalism. Subsequent efforts to set the Revolution within a broader chronological context led to a questioning of its significance as a historical event, however. Although, clearly, the revolutionaries had sought to remove some of the institutional obstacles to the development of a market economy, it appeared that in 1815 France was not so very different from France in 1789. It remained an essentially preindustrial society dominated by a landed élite. It was only during the nineteenth century, as the pace of socio-economic change accelerated, that a fundamental social transformation occurred. Even then, the complex of developments associated with industrialisation evolved far more gradually in France than in either Britain or Germany.

This insistence upon the significance of continuities across the revolutionary period was followed by the development of a second orthodoxy, as 'revisionist' historians stressed the importance of the ideological and political causes and impact of revolution rather than socio-economic factors. They claimed that a recognisably 'modern' political culture was created and widely diffused during these tumultuous years. Sovereignty was transferred from the king to the nation. Amongst the problems this caused was that of defining the 'nation', and the means by which it would intervene in politics. In the search for a solution a variety of constitutional proposals were considered. A wide range of political allegiances was created, and a set of agendas with which to inspire political activities on a global scale from that day to this, although, of course, these have been repeatedly reinterpreted to suit changing social and political conditions. Adopting a compromise position, the French Revolution might best be conceived as an integral part of a dual and permanent revolution whose bases were both socio-economic and political. It has inspired both hope and fear, at times with a dangerous religious-like intensity. Whilst republicans came to see 1789 as inaugurating the reign of liberty and as a major step towards the recognition of human rights and democracy, those of a more conservative bent focused their attention on the violence associated with the revolutionary Terror. As a result, it was not until the Fifth Republic that a genuine consensus on institutions was to be established. It is the impact of this dual revolution that we shall be concerned with in the next section of this book.

4

Revolution and Empire

The collapse of absolute monarchy was to be sudden and shocking to contemporaries. It heralded two decades of revolutionary turbulence and war, of unprecedented change, after a century or more free from serious internal disorder. Moreover, the stability of the social and state systems of most European countries were to be threatened and a new political culture established that still shapes our thought and action. Inevitably, explanations of these events have varied. The concept of the bourgeois revolution, invented by liberal historians such as François Mignet and François Guizot in the 1820s, and refined by Karl Marx, enjoyed a final flourish on the 150th anniversary of the Revolution in 1939 with the appearance of Georges Lefebvre's *Quatre-Vingt-Neuf* (subsequently translated as *The Coming of the French Revolution*). For its author, the Revolution represented the seizure of power by the bourgeoisie, a class created by the centuries-long development of capitalism in French society. That the representatives of this class were able to seize power, destroy aristocratic privilege and establish civic equality was due to the collapse of monarchical power. This had occurred because of the unwillingness of the landed aristocracy to contemplate fiscal and institutional reforms, which would have reduced their privileges, and the ability of bourgeois political leaders to take advantage of mass discontent in the countryside and amongst the urban poor, particularly in Paris, in order to defeat aristocratic and monarchical reaction. Lefebvre in effect identified four revolutionary movements: that of the aristocracy – which prevented monarchical reform; that of the bourgeoisie; the urban revolution, symbolised by the storming of the Bastille; and the peasant revolution. They were interlinked, but each had its own distinctive objectives.

This remained the dominant view amongst historians for some twenty years, until challenged by the British historian Alfred Cobban in a lecture entitled *The Myth of the French Revolution* in 1955. Cobban denied that the Revolution involved 'the substitution of a capitalist bourgeois order for feudalism'. He believed that it represented an effort by the traditional landowning and professional middle classes to gain access to office and political power. Rather than promoting the development of capitalism, the Revolution represented a major setback. Although condemned out of hand by Lefebvre as the work of a political reactionary, Cobban's essentially negative assault on the established view stimulated an extensive and ongoing debate. The appealing certainties of a narrow class-based explanation were lost for ever. In 1967 the American George Taylor claimed that 1789 was 'essentially a political revolution with social consequences and not a social revolution with political consequences'. In his challenging *Penser la Révolution française* (1978), the leading French revisionist François Furet, explaining the radicalisation of the Revolution, insisted that ideology rather than class was the essential determinant of political behaviour. His perspective was similar to that adopted during the Revolution by the British conservative Edmund Burke, in claiming that gradual change was preferable to a violent upheaval inspired by fanatics and descending inevitably into bloody chaos.

More recently, 'revisionism' has itself been criticised as an intellectual dead end. Efforts have been made to understand the context within which political ideas were diffused, and this has led to a reassertion of the importance of social 'class' as an explanatory factor, not in a rigid Marxist sense but in the form of interest groups 'reacting to opportunities in a fluid situation' (Popkin). It has come to be accepted that political events – the calling by the king of an Assembly of Notables, and the preparation for and meeting of the Estates-General in 1789 – revived and reinforced a complex of social tensions concerning the management of property and access to political power and focused the discontent of the middle classes, urban workers and peasants on the aristocracy. Whilst the actual outbreak of the Revolution has to be linked to a fortuitous combination of particular events, its fundamental causes were certainly deep-rooted in the structure of French society and its political system. The government's failure to cope successfully with mounting fiscal problems had reduced its prestige substantially, at the same time as this apparent ineffectiveness increased interest in proposals for constitutional reform. Support for the regime from many of its normal adherents declined, and, with it, its capacity for either reform or repression, so the mobilisation of opposition proceeded apace, culminating in the revolutionary overthrow of the *ancien régime*.

In theory at least, the French governmental system was based upon absolute monarchy, with the king's rights limited only by divine law. He was the source of all laws and of administrative authority, and had the right to appoint all officials, declare war or peace and levy taxes. In 1766 Louis XV declared: 'Sovereign power resides in my person alone.' As the clergy, present in every community, reminded the population constantly – this was God's will. One of Louis XVI's major achievements was substantially to weaken this age-old popular veneration for the person of the monarch.

In practice, as we have seen, severe limitations were imposed upon the powers of the central authority by the relationship of interdependence that existed between the king and social élites. These provided the senior personnel for the civil service and army, and for judicial institutions including those sovereign courts, and most notably the parlements, that claimed to act as guardians of the fundamental laws of the kingdom. Other limiting factors included the small size of the dependent bureaucracy and the fact that many officials had purchased their entitlement to office, which they saw as conferring considerable independence upon themselves. There was also the sheer physical difficulty of receiving information and maintaining control over a large territory with poor communications, although substantial road improvements had occurred during the eighteenth century. In other words, there was a marked and dangerous contrast between the monarch's

Plate 4.1 Louis XVI in his coronation robes. Painting by J.-S. Duplessis.
Musée Carnavalet, Paris. © Roger-Viollet/TopFoto.

political responsibilities and the resources available to fulfil these,
and nowhere was this more evident than in the areas of primary
governmental responsibility: the maintenance of justice; the waging
of war; and the levying of taxes to finance these functions.

Effective government involved a continuous process of compromise between the king, social élites and office holders. The reconciliation of complex conflicting interests was never easy. A solution of the grave problems facing the French monarchy in the late eighteenth century would have required leadership of an extremely high standard. All too often, the reign of Louis XVI has been perceived to be a mere prelude to revolution. Certainly, the rapid turnover of finance ministers suggests that he lacked the strength of character necessary to choose and consistently support an effective chief minister. Such a delegation of authority would have appeared to Louis to be inconsistent with his divine right to rule. This fundamental weakness of absolute monarchy, its excessive dependence upon the abilities and will of whoever inherited the throne, was intensified by the absence of an effective system for coordinating the activities of ministers and of a routine for presenting matters for the monarch's consideration. His interventions in government were unsystematic, frequently ill-informed, and influenced by vicious court intrigue. A king who hardly stirred out of Versailles, except to hunt, was physically – and, more importantly, psychologically – out of touch with the problems of his kingdom. Whether from natural stupidity or as a result of intense and disabling bouts of depression, Louis was unable to impose his authority. As a result, his policy decisions reflected the influence of a small circle of aristocratic advisors who regarded him with contempt and who were willing to contemplate only those reforms that did not threaten their own social status, access to patronage, and political power. Ministerial stability and consistent policies were always at the mercy of faction struggles within this inner circle. The situation was rendered all the more dangerous by the involvement of the queen, Marie-Antoinette, and her determination to support her personal favourites in advocating some form of decentralised aristocratic constitutionalism and to challenge the more traditional, and devoutly Catholic, absolutists favoured by the king.

On 20 August 1786 Calonne, the controller-general, warned Louis XVI that the state was on the verge of financial collapse. According to his – uncertain – calculations, in 1786 revenue would amount to around 475 million *livres* and expenditure to 587 million. A rise in debt on that scale could not be funded for

long. There were a number of policy alternatives. These included
economies; the scope for these was limited, however. Debts and
debt interest had to be repaid or confidence in the financial system
would collapse. Savings on the military account would threaten
France's international position. Reductions in spending on the
royal household and on public works were possible, but would
nowhere nearly cover the deficit. Another possibility was increased
taxation, but the widespread feeling that the burden was already
excessive and the bitter opposition likely from the privileged classes
made this a politically hazardous course of action. Nevertheless, in
a 'Summary of a plan for the improvement of the finances' presented to the king, and borrowing from the earlier schemes of
Turgot and Necker, Calonne proposed a massive reorganisation
of the state, according to rational principles. As approved by Louis
in the autumn of 1786, his plan proposed to introduce a land tax to
be levied in kind at harvest time, and from which no one would be
exempt, although, otherwise, nobles would continue to enjoy substantial tax exemptions. In an effort to conciliate the élite, the plan
proposed to create a network of local and provincial assemblies
elected by landowners, which would distribute taxation and supervise public works – but always under the strict control of the
government's *intendants*. Measures were also to be taken to stimulate economic activity through the abolition of internal customs
barriers and improved roads, as well as by relaxing controls over
the grain trade. In the short term, and to deal with pressing problems of indebtedness, Calonne proposed raising more loans, which
could easily be repaid once his reforms had begun to take effect.

   In order to secure support for these measures and overcome likely
opposition to registration of the new laws in the parlements, Calonne
proposed to convoke an Assembly of Notables, whose 144 members
would be selected by the king from amongst 'people of weight,
worthy of the public's confidence and such that their approbation
would powerfully influence general opinion'. He seems to have
assumed that such a hand-picked body could be expected to see
reason, and would appreciate that the nobility as such and its social
and political pre-eminence were certainly not under attack. Indeed,
this would have been inconceivable to a government composed of the
king and his nobles.

Made up of princes of the blood, bishops, leading nobles, magistrates and representatives of provincial estates and some cities, the Assembly opened at Versailles on 22 February 1787. It was soon clear that Calonne had badly misread the situation. Its members distrusted him, partly because of the more optimistic assessment of the financial situation by his predecessor, Necker. Seeing themselves as guardians of the public interest, they demanded detailed accounts. These representatives of the privileged classes were prepared to accept reductions in their fiscal privileges, but only in return for enhancement of their role in government and administrative decentralisation. Calonne sought to justify himself in a pamphlet, which only further alienated the notables and angered the king, who, typically, failed to support his minister against court intrigue and adverse public criticism. Calonne was replaced by Etienne Loménie de Brienne, Archbishop of Toulouse, whose credit was rapidly destroyed by a failure – partly on financial grounds – to support Dutch allies against a Prussian invasion. His efforts to secure support for reform were doomed to failure. The notables were dismissed and Brienne appealed instead to the Parlement of Paris, but its members, from self-interest, and supported by a public hostile to likely tax increases, only joined in the attack on the government. Whilst they would accept some of the proposed reforms – freeing the grain trade, commuting the *corvée* to a tax payment, and the establishment of provincial assemblies – they opposed the major fiscal measures and claimed that only an Estates-General could sanction new taxes. They had in mind a body of the kind last summoned in 1614, voting by order, with its proceedings safely controlled by the nobility and clergy.

Efforts to command the parlement's compliance by means of the ceremonial procedure known as a *lit de justice*, during which the monarch insisted that new laws were 'legal because I wish it', aroused new fears of royal despotism. Apparently anxious to avoid confrontation, Brienne abandoned the land tax, and thus, it seemed, the need to summon an Estates-General. More forceful measures were also introduced. On 8 May 1788 the keeper of the seals, Chrétien-François de Lamoignon, forced the registration of edicts that heralded the creation of a plenary court to assume many of the parlements' functions, and which would effectively emasculate them. The response was an extension of the so-called 'aristocratic revolt', in which nobles and members of the provincial parlements encouraged protests against ministerial 'despotism'. Public opinion was inflamed by a wave of pamphlets critical of the ministry and calling for constitutional reform. In Rennes and Grenoble, rioting was so serious that troops were called in. Determined repressive action would probably have mastered the situation, but the growing loss of public confidence in the regime, revealed by the indiscipline of noble army officers (setting a bad example to their subordinates, which would subsequently rebound on them), by the general unwillingness to subscribe to a new loan, and the imminent bankruptcy that threatened the government as a result, led Brienne to accept calls for an Estates-General and to fix a precise date for its meeting: 1 May 1789. Recognising his failure, he submitted his resignation. A new ministry under Necker abandoned the reforms under way. The parlements were restored. It is at this point, in August 1788, that the existing monarchical system can be said to have become completely discredited. The king and his close advisers seem to have lost any will to reform or to impose order on the nation. A dangerous vacuum of power existed. The question now was who would dominate the Estates-General, which it was assumed would introduce substantial constitutional reform.

The crisis was intensified further by a series of poor cereal harvests in the 1770s and 1780s, culminating in that of 1788, a year of drought followed by disastrous storms. The abundant wine harvest led only to glut and collapse of the price of what was for many peasants their only marketable crop. Cattle disease added to their problems. In 1788/9 the maximum cyclical increase in wheat prices was around two-thirds above the minimum of 1786 (it had been 100 per cent in 1770, and would be again in 1812 and 1817). As families were forced to spend growing proportions of their shrinking incomes on basic foodstuffs, so demand fell for building work, for textiles and for the other products of numerous rural and urban workshops. The Anglo-French trade treaty of 1786 increased the supply of manufactured goods just at the wrong moment. For much of the population, employment and earnings collapsed at the same time as the cost of living substantially increased. In normal times a male wage earner might spend around 70 per cent of his income on sustenance. In Paris a loaf of bread weighing 4 pounds cost 9 sous in August 1788 but 14½ sous by February 1789, at a time when a workman lucky enough to remain in employment earned perhaps 20 to 35 sous a day. A miserably cold winter added the problem of keeping warm to that of finding the wherewithal to purchase sufficient food. Insecurity and misery spread beyond the mass of habitually impoverished people into the ranks of normally quite comfortably off artisans and farmers.

In this situation there was frequent recourse to the traditional means of expressing a sense of grievance and of exerting pressure on the authorities to provide assistance. From January, and particularly from March 1789 and throughout the *soudure*, the period when the product of the previous year's harvest was almost exhausted and the coming year's not yet brought in, riots in marketplaces, the looting of bakers' shops, attacks on grain shippers and the enforced sale of grain and bread at a 'fair' price were common. These movements represented the widespread fear of hunger, the intense anxiety of the masses in a pre-industrial society, faced as they were with the permanent threat of destitution and informed by the persistent folklore of dearth, with its tales of people dying of hunger or reduced to eating rotten food, grass and weeds. Beggars were everywhere, voicing the age-old threat to burn down the homes of those refusing them alms; crime multiplied. Although urban workers were capable of organising strikes, as the silk weavers of Lyon had shown in 1786, it still seemed that – given the scale of the increase in the cost of food – the most effective action they could take to improve living standards was pressure to reduce prices rather than to increase wages; in other words, they reacted primarily as consumers. From the government's point of view, the most alarming disorders were the Réveillon riots in Paris. These were caused by an imprudent remark by Jean-Baptiste Réveillon, a wallpaper manufacturer, expressed at an electoral meeting, and subsequently distorted, in favour of wage reductions. Rumours spread, and on 27/8 April 1789 serious riots occurred, finally quelled only by military action, which killed or wounded some fifty people. Throughout the spring, in fact, the army was constantly deployed to prevent or repress disorder, and suffered growing fatigue and, because of doubts about government support, a loss of morale in the process.

Social tension was particularly inflamed by the fact that some individuals – bakers, merchants, farmers and landowners – actually appeared to be profiting from the general misery, by hoarding grain and thus forcing prices to rise. Merchants who naturally sought to profit from price differentials between places, and were encouraged to do so by the authorities, were accused of depriving people in the areas in which the grain originated. The increased transport of grains, which inevitably occurred in periods of dearth, seemed to many to prove evil intent. So too did the fact that price increases were proportionally far greater than the shortfall in the crop – the result both of speculation and of the panic buying up of stocks by consumers. All these factors reflect the underdeveloped character of the commercial system in an age of poor communications. Already, the development of commercial capitalism had intensified differences of interest between the more acquisitive and successful urban merchants and manufacturers and their workers, and in the countryside between landlords, the more substantial farmers and the remainder of the community. Now, at the moment in March 1789 when throughout the country members of the three estates were meeting to prepare their lists of grievances (*cahiers de doléances*) for the meeting of the Estates-General, a widespread sense of injustice, hatred and suspicion influenced debate.

The government's response to the subsistence crisis had been to protect and encourage the grain trade (which gave consumers the impression that it was protecting speculators), and additionally to allay fears by suspending exports, making bulk purchases abroad and offering import subsidies. Particular efforts were made to provision Paris. As a result of these policies, rumours spread that ministers were involved in a so-called 'famine plot'. The belief that powerful people were plotting with the grain merchants to punish the poor and secure huge profits reappeared during every crisis. Although the identity of the plotters varied between places, reflecting local social tensions, in a period of political crisis it was inevitable that ministers, who were already the targets of so much criticism, should now be blamed for the ultimate social crime: a plot to starve the people. Inevitably, too, governments, which normally claimed the credit for prosperity, were now blamed for misery. Poverty, together with the 'famine plot' mentality, also made the payment of seigneurial dues and tithes as well as taxes all the more intolerable. Together with declining economic activity, this sharply reduced the government's revenues. Popular attitudes during the economic crisis thus reflected, in extremely distorted fashion, the existing political situation, whilst the economic crisis itself made a substantial contribution to the politicisation of the urban and rural masses.

It was against this background that the preparation for the meeting of the Estates-General proceeded. On 25 September 1788 the Parlement of Paris declared that the constitutionally correct form for its meeting would be that of its predecessor in 1614, and in consequence each estate would deliberate and vote separately, and each would be able to veto the proposals of the others. This inevitably disappointed those whose model had been the British parliament or American state institutions. Amongst these so-called 'patriots' there emerged a particularly influential 'Society of Thirty', drawn from amongst the habitués of the socially prestigious Parisian salons. Of its fifty-five known members, fifty were nobles, almost all from old-established families, many of whom had felt excluded previously from office by court intrigue. In contrast with the desire of most aristocrats simply to limit the power of absolute monarchy, through the strengthening of traditional institutions that they had normally dominated, such as the parlements, the provincial estates and the Estates-General, these 'patriots' adopted the model of British constitutional monarchy as a more liberal and more efficient means of securing the predominant position of a wealthy and not exclusively noble élite. Not surprisingly, they were particularly influential amongst an audience drawn from the well-off, educated middle classes.

Through the circulation of pamphlets and model *cahiers de doléances*, the 'patriots' attempted to gain support for alterations in the procedure of the forthcoming Estates-General. They demanded that the Third Estate should have as many representatives as the other orders, and, by implication, that voting by head should replace voting by orders, thus destroying the noble veto. In response, an alarmist memoir signed by the princes of the blood, whilst offering to renounce fiscal privileges, attacked such proposals as 'likely to sacrifice and humiliate your brave, ancient, and worthy nobility' and as an affront to the monarch himself. It warned the king against a possible revolution in the principles of government, leading to an attack on property. This document, which would serve for nobles and their opponents alike as a sort of aristocratic manifesto, revealed not just the willingness of many nobles to make concessions and accept the loss of their privileged fiscal position but also their determination to preserve as much as possible of their social status and political power. By the end of 1788 the parlements also were clearly anxious about a possible threat to their own privileges, and were becoming more supportive of the monarchy.

Although many nobles welcomed a campaign against royal 'despotism' and were prepared to accept a loss of some of their privileges, most were unwilling to renounce aristocratic predominance within the Estates-General. In other words, they were unwilling to share political power, which appeared to be within their grasp. Thus the Parlement of Paris was prepared to concede increased numerical representation for the Third Estate but not voting by head, whilst, contradictorily, the second Assembly of Notables, convened by Necker in November 1788, was willing to accept voting by head but rejected numerical equality in representation. Without this the representatives of the Third Estate would remain in a strictly subordinate position. This debate on representation had the crucially important effect of realigning the political conflict. In response to noble exclusivism, the 'patriot' opposition was increasingly hostile to both parlements and the privileged in general. The growing number of resolutions, petitions and pamphlets written by men who were to achieve national prominence, such as Emmanuel Sieyès, Constantin-François Volney, Pierre-Louis Roederer and Jean-Paul Rabaut Saint-Etienne, as well as by a mass of more anonymous figures, was indicative of a rapid process of politicisation and the development amongst educated non-nobles, members of the Third Estate, of a sense of common purpose. Most influential of all was probably the Abbé Sieyès' pamphlet 'What is the Third Estate?'. His answer was 'everything' – in the sense that it was 'a complete nation', which could survive without the other two orders. 'Nothing can function without the Third Estate; everything would work infinitely better without the others.' Sieyès continued, however, 'What has it been until now in the political order?' The answer – 'nothing'. 'What does it ask? *To be something*.' In conclusion, he went so far as to suggest that, when the Estates-General came together, the Third Estate might meet apart from the other two estates and reconstitute itself as a National Assembly, competent to discuss and decide upon the affairs of the entire nation. This tract would come to serve as the programme of the 'patriot party' – not an organised party in the modern sense but a variety of groups, some, especially in Paris, already meeting as *clubs*. These provided a forum for speakers who had already achieved political notoriety – publicists such as Jacques-Pierre Brissot, *philosophes* such as the Marquis de Condorcet and liberal nobles such as the Marquis de Lafayette, the Duc de La Rochefoucauld, Charles Talleyrand and the Comte de Mirabeau. A similar effervescence was evident in such provincial centres as Aix, where Mirabeau's 'Appeal to the people of Provence' appeared, or Arras, which saw the publication of Maximilien Robespierre's pamphlet 'Appeal to the people of Artois'. The convocation of the provincial estates of the Dauphiné in June 1788 also contributed to an increasingly vigorous debate. Its deputies, meeting at Vizelle, had determined that in future representatives ought to be elected, rather than sitting as of right; that voting should be by head; and that the Third Estate should have as many deputies as the two other estates together. These proposals were accepted by the government, and would serve as a precedent both for the campaign to establish estates in other provinces and for the debate on the Estates-General. All this had the effect of provoking a growing alarm, and also intransigence, amongst nobles. The very nature of the political process was changing. As the expression of bourgeois resentment of privilege grew more commonplace and more extreme, so the alarm of members of the orders of clergy and nobles was intensified, and their determination to defend their distinctions and power reinforced. Social and political polarisation was developing rapidly.

Necker's announcement in the 'Result of the King's Council of State of 27 December' that representation of the Third Estate should equal that of the clergy and nobility was welcomed, but failed to satisfy 'patriot' opinion. Voting by head would be implemented only if all the orders agreed, which seemed unlikely. It was in response to this that Sieyès' pamphlet 'What is the Third Estate?' had vehemently denounced the nobility and clergy for their unwillingness to recognise the rights of their fellow citizens. Ominously, the journalist Jacques Mallet du Pan observed: 'The public debate has changed. Now the king, despotism, the constitution are merely secondary: it is a war between the Third Estate and the two other orders.' Efforts by members of the Third Estate to secure equal representation in the provincial estates of Provence, Guienne, Franche-Comté, Artois and Brittany added to the controversy, and in January 1789 led to fighting in the streets of Rennes between law students and supporters of the nobility. This clash was precipitated by the obvious and arrogant unwillingness of the Breton nobility to accept a compromise. A pamphlet entitled 'Discourse on the nobility of the Breton parlement' (December 1788) already referred to 'the dangerous insurrection of the Third Estate'. Significantly, the deputies elected to the Estates-General by the Third Estate in Brittany would be marked by their intransigent hostility towards the nobility. Meeting regularly as the Club Breton, joined by like-minded 'patriots' and corresponding regularly with their electors, they would make a significant contribution to the radicalisation of opinion both in the National Assembly and in the urban centres of Brittany.

On 24 January 1789 the government decreed that deputies to the Estates-General would be elected by each order in the *bailliages* and *sénéchaussées* – that is, within the basic administrative units. Although the regulations were extremely complex, with numerous variations, in most areas the members of the First and Second Estates would attend their electoral assemblies in person, whilst for the much larger Third Estate every male taxpayer over twenty-five years of age would be allowed to participate in a primary assembly to choose two delegates for every hundred households, who would take part subsequently in a *bailliage* electoral assembly. Most of the electoral assemblies were held in March and April 1789, against a background of economic crisis, widespread social disorder and political agitation. The government made no attempt to influence the outcome, leaving it to be determined by local circumstances and the influence of political ideas spread by numerous pamphlets.

Information on the numbers voting is fragmentary. In rural parishes around Rouen only 23 per cent of those eligible voted. In the city itself it was 40 per cent. In Alsace, 55 to 60 per cent turned out in Strasbourg and Colmar. Surprisingly, only around 30 per cent voted in Paris, suggesting perhaps that political awareness was much less developed than historians have sometimes led us to believe. Inevitably, those who attended the secondary assemblies of the Third Estate were drawn overwhelmingly from amongst the more literate, educated and better-off members of particular communities, and a dominant role in debate was taken by those who possessed the skills and confidence necessary to address public meetings – lawyers and officials in particular. Of the 1,318 deputies who actually took their seats in the Estates-General, 326 were members of the First Estate, of clergy. Reflecting divisions within the Church, a surprisingly high proportion (220) were members of the lower clergy – that is, parish priests rather than the noble bishops and abbots, canons and monks who had habitually ruled the Church. Amongst the 330 nobles were to be found representatives of the oldest, most prestigious and wealthiest families, including La Rochefoucauld, Luynes, Orleans, Noailles and Montmorency. A high proportion, 166, were essentially army officers, indicative perhaps of a determination amongst the previously powerless minor provincial nobility to curb the court aristocrats and parlementaires who had always assumed the right to speak for them. Significantly, only twenty-two members of parlements were elected, in what were often extremely tense and quarrelsome assemblies. Although the meeting at Versailles would reveal that around ninety of those noble delegates were politically liberal, a large majority of the Second Estate's representatives, if not entirely intransigent, were nevertheless quite clearly conservatives shocked by the course of events and determined to preserve noble pre-eminence, and to maintain their social distinctions. The humiliating exclusion of the recently ennobled from the ranks of the noble estate no doubt aroused bitter resentment, as they took their places amongst the lower order. The delegates of the Third Estate, with its representation doubled to 661, included 214 representatives of the liberal professions (including 180 lawyers). There were relatively few businessmen (seventy-six merchants, eight manufacturers and one banker). The remainder mostly described themselves as landowners – a characteristic shared by almost all the deputies of the Third Estate whatever their professional labels. It would be delegates with a legal education, many of them holders of venal offices – a relatively uniform group in terms of training, culture, and interests – who would dominate the Third Estate at Versailles, however.

Together with the preparation of *cahiers de doléances*, which accompanied them, the elections further stimulated political debate. They were especially effective in allowing the penetration of new political ideas into the countryside. More generally, they created a dangerous sense of expectancy. Why was the king asking for a state-ment of grievances if it was not his intention to do something about them? This led to a widespread assumption that seigneurial dues, tithes and taxes were about to be abolished, which frequently led to an immediate refusal to pay. Although the *cahiers* expressed great confidence in the king's intentions, they also helped to disseminate the increasingly widespread belief that a more liberal political sys-tem, a more egalitarian society and improved material living stand-ards were soon to be created. Inevitably, this belief represented a threat to the stability of the political system.

The *cahiers* themselves constitute a mass of documentation (some 40,000 were prepared) that, used with care, can provide important insights into the attitudes of substantial parts of the population towards society and politics on the eve of a major transformation of French institutions. Unlike the existing deliberative bodies of the Church, the assemblies of the First Estate were overwhelmingly rep-resentative of the parish clergy, who in many *bailliages* seized their opportunity to voice a range of accumulated grievances against the bishops and monastic priests. They condemned the impropriation of tithes and their own low incomes, criticised pluralism and non-residence and favoured diocesan government through elected synods and more open access to the highest positions in the Church. Nonetheless, greater emphasis was placed on the issues that united the clergy. For example, they were determined that Catholicism should remain the established religion and that the Church should retain control of education. They were hostile to the growing toler-ation of Protestants. Clearly, the influence of secularising 'philosophic' ideas was the cause of some anxiety. There was also a widespread willingness to accept a reduction in the fiscal privileges of the Church.

The *cahiers* drawn up at the meetings of the Second Estate reveal a similar willingness to renounce fiscal privilege (89 per cent of noble *cahiers*) as well as a desire to replace absolute monarchy with some form of constitutional monarchy. The existing system of government was condemned as despotic and corrupt, with this blamed not on the king but upon those ministers and courtiers who misinformed the monarch, wasted resources and monopolised office. The solution seemed to lie in regular meetings of an Estates-General, in ministerial responsibility to the elected body as well as to the king and in reform of the legal system to ensure the protection of individual liberty. Nobles generally assumed that *they* would play the predominant role within the new institutions, however, and retain their monopoly of high office in the bureaucracy, army and Church. Most noble *cahiers* insisted that voting in the crucial Estates-General that would introduce these political reforms should take place by order – as a means, according to the noble deputy Jean-Jacques d'Eprémesnil, of defending 'the just prerogatives of the nobility and the clergy' – although a significant minority accepted the replacement of voting by order with voting by head (38.8 per cent). Only 5 per cent of noble *cahiers* favoured equality of opportunity (probably most did not even consider the possibility), in comparison with 73 per cent of urban Third Estate *cahiers*. On the issue of seigneurial dues, it appears that nobles were divided between those with sufficient wealth to accept the loss and the mass of country gentlemen (*hobereaux*), less well off financially, who also made it a point of honour to defend the signs of their superior social status. Nevertheless, the most striking feature of these noble *cahiers* is the large area of agreement with those of the Third Estate – on the creation of a liberal and constitutional state.

The electoral process itself had contributed substantially to the politicisation of the bourgeoisie, which prepared the urban *cahiers* of the Third Estate. In the towns, such organised groups as the guilds, corporations and municipal councils, which focused in particular upon local grievances, dominated their preparation. In addition, they clearly favoured the regular convocation of Estates-General and voting by head, together with the abolition of noble fiscal exemptions and privileged access to office, as well as measures such as the abolition of internal customs barriers to stimulate the economy. On such matters as the abolition of seigneurial dues, of venal office or trade guilds, on the abolition of tithes or the confiscation of Church property, these *cahiers* were far more circumspect. They were reluctant to attack property rights and, if anything, favoured limited reform rather than drastic change. It was the *cahiers* from the larger urban centres that were most concerned with politics. They favoured constitutional government, the voting of taxes by an elected assembly and equal liability to taxation, and were more likely to support the abolition of the seigneurial system. Typically, whilst condemning most other forms of privilege, the representatives of the corporations – masters and journeymen – insisted upon the retention of their own rights to control entry into their trades and levels of production in order to restrict competition.

Although often following urban models, the rural *cahiers* – the great majority – were concerned mainly with such specific local grievances as the enclosure of common land and the denial of customary rights of access to pasture and forest. Hard times ensured complaints about the burden of seigneurial dues, the tithe and, in particular, what peasants saw as excessive taxation. Tension within the rural community – between rich and poor – was rarely represented in *cahiers* prepared by members of the rural bourgeoisie or the better-off peasants. More frequent was the expression of rural–urban hostility, based upon conceptions of the towns as the residence of tax officials, merchants, the 'parasitic' higher clergy and the absentee landlords who exploited the peasantry. Nonetheless, the fundamental institutions of the *ancien régime* were not really questioned.

The clear conclusion to draw from an analysis of the *cahiers* is the surprising degree of agreement between the representatives of the three estates. Fiscal and judicial reform, more open access to office and a modicum of representative government would probably have satisfied most of the population. The obvious question then, is: why, if this emerging consensus existed, was France drawn nevertheless into revolution? An essential part of the answer is the failure of the royal government to respond effectively to the appeals being made to it.

THE DEBATE ON A NEW CONSTITUTION

With absolute monarchy discredited and the creation of a power vacuum, a struggle developed between nobles, who in practice had shared political power with the monarchy through their quasi-monopoly of office holding, and non-nobles, who in questioning

aristocratic privilege were demanding equal rights of access to political power. The political crisis, beginning in 1787, which had had the
immediate effect of reinforcing noble opposition to the monarchy,
had, subsequently, through the process of the election of deputies to
the Estates, the preparation of *cahiers*, and the pamphlet war these
produced, stimulated an increasing assertiveness on the part of educated non-nobles. The growing tension and mutual suspicion was
apparent rapidly amongst the deputies who gathered at Versailles on
4 May 1789 to attend the Estates-General. In these circumstances,
the government's failure to provide effective leadership was to prove
disastrous. Speeches by the king and by Necker at the opening
session of the Estates-General proposed no programme. Whilst
accepting, in vague terms, that there might be a case for some
reforms, they warned against hasty action, and did nothing to resolve
the immediate issue of voting procedures. Such ineptitude left widespread feelings of disappointment and disaffection.

The procedural difficulties that ensued reflected and exacerbated
existing divisions. In the absence of a clear governmental lead on the
question of voting, representatives of the Third Estate, led by those
from the Dauphiné and Brittany, who had for the past twelve months
been engaged in conflict with the authorities and who were particularly hostile to noble pretensions, determined to establish their
position by pressing for the verification of credentials in common.
Initially, the First and Second Estates rejected this unseemly pressure,
although talks on procedure continued until the nobility's decision
(by 206 votes to sixteen) on 20 May that voting by order and a
mutual veto were fundamental rights and essential to the security of
the monarchy and the safeguarding of liberty. Finally, on 10 June,
Sieyès proposed to a meeting of the Third Estate that, if agreement
could not be reached, then it should proceed to scrutinise the election
results alone. This was adopted by 493 votes to forty-one. The
decision, which followed on 17 June, to adopt the title 'National
Assembly' (by a vote of 491 to ninety-three) was indicative of the
development of wider ambitions, made evident by its resolution
authorising the continued collection of taxes. Though essentially
moderate, the majority of the deputies of the Third Estate were
determined to make their influence felt and to implement constitutional reform. There could be no doubt now that the sovereignty of

the king and the social status and power of the nobility were being questioned.

Faced with a direct challenge to his authority, Louis XVI determined to hold a special session of the Estates-General on 23 June, at which he intended to present a programme and regain the initiative. Even this backfired, however, because officials forgot to inform the Third Estate that their meeting place would be closed until this royal session. Arriving on 20 June for a meeting, deputies assumed that the closure of the hall had to be the result of a royal plot, and gathered instead on an indoor tennis court. There they took an oath not to disperse until constitutional reform had been achieved. It seems to have been the king's original intention, on Necker's advice, to propose voting in common on important issues, regular convocation of the Estates, their consent to all new taxes, tax reform and decentralisation of local government by means of a network of provincial estates, together with guarantees of individual liberty and of equal access to official positions. These conciliatory proposals might have been effective, but, under pressure from the queen and his brothers, the king instead quashed the Third Estate's decisions of 10 and 17 June. His fundamental assumptions about his own rights and duties, as well as those of the privileged orders, no doubt made him unsympathetic towards reform proposals. Furthermore, he insisted that the separation of the orders had to be maintained, and that if on occasion they could engage in common meetings the privileged orders were to retain their right to veto proposals that affected themselves. Bitterly disappointed, the deputies of the Third Estate were left more determined to resist than ever. Necker, who had pointedly absented himself from this royal session of 23 June, was dismissed on 11 July.

The nobility, most of whom had welcomed the king's speech, were alarmed by the government's failure to disperse a Third Estate whose members, in arrogating to themselves the title of 'National Assembly', were so obviously challenging its authority. The determination of this assembly to resist royal pressure was encouraged when it was joined by most of the clerical deputies and, on 25 June, by forty-seven liberal nobles. On 27 June, hoping to gain time while troops were moved into the Paris region, the king ordered the remaining clergy and nobles to join the National Assembly. The news was greeted with enthusiasm in Paris, but Louis would never willingly concede the loss of his sovereign powers, and had determined to resort to military action. This might well have succeeded, if it had not been for the intervention of the popular classes.

Already, the government's inability to control the widespread subsistence disorders in the spring and early summer of 1789 had attracted mounting criticism from the propertied classes. The belief that the king would listen to the grievances expressed in the *cahiers* had only encouraged popular protest, and refusals to pay seigneurial dues, tithes and taxes. The demonstrators themselves blamed the government for its apparent unwillingness to offer assistance, whilst at the same time offering protection to the merchants and speculators, who appeared determined to starve the poor. More and more, the continuing rise in the price of bread was explained in terms of an aristocratic plot. The machinations of the privileged order were seen as intended to punish the poor and to obstruct the workings of the Estates-General, from whose gathering many expected better times. Additionally, rumours were generated by the government's decision to reinforce military garrisons in the Paris region with, wherever possible, mercenary regiments. In the meantime, however, because of the pressure of continuous activity and lack of firm leadership, military discipline and morale were deteriorating, intensifying the crisis of confidence amongst the king and his advisers. Continual political agitation was fired by the dismissal of Necker – regarded by 'patriots' as the only man capable of solving the regime's financial problems, and the only minister committed to reform – as well as by high food prices and talk of an impending military coup. These fears led to rioting in Paris on 12 July, involving the burning of the hated internal customs posts and efforts by crowds, composed of shopkeepers, small traders and workers, to arm themselves in order to resist royal tyranny. On 14 July the search for arms led to an assault on the royal fortress of the Bastille – a symbol of despotism towering over the popular *quartier* of the Faubourg Saint-Antoine – in which many deserters from such key units as the French Guard participated. This was widely taken to represent the collapse of royal power. Of more immediate practical significance was the establishment, by eminent middle-class citizens, of a 'Permanent Committee' to replace the royal municipality, which had clearly been overwhelmed by

Plate 4.2 The taking of the Bastille, 14 July 1789. Anonymous painting. Musée national du château de Versailles. Photo: Giraudon/the Bridgeman Art Library.

events, and the creation of a citizens' militia as a means of preserving order and protecting the city from attack. The dual objectives of this militia represented the ambivalence of the propertied classes – afraid of popular disorder, but dependent on their troublesome allies for support against the king and his soldiers.

The news from Paris, the anxiety as well as the sense of expectancy created by the breakdown of central authority, together with rumours combining the age-old belief in a famine plot with fear of nobility, encouraged a new paroxysm of unrest in the countryside. Normandy and lower Maine, parts of Flanders, upper Alsace and Franche-Comté, the Mâconnais and Dauphiné were the regions particularly affected. The peasantry sought to defend the interests of the village community against the exactions of a panoply of exploiters, including landlords, *seigneurs*, tithe and tax collectors and capitalistic farmers and merchants. Areas such as Languedoc, where the burden of taxation, seigneurialism and commercialisation was less intense, seem to have been affected far less by this outbreak. Although there was little personal violence, hundreds of noble châteaux were looted and

Plate 4.3 Châteaux burning as their owners flee, summer 1789. Anonymous engraving. Musée Carnavalet. Photo: Giraudon/the Bridgeman Art Library.

burned as peasants searched for hidden stocks of grain, and destroyed the records of seigneurial obligations. Often a festive atmosphere prevailed as peasants celebrated a victory for popular justice. The economic crisis had created widespread misery and fear of starvation. The preparation of the *cahiers* had encouraged hopes and aspirations for a more secure existence. Now that this seemed to be threatened by the determination of the king and his nobility to preserve their exclusive rights, direct action seemed justified. Panic spread – turning between 20 July and 6 August into the manifestation of popular hysteria that historians have labelled the 'Great Fear' – as rumours rapidly circulated that the château burning was the work of marauding brigands intent on murder, pillage and rape, and the destruction of the ripening crops. Throughout the provinces, as in Paris, municipal administrations and civic militias were created in an effort to restore order. They were armed with weapons seized from arsenals or freely handed over by troops. Evidently, local élites had lost confidence in the ability of the monarchy to fulfil its fundamental responsibility for the maintenance of order. They additionally suspected the sincerity of both the king's and the aristocracy's commitment to constitutional reform. The composition of these new bodies varied from place to place, according to the character of local élites, the balance between political groups and the degree to which popular pressure was exerted. They represented not only a determination to preserve social order but also the dissolution of royal government. They would look to the National Assembly for inspiration, rather than to the monarch.

On 16 July the war minister, the Duc de Broglie, advised the king that the army could be relied upon no longer. The regime had lost its monopoly of armed force. In despair, the king recalled Necker, and, in front of an armed crowd, on the steps of the Hôtel-de-Ville in Paris, donned the tricolour cockade, which united the white of the Bourbon family with the red and blue of the city. Furthermore, he accepted the appointment of the 'patriots' Jean-Silvain Bailly as mayor and Lafayette as commander of a militia whose new title of 'National Guard' signified its political aspirations. On 4 August the National Constituent Assembly, as it now called itself, with clergy and nobles such as the Duc d'Aiguillon and the Vicomte de Noailles to the fore, accepted the need to abolish the seigneurial system. In what Lefebvre has referred to as the 'death certificate of the old order', deputies, in euphoric mood, decided to destroy entirely the feudal regime and thereby to abolish serfdom, labour services, seigneurial justice and exclusive hunting rights and *banalités*, together with tax exemptions, seigneurial dues and tithes. These were desperate measures, intended to pacify the countryside. In the cold light of day, however, deputies, many of whom had profited personally from the system, were to have second thoughts. They had wanted reform, not revolution. The changes they had introduced must have represented an immense shock to their constituents. A committee was established, which confirmed the abolition of all forms of personal

Plate 4.4 The night of 4 August 1789: a social revolution. The Constituent Assembly votes for the abolition of the seigneurial system. Engraving by I. S. Helman, after a painting by C. Monnet. Bibliothèque nationale. Photo: Giraudon/the Bridgeman Art Library.

servitude but required peasants to repurchase dues that were based upon a more or less fictitious 'contractual relationship' and therefore represented property rights. The price was established at twenty-five times the annual value – a rate that satisfied no one. Moreover, it was stipulated that arrears owed from the past thirty years would have to be paid – a decision that encouraged a further wave of attacks on châteaux. The heightened expectations of peasants, who had neither the resources not the inclination to compensate seigneurs, encouraged them to ignore the Assembly's second thoughts. The law was enforced rarely, and redemption payments were hardly ever paid. Finally, on 15 July 1793, in the aftermath of another massive wave of rural protest caused by poor harvests and suspicion of noble intentions and because of the need to stimulate support for the war effort, dues were abolished finally without compensation by the National Convention. These measures implied a major recasting of social

relationships. As well as causing substantial financial loss for seigneurs, they destroyed the legal basis for noble power in the
countryside.

On 26 August the Declaration of the Rights of Man and of the
Citizen was promulgated. Adopting a universalistic language, it
provided an inspiring statement of principle as well as implicitly
condemning the fundamental bases of the *ancien régime*. Partly
drafted by Lafayette, and closely following the American
Declaration of Independence, it also reflected a European natural
law tradition. The declaration affirmed a commitment to the rule of
law, to equality before the law, to representative government, to
freedom of speech, association and religion and to equal access to
office. It represented a renewed assault on privilege and an affirmation of the sovereignty of the nation, in place of a monarchy that had
lost its status as a sacred institution. The declaration also guaranteed
private ownership of property as one of the 'natural and imprescript-
able rights of man', and as the basis of social and political order.
After all, this was an assembly made up of men of property. On 19
June 1790 the momentous decision to abolish hereditary nobility
was taken. Although the proposal was supported by such eminent
nobles as the Lameth brothers, Noaille and Lafayette, it also reflected
the declining influence of deputies drawn from the privileged orders.
Even though the nobility were to remain a major status group with
much of their wealth intact, this assault on the hereditary élites,
which had, since time immemorial, shared power with the king,
had a traumatic effect and was resented bitterly. The ideal of the
National Constituent Assembly was to create a situation in which,
henceforth, individuals would be free to dispose of their talents and
property, restricted only by the stipulation that their actions should
do no harm to others.

Measures were also introduced to stimulate economic activity.
These included the elimination of internal customs barriers, the
ending of restrictions on the grain trade (August 1789), the legalisation of loans at interest (12 October) and suppression of the craft
and mercantile guilds and of official controls on manufacture (loi
d'Allarde, 2 March 1791) – reforms that had been discussed for
decades. Many landowners and peasants also benefited from the
elimination of tithes and seigneurial dues. Much of the rural

population would retain more produce, either to sell or consume. In the manufacturing economy, however, successive upheavals created an atmosphere of uncertainty more conducive to speculative than sustained entrepreneurial activity. The needs of war would soon lead to the reimposition of economic controls. Soaring inflation would threaten paralysis. Not surprisingly, the desire for security together with an active land market would encourage the diversion of capital from commerce and manufacture, with industrial production probably reaching its lowest level in 1796. Subsequently greater internal security and the widening of the frontiers provided better opportunities, but the maritime war, in which British domination was more complete than ever before, would continue to have a devastating impact on the ports and their hinterlands, previously the most dynamic sectors of the economy.

The abolition of seigneurial courts and of venality (11 August 1789), with far from generous compensation, cleared the way for a thoroughgoing reorganisation of the judicial and administrative systems. The complex chaos of conflicting jurisdictions that had made up the *ancien régime* administration, as well as the cost of justice, had long been subject to criticism. The rational restructuring that ensued provided for a hierarchy of communes, districts and departments. The other guiding principles, representing a reaction against absolutism and a determination to weaken the power of the executive, were decentralisation together with the election of officials. The basic ideals of popular sovereignty and elective representative government were recognised by a law of 14 December 1789. It stipulated that deputies and officials were to be elected by 'active' citizens, those paying the equivalent of three days' labour in taxes. The poorest, property-less members of society, who lacked the independence thought to be a prerequisite for voting, were to be excluded. The issue of political rights for women was rarely considered worth debating. Even so, a mass electorate was constituted, made up of 4.3 million electors, including 77,590 in Paris. The essential restrictions on political participation were the higher (ten-day) tax qualification required of those eligible for office and, particularly, the principle of indirect election. This helped ensure the dominance at both municipal and national levels of a wealthy élite of 'notables'. The limits to the deputies' radicalism were also evident in such

measures as the Le Chapelier law (June 1791), which banned workers' associations and strikes as restraints upon individual freedom,
and in the use of force against hostile demonstrations.

The inspirational phrases of the Declaration of the Rights of Man
and of the Citizen were one thing; the implementation of practical
measures of reform, and the solution of the financial problems that
had occasioned the summoning of the Estates-General, were another.
It was soon clear that it was easier to overthrow one regime than to
reach agreement on what should replace it. The debate on the new
system of government and the inevitable competition for power that
ensued would open up increasingly bitter divisions amongst the country's new rulers; assisted by the pressures of war, it would promote
major political realignments and a process of politicisation that threatened to bring the masses into politics. Certainly, there were pressing
problems. These included the need to redefine political authority and
to re-establish effective government. To a substantial degree, the policy
decisions taken by the Assembly reflected its social composition. Most
deputies were relatively well off and anxious to safeguard a social
order still conceived of in basically agrarian terms, as well as to
preserve the monarchy as the essential guarantor of this social order.
The solution incorporated into the constitution of 1791 was to accord
considerable formal authority to the king as head of the executive
whilst seeking to control its use by insisting that royal orders were
valid only if countersigned by ministers who were responsible to the
elected assembly as well as to the monarch. The king's right to veto
legislation would only delay its implementation (for two to six years),
and did not apply to financial bills. These stipulations reflected a
fundamental lack of trust, which made the harmonious working of
the new system of constitutional monarchy extremely unlikely.

The disorders that had preceded and accompanied the Revolution,
and the widespread refusal to pay taxes, had greatly intensified the
government's financial problems. Summoned originally to solve
these, the Assembly felt obliged to take exceptional measures. On 2
November 1789 it determined to adopt a proposal made by
Talleyrand, Bishop of Autun, that Church property be sequestrated.
In March 1790, as the financial crisis deepened, it was decided to
issue Treasury bills (*assignats*), the repayment of which would be
guaranteed by the value of the confiscated land (*biens nationaux*).

Subsequent overissue of this paper currency would lead to its rapid depreciation. The impact of these measures was to be considerable. The Assembly had certainly not planned to threaten the existence of a Church still seen as the basis of moral order. It was intended that the clergy, as well as the educational and charitable work they supported, should be provided for by the state. There was little sympathy, nonetheless, for either the 'useless' contemplative religious orders or even the teaching and charitable orders, widely regarded as wasteful and inefficient, and their dissolution was to follow (decrees of 13 February 1790 and 18 August 1792). Unfortunately, although the various assemblies were full of good intentions in the spheres of education and welfare, their achievement was an essentially negative one. The pressing financial needs of war would soon frustrate any real achievement, although the principle of state responsibility for the provision of public assistance, and in particular free and obligatory instruction as the means of promoting enlightenment, civic virtue and linguistic and national unity, survived to inspire the left throughout the following century. More immediately, from October 1789 the Assembly began to take an active role in the reorganisation of the Church. Together with the guarantee of freedom of worship enshrined in the Declaration of Rights, this threatened the autonomy and exclusive rights of the Catholic clergy. The Civil Constitution of the Clergy (July 1790) extended the principles of administrative reform to the Church by providing for the election of (suitably qualified) parish priests and their bishops by the local and departmental electoral assemblies. In response to this extremely radical document a clear division was evident between deputies drawn from the former privileged orders and those originating in the Third Estate. The Church was to be subordinated to the state and to civil society in ways the Pope could not accept. Pius VI temporised, but the oath of loyalty required of priests in their new position as employees of the state (decree of 17 November 1790) was too much, and he felt obliged to condemn the reforms in March/April 1791. Initially priests had often welcomed the democratisation of the Church but the papal decision forced many of the 50 to 60 per cent who had already accepted the oath to retract. To a considerable degree their original decisions had reflected the attitudes of their parishioners towards the revolutionary regime, and, significantly, a map representing these juror–non-juror decisions in 1791 would continue to correspond quite closely to those illustrating the left–right political divide until the 1950s.

   As the authorities sought to impose their will on the Church, the increasingly anticlerical and then anti-religious policies introduced would reinforce the determination of many communities to defend their right to a parish priest, the vital intermediary between man and God. More than anything else, this created the potential for mass resistance to the Revolution. Religious issues would remain central to political conflict throughout the following century. More immediately, by February 1791 some 200 deputies – mostly nobles and priests – had ceased to attend meetings of the National Constituent Assembly and were turning towards extra-parliamentary forms of resistance. Nevertheless, there was widespread support for a regime that had eliminated or eased the burden of seigneurial dues, tithes and taxation. The revolutionary land settlement was to be an additional element in this creation of a pro-revolutionary party. The confiscation of Church property, and subsequently that of émigrés (only about a half of whom were nobles) by a decree of 3 June 1793, would affect around 10 per cent of the national territory. Although initially it had been intended to facilitate access by the poor to property by dividing estates into small portions and allowing payment over twelve years (decree of 14 May 1790), the urgent need to increase state revenue led instead, in May 1791, to the requirement of a deposit of 30 per cent and the balance over four and a half years with sale to the highest bidder. The more egalitarian decrees of 3 June 1793 and 4 Nivôse year II had little impact and were soon reversed. Thus, not surprisingly, it was those with money to spare who were best placed to take advantage of the favourable opportunity to purchase provided by such extensive sales. The impact on social structures varied considerably between regions according to the amount of land for sale. Church property had been particularly extensive on the rich northern plains, reaching 30 to 40 per cent of the land in Picardy, but fell to as little as 3 per cent in parts of the south. The majority of nobles, perhaps as many as four-fifths, sat out the Revolution, intensely annoyed by their loss of titles, power and status, and frequently insecure and frightened, but suffering little further material loss after the abolition of seigneurial dues, and

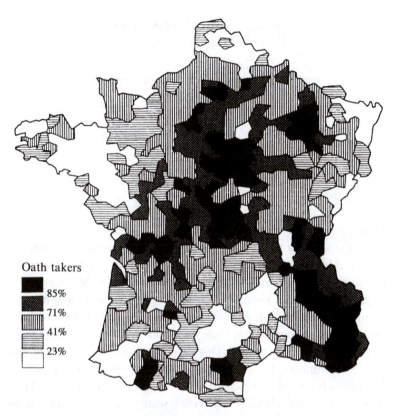

Figure 4.1 The Civil Constitution of the Clergy (percentage of oath takers). (Source: M. Vovelle (ed.), *L'état de la France pendant la Révolution*. Editions La Découverte, 1988.)

they were often able to take advantage of the sales of *biens natio-naux*. Subsequently, by one means or another, many former émigrés were able partially to reconstitute their estates, but there can be no doubt that the nobility as a group lost heavily as a result of the Revolution. This was especially the case in a frontier department such as the Nord. Lefebvre has estimated that shares in land owner-ship there evolved as shown in Table 4.1.

The Nord was unusual in the share purchased by peasants but even there it was bourgeois purchasers – that is, existing landowners, professional men, merchants and manufacturers – who acquired two-thirds of the land sold, increasing the economic dominance of

Table 4.1 *Share in landownership,*
Department of Nord (per cent)

Department of Nord

	1789	1802
Clergy	20	0
Nobles	22	12
Bourgeois	16	28
Peasants	30	42

many towns over their rural hinterlands. Landownership offered security and enhanced social status as well as providing a decent income. Although a considerable number of better-off peasants were able to acquire land, and many more benefited from the abolition of seigneurialism, the situation of most of the rural population remained little changed. Already possessing 40 to 45 per cent of the land before the Revolution, they were able to increase this only by some three percentage points. This engendered bitter disappointment and a determination to oppose the implementation of decrees such as that of 10 June 1793, which sought to facilitate enclosure and the division of common land. It was widely seen as an attack on customary collective practices crucial to the survival of the poor. The revolutionary conception of property as an individual right free from restriction had little support in many rural communities. The rural masses were to remain divided. Although they would remain bitterly hostile to any hint of a restoration of seigneurialism or of the tithe, most peasants lacked a real sense of positive commitment to the new regime and soon relapsed into an indifference towards those political affairs that did not affect them directly. Even so, the national debate on the new constitution, together with the competing interests of individuals, families and clan and social groups in countless towns and villages, ensured that the political crisis would be prolonged.

Clearly, the Revolution had passed its point of no return. Fundamental commitments had been made to the principles of equality before the law, the sovereignty of the nation and representative institutions. A new political culture had been created. It was quite clear that the deputies intended to restrict substantially the powers of the monarchy, although the search for a compromise with the king would continue; indeed, the alternative was unthinkable for some time to come. In spite of these massive innovations, when the deputies gathered for the final session of the Constituent Assembly, on 30 September 1791, a broad consensus in favour of the Revolution still existed. There were ominous signs of future conflict, however. By early 1790, disgusted by the turn of events, many noble and clerical deputies had already withdrawn from the Assembly. The king appears to have assumed that he had little alternative but to make concessions, whilst playing for time in the hope that intervention by the European powers would bring his subjects to their senses. Nevertheless, many of his courtiers, headed by his brother, the Duc d'Artois, together with *ancien régime* bishops and parlementaires, found their situation intolerable, and made up the first wave of émigrés. They would soon be joined by growing numbers of noble army officers – some 6,000 – unable to endure indiscipline or feeling honour-bound to support the king. Although many officers remained and would, like the young Napoleon Bonaparte, benefit from accelerated promotion opportunities, these émigrés constituted the cadres for counter-revolution.

RADICALISATION OF THE REVOLUTION

A process of political and social radicalisation, culminating in the Terror, would follow this first, 'creative' phase of the Revolution. Whereas historians in the 'orthodox' tradition, including successive holders of the chair in the history of the French Revolution at the Sorbonne, such as Albert Mathiez, Lefebvre and Albert Soboul, celebrated the democratic and egalitarian achievements of this period, from the 1970s 'revisionist' historians such as François Furet have forcefully insisted that 1789 had sown the seeds of an authoritarian and fundamentally destructive radicalism that they dismissed as an unnecessary aberration. The efforts of the revolutionary militants of the year II to defend the Revolution against its internal and external enemies have been condemned. Aspects of the Terror were certainly odious but, supported by the conservative media, some historians have gone so far as to present it as the first step towards the twentieth-century revolutionary terrorism represented by Stalin's *gulags*. Frequently exaggerating the number of deaths, they have described the repression of counter-revolutionary movements in the Vendée as heralding Nazi genocide. This essentially ahistorical, and indeed hysterical, approach can only be understood as a feature of the politics of the reactionary right of our own time. It ignores the threat posed to the achievements of 1789 by the reactionaries of that time and their foreign supporters. Although the challenge to privilege and the sense of expectancy that this produced had undoubtedly created a powerful political dynamic and widespread social tension, it was above all the counter-revolutionary menace that provoked the radicalisation of the Revolution.

The continuing collapse of the authority of the royal government was another major factor. Louis XVI's inability to offer an effective lead to contending groups within the Constituent Assembly ensured that whatever initiatives did come developed out of that body itself. This was to be a process fraught with difficulty. Initially within the Assembly there had been an almost universal commitment to monarchy, although, significantly, Louis XVI was now deemed to reign not only 'by the grace of God' but also 'according to the constitutional law of the state'. The debate continued concerning the nature of the monarchy and the respective powers of the king and the elected assembly – that is, about who should hold power. Loosely organised groups argued over the forms of the new political community. A majority of socially conservative politicians such as Lafayette, Bailly, Sieyès, Talleyrand and Mirabeau – who secretly took the king's money – were anxious to finish the Revolution by conciliating the monarch. Increasingly, the more radical deputies looked outside the Assembly and towards the popular classes of Paris for support. There the level of mobilisation of the masses, low at first, rapidly developed due to the activities of a network of political clubs, meeting in such places as the former Cordelier and Jacobin convents, and the printing of innumerable pamphlets and (often ephemeral) newspapers, including Jean-Paul Marat's *Ami du people* and Brissot's *Patriote français*. Competition, initially between such bourgeois groupings as Feuillants, Girondins and Jacobins, and their various efforts to win popular support, resulted in a democratisation of politics, but additionally in the escalation and nationalisation of conflict. Campaigning journalists sought to further their cause as well as to expose the corrupt machinations of their opponents. Influenced by the professional men and journalists who spoke in the clubs, popular societies were created, with affiliates in the provinces, which increasingly agitated for a wider franchise, for referenda and for the right to recall deputies. The lower middle-class traders and artisans, and the skilled workers who largely made up these groups, shared a growing commitment to democracy, contempt for the moderation of the Constituent Assembly and suspicion of the king. This was evident as early as 5 October 1789 in the action of crowds, largely made up of women anxious about the cost of bread, when they humiliated the monarch by forcing him to move from his palace at Versailles to the Tuileries in Paris. The Assembly followed. This would allow the exercise of continuous popular pressure on both. A process of political education, and indeed of the politicisation of everyday life, was under way in which women, though lacking formal political rights, were active participants. The content and objectives of politics were being transformed.

It rapidly became apparent that, while he might make concessions under pressure, Louis XVI remained an unwilling participant in the process of political reform. He probably could not have conceived of anything more radical than an aristocratic monarchy on the British pattern. His disillusionment grew. On 23 June 1791 the royal family tried to escape from France, leaving behind them a justificatory memorandum complaining about the limits imposed on the royal right of appointment to office, on the king's ability to veto legislation, on his freedom to conduct diplomacy and about the growing influence of the radical clubs. For many, this so-called flight to Varennes (where the king was arrested) finally broke the spell of monarchy. Evidently, the king was willing to conspire not only with the internal opponents of the Revolution but with émigrés and foreign rulers. Engravings such as 'The family of pigs returned to the table' spread contempt. A renewed panic swept through the provinces. National Guards were mobilised to meet invading armies and prevent aristocratic treason. At the same time the determination of a large number of deputies to continue to seek an accommodation with the discredited king intensified political tension. In the Assembly, moderates such as Antoine Barnave were anxious to preserve a strong monarchy through fear that a republic would herald a descent into anarchy. On the other hand, radicals such as Georges Danton, Camille Desmoulins and Robespierre agitated for the trial of the king they claimed had proved himself to be a traitor and perjurer. On the streets rising social tension was clearly evident. On 17 July a peaceful crowd, which had gathered on the Champ de Mars to sign a petition against the rehabilitation of the king, was brutally dispersed by middle-class National Guards commanded by Lafayette. They left behind some fifty dead. At this stage, nevertheless, many former liberals were themselves advocating the radical step of establishing a republic. By the time the Constituent Assembly had completed its work and given way to a Legislative Assembly with the promulgation of the constitution on 13 September, the monarchy was widely discredited.

The period during which this new assembly sat (1 October 1791 to 20 September 1792) was short but of crucial importance. It saw the abolition of the monarchy, and a further radicalisation of the Revolution, in a situation of war, threatened counter-revolution and the popular disorder consequent upon a poor harvest and inflation. The members of this assembly were all new to national politics, the Constituent Assembly, in an exceptional self-denying mood, having determined that its members should be disqualified from re-election. There were fewer clerics and (ex-)nobles, though most deputies came from the prosperous landowning and professional middle classes with experience in local government. Doubtless, a large majority would have favoured moderate policies. Thus 250 of the 745 joined the Feuillant club and only 136 joined the Jacobins; included in the latter number were future Girondins, a group that came to owe its label to the fact that many of its leaders, including Pierre Vergniaud, Marguerite-Elie Gaudet, Armand Gensonné and Jean-François Ducos, represented the Gironde department. In spite of their differences, the deputies were overwhelmingly committed to the defence of the principles of 1789. For this reason, even moderates, as *patriotes*, believed in the urgency and legitimacy of repressive measures against the émigré nobility and non-juror clergy – the *aristocrate* party – and sided with the Jacobins rather than the more cautious Feuillants. They also shared in the decision taken on

20 April 1792 to engage in military action against the émigrés gathering on the frontiers and the 'despots' who supported them. This decision, which, in effect, forced war on the European powers, was very much influenced by internal political strife. The king accepted the resolution in the hope that the Revolution would be defeated and destroyed. Lafayette and his associates believed that the prestige derived from a successful war would allow them to crush the Jacobins. Brissot and the Girondins, who were convinced that there was an international conspiracy to restore the *ancien régime* by means of invasion and internal subversion, had faith in the capacity of a revolutionary army to overwhelm its opponents and liberate Europe. This was a dream that attracted most Jacobins, with Robespierre, warning of the dangers of war in the Jacobin club, almost a lone opposing voice. In the event, the military situation rapidly deteriorated. The army had been weakened by the emigration of most of its officers. By July it became necessary to declare the fatherland in danger (*la patrie en danger*). The war also had a decisive impact on the internal political situation.

By this time the differences between deputies who still sought a compromise with the king and those political militants determined to secure victory at all costs had become unbridgeable. In August, following the publication of a threatening counter-revolutionary manifesto by the Duke of Brunswick, commander of the invading Prussian and Austrian armies, popular support grew for action against the king, other subversives and corrupt politicians. A conflict of authority developed between the Assembly, the Paris Commune and radical clubs as news was received of Prussian military successes on the eastern frontier and fear grew of counter-revolutionary plots. On 9/10 August some 25,000 members of the popular societies and of the now democratised National Guard attacked the Tuileries Palace, massacring 600 of the king's Swiss Guards and securing the imprisonment of the monarch. Lafayette, who attempted to march on Paris and restore constitutional monarchy, was deserted by his troops. Between 2 and 6 September the growing threat of invasion and fear of treason led to the massacre of some 1,400 political prisoners held in Parisian prisons. This heralded the violent establishment of a revolutionary dictatorship. Most conservative members of the Legislative Assembly fled, leaving it under the control of a

Plate 4.5 The attack on the Tuileries, 10 August 1792. Painting by J. Bertaux. Musée national du château de Versailles. Photo: Giraudon/the Bridgeman Art Library.

Girondin majority that, under constant popular pressure, voted for the suspension of the king from his functions and the summoning of a National Convention to prepare a new constitution that, now that the age of kings was finally over, would guarantee liberty and popular sovereignty. It was to be elected by manhood suffrage (with the exception of domestic servants, deemed to be lacking in independence) but again with the safeguard of indirect election. In the succeeding weeks the Girondins ordered the deportation of refractory priests, the final abolition of seigneurial dues without compensation and the sale of émigré property – measures that the king had previously obstructed. Even amongst those committed to victory, however, there emerged differences over political and military tactics that would lead the members of competing groups to accuse each other of treason. In spite of these seemingly radical measures, therefore, Girondin leaders were to be increasingly subject to criticism by Parisian radicals because of their opposition to the uprising of 10 August and to the final dethronement of the king, and reluctance to introduce controls over the supply of food.

The National Convention was to govern France from September 1792 until November 1795. Only around 700,000 of a potential electorate of 7 million participated in its election, reflecting both popular indifference and the limits to politicisation. Like previous assemblies it was made up predominantly of comfortably off bourgeois. On 10 August 1793, the first anniversary of the attack on the Tuileries, it promulgated a new constitution. Although its introduction was suspended because of the military crisis, this represented a determined effort to win popular support and provided for a unicameral legislature elected by direct manhood suffrage, which would itself elect an executive. In addition to the liberty proclaimed in the Declaration of Rights in 1789, the preamble guaranteed the rights to public assistance, education and even to insurrection to resist oppression. This, the most democratic constitutional document of the period, was soon overshadowed by bitter factional divisions, however, especially between Girondins and Montagnards (the mountain dwellers – that is, the radical deputies sitting on the left and at the top of the steeply banked seats in the assembly), the latter based on the Jacobin club and led by eminent members of the Paris delegation, most notably Robespierre, Danton and Marat. Both groups sought to appeal for support to the majority of uncommitted deputies, the so-called Plain. In the absence of parties in the modern sense, the membership of these groups – many of them lawyers – remained fluid and based upon personal networks and shared political sentiments, as well as mutual antipathy. If there was a general consensus on such fundamental matters as the need to secure the protection of private property and to defend the Revolution, and in favour of an aggressive foreign policy in order to bring 'fraternity and assistance' to the oppressed peoples of Europe, explosive political differences remained. The Montagnards were convinced that their opponents were insufficiently committed to the campaign against counter-revolution and half-hearted in their support for the trial and, finally, the execution of the king – traitor or martyr, depending on one's perspective – which took place on 21 January 1793. On the other hand, the Girondins suspected the Montagnards of planning to use violent popular support in order to establish the dictatorship of Paris over the provinces. As the military crisis deepened in the spring and summer of 1793, exceptional measures to combat the internal enemies of the republic came to seem even

Plate 4.6 The execution of Louis XVI, 21 January 1793. The final symbolic
breach with the *ancien régime* and an act in defiance of the crowned heads of
Europe. Photo: the Stapleton Collection/the Bridgeman Art Library.

more necessary. News of the treasonable contacts between General
Dumouriez and the Austrians and the popular demonstrations this
provoked in Paris helped to establish parliamentary support for a
purge of leading Girondins and for a terror directed at the nation's
enemies. The more extreme Jacobins called on the 'people' to save the
Revolution from the treason of the 'rich'.

The military effort caused massive problems. Armies had to be
raised, equipped and fed. The state's financial crisis deepened.
Printing more paper money (*assignats*) heightened inflation. In spite
of the reasonably good harvest of 1792, the disruptive impact of war
and inflation caused serious food shortages and widespread rioting
during the winter of 1792/3. The effort to mobilise men and resources would lead to growing internal dissent. In part this was due to the
very scale of the effort implied by the universal call to arms (*levée en
masse*) and, when the stream of patriotic volunteers became inadequate, by the growing resort to conscription. By the summer of 1792
there were already 400,000 men under arms, mostly enlisted since
1789, and by the autumn of 1793 over 750,000. Weight of numbers,

rather than tactical innovation or even ideological commitment, explains the victory over the Duke of Brunswick at Valmy on 20 September 1792, which saved the Revolution and led to the 'liberation' of the left bank of the Rhine. Subsequent victory at Jemappes permitted the occupation of the Austrian Netherlands (essentially, modern Belgium), but almost inevitably the threat this posed to the strategic and commercial interests of Britain and the Netherlands led to war with these powers, declared by the Convention in February 1793. From that month, however, what was left of the old royal army and the new volunteer battalions were amalgamated to constitute a more effective fighting force. In spite of the massive emigration of nobles, the officers were mainly professional soldiers, owing their often-rapid promotion to their own abilities and to the Revolution itself.

To a very large extent, the establishment of the system of government known as the Terror has determined the attitudes of both contemporaries and later commentators towards the Revolution. It should not be viewed simply as mindless violence, however. Many of the measures taken could be justified as responses to the defeats of spring 1793, to the renewed threat of invasion and counter-revolution and to the demands for punitive action articulated by the Parisian clubs and popular societies. The Terror was intended as a temporary expedient. As a decree published in October 1793 put it, the government of France would be 'revolutionary until there is peace'. The will of the Convention was now to be enforced by requiring ministers to report to its committees and especially to the Committee of Public Safety, a kind of war Cabinet exercising a general supervisory role, and to the Committee of General Security, responsible for policing the country. These bodies would largely supplant the legislative body for as long as the emergency lasted. In the provinces they acted through the elected local authorities, the revolutionary committees and the popular Jacobin clubs. Delegates of the Convention, the *représentants en mission*, had overriding authority, however. When necessary, they could call upon the support of the army, National Guards or the armed civilian *armées révolutionnaires* found in around one-third of departments. The latter were composed of enthusiastic urban Jacobins determined to impose republican virtue and the style of an essentially urban revolution upon an often recalcitrant countryside. These developments represented an effort to reinforce the role of the state, following the brief experiment with decentralisation. Moderation was often equated with treason. In practice, however, the implementation of the Terror was far from systematic. Officials in Paris remained inescapably dependent on the goodwill of local officials, themselves often heavily engaged in faction fighting and either indifferent to outside events or hostile to growing interference in their affairs by representatives of the state. In many communities nothing much happened. Support for the radicalisation of the Revolution appears to have been particularly widespread in the neighbourhood of Paris and other major cities, in the threatened frontier regions and in parts of the centre and south-west. An estimated 17,000 'legal' executions took place, together with 30,000 to 40,000 unauthorised killings. The judicial murder and the massacre of prisoners can be explained, but under no circumstances justified. A large majority of those killed were manual workers or peasants, although proportionate to their numbers the nobility no doubt suffered most. The impact of the Terror was further intensified by widespread arrest and imprisonment (affecting about 500,000 or 3 per cent of the adult population), as well as by rumours, which added to the intense sense of anxiety and of shock in even the most isolated village.

Military mobilisation, the need to feed the growing armies and the disruption of the food-marketing system this caused, as well as civil disorder, inflation and poor harvests, added a sometimes overwhelming concern with subsistence to these other tensions. The diminution of purchasing power and widespread unemployment this would anyway have caused was made all the more severe by the loss of external markets due to the war. Rising social tension and widespread popular protest involving numerous marketplace riots and efforts to disrupt the commerce in foodstuffs threatened to disorganise the provisioning of the cities. Hostility grew towards a government that could not ensure the sustenance of the poor. In this situation the Convention, although favouring free trade, felt bound in May and September 1793 to impose maximum levels on the price of grain and to make speculative hoarding a capital offence. Robespierre insisted that 'existence is the first of all rights', but these measures were intended to be nothing more than a temporary expedient, a concession to the war effort and to pressure from the Parisian shopkeepers, artisans and workers. These were the so-called *sans-culottes* – that is, those who wore trousers, rather than knee-breeches, and who, by implication, worked with their hands. In practice, the lack of effective means of enforcement in the face of the ill will of merchants and peasants attracted by black market prices and the obstructionism of many rural municipalities made the enforcement of price controls extremely difficult. The very attempt, combined with requisitioning, caused considerable agitation, however, so that the revolutionary government itself became increasingly anxious to end the experiment, and this economic terror was noticeably relaxed even before the fall of Robespierre and its final abolition on 24 December 1794.

Another manifestation of the Terror was the campaign of dechristianisation waged in some areas during the autumn of 1793 and spring of 1794. This combined intellectual anti-religious feeling with popular anticlericalism and was further stimulated by association of the refractory clergy with counter-revolutionary fanaticism. It manifested itself in pressure on priests to resign their functions, in the destruction of religious images and the closure of churches, in the hunt for dissident clerics and, ultimately, in the effort to create a new revolutionary Cult of Reason and the Supreme Being, designed to promote civic virtue and the regeneration of humanity. The prospect of enhancing future 'happiness' could be used to justify the extirpation of its enemies. The effort to desacralise daily life also involved the introduction of a revolutionary calendar that abolished Sunday, to mark the dawn of a new era. The effects varied. A great deal depended on the enthusiasm of particular *représentants en mission*. Certainly, the credibility of the official constitutional Church was destroyed and the habit of religious observance weakened in many places, especially in parts of the Paris region, Normandy, the Rhône corridor and areas of central France where the influence of the Church was already often tenuous. In many other places support for the clergy, particularly amongst women, was strengthened in reaction to the assault on traditional religious practices.

In deciding on these various measures, to an important degree the Convention was making concessions to the Parisian popular classes, the workers and masters of the Paris trades who had participated in every major demonstration from the taking of the Bastille. Only with their aid had the Revolution prevailed. The outbreak of war and counter-revolution had both radicalised the revolutionary leadership and reinforced its dependence on mass support. Political factions within the Convention could appeal to those outside its walls. Between 31 May and 2 June 1793 representatives of the organs of Parisian local government, of the *sections* and municipality, petitioned for the arrest of leading Girondins and for the more energetic waging of the war. Then, and again on 4–5 September, when further demonstrations demanded the establishment of 'revolutionary government', a majority of deputies felt bound to agree. To impose food procurement and political repression in the absence of a substantial state bureaucracy or monolithic party, the government had little alternative but to use the local popular societies and the *armées révolutionnaires*, with their largely *sans-culottes* membership and reverberating slogans: *Guerre aux tyrans* (War on the tyrants), *Guerre aux aristocrats* and *Guerre aux accapareurs* (hoarders or speculators). The clubs had proliferated, and by the year II they had spread into many rural areas. Estimates of their number varied between 5,000 and 8,000, with anywhere between 500,000 and 1 million members – that is, one adult male in twelve, or six, although regular activists must have been far fewer. Their leaders remained predominantly bourgeois professionals or landowners, but, as a result of the development of popular political awareness, some democratisation was evident.

The *sans-culottes*, and particularly the more militant amongst them, were a socially disparate group with diverse interests, made up mainly of master artisans, journeymen and shopkeepers – that is, the better-off, more literate element amongst the popular classes. The poorest remained indifferent or else felt excluded. Locksmiths, joiners and cabinetmakers, shoemakers and tailors appear to have been amongst the most active. They were given a sense of unity by craft and neighbourhood loyalties, and in some provincial cities and in the various *quartiers* of the capital they were able to organise political action through meetings and demonstrations, and in Paris by means of regular meetings of the *sections*. A 'language of exclusion' developed that condemned, in the most ferocious terms, all those suspected of being lukewarm towards the Revolution, and above all the 'rich and corrupt' – all those, whether aristocrats, financiers, landowners, merchants or speculators in general, who were believed to be exploiting the poor. Their hostility was in part a diffuse form of class antagonism but they subscribed to a set of egalitarian moral values rather than a systematic political ideology. It seemed so obviously unjust that some citizens had substantial property whilst others endured constant insecurity, that some consumers had food and drink in plenty when others frequently went without. The *sans-culotte* ideal was a community in which all should work, in which every family would gain status and security through the possession of a small property and in which the rich would be deprived of their superfluity in order to provide for the poor. Although committed to the private ownership of property they believed that absolute rights of ownership should be restricted by the 'needs of the people'. This was symbolised by the question of bread, which ought to be available to all at an affordable price. They demanded additionally the right to influence government decisions, not only through elected deputies, who should be subject to recall when they diverged from their instructions, but by means of mass petitioning, a form of popular sovereignty that constituted an obvious threat to the rights of elected assemblies. The masses thus began to adopt and adapt the slogans and ideals of the political groups engaged in the struggle for power and threatened to become an independent political force. Neither in Paris nor the provinces, however, did the leaders of this movement give much thought to developing an effective means of coordinating their actions. Their activities remained essentially local.

The primary link between this popular movement and the Jacobins was a shared commitment to the defence of the Revolution. The threat of counter-revolution initially represented by the émigré nobles, who had in 1789 gathered in Nice, Turin, Lausanne, Mannheim, Coblenz and Brussels, who sought support from the European powers and who had begun to organise conspiratorial networks in France, was substantially reinforced by the growth of mass resistance to the Revolution. It seemed transformed into a 'vast conspiracy against the liberty of France and the future liberty of the human race' (Hérault de Séchelles). The reasons for this development were varied. One characteristic of the movement, and indeed its fundamental weakness, was its localism. Certainly there was widespread resentment of growing interference in communal affairs by the new administrators who, through the army, the urban National Guards and the *armées révolutionnaires*, possessed a coercive power much greater than that of the *ancien régime* in many areas. Moreover, from as early as 1790 much of the population began to feel that the sacrifices they were being asked to make far outweighed the gains they had made from the Revolution, although rejection of Jacobinism certainly did not necessarily imply support for counter-revolution. The main centres of mass support for armed opposition were to be characterised by the significance of the religious issue. Conflict frequently reflected pre-revolutionary tensions. In the Midi, and especially the Montauban and Nîmes areas, as early as spring 1790 there was a reaction against the growing Protestant role in local affairs, and rumours that Catholics were about to be massacred encouraged renewed sectarianism. Together with subsequent attempts to raise the peasants of the Lozère and Ardèche in July 1792 and at the beginning of 1793, these movements were crushed with relative ease. Elsewhere, support for those clergy who refused to accept the Civil Constitution was a more dangerous threat.

In areas of intense faith the refractory priest represented the religious idealism of his community, and had powerful and important functions to perform. Efforts by outsiders to deny this were bound to be resisted. The attack on Christianity, involving the closure of churches, widespread iconoclasm and the persecution of priests, must have represented a profound shock. Even then, as a cause of counter-revolutionary mobilisation, religious issues have to be considered alongside disappointment with the revolutionary property settlement, hostility towards taxation and conscription, and the requisitioning of foodstuffs and horses in return for increasingly devalued paper money. Peasant land hunger was such that even in areas where they supported refractory priests they often did not hesitate to acquire former Church property. Where the land settlement was favourable to influential groups within the village community they tended to favour, or at least not actively oppose, the Revolution. Where, in contrast, they felt deprived of the opportunity to purchase land, usually by bourgeois speculators from nearby towns, their frustration was intense, particularly when even the abolition of the tithe failed to benefit tenant farmers, who found it reincorporated into their rents. Conscription and especially the decree of 24 February 1793 added fuel to the flames of resentment. In the west, widespread violence occurred in the spring and summer of 1791, developing in 1793 into full-scale rebellion in the Vendée and southern Anjou and to a lesser degree in parts of Brittany and Normandy. This lasted into 1796, and intermittently until 1799 and beyond. In the four departments of the Vendée *militaire* some 170,000 people are estimated to have lost their lives as a result of guerrilla warfare and brutal repression, though even these statistics probably underestimate the impact of frequently indiscriminate military efforts to clear the countryside of insurgents and all those who might lend them succour. Military casualties were also heavy in these domestic conflicts. Violence was thus a primary characteristic of counter-revolution as well as the Terror. It was most dangerous where rural artisans and peasants accepted the leadership of nobles with military experience. Their relationship was often a tense one. Even where, apparently, artisans and peasants fought for the same cause as nobles this certainly did not mean that they favoured the restoration of the *ancien régime* in its entirety.

The danger to the Revolution was exacerbated by 'federalism'. To many moderates it appeared as though a minority of deputies, supported by the Paris popular movement, were usurping the rights of the nation's elected representatives. The democratisation of local government and the emergence of a relatively 'extreme' popular Jacobinism, together with the threat this posed to established social relationships, caused widespread alarm. Thus a movement of resistance to the Terror developed in the spring of 1793. It attracted liberal royalists but mainly involved socially conservative republicans in cities such as Bordeaux, Lyon, Marseille, Nîmes, Montpellier, Toulon and Caen, with upper middle-class leaders anxious to defend liberty, order and property against the threat of anarchy implicit in proposals for an agrarian law to involve land redistribution and to levy forced loans on the 'rich'. At a time when events in the Vendée as well as external war were imposing intense strains on military resources this new threat to the survival of the Republic was regarded by Jacobins as a particularly heinous form of treason. When, in desperation, the federalists of Lyon and Marseille appointed royalists to command their armies and those at Toulon called in the British and handed over much of the French fleet in the process, they clearly exposed themselves to the prospect of brutal retaliation.

By August 1793 royalist or federalist activity affected around twenty departments. Shortages of troops ensured that the central government lost control over large areas. Nevertheless, the Republic was to survive. The uncoordinated military effort mounted by the federalists was overcome with relative ease. Able to mobilise some 30,000 men, the Vendéans were militarily a greater problem, but by the end of the year their main effort had been crushed. Continued guerrilla activity – the *chouannerie* in parts of the Vendée, of Brittany and Normandy – so difficult to terminate entirely where activists enjoyed the advantages of local knowledge, a protective topography and community support, only intensified an increasingly vicious cycle of massacre and reprisal and created enduring hatreds.

For as long as the Revolution seemed threatened, an overriding sense of unity survived amongst its defenders. In the autumn and winter of 1793, however, military success against both external and internal enemies allowed the fissures to break open. Faction fighting was intensified. From as early as the autumn of 1793 Danton and his associates pressed for a relaxation of the Terror. In contrast, Jacques Hébert appealed for its intensification. Robespierre and his supporters isolated both of these groups politically, and their leaders were guillotined in March/April 1794. The Committee of Public Safety was also determined to restore governmental authority in the capital, and to control the popular movement that placed it under constant radicalising pressure. This became easier as many militants were incorporated into the burgeoning bureaucracy and army. Others were too frightened, disillusioned or fatigued to continue their political involvement. In all probability, a considerable loss of spontaneity was inevitable. Between January and April 1794 the leadership and organisation of the Parisian popular movement was destroyed. Subsequent efforts by surviving *sans-culottes* militants to resort to force to defend their conception of popular democracy were crushed rapidly. By their success, however, the Jacobins isolated themselves from the mass support that had brought them to power in the summer of 1793. Furthermore, the Terror had been acceptable to most members of the Convention only as an expedient. The military victories of June/July 1794, won by the superior generalship of

Plate 4.7 Emergence of the conservative republic, Thermidor, year II (28 July 1794). Troops loyal to the Convention arrive at the Hôtel-de-Ville in Paris to arrest Robespierre. Engraving by I. S. Helman, after a painting by C. Monnet. Bibliothèque nationale, Cabinet des Estampes. Photo: Giraudon/ the Bridgeman Art Library.

officers promoted on merit, by weight of numbers and because of divisions amongst the allies, ended the immediate threat of invasion and made revolutionary terrorism much less tolerable. A majority of deputies found Robespierre's apparent determination to turn terror into a permanent form of government, a means of creating a new moral order, increasingly abhorrent. They objected also to the judicial murder of some of their own, in particular Danton. Who could feel safe? The Committee of Public Safety was divided itself, along both personal and political lines. When on 26 July 1794 Robespierre denounced Joseph Cambon, Jacques-Nicolas Billaud and others in the Convention they defended themselves vigorously and attracted vocal support. On the following day the assembly voted the arrest of Robespierre and his associates, and secured their rapid execution. Although they would serve as useful scapegoats, the Convention itself would share in their discredit. This reassertion of the sovereign powers of parliament was followed by the curtailment of the powers of its committees. The administration and National Guard were purged energetically of both suspected Jacobins and *sans-culottes*, and the popular societies subjected to repression or closure. Political prisoners were released and the surviving Girondin and federalist deputies recalled. These events, in the month of Thermidor, year II, in the revolutionary calendar, marked the beginning of the transition to a more conservative regime.

THE CONSERVATIVE REPUBLIC

The context was one of widespread and extreme misery, with the worst subsistence crisis since 1709, resulting from the poor harvest of 1794 and the harsh winter of 1794–5. Popular risings in Paris on 1 April and 20–23 May 1795, induced above all by the desperate desire to reduce bread prices, but employing the slogan 'Bread and the constitution of '93', were easily crushed by the army and the National Guards of the better-off western *quartiers* of the capital. This marked the end of the *sans-culottes* as a significant political movement for some thirty-five years. On 23 August it was decreed that the surviving political clubs and popular societies should be closed. Cold, hunger and repression had taken their toll. Arbitrary judgements by military courts were employed increasingly against dissidents. The subsequent conspiracy to seize power led by François-Noël Babeuf, a proponent of the abolition of private property, ended prematurely with his arrest in May 1796 and provided yet another excuse for the detention of suspects. The Convention was now able to complete its task of preparing yet another constitution. The democratic constitution adopted but never implemented during the summer of 1793 had come to appear dangerously egalitarian. In contrast, the constitution of the year III provided for the election of a binary legislature made up of a Council of the Ancients and a Council of the Five Hundred, with a system of indirect election in which a mass electorate of around 6 million (only 20 per cent of whom would feel motivated to vote) elected delegates to departmental electoral assemblies, whose 30,000 members ultimately selected deputies. These were all wealthy men qualifying through the payment of taxes equivalent to the wages earned for between 100 and 200 days' labour. Manhood suffrage had come to be seen as a recipe for anarchy or despotism. Furthermore, as a safeguard against a possible royalist election victory, it was also stipulated that two-thirds of the deputies to be elected to the Conseil des Cinq-Cents and Anciens should be members of the Convention. The commitment to equality before the law survived, and property rights were firmly guaranteed, but this document was silent on the right to work, to assistance and to an elementary education, upon which the Jacobins had previously insisted. These were to be the responsibility of the individual and not the state. Indeed, the final ending of the economic controls associated with the Terror seemed to confirm the regime's indifference to popular suffering. Executive authority was conferred on a Directory of five, all of them regicides, although, in order to prevent a repetition of the dictatorship they had just endured, deputies were now determined to enforce a rigorous separation of powers.

This was to be a regime constantly aware of the threats from both the Jacobin left and the royalist right, and desperately in need of a social and political base it could call its own. The danger implicit in its balancing act was rapidly made clear. Resentment of the Convention's perpetuation of its own power led to a royalist demonstration in Paris on 5 October 1795, forcing the regime to look to the left for support, but this served only to alienate those moderate notables who were its natural constituents. In any event, the alliance with the left could be only a short-lived tactical manoeuvre. Although, on several occasions, the monarchist threat would promote efforts to increase republican unity, anxiety within governing circles that this might encourage the rebirth of the alliance between the Jacobins and the popular classes always led to a renewal of repression. Similarly openings to the right, as in the case of the decree of 21 February 1795 establishing freedom of conscience in religious matters, were hedged around with too many restrictions to enjoy real success. Certainly, the monarchist menace seemed very real. It could be seen daily in the dress, affectations and arrogance of the so-called *jeunesse dorée* (gilded youth) in Paris. It manifested itself in continued insurrection in the west, against which a reinforced military effort under General Hoche was deployed, with as many as 100,000 men sweeping through the countryside in flying columns in the spring of 1795. In communities in the Rhône valley and throughout the south-east, the excesses of former Jacobin militants, denounced as 'terrorists' and 'drinkers of blood', were avenged. They were subjected to ostracism and intimidation and not infrequently murdered. If 1795 was the bloodiest year of this White Terror it continued at least until 1802, and represented both revenge and the reassertion of social hierarchy. The purge of Jacobin sympathisers from the administration and the widespread collapse of local government in the face of desertion, draft dodging and brigandage left former militants cruelly exposed. Overt royalist political activity was also evident. In spite of the inept intransigence of the demand made by the former king's brother, the Comte de Provence, in the Verona declaration of 24 June 1795, for a restoration of the 'ancient constitution', subsequent elections revealed considerable support within the wealthy electorate for monarchists. So much so that on 4 September 1797 – the so-called coup d'état of 18 Fructidor, year V – the Directory felt obliged to annul the election results in over half the departments and to reactivate legislation against émigrés and priests as well as to engage in a further purge of the administration. The constitution had been violated.

The so-called Thermidorian and Directorial regimes have generally received a bad press. The seriousness of the problems they faced ought to be borne in mind, however. Ending the Terror did not end the problems caused by civil and external war, and by poor harvests. Although the Directory made substantial progress towards ending the financial instability caused by the massive depreciation of the *assignat*, repeated purges of both the bureaucracy and parliament considerably weakened the authority of the central government and increasingly left it isolated. It survived for as long as it did because of the ability of men such as the Vicomte de Barras and Lazare Carnot, and especially because of the divisions and weakness of its adversaries. There were obvious dangers, however, in a situation in which war and its own isolation forced the government to rely increasingly upon the support of the army. Lyon and Marseille, as well as substantial parts of the countryside, were subject to martial law. Military victories leading to the annexation of the Low Countries and Rhineland and the creation of 'sister' republics in Italy kept most of the army outside France. In the conquered territories soldiers engaged in a systematic policy of looting and living off the land, which considerably eased the regime's financial difficulties.

Moreover, the army's senior officers were opposed to both a royalist restoration, which would threaten their own status, and to a Jacobin revival, which would seek to reimpose civilian control over their activities. Ominously, however, efforts to control the generals were often rejected contemptuously. The revolutionary army had been transformed into an increasingly professional force, divorced from civil society.

THE CONSULATE AND EMPIRE

By the end of the 1790s the Republic, in the persons of its squabbling politicians, was discredited. Even amongst deputies there was a widespread desire for strong government, which would more effectively safeguard social order, whilst respecting personal liberty and equality before the law – that is, the fundamental gains of 1789. There was little agreement as to how these objectives might be achieved. Various groups were looking for the support of an influential general, however. Jean-Baptiste Bernadotte, Barthélemy Joubert, Victor Moreau and then Bonaparte were all cast in this role. For Sieyès and his faction, frightened by a neo-Jacobin renewal of the Directory in June 1799, Bonaparte had obvious virtues. Besides his talent as a soldier, he possessed useful contacts within the intellectual and political élites, and, a brilliant self-publicist, he was popular both in the army and amongst civilians. Abandoning his army in Egypt, the youthful hero of the war in Italy returned to France in time to participate in the conspiracy. Using the pretext of a Jacobin plot, the legislature was persuaded to transfer itself to Saint-Cloud, just outside Paris, and once there, on 18/19 Brumaire, 1799, was surrounded by troops and pressured into establishing a ruling Consulate made up of Sieyès, Ducos and Bonaparte. The coup had been planned as a means of affirming the authority of Sieyès and his supporters but it rapidly became evident that real power lay in the hands of Bonaparte, the man with military support. The constitution of the year VIII (1799) provided for his appointment as First Consul for ten years with substantial executive power. Although virtual manhood suffrage was also recognised, as before democracy was kept at bay by means of a complex process of indirect election culminating in the selection of deputies for a legislative assembly (Corps législatif) by members of a senate, itself formed by cooption. Moreover, the press and political activity were subject to constant and effective repression. Provision was also made for a plebiscite, with its results carefully manufactured, as the means of legitimising these arrangements. Meaningful popular participation in politics, already fatally weakened, was finally destroyed. Although Bonaparte owed his power to the army, his regime, whilst certainly authoritarian, was not to become a military dictatorship. The supremacy of the civilian administration was to be preserved even if much of its energy was to be absorbed in the incessant task of providing the means for waging war.

The immediate problem was to impose governmental authority upon a country plagued by widespread banditry and political disaffection and in which local administrators had lost confidence. A combination of military action against royalist insurgents in the south and west, together with concessions to Catholics to allow Sunday worship, and a generous amnesty for both royalists and Jacobins, sought to impose order and create a consensus in support of the new regime. This was followed by measures that would permanently increase the effectiveness of the administration, and represent another important stage in the creation of a centralised state – an *état bureaucratique*. A law of 7 February 1800 established the prefectoral system. The revolutionary principle of the election of local officials was replaced by their imposition from above and the creation of a hierarchical structure whose officials, as the representatives of the state in each department, would enjoy high salaries and status. Significantly, 40 per cent of the 281 prefects appointed between 1800 and 1814 would be *ancien régime* nobles. Although these measures increased the ability of the central administration to implement government policy in the provinces, it ought to be borne in mind that the relatively small number of officials, as well as poor communications, ensured continued reliance on the cooperation of local élites, particularly those selected to serve as mayors in some 40,000 communes. Much of the statistical information so assiduously collected by Napoleonic officials in an effort to assess the nation's manpower and economic resources was definitely of doubtful veracity.

In spite of his own ignorance of administrative and financial matters, and his frequent absences, Bonaparte proved to be immensely energetic and willing to accept the reforming proposals of experienced administrators such as Charles-François Lebrun and Charles Gaudin, the latter – as finance minister – a former collaborator of Necker. Financial confidence was to be restored by means of the more efficient collection of taxes (law of 24 November 1799) and the establishment of a central bank. There had been considerable progress also in the preparation of new legal codes before the establishment of the Consulate. They provided France for the first time with a uniform legal system and confirmed the basic principles of personal liberty and legal equality established in 1789. At the same time, the conservative principles associated with the patriarchal family and regulation of the transmission of private property were reinforced. Following the destruction of the society of orders, property had indeed become the essential source of social status. As a means of conciliating colonial and mercantile élites, considerable resources were also devoted to the re-establishment of slavery in the colonies, which had been abolished in the year II.

The prestige of the regime was further heightened by a string of military victories, leading to the Peace of Lunéville (8 February 1801), which restored French dominance over northern Italy and the left bank of the Rhine, and to the Treaty of Amiens (25 March 1802) with Britain. In the longer term neither Austria nor Britain would be able to tolerate the prospect of French hegemony. More immediately, however, peace released troops for internal repression, in combination with which Bonaparte felt able to take further conciliatory initiatives. In April 1802 an amnesty was offered to all save 1,000 émigrés provided they took an oath of loyalty and accepted the revolutionary land settlement. Furthermore, a Concordat, finally published at Easter 1802, was negotiated with the papacy. It represented Bonaparte's cynical appreciation of the value of religion as a means of social control. It also made it easier for Catholics to accept his government, and substantially weakened the royalist cause. Although it accepted the pre-eminence of Catholicism as the religion to which most of the population adhered, the agreement also recognised the principle of religious toleration. Whilst accepting the spiritual leadership of the Pope, the Concordat, together with the organic articles necessary to implement its provisions (on which the Pope was not even consulted), furthermore provided for extensive and much-resented state control over the clergy and required them once again to preach submission to the established authorities. Nevertheless, it was generally welcomed as bringing to an end a period of vicious conflict between Church and state that had threatened the very existence of established religion. The urgent work of religious reconstruction could begin. Even Napoleon's subsequent occupation of the Papal States and excommunication by the Pope failed to shake this new internal consensus.

On 6 May 1802, in gratitude for Bonaparte's achievements, the senate proposed that his authority be extended for a further ten years; instead, the Conseil d'Etat (State Council) suggested a plebiscite to ask the nation to establish him as consul for life with the right to nominate his successor. In this way legislative bodies made up of wealthy property owners, rarely consulted but repeatedly purged until they were composed overwhelmingly of proven adherents of the regime – and recipients of its patronage – gave power to Bonaparte as a means of avoiding the uncertainties of election and parliamentary government. After years of repression, the mass of the population remained indifferent. The establishment of the hereditary Empire on 18 May 1804 – sanctioned by a further dubious plebiscite – was another means by which those who served the regime sought to increase their security in response to a series of royalist assassination plots. Although it had little real effect on the institutions of government, this re-establishment of monarchy had immense symbolic value in bringing the era of revolution to a close. Like the conservative republic that had preceded it, this was to be an authoritarian regime, devoted to the preservation of the social status quo. Public opinion was manipulated through censorship and imperial self-glorification. Opponents faced arbitrary arrest or repressive action by the imperial gendarmerie or army.

Napoleon's essential objectives remained the establishment of effective government, the reinforcement of social order, assurance of French military and political predominance in Europe and the secure establishment of his dynasty. A new status hierarchy was to be constructed, based upon service to the state, and formalised at its summit through the etiquette and luxury of the Tuileries Palace.

Plate 4.8 The battle of Austerlitz, 2 December 1805, confirmed French military predominance following the occupation of Vienna, a fact recognised in the Treaty of Pressbourg. The Austro-Russian force was defeated with the loss of 37,000 dead and 30,000 prisoners; 8,000 French troops lost their lives. Engraving by J. L. Rugendas II. © Paris – Musée de l'Armée, Dist. RMN–Grand Palais.

Drawn from wealthy bourgeois and noble families, its future members were to be trained in the *lycées* (law of 1 May 1802) under close state supervision. Their achievements were to be recognised with membership of the Legion of Honour (May 1802) and of the imperial nobility (1808). Men from a variety of social backgrounds were to be attracted by the prospects offered by the extended Empire. Former *ancien régime* nobles made up 22 per cent of the 3,263 new nobles, with 20 per cent coming from the popular classes and 58 per cent from the bourgeoisie. Additionally, 59 per cent would have a military background. Shared objectives served to reduce political disunity. Although, at first, most members of the old nobility chose to remain inactive, as time passed few families were not represented in the civil administration or officer corps. The regime's successes and growing air of permanence encouraged

Plate 4.9 Napoleon distributing Europe between his brothers. Engraving by
J. Gauthier. Musée Carnavalet. © Roger-Viollet/TopFoto.

many to overcome their initial disdain for the 'usurper'. As under
the *ancien régime*, the bourgeoisie continued to view office holding
as a primary means of achieving upward social mobility. Grateful
for the re-establishment of social order, many former republicans
also assumed that, if the alternative was a Bourbon restoration,
Bonaparte was the lesser evil.

As the administration became more effective, so the regime became
more dictatorial. Representative institutions were largely ignored. At
the top, the emperor's growing intolerance of dissent led to the
replacement of able ministers such as Jean-Antoine Chaptal,
Talleyrand and Joseph Fouché and left the regime increasingly
dependent on the will and ability of a dictator who seems to have
come to believe increasingly in the idealised image of the 'hero', the
'man of destiny', that – with the enthusiastic support of artists and
writers – he had worked so hard to construct. As a result, decision
making would become less rational. In the short term religious peace,
social order, material prosperity and the seemingly endless list of

military victories protected the regime from dissent. Those workers whose age, family responsibilities and luck in the draw enabled them to escape military service profited from the reduction in the size of the labour force and rising wages. Urban consumers and most of the rural population benefited from the series of good harvests between 1802 and 1809, an episode of always fragile prosperity for which the regime inevitably claimed credit.

This period was terminated by the poor harvest of 1810 and the deteriorating military situation. To a large degree it had represented merely recovery from the losses of the revolutionary period. Although localised examples of innovation and growth can certainly be identified, most notably in the textiles and metallurgical industries in Paris, Rouen, Lille and Mulhouse areas, protected by war from the full rigours of British competition, French technology had increasingly fallen behind that of its rival.

Perpetual war, unwillingness to compromise and the sheer intensity of the struggle were to lead to the Empire's collapse. Although he posed as a peacemaker, Napoleon's determined effort to impose French political hegemony on Europe, together with the unrestrained extraction of men, money and supplies from allies and former enemies by an often brutal occupying power, was bound to provoke resistance. The situation was exacerbated by efforts to establish France as the dominant economic power by means of the Continental System (1806), intended to weaken Britain by excluding its goods from the Continent, which would then serve as a market and source of raw materials for French manufactures.

In spite of his monarchical pretensions, the emperor was perceived by the allies to be the embodiment of an aggressive and revolutionary foreign policy. Moreover, the lack of definable long-term goals other than complete domination was all too likely to cause Napoleon to overreach himself. Careful reorganisation of the army between 1800 and 1804, and his tactical genius and disregard for human life, could offer only temporary advantage. The remarkable victories during the Austerlitz campaign, and at Jena and Auerstadt, notwithstanding, his opponents, repeatedly defeated, learnt their lessons the hard way. The Peninsular War (1808–14) proved to be a serious drain on resources. The invasion of Russia in 1812, undertaken in spite of advice to the contrary and inspired by a determination to punish the tsar for withdrawing from the Continental System, proved to be catastrophic. The numerical advantages offered by the size of the population of military age in France and its annexed territories were lost as the armies retreated, and, with the declining ability to make the defeated pay, so the costs of war, in terms both of men and money, increased. Political opposition grew. Its strength is difficult to gauge. Generally, administrative reports told the emperor and his ministers what it was presumed they wanted to hear, repeatedly stressing the people's loyalty and great love for their ruler. There were three main elements of antagonism, however: republicans, royalists and – most dangerous of all – the war-weary. Following earlier repression and a renewed wave of arrests in 1801, republican and popular opposition had largely been relegated to the verbal, to little more than anonymous yells of 'Down with [*A bas*] Bonaparte' and private discussion by groups of old Jacobins. Police surveillance and occasional prosecutions combined to create an atmosphere of fear and to encourage restraint. Royalist groups, of which the Knights of the Faith (Chevaliers de la Foi (1809)) were the most notable, were more active, engaging in assassination plots and creating underground networks linked with émigrés and the British. Within high society, contempt for the regime was expressed frequently in the privacy of the home. Many of those who had rallied to it and held office had done so on a conditional basis and only for as long as there was no alternative. Even within the army, generals such as Bernadotte, Moreau and Jean-Charles Pichegru had long questioned the motives of a man who had been prepared to abandon his troops, first in Egypt in 1799 and then in 1812 in Russia, and who appeared to be making excessive demands upon the army for his own personal glory.

War-weariness increased rapidly with the failure of the Russian adventure and during the defensive campaigns of 1813/14. The British blockade intensified the commercial crisis caused by poor harvests in 1811 and 1812. An extremely harsh winter added to popular misery and discontent. The burden of taxation, raised primarily through consumer taxes, had always fallen disproportionately on the poor. Sharp increases from 1809 were all the more difficult to support. Draft dodging increased. More effective policing and the greater prestige of the regime had previously ensured that it

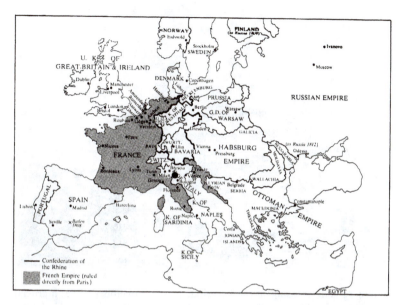

Figure 4.2 Apogee of Empire, 1812. (Source: R. Gildea, *Barricades and Borders: Europe 1800–1914*. Oxford University Press, 1987.)

had been a far less serious problem than during the Republic or Directory. Those who could afford to could in any case hire replacements. It is worth noting too that between 1800 and 1814 conscription took only some 7 per cent of the total population, a high enough figure but not when compared with the 20 per cent mobilised between 1914 and 1919. By the end of 1813 the allies had crossed the Rhine, however, and the Duke of Wellington was advancing through the Midi. In December even the normally docile Corps législatif voted (by 229 to thirty-one) in favour of peace on the basis of France's 'natural frontiers' (essentially those of 1792), and had its session adjourned for its pains. As casualties mounted and morale declined, banditry, together with endemic guerrilla warfare in the west, revived as unwilling conscripts took to the hills. In many parts of central France the call to arms to defend the nation by the distant government in Paris seemed threateningly irrelevant to daily life. Together with widespread subsistence disorders and unemployment, this contributed to a breakdown in law and order, particularly in the still under-policed countryside. Defeat and internal strife also

Plate 4.10 The crossing of the Berezina, 25–29 November 1812: a crucial moment in the disastrous retreat from Moscow. Lithograph by V. Adam. Bibliothèque nationale, Cabinet des Estampes. Photo: Giraudon/the Bridgeman Art Library.

threatened the conditional loyalty of the propertied classes predicated upon the promise of security and prosperity. On 31 March 1814, in spite of an often brilliant defensive campaign, the allies entered Paris; on 2 and 3 April the senate and Corps législatif voted to deprive the emperor of his throne. On 6 April his own marshals forced him to abdicate at Fontainebleau. This collapse represented a massive withdrawal of support by the notables. To a large degree, the masses remained indifferent to the proceedings. As Napoleon had himself predicted when asked how the people would react to his disappearance: *On dira 'Ouf'*!

A new constitution was now prepared by the senate, a body made up of imperial dignitaries, officials and landowners, many of them former members of the old revolutionary legislatures. The proposals that emerged, the bases for a new constitutional charter, closely resembled the constitution of 1791 in providing for a constitutional monarchy, with the king enjoying considerable power as head of the executive, and incorporating the other crucial gains of 1789, including equality before the law and freedom of religion and the press. It also guaranteed the revolutionary land settlement. The lower house of parliament was to be elected on a very restricted franchise, ensuring that only the wealthy – those with a 'real' stake in society – would share in political power. Under pressure from the allies, and in order to secure the restoration of legitimate monarchy, the former Comte de Provence, who, following the death of Louis XVI's young son in prison in 1795, had adopted the title of Louis XVIII, although rejecting the tricolour as the nation's symbol, otherwise felt obliged to accept this compromise. The Charter was proclaimed on 4 June.

It took a considerable degree of incompetence on the part of the restored monarchy and its supporters to make Bonaparte popular again. The deposed emperor was able to take advantage of his continued popularity in the army and the widespread resentment aroused by the inescapable need to reduce substantially the size of the administration and army in a France restricted to its old frontiers and requiring only a peacetime military establishment – a process used by the royal government, moreover, to purge the potentially disloyal, reward its own supporters and place trusted personnel in key positions. This seemed to herald a far more thoroughgoing counter-revolution. In the countryside there were widespread rumours about the repossession of their land by former émigrés and the reimposition of feudal dues and tithes.

Napoleon's return from exile on the island of Elba on 1 March 1815 and the rapid flight of Louis XVIII to Ghent seem to have reanimated radical anti-noble, anticlerical and nationalistic feeling – a neo-Jacobin revival, which caused great anxiety amongst 'respect-able' property owners, as did the prospect of renewed war. In an effort to win them over, Napoleon indeed felt obliged to promise the establishment of a constitutional, parliamentary regime in an 'Additional Act' similar in many respects to Louis XVIII's Charter.

Support for the emperor's return would remain far from univer-sal, however. It was most wholehearted in the north and east, in areas that had suffered considerable depredations as a result of the allied invasion. Elsewhere the response was often indifference or active opposition, as in those coastal regions that anticipated a renewal of the British blockade, and especially areas in the south and west in which popular opposition to the religious policies of the

Revolution and subsequently to conscription had been most intense. It was in these regions that often brutal reprisals would be taken against Bonapartist sympathisers when Waterloo brought this new adventure – Napoleon's Hundred Days – to a bloody climax. This overwhelming defeat forced the emperor to abdicate for a second and final time, on 22 June 1815, and was followed by his imprisonment at a safe distance, far out in the Atlantic, on the island of Saint Helena. There, he would employ his energy in the construction of a self-justifying and, as we shall see, politically potent Bonapartist myth.

The total collapse of Napoleonic imperialism would indeed fail to persuade those who continued to admire the emperor's achievements, as well as the generations of popular historians who persist in worshipping at the imperial shrine, to reflect sufficiently on the dangers implicit in the dictatorship of a supremely egotistical individual obsessed with military concepts of honour, sacrifice and glory. The ultimate outcome of his bloody campaigns might otherwise suggest that French military history should be characterised less by its glorious triumphs than by the frequency of catastrophic failure.

CONCLUSION

The closure of the long period of upheaval beginning in 1789 did not mean the end of political turmoil in France. The Revolutionary–Napoleonic era had destroyed old landmarks and had fundamental effects on the ways in which people thought about politics. Liberal and democratic principles had been laid down, the sovereignty of the nation recognised. Monarchy had been abolished and a king and queen executed. The Church and aristocracy had been subjected to sustained assault. Precedents had been established and allegiances formed that were to be passed on to succeeding generations. The fears and aspirations that had been generated created agendas for the following century. In part this was due to the entry of the masses into the political arena. The emergency that had led to the Terror had, however incompletely, politicised much of the population. It would prove impossible for even the best organised of police forces to reverse this entirely. The experience had also, of course, polarised political opinion, for or against the Revolution.

In recent years it has become fashionable, and not only amongst politically conservative 'revisionist' historians, to decry the significance of the Revolution (and by implication of revolutions), to seek to reduce it to the status of a passing epiphenomenon – the Revolution as continuity – with few lasting effects, and these essentially negative. There are indeed good grounds for arguing along these lines. The basic pre-industrial structures of the French economy remained unchanged, with the predominance of a low-productivity agriculture, slow and high-cost transportation systems and fragmented commercial networks and small-scale manufacturing. The costs of revolution and war were high. The gradual processes of change represented by growing commercialisation and increasing productivity, already evident in the previous century, had been slowed rather than stimulated.

In social terms too it seems quite correct to stress the continuities between the pre-revolutionary period and the early nineteenth century. It was the structure of the élite that had been most dramatically affected by the Revolution and Empire. The decline of the society of orders had been well under way before the Revolution, however. The abolition of noble privilege and recognition of civil equality confirmed as much as completed this process. Although substantial land transfers reduced the economic and social power of the nobility and the Church, their main consequence was to consolidate existing patterns of landholding and the position both of the rich, amongst whom the nobility remained conspicuous, and of peasant cultivators. In a still primarily agrarian society, in which the wealth necessary to fund appropriate lifestyles and to provide the education that allowed access to the professions or political office, was derived primarily from the land, it followed that the social élite, this class of *notables*, even if enlarged by the inclusion of many non-nobles, retained many of its pre-revolutionary characteristics. Certainly the years after 1789 had provided opportunities for upward mobility, particularly through state service and speculation on the value of land and military supplies, but the aspirations of the new men had been defined according to models established by the old. The Revolution had, furthermore, created an intense sense of insecurity. Political conflict and competition for power had left bitter divisions within the élite, as well as arousing the more or less clearly formulated aspirations of other groups.

Plate 4.11 The beginnings of industrialisation: a coal mine near Liège. Note the use of a steam engine for drainage, and the anxious crowd gathering following news of an accident on 29 February 1812. Musée Carnavalet. Photo: Giraudon/the Bridgeman Art Library.

A new political culture had certainly been created and new institutions established, which, centred on conceptions of the rights of man, were to affect fundamentally, and for the good, the ways in which we conceive of social relationships. Thus, although it is important to reject the exaggerated notion of revolution as the essential 'motor of history' in the Marxist sense, this should not lead us to ignore the impact of political upheaval. It would take generations to work through the agenda established by revolution, and the effort to do so would profoundly mark the succeeding century, as the proponents of *mouvement*, to complete the revolution, clashed with the supporters of *résistance* to further change.

5

The nineteenth century: continuity and change

The restoration of the Bourbon monarchy in the person of Louis XVIII, brother of the king executed in 1793, was far from representing a return to the pre-revolutionary status quo. The gains of 1789 – constitutional monarchy, representative government, and equality before the law – were recognised in the Charter granted by the king to the nation. In many respects the agenda for political debate throughout the forthcoming century had been established during the long years of internal strife and external war between 1789 and 1815. Sustained mobilisation had created a new political culture. Those who had directly experienced these events transmitted durable mental habits to their children. A wide range of political options had emerged, including reactionary Catholic monarchism, commitment to the liberal principles of 1789, *sans-culottes* egalitarianism, Jacobin nationalism and Bonapartism. Each of these signified adherence to highly selective references and images of the Revolution (the Declaration of the Rights of Man, the execution of the king, the dominance of Robespierre, of Bonaparte, and so on) that signified fundamentally different value systems, around which political 'parties' (not organised bodies until the twentieth century) coalesced and wider support might be mobilised in order to reaffirm or challenge the legitimacy of existing institutions. Over time these ideas underwent frequent, more or less conscious, reinterpretation under the impact not only of political processes but also of socio-economic change already under way during the old century and accelerating in the new. The chronology of change in the economy and society was very different from that in politics, however. Thus the history of the nineteenth century has to be looked at against the background of two revolutions: the industrial as well as the political.

ECONOMY AND SOCIETY

Revolution and war had distorted earlier patterns of growth. Maritime blockade had largely destroyed the prosperous overseas trade, whilst industries contributing to the military effort or with their markets enlarged by frontier changes had prospered. Within the reduced boundaries of 1815 essentially pre-revolutionary patterns of growth were resumed. Growing population and urbanisation stimulated the commercialisation of agriculture. Productivity gradually increased as the more intensive cultivation associated with mixed farming spread. In manufacture, artisanal workshop production developed through increases in the numbers of workers employed in town and country, as well as efforts to increase productivity by means of greater specialisation. In many respects, however, the economic and social structures of the *ancien régime* survived, with repeated crises, reflecting low levels of productivity, sharp rises in food prices, as a consequence of poor harvests, and widespread misery, resulting in a decline in the demand for manufactured goods. The beginnings of structural change and modern industrialisation were also evident, nevertheless, stimulated both by rising levels of demand caused by population growth and a slow increase in per capita incomes, and by the impact of technological advance on the supply of agricultural and manufactured goods. At first gradually, a series of innovations occurred affecting most notably the production of textiles, metallurgy and engineering. From the 1840s the pace of change accelerated, stimulated by substantial reductions in the cost of transporting goods and people by rail, and by the diffusion of information as a result of increased literacy, development of the media and the spread of the electric telegraph. The adoption of steam as a relatively cheap, flexible and plentiful source of power was a striking feature of these developments. In total, they represented the transition from a civilisation based upon wood and water to one built upon coal and the steam engine as the primary sources of heat and energy. This was transformation on a scale

Table 5.1 *National income at constant prices*
(1905–13 francs)

Years	Total national income (millions of francs)	Per capita national income (francs)
1825–34	10,606	325.6
1835–44	13,061	380.5
1845–54	15,866	443.0
1855–64	19,097	510.9
1865–74	22,327	602.0
1875–84	24,272	644.2
1885–94	26,713	696.6
1895–1904	30,965	794.7
1905–13	34,711	876.4

comparable with that brought about by the information technology revolution of our own time.

Nineteenth-century growth differed from that of previous centuries, moreover, in that it was sustained and accumulative and resulted in major structural changes in both the economy and society. One crucial characteristic was the substantial increase in per capita production revealed in Table 5.1. The statistics should be treated with caution, but they can be treated as indicators of general trends. There is no simple explanation of these economic changes. Regarded with a mixture of admiration and horror, Britain offered a model of the future. As well as the threat of competition, the desire to emulate provided important stimuli to change, although the high levels of tariff protection introduced in 1816 weakened this. Nevertheless, economic change in France has to a large degree to be explained in terms of the specific French context, in relation to particular geographic conditions, market structures and the supply and cost of the factors of production.

Sustained growth meant breaking out of the vicious circle that, in a traditional society, resulted in low real incomes because of low per capita productivity, caused by low levels of investment in capital equipment, which in its turn was the result of low levels of demand due to low real incomes. The problem was intensified by a tendency for population growth to accelerate in the early stages of development, at a time when industrial expansion, and the provision of employment opportunities outside the agricultural sector, remained slow. To a substantial extent per capita income and the whole cycle of economic growth thus depended upon rising agricultural productivity, both to feed this population and to provide resources for industry. A long period of increased demand was necessary to encourage economic innovation, the shape of which was determined by the range of techniques available and the capacity of potential innovators to make use of them, itself determined by the availability of capital and of labour with the appropriate skills. New techniques tended to be more readily accepted the more easily they fitted into existing productive systems, the lower their capital cost and the greater the possibility of financing them through self-investment. In effect, modernisation involved not the substitution of 'modernity' for 'tradition' but the interpenetration of various attributes of both, and needs to be considered within the context of established local and regional economic systems.

The structure of demand was transformed decisively by transport innovation, which increased the size of potential markets by reducing the cost of transporting commodities. Undoubtedly, progress was made before the construction of a railway network, as a result of investment in roads and waterways. Nevertheless, the high cost and the slowness of movement remained major obstacles to the development of a more unified market and a substantial disincentive to increased production. Prior to the development of the rail network, with the exception of regions close to the sea or waterways, high transport costs had made it difficult to break out of an economic system based upon small-scale production for localised demand. Comparisons might be instructive. Britain, a much smaller country, possessed the advantages of a relatively dense seaborne and waterway transport system, which facilitated the establishment of an integrated market. France had more in common with a large landmass such as Germany, in which it took the railway to secure a major transformation of market structures. Construction of the railways, furthermore, created a substantial demand for high-quality engineering products, including locomotives and rolling stock, rails and construction materials. Massive amounts of capital had to be raised and complex bureaucratic organisations created to provide for the secure and profitable running of trains. The first important lines, from Paris to Orléans and to Rouen, were opened in 1843. Subsequent construction was slow, and interrupted by the long mid-century crisis. At the end of 1847 only 1,830 km of track were in use. By 1870 the figure had risen to 20,000 km, and by 1914 to 40,770 km, together with over 7,000 km of narrow-gauge rail and tramway. Whilst the volume of goods moved by road and waterway increased slowly to reach 2.9 and 3.8 billion kilometre/tonnes by 1905/14, that transported by rail reached 21. The establishment of a viable network, especially during the 1850s, along with improved road links to railway stations, transformed commercial practices. The creation of larger and more competitive markets intensified innovatory pressure throughout the economy. Transport changes also profoundly affected the spatial structures of economic activity. The importance of towns as poles of growth, attracting enterprise, capital and labour, and as markets for agricultural and industrial products alike was reinforced. Amongst towns, a more clearly defined functional hierarchy emerged. The new forms of transport also favoured the more developed areas of plain and valley, with their higher productivity, incomes and investment potential. Thus a 'dual' economy emerged, as investment tended to be concentrated in the more dynamic regions. The more 'modern' and the more 'traditional' sectors were not isolated from each other, but were distinctive in terms of the scale and capital intensity of production. In agriculture, the more market-centred capitalistic farms were more clearly distinguished from peasant farms orientated towards the satisfaction of family needs.

The basic factors influencing demand for agricultural products were the growth of population and per capita consumption. The diversity of French agriculture had long been evident, and it is partially revealed by Figure 5.1. Productivity was highest in areas, especially in the north, with superior soils and access to markets. Over centuries large farms had developed with higher livestock densities, more draught power and manure, better equipment and more complex rotation systems. Nevertheless, prior to the communications revolution, in an overwhelmingly rural society with low average incomes, diet and patterns of demand were slow to change. The fragility of a food supply system based upon what remained, in spite of improvement, low-productivity agriculture, and on a fragmented marketing system, was evident from repeated subsistence

crises. Traditional agricultural economies were thus based on delicate internal balances. Groups of plants needed to be integrated
in such a way as to facilitate the division of labour throughout
the farming year. Of even greater importance was the production
of a range of commodities in a polycultural system. Plants with
different vegetative cycles provided some guarantee against the failure of any one crop due to bad weather. Although never absent,
innovation normally depended upon almost certain confidence that
the replacement of one element in the cultural system would not
upset the equilibrium of the whole. Concerned above all with family
subsistence, the peasant cultivators who dominated much of French
agriculture required empirical proof of the value of innovation
before engaging in it themselves. The reduction of risk was their
primary concern rather than profitability.

Innovation occurred normally by means of a slow accumulation
of experience, usually gained in the first instance by the larger
farmers who possessed sufficient land and capital to take risks.
Nevertheless, and in spite of often poor access to markets, not even
the most traditional of peasant families could isolate themselves
entirely from commercial considerations. It was necessary for every
family to cultivate a cash crop or else hire out labour, work in rural
industry or have recourse to temporary migration. The widest possible range of activities was necessary in order to enhance security
and to obtain the cash resources vital for the payment of taxes or
purchase of necessities that were not produced locally, or to save to
realise the peasant's dream of acquiring more land. In the earlier
part of the century, however, farmers continued to focus upon the
production of cereals. Only once their food supply was secured
by the improvement of communications would they feel sufficiently
confident to specialise further in the production of what naturally
grew best and become more responsive to the demands of rapidly
growing urban markets for meat, dairy products, fruit and wine.

The initial improvement of access to markets through the construction of the primary rail network took place between the 1840s
and the 1870s. Together with the provision of secondary rail and
road links, this encouraged substantial increases in productivity and
in commercialisation. The combination of increasing production
with high and rising prices brought prosperity. In the last third of

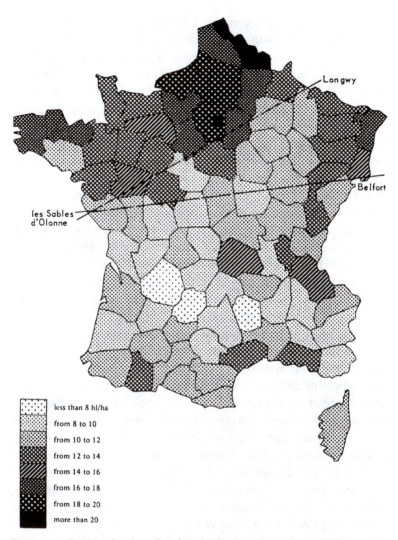

Figure 5.1 France, developed and underdeveloped, I: wheat yields in 1840. (Source: R. Price, *An Economic History of Modern France*, c. *1730–1914.* Macmillan, 1981.)

the century, however, the stimulus afforded by the establishment of more integrated national and international markets as a result of the communications revolution and, from 1859/60, of reductions in tariff protection resulted in overproduction, especially of wheat

and wine. Falling prices combined with rising costs of production
and the devastating impact of phylloxera on the vines to cause a
severe crisis and a decline in the rate of increase of productivity.
The reintroduction of high levels of tariff protection limited competition from imports but further reduced the pressure to innovate.
Recovery commenced in the mid-1890s, but was hesitant and limited.
Thus, in many respects, French agriculture on the eve of the First
World War remained archaic. This was particularly evident in the
survival of large numbers of small peasant farms and in those regions
that remained relatively isolated and where natural conditions
were not favourable to the creation of a modern agriculture. In spite
of the limits to change, however, the period from the 1840s, during
which the operating context for farmers was transformed, was one
of crucial significance for the long-term evolution of French farming.
It saw the final disappearance of the age-old subsistence crises.
More substantial innovation occurred within the space of three or
four decades than had previously occurred in as many centuries; this
marked a decisive break with the past.

On the basis of international comparisons, French businessmen,
just like farmers, have frequently been condemned for their lack
of enterprise. This approach does have its limits, however. It fails to
take account of differences in social and economic structures leading
to different but equally rational forms of industrial growth. Estimates
of nineteenth-century industrial growth rates vary considerably
(between 1.8 per cent and 2.9 per cent per annum). Nonetheless,
production seems to have increased sixfold by 1913. The period
between 1815 and 1846 was characterised by slow, regular growth,
interrupted by minor fluctuations; 1846 to 1851 saw major political
and economic crises, followed from 1852 to 1857 by a period of rapid
growth. 1858 and 1859 were years of depression, succeeded from
1860 to 1882 by slow growth interrupted by war and political crisis in
1870. Another lengthy period of depression from 1882 to 1896 ended
with the onset of prosperity, terminated only by the First World War.
Throughout, industrialisation, involving fundamental changes both
in the structure of the economy and in productivity, represented a
response to changing market conditions, and to new opportunities
and competitive pressures. A complex of factors, including the scale
of demand for a product, the comparative cost of labour and of

machinery, and the availability of capital, influenced technological change in particular industrial sectors, with development largely taking the form of the piecemeal application of innovations to meet the particular circumstances of time and place.

There was thus no abrupt change in the structure of French industry. Initially, poor communications ensured the survival of a decentralised market and the dispersal of production as artisans and merchants produced and redistributed goods to geographically limited hinterlands. Inefficient high-cost producers were protected from competition by high transport costs. The most obvious method of responding to increased demand was simply to produce more in the same old way. This was not necessarily perverse or lazy, but could represent an intelligent use of existing resources. It was encouraged by the availability of cheap labour and the continued fragmentation of the market until at least the 1850s. The structure of demand was complicated. It depended not only upon the size of population and its per capita income but upon a mass of decisions about expenditure and personal taste.

Moreover, the rate of increase in demand continued to be restrained by the relatively sluggish growth of the French population, by the survival of peasant farming and by slow urban development. Whilst a low-wage economy reduced employers' costs, it also restricted purchasing power and increased social tension. The situation further deteriorated during periods of depressed agricultural prices. Furthermore, and throughout the century, the distribution of a large part of total income in the form of rents, interest and dividends, and, conversely, the restraints imposed on the growth of earned incomes, helped to preserve a highly individualised bourgeois demand for luxury products that hindered the development of mass production. To some extent, export markets compensated for the limitations of internal demand. After the disasters of the revolutionary–imperial wars, however, exports increased primarily where they were not in competition with British factory production – that is, particularly in the markets for high-quality goods such as silks and *articles de Paris*, traditionally produced on a small scale and particularly vulnerable to trade recessions.

Once introduced, new equipment might be employed for fifty years or more, although with occasional modifications. The major

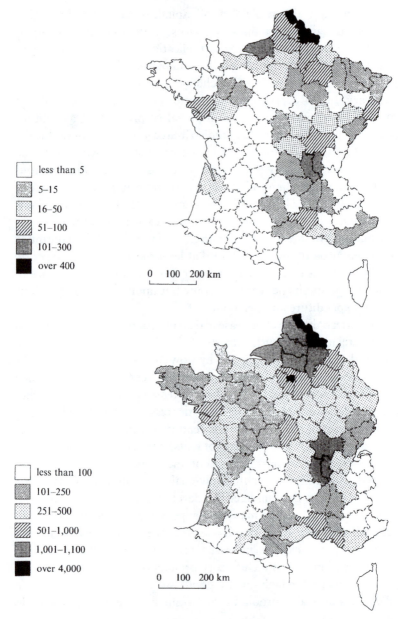

Figure 5.2 France, developed and underdeveloped, II: the steam engine as an indicator of industrialisation (number per department in 1841 and in 1878). (Source: G. Dupeux *et al.*, *Atlas historique de la France contemporaine*. Armand Colin, 1966.)

exceptions involved the construction of large-scale integrated metallurgical establishments and the development of the railway network. Technological changes in these two sectors had fundamental effects on the whole economy, through the provision of large quantities of iron and steel and the availability of a low-cost means of bulk transport.

The pace of change accelerated as a result of improved communications, market integration and the transition from relatively closed to more open local communities. The demand for such goods as iron tools and cotton garments rose with farm incomes and, especially, the reduction in their cost. This had vital effects in terms of the creation of substantial homogeneous markets and high levels of demand for standardised products. The growing predominance of factory over artisanal forms of production and of the industrial economy over agriculture became increasingly evident. Poles of growth emerged in and around Paris, Lyon, Lille, Rouen, Mulhouse and Marseille – cities well placed in terms of access to supplies of capital, labour and raw materials and, by waterborne and rail transport, to potential markets. For many small producers the spread of capital-intensive methods of production heralded a period of crisis and decline. The rate of growth in large-scale mechanised industry between 1835 and 1844 and 1855 and 1864, for example, has been estimated to have been twice as great as that for industry as a whole. In twenty years its share of the total industrial product rose from one-quarter to more than one-third. Small-scale enterprises were disadvantaged in an increasingly competitive market by their inability to enjoy economies of scale, their poor links to commercial networks, low profit margins and limited access to external credit, which made innovation difficult and left them vulnerable to short-term economic fluctuations. They survived largely by means of hard work and greater specialisation. The enlargement of markets and the growing complexity and cost of technology favoured large enterprises, and an emerging managerial capitalism, as well as, towards the end of the century, the concerted application of science to production and the advent of a 'second' industrial revolution, characterised by the development of electrometallurgy and chemicals on a large scale, and subsequently by the emergence of the internal combustion engine and the motor car.

Table 5.2 *Population increase (1750–1911)*

Year	Population (millions)	Year	Population (millions)
1750	21	1861	37.4[*]
1801	27.3	1872	36.1[*]
1821	30.5	1881	37.7
1831	32.6	1891	38.3
1841	34.2	1901	38.9
1851	35.8	1911	39.6

[*] Affected by territorial changes.

The growth of the service sector was another important feature of economic modernisation, involving the concurrent development of communications and financial and commercial networks. Structures and habits were transformed as the volume of goods produced and marketed multiplied. The traditional fairs declined. As the scale of production increased and investment levels rose, manufacturers adopted less passive attitudes towards their markets. They started to prospect for new customers – the commercial traveller appears in the 1820s – and to advertise their wares. The growth of a mass-circulation press was vital in this respect. As incomes grew, the retail trade too was transformed by the establishment of growing numbers of department and chain stores, and especially of corner shops. Mail-order catalogues were distributed to the most isolated communities. By the end of the century a mass consumer society had been created.

In all these ways the pre-industrial economy, which had survived until the middle of the nineteenth century, was transformed, and in the process a major social revolution occurred. The renewal of economic structures made possible improvements in nutrition, living conditions and social aspirations, the effects of which were clear in the decline in birth as well as mortality rates. In addition, the town came close to replacing the village as the main place of residence. France was to be distinguished amongst the industrialising nations of the nineteenth century, however, by its relatively early transition to a 'modern' demographic regime, and its low rate of population growth. The practice of birth control, essentially through withdrawal (*coitus interruptus*), had been spreading since the eighteenth century, and more rapidly as a result of the revolutionary upheavals that had challenged established norms of behaviour. By the 1830s, as the birth rate fell below thirty per thousand, contraception had become a mass phenomenon, although with major regional and social variations. These demographic trends had complex effects on the supply of labour and on demand for goods but also ensured that, in comparison with contemporary underdeveloped countries, population pressure on resources was far less intense. The substantial reduction in the numbers of men available for military service would arouse growing concern, however.

Within the period from 1815 to 1914 three major phases of demographic evolution can be identified. The first, from about 1815 to around 1848, was characterised by slow change. In many regions growing population increased pressure on resources and maintained dietary standards at low levels. This was essentially a period of continuity with the second half of the eighteenth century, with both high (though declining) death and birth rates. It culminated in an intense economic, social and political crisis between 1846 and 1851. A second period roughly corresponded to the Second Empire and was characterised by accelerated industrialisation, the transport revolution, rapid urban growth and increased migration from the countryside. Certainly, living standards appear to have improved, although an earlier tendency for the birth rate to decline seems to have levelled off. The third period, from about 1871 to 1914, saw a renewed decline in birth rate, with the impact on overall levels of population partly compensated for by reductions in mortality, and particularly the infant death rate, as economic development brought further improvements in living conditions. During these years migration from the countryside grew far more intense. Urbanisation was accompanied by the transformation of towns, which had remained almost medieval in character, into recognisably modern urban centres. This was a complex development, with the character and scale of growth depending upon pre-existing socio-economic structures, which were far from homogeneous, and the nature of regional economic change. Whilst stressing the importance of urbanisation, it is also important to remember its relative slowness in comparison with other parts of western Europe. The period of Revolution and Empire had been one of stagnation, and the growth rate of towns in the first half of the nineteenth century was probably lower than it had been for much of the eighteenth. Nevertheless, 25.5 per cent of the population was classified as urban in 1851, and the proportion had reached 44.2 per cent by 1911.

The most notable development was the growth of Paris as a dynamic social space. In 1851 3 per cent of the French population lived in the capital and its suburbs; by 1911 this had risen to 10 per cent. The economic structure of the city had become increasingly complex. In the early decades of the century artisanal forms of production had been dominant. Subsequently heavy industry had developed, particularly engineering and chemicals, on the northern and eastern outskirts, whilst inner-city areas, although continuing to shelter the various artisanal trades, proved increasingly attractive to the development of administrative, financial and commercial enterprise. Particularly during the Second Empire, substantial urban reconstruction cleared some of the worst slums, considerably improved water supply and public hygiene and created a sanitised inner city, with its theatres, stores and cafés, and broad avenues along which traffic, and if necessary troops, could move with relative ease. The development of mass transport facilities from the 1870s, with suburban railways, tramways and finally bus and – from 1900 – underground services, made it increasingly feasible to live some distance from one's place of work.

Since time immemorial the primary cause of migration to the towns had been rural poverty. The cost of housing had forced low-wage earners to reside in overcrowded and insanitary conditions, however, wherever work was available, in both city centres and more peripheral *quartiers*. By the 1840s severe strains were being imposed on the urban fabric. Subsequently, accelerating industrial and commercial development substantially increased urban labour needs. The underemployed 'underclass' that had previously caused intense social fear rapidly diminished in size after the middle of the century. The towns became more attractive to potential migrants because of enhanced employment opportunities, which offered higher wages, greater security, less hard work (especially for women) and increased leisure. Especially from the 1850s, urban living conditions slowly improved, whilst industrial concentration reduced the employment opportunities in rural industry on which so much of the population in the countryside had previously depended. Furthermore, better communications made the rural population more aware of the contrasts between urban and rural life.

Inevitably, the process of socio-economic transformation was accompanied by major changes in popular culture and behaviour. A working class came into existence, with a diffuse sense of collective identity created by the shared difficulty families faced in making ends meet and a bitter resentment of social inequality, of exploitative employers and a repressive state. Secularisation and rising mass literacy were other indicators of cultural change. Although the harrowing experience of the Revolution was followed by an often intense religious revival, the Church must frequently have appeared to have less relevance in an increasingly urban environment and when dependence upon nature was becoming less absolute. On the other hand, education was of increasingly obvious practical value in an industrialising, more commercial and highly administered society. For the élites who took the crucial decisions concerning investment in schools, instruction promised to be the most effective means of 'civilising' the masses and of safeguarding their own power.

SOCIETY AND POLITICS

The abolition of legal privilege in 1789 had left wealth as the primary social distinction. The continued importance of traditional forms of wealth creation meant that in 1815 France remained dominated by a pre-industrial social élite predominantly made up of landowners, both nobles and non-nobles, many of whom served or had been employed in government service, together with growing numbers of professionals and businessmen. Internal tensions survived, particularly between nobles and bourgeois, and in relation to complex assumptions about status, political allegiances, and professional and regional identities. Nevertheless, it was still possible to recognise an élite that shared in the possession of certain generally desired attributes including wealth, social influence and political power, and that served as a reference point for other social groups. In national politics the predominance of these *notables* lasted until the 1870s, reflecting the survival of traditional social structures and patterns of behaviour, only slowly transformed by economic change. Throughout the period of constitutional monarchy (1815–48) this was enshrined in an electoral system based essentially on a property qualification that, reinforced by the economic protectionism introduced in April 1816, was intended to limit instability and safeguard vested interests. These were the means of avoiding democracy and the threat posed by the poor and ignorant to what was perceived to be genuine liberty, and to Christian civilisation itself. Property symbolised capacity. Lack of property represented proof of intellectual and moral inadequacy. Furthermore, the system facilitated the maximum exercise of personal influence. The *notable* was typically an individual whose standing within the local community depended on the wealth and reputation of his family, enhanced by the social and charitable activities of wives and daughters, who might otherwise be largely confined to 'separate spheres' by their supposed physical, intellectual and emotional weaknesses. The combination of high social status, a worthy lifestyle, dual residence in town and country and education in the classics and law were such as to allow the *notable* a foot in both the local and the enveloping national society. He had the means to accumulate social capital and develop career prospects through participation in the overwhelmingly male social networks, which, in the absence of 'parties', also provided the organisational bases for political activity. The centrality of Paris within these socio-political processes is obvious.

In general, these *notables* were opposed to the extension of political rights to the poorer and inferior classes, and with even greater determination resisted any threat to their rights as property owners. They constituted a powerful conservative commitment to *résistance*. Their wealth and education allowed them to exercise substantial influence as politicians, officials, landowners, employers and dispensers of charity (in a pre-welfare state). This access to multifaceted means of exercising pressure and influence gave them tremendous advantages in the political game. For them, and probably most of the population, the experience of the Revolution had been profoundly disturbing. It had come to represent the confiscation of property, punitive taxation, conscription, an assault on the Church, the Terror and the threat of further social anarchy. The nineteenth century was to be beset by the threat of revolution, however. This was largely because of widespread disappointment with what was felt to be the incompleteness of political and social change. Some of the discontented – those in favour of *mouvement* – were to gain satisfaction through the limited extension of the franchise in 1830, others by means of the introduction of manhood suffrage in 1848, more when the Republic was definitively established in the late 1870s. Each of these crises also revealed the capacity of existing élites to employ their social influence as a means of adapting to changing political circumstances. Moreover, the structure of the élite itself gradually changed as the process of concentration in finance and industry created new conditions for amassing wealth. Expansive conditions provided opportunities for upward mobility for the few. The scale of accumulation also changed. Although the absolute wealth of landowners did not decline before the 1870s to 1880s, relative decline began much sooner. The agricultural depression of the last third of the century accelerated the process. Landowners were slow to transfer their capital to more lucrative forms of investment. Increasingly, a *grande bourgeoisie*, composed of financiers and major industrialists, assumed economic predominance as well as the ability to exercise formal and, through pressure group activity, informal political power.

Although French society would remain profoundly inegalitarian, increasingly democratic political processes ensured that substantial political power was diffused down the social hierarchy, and in particular to the professional middle classes. To a considerable extent, however, decision making continued to be the purview of an inner circle of ministers, senior civil servants, particularly influential deputies, and the representatives of powerful pressure groups. Thus, whilst it is tempting to focus upon dramatic political events, this should not lead us to neglect important continuities. Access to political power and especially to the key positions in government, parliament and the administration continued to depend upon possession of the income and education that fitted men for public life. The cultural and political hegemony of the propertied classes was challenged only ineffectively. Privilege in these spheres was defended by the brutal deployment of military force, if necessary, as in June 1848 or against the Paris Commune in 1871. To an important degree, the political history of nineteenth-century France can therefore be seen as a continuous search for stability. Eventually this was to be secured, but only from the 1870s, through the establishment of a strong centralised state, the

Third Republic, better able than its predecessors to influence and control the social groups and regional societies that divided the nation; this was attributable to the modernisation of the techniques of government, more effective political socialisation, the institutionalisation of protest and the growing legitimisation of the regime.

The nineteenth-century state thus functioned primarily as an *état-gendarme*, above all committed to safeguarding law and order by means of the expansion of policing – frequently involving deployment of the army and harsh penal retribution. Defence needs – the provision of increasingly costly weapons systems and the enrolment of growing numbers of men (*c.* 390,000 by 1850 and 620,000 by 1900) – imposed substantial financial burdens. The machinery of state remained under the control of senior officials recruited primarily within the social élites, their origins undoubtedly influencing their decision making. In order to secure social order they accepted the need to extend the role of the state, taking advantage, for example, of new communications technologies (rail and electric telegraph), which immeasurably increased the effectiveness of political and administrative centralisation. The number of government employees (including postal workers and teachers) rose from around 300,000 in 1850 to 583,000 by 1910. A system of mass instruction was also established (most notably through the laws of 1833, 1850 and 1882) as the means of ensuring greater cultural homogenisation and closer social control. A sense of national unity was promoted assiduously. Certainly, primary instruction, which was all that the vast majority of children received (even in 1914 only 5 per cent of boys enjoyed a secondary education), was established as a 'system of subordination' (Bayly) rather than a means of promoting social mobility. Something needs now to be said about the complex evolution of nineteenth-century politics and the changing distribution of power.

THE RESTORATION

The return of the Bourbons in 1814/15 was due to military defeat and the inability of the victors to identify a viable alternative; not the most auspicious of beginnings. Although there was little enthusiasm for their return it did at least bring peace. Moreover, Louis XVIII accepted the need to reassure the social and political élites by promulgating the Constitutional Charter. Granted by the monarch to his subjects as an act of grace, and full of dangerous ambiguities, this accorded to the king powers far greater than those granted in the constitution of 1791. It stipulated that 'the person of the King is sacred and inviolable' and insisted that '[e]xecutive power belongs to the King alone', including the sole right to initiate legislation and to dissolve parliament at will. It did retain key liberal provisions, however, designed to restrain rulers, and particularly the need for parliamentary consent to taxation. Furthermore, the Charter promised that the king would respect personal liberty, recognise equality before the law and make provision for both a hereditary chamber of peers and a lower house that would be elected by those whose capacity for rational decision making was guaranteed by the possession of property, education and leisure. Increasingly, political life would focus on parliamentary debate. The basic freedoms necessary for political activity were also recognised.

Plate 5.1 The royal family in May 1814. From left to right: the king's brother, the Comte d'Artois (the future Charles X); Louis XVIII; his niece, the Duchesse d'Angoulême (daughter of Louis XVI); and the Duc d'Angoulême and Duc de Berri, both sons of the Comte d'Artois. Musée Carnavalet. Photo: Giraudon/the Bridgeman Art Library.

Equally important as a means of drawing a curtain on the past was the promise that established status and property rights would be respected, including possession of land confiscated from the Church and émigrés during the Revolution. Amongst the élites there was a general willingness to accept a compromise, which offered protection against both a return to the *ancien régime* and the dangers of popular sovereignty. Thus, with the support of most senior military commanders and of royalist sympathisers in the administration, the change of regime was relatively easy. The masses welcomed the end of conscription; businessmen, particularly in the ports, looked forward to renewed prosperity; but it was above all the nobility who fêted what they hoped would be a return to a mythical golden age in which their dominance had been unchallenged. The main effect of Napoleon's return during the Hundred Days and the reawakening of popular revolutionary patriotism and of incipient Jacobinism was to reinforce concern about social order.

Opposition would subsequently be slow to voice itself. This was partly because of the renewed 'White Terror' that followed Waterloo. The Bourbons, in spite of previous criticism of the centralised imperial state, gratefully assumed control over the existing apparatus of surveillance and control. In addition, the politically aware were initially uncertain about the character of the new regime. Besides the general desire for peace and order, most *notables* would probably have wished for a moderate constitutional monarchy, avoiding all excesses in domestic and foreign policy of the kind that had become only too familiar since 1789. Many non-nobles, whether landowners, professionals or businessmen, even if not enthusiastic adherents of the Bourbons, were prepared to accept the regime provided it respected these basic aspirations. In contrast, real enthusiasm was to be found amongst nobles and the clergy and members of other social groups subject to their influence. Encouraged by the king's brother, the Comte d'Artois (the future Charles X), and his entourage, they were confident that at last they would receive compensation for the sufferings they had endured during the Revolution and be assured of predominance within the state and army. Many of them believed that it was God's will that France should be cleansed of the remains of Jacobinism and atheism and endure punishment for the murder of Louis XVI. They were inspired by a sense of *noblesse oblige*, a commitment involving a distinctive lifestyle and manners, membership of particular social networks, an arrogant disdain for social inferiors and an idealised conception of a Christian society, with the château at its heart in every village.

The election of the first parliament of the regime, to be known as the Chambre introuvable, took place in an atmosphere of political terror in August 1815. Some 50,900 electors selected 402 deputies. Of these, 78 per cent were clearly very conservative, and amongst them 52 per cent were *ancien régime* nobles. Of the others, most were not opposed to the regime, but only to the exaggerated demands of its more extreme adherents, the so-called *ultras*, with their semi-secret organisation, the Chevaliers de la Foi. Influenced by Napoleon's former minister Fouché, Louis XVIII was himself unwilling to risk the politically divisive measures demanded by the *ultras*. He dissolved the chamber in September 1816 and, partly through the use of government influence, was able to secure the election of a far more moderate majority. Amongst its achievements were to be the electoral law of 1817, which by means of a F300 tax qualification restricted the electorate to 100,000, primarily made up of landowners. The requirement that candidates for election should be at least forty years old and pay F1,000 in direct taxation ensured that only around 1,650 were eligible. The government also proceeded with a purge of *ultras* from the administration and allowed the return of political exiles. Reconciliation could go only so far, however. Liberal election successes frightened the ministry led by Elie Decazes into introducing a more restrictive electoral law. Then the assassination, in 1820, of the heir to the throne, the Duc de Berri, the last in the direct line of Bourbons until the posthumous birth of his son, precipitated a major crisis. Together with the uncovering of Bonapartist plots in the army, it appeared to justify exceptional measures of repression, including detention without trial for three months, tighter censorship and yet more restrictive electoral legislation. These procedures intensified the processes of political polarisation occurring between ultra-royalists and out-raged liberals, between nobles and non-nobles within the élite and, on a regional basis, between the west and south and other areas. Above all, these developments signified the effective end of

Plate 5.2 *The Solemn Blessing of a Cross.* The restoration of moral order, or Catholic reconquest, 1826; one of the many missions attempting to re-establish collective piety. Engraving by J. Massard. Bibliothèque nationale.

efforts to broaden the base of support for the regime and to rule by consensus. Nevertheless, the situation was far from being irredeemable. Successful military intervention in Spain in 1823 considerably enhanced the status of the regime.

The accession of Charles X in September 1824 again fundamentally transformed the situation. The new king, and the courtiers, who exercised a largely unrecorded influence on him, had a conception of his rights and responsibilities hardly compatible with constitutional monarchy. They also shared a dangerous capacity for wishful thinking. Initially, a ministry led by the Comte de Villèle and an *ultra*-dominated chamber, elected in 1824 in the aftermath of the assassination crisis, supported the king. Three-fifths of the deputies were nobles and one-half former émigrés. This majority was to be characterised by bitter divisions, however, between the proponents of an aristocratic and clerical monarchy, such as François La Bourdonnaie, and constitutional monarchists inspired by the Vicomte de Châteaubriand, and those broad divisions were themselves splintered by personal feuds and competition for influence and office. The provision of compensation for former émigrés whose land had been confiscated during the Revolution was described by liberals as a fine on the nation imposed by a self-seeking noble majority. Concern about the regime's intentions was increased by its efforts to lend support to a Church intent upon restoring 'moral order'. As well as introducing dire penalties for the crime of sacrilege, officials encouraged ostentatious religious missions conducted by an increasingly aggressive and triumphalist ultramontane clergy. Additionally, subsidies were provided in order to restore the material fabric of the Church and 'the beauty of holiness'. The work of reconstruction following the depredations of the Revolution also required the urgent re-establishment of seminaries to educate growing numbers of secular clergy and encouragement of the expansion of the religious orders, particularly those female communities so useful in providing care and instruction for the poor. A close alliance between throne and altar would promote the supreme objective of reinforcing religious faith. It would also ensure that religion remained a politically divisive issue.

In addition, the government continued to manipulate the electoral system, reducing the number of voters from 100,000 to 89,000 between 1817 and 1827. Together with the preferential treatment of nobles within an army and administration already considerably shrunken with the return to peace, and the pressure for restitution frequently exerted by parish priests on those who, during the Revolution, had purchased former Church property, government policies created an increasingly widespread belief that a return to the *ancien régime* was planned.

The regime's critics were essentially liberals committed to constitutional monarchy who, initially at least, had seen the Bourbons as more likely to guarantee liberty and order than either Bonaparte or a republic. Few republicans dared to discuss their ideas openly, and the death of the former emperor in May 1825 left Bonapartists without an obvious leader, although a semi-religious, romanticised, cult of Napoleon continued to evolve in songs, pictures, poems and memoirs, and as part of both 'high' and popular culture. In most regions there appears to have been little sustained interest in politics outside the narrow circle of men with money and leisure. The cadres for opposition nevertheless already existed. Police reports claimed that most liberals were lawyers or merchants, or displaced members of the former imperial service élite and army officers retired prematurely on half-pay. In every little town they met regularly in cafés and clubs to read newspapers and discuss their contents. Because the electoral system required that parliamentary candidates were wealthy, however, and because of the publication of parliamentary speeches, opposition leaders tended to be members of the landowning élite. Significantly, by 1825, whilst 20,000 subscriptions to pro-government newspapers were recorded, twice as many subscribers received opposition papers. Although these numbers were small, the press offered not just news and comment but also leadership, a means of organising election campaigns and the sense of belonging to a movement. Multiple readership, of course, substantially widened access.

Liberal successes in the 1827 election persuaded the king to replace Villèle with the more liberal Vicomte de Martignac, a move he rapidly perceived had only stimulated further opposition. Charles X, who had already, between 1789 and 1792, through his counter-revolutionary activities done so much to discredit the Bourbons, now surpassed himself. In August 1829 he appointed his old friend the Duc de Polignac, a religious mystic, to head a ministry that, in the persons of La Bourdonnaie and Marshal Bourmont, was widely taken to symbolise defeat, national humiliation and the White Terror of 1815, and that, by ignoring the liberal electoral gains in 1827, completed the process of political polarisation. The formation of this government seemed to confirm the growing suspicion that the king was plotting a coup d'état. In response, the liberal association Aide-toi le ciel t'aidera (Heaven helps those who help themselves), originally formed to encourage the registration of voters, called for a nationwide refusal to pay taxes. Its leaders, moderate and legalistic figures such as the Protestant historian Guizot, found themselves at the head of an increasingly alarming coalition that included young republican activists. Poor harvests, high food prices, unemployment and misery added to the sense of crisis. Two successive elections in 1830 returned majorities hostile to the government. In the second, and in spite of the efforts of officials and government supporters to exercise pressure and personal influence within the small, face-to-face, electorate, 270 liberals were returned and only 145 government supporters. These liberal deputies most certainly did not want revolution, and would probably have been satisfied if Charles had been prepared to accept the electorate's verdict on Polignac and recognise that in future his ministers should enjoy the confidence of both king and parliament. Both sides were determined to abide by their mutually exclusive interpretations of the Charter, however. Charles X believed that concessions would take him down the slippery road to revolution. He responded by invoking the emergency decree powers he possessed under the terms of article 14 of the Charter, and in July introduced ordinances that tightened censorship, dissolved the newly elected chamber before it had even met, revised election procedures to increase administrative influence and reduced the electorate to its wealthiest quarter, made up of 23,000 mainly noble landowners. This brought the crisis to a head. It forced members of the social and political élite to choose, unwillingly, between 'liberty' and the Bourbon monarchy. Although the liberal leadership included nobles such as the Duc de Broglie and Comte Molé, a large majority of nobles were undoubtedly sympathetic towards the king. Amongst the opposition, wealthy landowners, former imperial officials and members of the liberal professions played leading roles. Once again, however, constitutional conflict would be settled on the streets of Paris.

The liberals gave the signal for resistance with a poster, written by Adolphe Thiers and Charles de Rémusat, calling, in rather ambiguous terms, for protest. No doubt only peaceful action had been envisaged, but this was to degenerate into violence. The call to defend 'liberty' mobilised a disparate coalition drawn from the middle and working classes of the city. Around midday on 27 July the first clash occurred between demonstrators and *gendarmerie* units attempting to disperse crowds on the Place du Palais Royal. In the afternoon, exasperated by the taunts and stones thrown at them, troops seem to have fired without orders. This was followed by the construction of barricades and bitter street fighting in the poor *quartiers* of the capital, in which some 850 civilians and soldiers would be killed. Although the garrison amounted to some 11,000 men, contingency plans for dealing with a major insurrection had not been prepared, and ammunition and food stocks were low. Marshal Marmont, the military commander, was both unpopular and unsure of himself. The army was not trained for street fighting. On 28 July three columns were ordered to converge on the Hôtel-de-Ville, clearing barricades as they went. They achieved their objective, but the barricades were simply reconstructed after they had passed. Isolated, tired and hungry, troops began to fraternise with insurgents, amongst whom there were many former veterans of the imperial armies. There remained the possibility of awaiting reinforcements from the provinces, but Charles X was increasingly disheartened by reports that they could not be depended upon. Almost everywhere the royal administration simply collapsed, its members quickly replaced by representatives of the liberal opposition. On 31 July, in the hope of saving something from the débâcle, the king accepted the appointment as *lieutenant-général* of the kingdom of the Duc d'Orléans, a descendant of Louis XIV's brother, and a prince with a liberal reputation who had fought for the revolutionary cause at Valmy and Jemappes. On 2 August Charles X abdicated in favour of his infant grandson, the Comte de Chambord, withdrew the ordinances and agreed to new elections. It was too late.

Plate 5.3 Fighting in the boulevard des Italiens, 28 July 1830. Lithograph by V. Adam. Musée Carnavalet. Photo: Musées de la Ville de Paris. © SPADEM.

The July Revolution had occurred because many essentially moderate members of the élite had withdrawn their normal support from a regime that had threatened the fundamental principles of representative government enshrined in the constitution. Moreover, Charles X had shown excessive favour towards one element of this élite, the nobility, and in so doing threatened the status that other *notables* had enjoyed since 1789. The loss of legitimacy that the regime had suffered as a consequence appears to have been felt by even its most determined supporters. Events had developed so rapidly and in such an unexpected direction that even opposition leaders were unprepared for the outcome. The armed crowds, which had taken over the streets, frightened them, as did the shouts of *Vive* [Long live] *Napoléon II* and *Vive la République*. The prospect of a renewed popular intervention in politics filled them with horror. Convinced that the result would again be civil and foreign war, liberal leaders vested Lafayette, the ageing hero of the previous revolution, with command of a National Guard and, just as in 1789, established a municipal commission to restore order. On 30 July, to end the power

vacuum, they offered the throne to the Duc d'Orléans on condition
that he agree to respect the principles of constitutional monarchy.
A proclamation written by Thiers, a journalist and historian, presented the new king as 'a prince devoted to the cause of the revolutions', as a 'citizen-king'. On 31 July, as Louis-Philippe, he appointed
a government and convened a meeting of the Chamber of Deputies.
On 8 August the Chamber voted in favour of a revision of the
constitution that significantly altered the balance of power between
king and parliament in the latter's favour. On this occasion the
contractual character of the relationship between king and nation
was affirmed clearly, with Louis-Philippe obliged to swear on oath to
respect this revised and more liberal Charter. A substantial purge of
the administration, together with the withdrawal of many nobles
from public life because of their unwillingness to serve the 'usurper',
confirmed the defeat of aristocratic reaction.

Plate 5.4 Lafayette receiving Louis-Philippe at the Hôtel-de-Ville, Paris, 31
July 1830. Painting by E.-F. Féron. © RMN–Grand Palais (Château de
Versailles)/Droits réservés.

THE JULY MONARCHY

In spite of the surprisingly rapid re-establishment of the authority of the central government, the political situation remained tense. Conflicts of interest were inevitable between the diverse groups that had overthrown the Bourbons. Having achieved their aims, most liberals became political conservatives, interested in the protection of their personal liberty and property. The *liberté* for which many had fought had diverse meanings, however. In the aftermath of the Revolution people felt free to discuss them at meetings and in newspapers. Dissatisfaction was expressed with a new electoral law, which simply reduced the tax qualification for voting from F300 to F200. This significantly reduced the weight of nobles within the electorate whilst enfranchising mainly landowners (who, together with farmers, made up about 56 per cent of voters in 1846), officials (about 8 per cent), professionals (about 10 per cent) and businessmen and a small proportion of the more prosperous artisans (about 26 per cent). It continued to exclude the vast majority of lower middle-class, peasant and worker citizens. Thus, whereas in Britain the 1832 electoral law would enfranchise one in twenty-five of the population, in France the corresponding figure was only one in 170, although growing prosperity gradually enlarged the national electorate from 166,000 to 241,000 by 1846, whilst the 1831 municipal election law gave the vote to some 3 million. This enlarged, but still small, electorate would consistently provide the regime with solid parliamentary support. To some at least of those who were excluded, however, this was all very arbitrary. Still a small minority, republican militants complained about the way a rump of the Chamber of Deputies, rather than a newly elected Constituent Assembly, had taken the crucial constitutional decisions. Even within the government there were fundamental disagreements over the degree to which political liberalisation ought to be pursued. The minister of justice, Jacques-Charles Dupont de l'Eure, resigned and subsequently denounced the regime for 'repudiating its authors and natural supporters, and returning with an incontestable predilection to the traditions and the men of the Restoration'. In Paris a revival of the republican press occurred. In the provinces the network of committees established to oppose the absolutist dreams of Charles

X was partially reactivated. Moreover, the Revolution re-established the masses on the political stage, and this to a large degree explains the increasingly conservative – and, indeed, repressive – character of the government. Official praise for their courage encouraged Parisian workers not only to take to the streets to demand the trial and punishment of Charles X's ministers but also, through petitions and strikes, to demand higher wages, a shorter working day and the banning of employment-threatening machinery. They were demanding that a regime that they believed they had created should recognise the basic human right to a living wage. They were to be disappointed by the government's negative response, especially as living standards were to deteriorate sharply in the economic crisis that followed the Revolution.

These popular demands were met with incomprehension by a government committed to 'the principle of the freedom of industry'. The brief seizure of control over the city of Lyon by armed workers in November 1831 and their slogan 'Live working or die fighting!' caused a great stir. The journalist Saint-Marc Girardin wrote that this insurrection had 'revealed a great secret', which was that 'the Barbarians who threaten society are not...on the steppes of Tartary...they are in the suburbs of our manufacturing cities'. The government was increasingly determined to bring political agitation to an end and to eliminate the growing numbers of associations created by workers to protect their 'rights'. It combined repression with an effort to safeguard 'social order' in the longer term by means of the introduction, in 1833, of a major law on primary education intended to 'moralise' the lower orders through religious instruction, to encourage the use of French in place of regional languages and generally to enhance the sense of national identity. Those communes that still lacked a school (about one-third) were required to establish one, and each department to make provision for teacher training. Provision for girls – to be carefully socialised into appropriate gender roles – would soon follow. As yet, however, compulsory attendance at school was hardly on the agenda.

In response to growing government repression, small groups of middle-class republicans began to look outside the narrow electorate for support, and attempted to politicise discontented workers through organisations such as the Société des Droits de l'Homme

(Society for the Rights of Man). This gradual coming together of young republican militants and workers was to be vital to the intellectual development of both. It led to an interpenetration of republican political ideas and those derived from a traditional artisanal corporate culture. The period of post-revolutionary agitation would largely be terminated, however, in the wake of a law banning political meetings introduced in April 1834. The government's response to the wave of insurrectionary protest that this set off was increasingly brutal, immortalised by Honoré Daumier's drawing of the slaughter of a family by troops and bourgeois National Guards in the Cloître Saint-Merri in Paris. These events were to prove central to the development of class consciousness and an interest in republican politics amongst the lower middle class and artisans, and to a widening of support for the republican movement. In the immediate future these developments were to be restricted and fragmented by coercive government action. Nevertheless, from the 1840s, as the capitalistic transformation of the economy grew more intense and threatening to artisanal traditions and work practices, the socialist conception of a more egalitarian society based upon self-regulating producers' cooperatives attracted growing interest.

The political peace of the years that followed 1834 was due in part to firm, repressive government, but additionally to support from the small number of electors for a regime that, through parliament, allowed them to represent their own particular interests. Successive governments sought to guarantee order not only through police activity but by means of economic protection, an essential 'conservative principle' (Guizot, the prime minister), and efforts to ensure prosperity on the basis of a major public works programme involving most notably railway construction. As head of the executive, the king made full use of his powers, and insisted that ministers sympathised with his objectives. Responsible also to parliament, governments sought to maintain majority support in part through the extensive use of patronage. The Orléanist monarchy lacked the mystical appeal of its 'divine right' predecessor. Support for it was to a much greater degree conditional. Nevertheless, throughout its existence, opposition both within and outside parliament was weak and divided. It ranged from the supporters of another Bourbon restoration, the Legitimists on the right, to the republicans on the left. Its most numerous and vocal critics were drawn from the ranks of the so-called 'dynastic' opposition, whose representatives, in newspapers such as *Le Siècle*, employed the language of 1789 to attack the dominant *aristocratie bourgeoise*. Politicians excluded from power condemned the corruption of the representative process through the abuse of government influence in elections and, particularly following their dismal failure in the 1846 general election, sought to change the rules of the game by means of franchise reform. It was not their intention to enfranchise the masses but to secure the wider representation of the property-owning middle classes. From a position of apparent strength, however, Guizot was determined to reject reforms that might result in electoral defeat for the government. He was convinced that widening the franchise would only politicise the less able and responsible members of society – those most likely to bring about further revolution.

Certainly, the position of the regime was not as secure as it appeared. Even in the 1846 election there was substantial support for the opposition in the major cities. The regime's foreign policy appeared to many to be subservient to British interests. In 1840 Louis-Philippe's determination to avoid war, and also to assert his own authority, had led to the dismissal of Thiers, though not before that vainglorious minister had secured the return of Napoleon's remains from Saint Helena and their interment with great pomp in the Invalides. The regime's credit also suffered from scandals in high places, from continuous opposition criticism of electoral corruption and the use of patronage to control deputies and, especially, from the severe economic crisis beginning in 1845/6 and the resultant widespread popular protest. The image of prosperity that had previously been cultivated by the regime was shattered and replaced by widespread pessimism and anxiety. Political agitation multiplied, as a result in particular of the 'banquet' campaign, its form a means of circumventing the laws against political meetings. This was initiated by members of the dynastic opposition such as Odilon Barrot, who favoured a limited extension of the franchise by means of a reduction in the tax qualification to F100. These moderates rapidly lost the initiative to republicans such as Alexandre-Auguste Ledru-Rollin, however, who at Lille in November 1847 demanded manhood suffrage. A true romantic, he idealised the 'people' as the '*Ecce Homo* of modern times', whose 'descent from the cross' and 'resurrection' was close. He assumed that political reform was necessary in order to avoid another bloody revolution, and that this would need to be accompanied by (unspecified) social reforms, which would end the people's suffering. The government's intransigence, revealed in an aggressive speech from the throne on 28 December, only encouraged more virulent opposition. In its turn, this heightened conservative fear of 'anarchy' and 'communism'.

The 'banquet' campaign, attracting widespread support in the centres of opposition strength in the north and east, was planned to culminate in a mass banquet in Paris. Afraid of disorder, the government banned this gathering – a move that was accepted with a certain sense of relief by liberal and moderate republican politicians. More anonymous and radical figures, however, called for a protest demonstration. On 22 February 1848 crowds of students and workers gathered at the Madeleine and on the Place de la Concorde, and sporadic violence occurred as the police attempted to disperse them. On the following day elements of the solidly middle-class National Guard made clear their support for reform and their alienation from a regime that seemed to represent the interests solely of the upper classes, the so-called *grande bourgeoisie*. This seems to have persuaded the king and his advisors of the wisdom of reform, and news of replacement of the intransigent Guizot with the more liberal Louis-Mathieu Molé as prime minister was well received in the ranks of the citizen militia. In contrast, the construction of barricades was under way in the working-class *quartiers*. Nevertheless, the situation might have been stabilised if it had not been for a murderous fusillade, which killed some twenty people, fired at around 10 p.m., without orders, by nervous troops guarding the Foreign Ministry in the Boulevard des Capucines. An enraged population began to construct hundreds of barricades in the narrow, tortuous streets of the old city, which could easily be blocked by an overturned cart, barrels and paving stones. In an attempt to save the rapidly deteriorating situation an increasingly indecisive monarch was encouraged to abdicate, and members of the dynastic opposition, including Barrot and Thiers, vainly attempted to establish a regency for his grandson. At the same time, republican leaders at the offices of the newspapers *Le National* and *La Réforme* were beginning to realise that a more radical outcome was now possible. On the morning of 23 February probably only a small minority of the Parisian population had been committed republicans. By early morning on 24 February there were 1,500 barricades and a mass insurrection was under way against a king who 'murdered his people'. With a loss of confidence amongst the political leadership and in the absence of clear instructions, the efforts of Marshal Bugeaud, a commander with a well-merited reputation for brutality, to clear the streets soon lost momentum. He was forced to withdraw his increasingly disorganised forces towards the Tuileries. In the late afternoon, amongst scenes of great disorder and public euphoria, a provisional government made up of well-known republican politicians and journalists was proclaimed by the crowds at the Hôtel-de-Ville. Like the First, the Second Republic was to have a major impact on political culture. Slowly reinterpreted during decades of gradual economic and social change, the themes of the earlier Revolution were now to undergo accelerated revision. New perceptions of society and politics were to be fashioned, which were to determine the options available in the succeeding decades.

THE SECOND REPUBLIC

A revolution had occurred because, in a situation of economic and social crisis, the regime had lost the support of many even of its habitual adherents. As the desire for political reform had become more widespread the regime had failed to sanction concessions soon enough. A chance incident had then finally destroyed its legitimacy, at least for many of the citizens of its capital. To their great surprise, a small group of active republicans had been able to take advantage of governmental collapse and take over the reins of power. It was then that their problems really began. The members of this provisional government were divided socially, personally and politically. They lacked experience of government. A majority of moderates, with at their head the aristocratic poet and historian Alphonse de Lamartine, saw their role as essentially one of preserving order and administrative continuity, whilst otherwise keeping their acts to a minimum, until the election of a Constituent Assembly. The sense of expectancy amongst the crowds in Paris, however, ensured that even these cautious men felt bound to recognise manhood suffrage, the democratisation of the National Guard (which meant arming the masses) and freedom of the press and assembly. A minority, made up of Ledru-Rollin, the socialist Louis Blanc and the worker and secret-society veteran Albert Martin, favoured more radical action. It was becoming evident that it had been easier to agree on opposition to the deposed regime than on the form its successor would take.

Alexis de Tocqueville later remembered Paris 'in the sole hands of those who owned nothing. . . Consequently the terror felt by all the other classes was extreme. . .the only comparison was with the feelings of the civilised cities of the Roman world when they suddenly found themselves in the power of the Vandals or Goths.' Outside Paris too news of the Revolution came as a great shock and caused considerable alarm amongst those who still tended to associate the Republic with the Terror. In the absence of any alternative, the change was accepted grudgingly by conservatives, reassured in part by the presence of the likes of Lamartine in government. In contrast, many, particularly amongst the lower middle and working classes, reacted with enthusiasm to their enfranchisement and what promised to be the dawning of a new era. This sense of expectancy created a difficult situation for a government that was concerned to establish its authority and, in any event, was faced with massive problems. Amongst these were the organisation of elections and providing assistance to those thrown out of work by the loss of business confidence in the aftermath of the Revolution. The political education of the masses proceeded apace in the host of newspapers, political clubs and workers' associations created to take advantage of the new freedom. Probably only a minority of workers and peasants conceived of politics in terms of institutions or a formulated ideology, but particularly in the major cities slogans in favour of the 'organisation of work' and the *République démocratique et sociale* were popular. These represented the demand for state assistance in the creation of a network of producers' cooperatives to replace capitalist exploitation. The discourse in Parisian clubs such as Auguste Blanqui's Société républicaine centrale or Armand Barbès'

Club de la révolution was frequently extreme. The latter's manifesto announced that 'we have the republic in name only, we need the real thing. Political reform is only the instrument of social reform.' These radicals were determined to prevent a repetition of what they regarded as the betrayal of 1830, and organised mass demonstrations in order to maintain continuous pressure on the government.

Already, on 25 February, the provisional government had recognised the right to work, appearing to promise far-reaching reform when all that was intended was the traditional expedient of charity workshops for the unemployed, providing low-paid manual work. So-called National Workshops were established in Paris and most other urban centres. The establishment of the Luxembourg Commission, composed of representatives of government, employers and workers to enquire into working conditions and propose reforms, reinforced the belief that major changes were imminent. In practice, the main concern of the government was to promote economic recovery through the re-establishment of business confidence, which required the preservation of public order and avoidance of 'socialistic' measures. The first of these objectives, together with the threat of foreign intervention to enforce the provisions of the 1815 peace settlement, threw the regime into early dependence on the army. Widespread peasant protest against the capitalistic threat to customary agricultural practices had the same effect. Any lingering peasant hopes for sympathetic government action were soon destroyed by the introduction of a 45 per cent supplement to the land tax designed to help balance the budget and pay for the National Workshops. The government was increasingly isolating itself from potential mass support and reinforcing its dependence on social élites, which, regardless of former political persuasion, were now united by the desire to prevent social reform.

The introduction of 'universal' (male) suffrage, which at a stroke increased the size of the electorate from 250,000 to close on 10 million, was the realisation of a dream for radicals. An enormous – an unrealisable – sense of expectancy built up. For the first time in history the entire male population, in a major state, was qualified to vote, and, indicative of a growing political maturity, 84 per cent would do so in April 1848. Women remained disenfranchised. Limited feminist incursions into politics in 1848 would indeed arouse considerable concern. Such involvement ran counter to the ideals of domesticity and belief in the intellectual inferiority of women, shared by men of every political persuasion, and even by many women. Republicans were additionally concerned, and probably with reason, that votes for women – as well as their informal influence – would increase the influence of the clergy. In any case, for conservatives, the extension of the right to vote was a nightmare, the first step possibly towards a complete revolution in society.

In practice, however, democratic aspirations were to be disappointed. In the absence of organised parties the choice of candidates in most areas, and especially in rural constituencies, remained dependent on the activities of small groups of politically experienced *notables*. Alarmed at the threat posed by democracy to their own 'liberty', their divisions temporarily forgotten, conservatives were able to take advantage of superior organisational resources and experience to mobilise support. Faced with a plethora of candidates, many voters turned to those whose wealth, education or functions gave them status in the local community, including the clergy. Certainly, one result of the introduction of manhood suffrage was to establish a clear correlation between religious commitment and political conservatism, in opposition to what was represented as a challenge to the eternal values of religion as well as to social order. When influence was insufficient, intimidation could be employed. The poor needed to be prudent. Republicans had little time to counter this before balloting on 23 April. Most of the successful candidates were to be conservatives and former monarchists, even if, reflecting a continuing crisis of confidence, they adopted the republican label. Indeed, when they met as a Constituent Assembly they elected an Executive Commission made up essentially of the more moderate members of the previous provisional government.

The election results inevitably caused great dissatisfaction amongst radicals. A major demonstration in Paris on 15 May, which culminated in the chaotic invasion of the Assembly's meeting place by the crowd and a call for the establishment of a committee of public safety to levy a wealth tax to finance the immediate creation of producers' cooperatives, strengthened the conservative determination to restore order. The National Workshops, which to radicals symbolised the hope of a better world, increasingly represented the revolutionary menace for their opponents: '80,000 workers paid by the state to learn about revolt in the idleness of the *cabaret*' was one newspaper's description of the Parisian scheme. On 22 June their closure was announced. No effort was made to reassure the tens of thousands of unemployed that relief would still be provided. Indeed, the government's threat to resort to force only reinforced the widespread disillusionment with legal political processes and the belief that with such an uncaring regime there was little alternative but to *recommencer la révolution*. On 23 June, inspired by the slogan 'Liberty or death!', barricades were constructed throughout the poor eastern *quartiers* of the city. The insurgents had no overall plan, no collective leadership emerged and the rising rapidly degenerated into a desperately fought defence of isolated neighbourhoods.

Estimates of the numbers involved vary, but a substantial number of men and women (perhaps 20,000 to 30,000) felt sufficient disappointment with the outcome of the Revolution to risk their lives in an attempt to establish a regime more responsive to their needs. They believed they were fighting for justice. Against them were ranged the forces of 'order', including National Guards from the wealthier western *quartiers*, about one-fifth of them workers; the Mobile Guard, recruited from amongst young, unemployed workers, not yet integrated into craft and neighbourhood solidarities, who remained loyal to comrades and the government, which paid them; and the regular army, which was to become, in the eyes of the propertied classes, the 'saviour of civilisation'. Overall command was in the hands of the defence minister, General Cavaignac, who additionally, at the request of the Constituent Assembly, became head of government. Anxious to avoid a repetition of February, when dispersed groups of soldiers had been overwhelmed, he concentrated his forces, a tactic that initially allowed the revolt to spread; then, when concentration had been achieved, he smashed the insurrection in three days of vicious street fighting. The artist Ernest Meissonier 'saw defenders shot down, hurled out of windows, the ground strewn with corpses, the earth red with blood'. Around 4,000 combatants were killed. The Parisian left was to be decapitated for a generation. Whatever the precise sociological character of the conflict, and despite the fact that workers fought on both sides, contemporaries saw it as one between *bourgeois* and *peuple*, as a form of class struggle. According to de Tocqueville, the insurrection was a 'brutal, blind but powerful attempt by the workers to escape from the necessities of their condition, which had been described to them as an illegitimate oppression... It was this mixture of cupidity and false theory which rendered the insurrection so formidable... These poor people had been assured that the well-being of the rich was in some way based upon theft from themselves.'

Plate 5.5 June 1848: barricade in the rue Saint-Antoine. Lithograph by E. de Beaumont and E. Ciceri. © RMN–Grand Palais/Agence Bulloz.

The conservative press depicted the events as an outbreak of mindless savagery, as a rising fought for 'pillage and rape'. Their initial cry of triumph at the 'victory gained by the cause of order, of the family, of humanity, of civilisation' was mixed with fear, however, and was soon followed by demands for more thorough repression. Political activity was severely restricted. The new constitution promulgated on 4 November 1848 provided for the election of a president with strong executive authority.

The successful candidate on 10 December was to be Louis-Napoleon Bonaparte, with 74 per cent of the vote, compared with Cavaignac's 19 per cent. The author of two pathetic attempts to overthrow the July Monarchy, and of well-known pamphlets outlining 'Napoleonic ideas' and extremely vague means of securing the 'Extinction of poverty', the emperor's nephew was able to take advantage of the messianic cult of the great soldier and political leader created by the outpouring of books, pamphlets, lithographs and objects of devotion over the previous thirty years.

Bonaparte's appointment of a ministry made up mainly of figures associated with the Orléanist monarchy seemed to confirm his commitment to the so-called 'party of order'. Its members aware of their growing political isolation and subject to pressure from the new government, the Constituent Assembly voted its own dissolution on 29 January. The election that followed, on 13 May, was, especially in the provinces, far more politicised than that of April 1848. A clear right–left division emerged between a reactionary conservatism and a radical republicanism with the centre, the moderate republicans, squeezed in between. The *démocrate-socialiste* or Montagnard movement, which might be seen as the first attempt to create a modern national party, incorporated both democrats and socialists determined to defend the republic and work for genuine social reform. Some 200 Montagnards were elected, and although this compared badly with the 500 conservatives the latter were alarmed by such an unexpected radical success. Not only had the working-class areas of Paris and Lyon supported the 'reds' but so too had voters in some parts of the supposedly 'incorruptible' and conservative countryside. Where might this lead? An apocalyptic perspective of an eventual socialist electoral victory and of the threat to private property, religious faith and the family began to develop. Moreover, in spite of constant repression, in some areas *démocrate-socialiste* organisation and propaganda in the form of newspapers, pamphlets, almanacs, engravings and songs managed to survive. It presented a social programme based on a few simple slogans that linked people's everyday problems to the political objectives of the left. Politics was made to appear relevant to the masses. State taxation, exploitation by the rich and the tyranny of capitalism in general and of usury in particular were denounced. In a period of continuing economic depression the establishment of a *République démocratique et sociale* that would provide cheap credit to satisfy peasant land hunger and to protect those who felt threatened with expropriation for debt had considerable appeal. So too did the promise of free education, a guaranteed right to work, and state support for the establishment of producer and consumer cooperatives. This was to be the road to liberation for the *prolétariat*. These measures were to be paid for by means of higher taxation of the rich and the nationalisation of such key sectors of the economy as the railways, canals, mines and insurance companies. The ideal of a society of small, independent producers, that of the *sans-culottes* of 1793, was thus to be reconciled with the development of a modern capitalistic economy.

In response, conservative parliamentarians once more sought to change the rules of the political game. It was intolerable, as one judicial official put it, that 'the communists [be offered] the possibility of becoming kings one day through the ballot. Society must not commit suicide.' A new electoral law introduced stricter residential qualifications that removed around one-third of the poorest voters from the rolls, and ever more intense action was directed at surviving left-wing newspapers and organisations, driving many of those that survived underground. In an effort to safeguard the future, another law on primary education (*loi Falloux*) reinforced the religious and socially conservative message delivered in the schools as well as the supervisory powers of the clergy. The Church was closely associated with 'reactionary' political forces, although the clergy would remain dissatisfied with anything less than total control over the instruction of the young. Even these measures did little to relieve conservative hysteria. As the 1852 legislative and presidential elections came closer rumours of socialist plots abounded, placing

Louis-Napoleon, as the incumbent president, in an increasingly strong position. Although the constitution debarred him from a second term of office the conservative factions were unable to agree on an alternative. Moreover, Bonaparte himself was determined not to hand over power with what he believed to be his historical mission – the regeneration of France – unachieved.

As head of the executive he was well placed to mount a coup d'état, which he did on 2 December 1851. Although directed against both the monarchist groups represented in the National Assembly and the radical republicans, the fact that only the latter offered resistance gave it an essentially anti-republican character. The coup could be seen as the culmination of a long period of repression directed at the left. In Paris only very limited resistance occurred, reflecting preventative arrests, and obvious military preparedness. Few workers were prepared to risk a repetition of the June insurrection to defend the rights of a monarchist assembly against a president who promised to restore manhood suffrage. Similarly, only short-lived demonstrations occurred in other cities. In some 900 rural communes and small towns, however, mainly in the south-east, around 100,000 men did resist. They came from regions of predominantly small-scale peasant farming in which the difficulties caused by growing population pressure on the land had been intensified by the persistent problems of market-orientated activities such as vine and silk cultivation, forestry and rural industry in general. More significant was the survival of clandestine democratic socialist organisations, through which they were mobilised to defend the *République démocratique et sociale* and the new era of security and happiness that had been promised for 1852. The naivety of their beliefs should not be allowed to detract from their very real faith in progress and the triumph of democracy. The columns of troops that moved into the countryside, once the security of their urban garrisons was assured, easily crushed their movements. A settling of accounts with the left, with over 26,000 arrests throughout France, followed this, with not too much attention paid to the rule of law. Conservatives had been badly frightened by grossly exaggerated accounts of 'red' atrocities. Now they gave thanks to God for their deliverance: salvation seemed to be offered by the police state. On 20 December a plebiscite was held to sanction the extension of the prince-president's authority.

Louis-Napoleon was determined to secure a large majority. It was made clear to all officials that their continued employment depended upon enthusiastic campaigning. The basic theme was the choice between 'civilisation and barbarism, society and chaos'. In place of the era of disorder opened in 1848, a new period of order, peace and prosperity was promised. The result was predictable: 7,500,000 voted 'Yes', 640,000 'No', and 1,500,000 abstained, with opposition concentrated in the major cities. In symbolic promise of things to come, the image of the Republic on coins and stamps was replaced by that of *Son Altesse Impériale Monseigneur le Prince-Président*. On 1 January 1852, at a solemn service in Notre Dame, the Archbishop of Paris chanted the *Domine salvum fac ludivicum Napoleonem* as though the Empire already existed, and on 12 May new flags bearing their imperial eagle were distributed to the army. Relieved of their terror, in 1852 the upper classes celebrated carnival with great enthusiasm.

What was the long-term significance of the mid-century crisis lasting from 1846 to 1852? It had certainly aroused fear of social revolution and demonstrated the willingness of social élites to resort to violent repression to protect their privileges. It also constituted an important stage in mass politicisation, however. The introduction of manhood suffrage had encouraged political mobilisation in support of both left and right. In spite of subsequent repression, it was during these years that the idea of the Republic gained precision and mass support. Although substantial differences remained between moderates and radicals, to an important degree they still shared the universalistic ideals of 1789 to 1794. If it had much in common with 'primitive' traditions of popular protest, the resistance to the 1851 coup d'état was nevertheless inspired by political ideology. With some success, *La Bonne, la République démocratique et sociale*, had been presented as the means of creating a more egalitarian and just society. The coup had smashed these hopes. For the second time, supported by the army, a Bonaparte had destroyed a republic. Within a year, following another carefully orchestrated campaign, a second plebiscite (on 21–22 November 1852) approved the re-establishment of the hereditary Empire, which was proclaimed on 2 December, the anniversary of Austerlitz. Its constitution was based very much on that of the first Empire, arrogating immense authority to the head of state.

THE SECOND EMPIRE

The intentions of the new emperor, Napoleon III, have been the subject of frequent debate. The reputation of this strange man, inspired by a belief in his own destiny, suffered irreparably from the military disaster of 1870. He cannot be simply dismissed as he was by Victor Hugo as *Napoléon le petit*, however. His objectives were clear: to depoliticise government through the establishment of a strong and stable executive power capable of promoting economic and social modernisation, and by this means to 'close the era of Revolution by satisfying the legitimate needs of the people' (2 December 1853). It was in the first decade that the personal power of the emperor was greatest. Ministers were convoked once a week to discuss an agenda he had prepared. They provided information. He took decisions. The tradition of ministerial responsibility to parliament gradually built up since 1814 was effectively annulled, and the Corps législatif rendered largely quiescent. These were years in which continued political repression and close cooperation with reactionary and clerical forces characterised the regime and in which elections were carefully managed through the support given to 'official' candidates. Even in this period, however, the implementation of government policy was to be obstructed by a complex of often conflicting vested interest groups, as well as the practical difficulties of administrative control, finance and vacillation on the part of the head of state himself. In practice, the new regime was inescapably dependent on the aristocratic and *grands bourgeois* servants of previous governments. The majority of ministers were conservative ex-Orléanists (Pierre Magne, Achille Fould, Eugène Rouher, Jules Baroche). There were remarkably few genuine Bonapartists. As the former Orléanist prime minister Guizot pointed out, 'An insurrection can be repressed with soldiers; an election won with peasants. But the support of soldiers and peasants is not sufficient to rule. The cooperation of the upper classes who are naturally rulers is essential.' Napoleon appears to have assumed that the *notables* would rally to his government. He was, to an important degree, to be disappointed.

Plate 5.6 Napoleon III, the empress and the Prince Imperial, surrounded by their people. One of the numerous popular engravings; the image of Napoleon I, founder of the dynasty, can be seen in the background. Engraving by L. Flaming. Bibliothèque nationale, Cabinet des Estampes.

Nevertheless, in the early years strong government and political stability, accompanied by economic prosperity, certainly enhanced the regime's status. The emperor's claim to be the 'saviour of society' was widely recognised throughout the property-owning classes. Substantial investment in the transport infrastructure provided a major stimulus to the economy. The emperor's determination to create a 'modern' capital city and ward off the threats of revolution and cholera would be realised in part with the support of private investors and government engineers mobilised by Baron Haussmann, the forceful prefect of the Seine. Much of the rural population upon whose electoral support he depended saw him as 'their emperor', offering protection both against a restoration of the *ancien régime* and revolutionary chaos. In addition to extracting resources through taxation and conscription, this was a regime that brought benefits in the shape of railways and roads, and offered subsidies for the construction or renovation of churches and schools. Although republican historiography tended to minimise its significance, many workers were also attracted by the Napoleonic legend and the emperor's show of sympathy for the poor.

The Crimean War (1853–6), fought to defend a crumbling Turkish empire against Russian 'barbarism'and the threat it posed to European civilisation, and with the commitment of as many as 310,000 soldiers and sailors (compared with 98,000 British), revealed the superiority of the French army over both its allies and opponents. Success appeared to have restored France to a pre-eminent place in Europe. The emperor's subsequent departure for the war in Italy against Austria in 1859 was greeted with a display of bellicose nationalism even in such centres of opposition as Paris and Lyon. Public ceremonies, including religious celebrations, military reviews, and fireworks and dancing, regularly glorified the regime. The Second Empire thus enjoyed a broader consensus of support than had its predecessors. Election results suggest that this reached its peak in 1857, when official candidates received 5.5 million of the votes cast, compared with 665,000 for the opposition. There were a substantial number of abstentions, however. Prefects remained concerned about public opinion, especially in the cities, where supervision of the electorate was so much more difficult. Much of the support for the regime, particularly from the social élites, had always been conditional and far from wholehearted. It declined as the threat of a revolutionary upheaval receded. With order apparently restored, *notables* would press increasingly for the re-establishment of a parliamentary system as the means by which they could participate more fully in political decision making and protect their own vital interests. The growing number of critics therefore ranged from those who had initially welcomed the coup but no longer saw any need for authoritarian rule, including most notably socially conservative liberals, to republicans, the victims of the coup, who rejected the Empire and all its works.

Republican opposition remained weak throughout the 1850s and for most of the following decade. In most regions, the process of politicisation during the Second Republic had not lasted long enough to establish a permanent mass commitment to the Republic. Repression had been effective. Knowing themselves to be marked men, many former activists had adopted a submissive stance. Administrative reports from the provinces in the 1850s were marked by a sense of security, in sharp contrast with their alarmist tone prior to the coup d'état. In the 1852 elections republicans generally either voted for conservative opponents of the government or abstained. The moderate republicans Cavaignac and Hippolyte Carnot, elected in Paris, and Jacques-Louis Hénon, in Lyon, refused to take the oath of loyalty to the emperor and were unseated. Nevertheless, in most parts of France, republicans continued to meet, cautiously gathering at work and in bars and private homes, and using the multiplicity of voluntary associations as a disguise for political activity. The cadres necessary for the eventual re-emergence of the republican party thus remained in existence or were reconstituted.

From 1860 the context for political activity was to change. The regime of Napoleon III, unlike that of his illustrious uncle, was not to take an increasingly authoritarian form. Significant steps were to be taken towards the creation of a parliamentary regime. Encouraged by his half-brother the Duc de Morny, by Alexandre Walewski (the illegitimate son of Napoleon I) and by his cousin Prince Napoleon, and anxious to create a constitutional regime less dependent on his own survival, the emperor conceded to the Corps législatif – by a decree of 24 November 1860 – the right to discuss the address from the throne at the beginning of each parliamentary session; and further agreed to nominate ministers without portfolio to explain and defend government policy before the elected assembly. Moreover, debates were now to be reproduced in full in the press, according much-needed publicity to the views of supporters and, in particular, opponents of the regime. This was in spite of the misgivings of the more authoritarian ministers, and especially Baroche, Fould and Rouher. In December 1861 Napoleon further responded to anxiety within financial circles about the growth of the national debt and Haussmann's unorthodox arrangements for financing the reconstruction of central Paris, by allowing increasing parliamentary control over the budget. This provided a vital means of enhancing the influence of the representative assembly. Throughout the decade, too, although repressive legislation remained intact, much greater tolerance was displayed towards the press. A new political climate was being created.

It seems likely that the emperor had always intended, once order had been restored, to introduce reforms designed to reconcile liberals and republicans. Authoritarian government was seen to be an obstacle to economic and social modernisation. Initially, at least, the policy of liberalisation represented confidence in the stability of the regime. A series of measures would have complex and often contradictory effects, however. These included an amnesty for republicans; alliance with Piedmont against Austria and in support of a 'Europe of the nationalities'; a loosening of the alliance between Church and state; the 1860 commercial treaty with Britain, designed to intensify competitive pressures and to force the pace of modernisation; and the enhanced role of parliament. The realisation that the regime was unlikely to resort to brute force against its opponents encouraged growing criticism from all those who felt that the new policies and the emperor's willingness to use his personal power threatened their vital interests. Amongst the most vocal were clericals anxious about the threat posed by Italian nationalism to the papacy's temporal power and political liberals concerned about the economic dislocation that might result from free trade, and especially its impact on agricultural prices and on the metallurgical and textile industries. They demanded further liberalisation of political institutions to facilitate greater parliamentary control over government policy and restore the influence of established social élites.

The vitality of this opposition made it clear that the regime had failed to engineer a national reconciliation. In this situation, unlike his predecessors, Napoleon III was prepared to adapt. Liberalisation became the means of reassuring the élites upon whose willingness to cooperate the regime ultimately depended. The prolonged and at times apparently grudging nature of the process was to ensure that these predominantly conservative liberals proved less grateful than they might otherwise have been. Efforts by the regime to create an opening to the left only increased their suspicions. This involved conciliatory overtures to workers through a discussion group established in 1861 by the emperor's nephew, the 'republican' Prince Napoleon, and the dispatch of a workers' delegation to the London International Exposition in 1862, which led on to the legalisation of strikes in 1864 and to growing toleration of still illegal union activity. It was no substitute for conservative support, however. As this weakened, the regime had little alternative but to make further concessions to the *notables'* determination to re-establish the sort of institutional arrangements that had made the July Monarchy so responsive to their interests. Further liberalisation thus represented concessions by the regime to pressure.

The increase in this pressure was clearly evident in the gradual collapse of the system of official candidature, beginning during the 1863 parliamentary election campaign. The system was challenged in the first place by an increase in the number of opposition candidates and consequently of political agitation; and by the willingness of clericals and protectionists – former government supporters with secure local political bases – to criticise the regime. In the absence of the wholehearted support of local élites, electoral

Table 5.3 *Legislative election results*

	Registered voters	Votes for government	Votes for opposition	Abstentions
1852	9,836,000	5,248,000	810,000	3,613,000
1857	9,490,000	5,471,000	665,000	3,372,000
1863	9,938,000	5,308,000	1,954,000	2,714,000
1869	10,417,000	4,438,000	3,355,000	2,291,000

management became increasingly difficult. The electorate was encouraged to reject official interference with the 'dignity' and 'independence' of voters. There was a growing possibility that official 'advice' on voting might simply be rejected, thus throwing the whole system into question.

The 1863 election saw the reconstitution of an extremely heterogeneous but increasingly effective parliamentary opposition, which included the growing number of Legitimists determined to defend the interests of the Church and willing to ignore the instructions of the Comte de Chambord, the Bourbon pretender, to abstain from political activity; irreconcilable Orléanist *notables*; and independent liberals and republicans. Although only thirty-two outright opponents of the regime were successful they combined with some of its more liberal adherents to constitute a Third Party. Together with the scale of support for opposition in the major cities, this caused considerable disquiet amongst the regime's supporters. Further concessions were made, most notably the liberties accorded in 1868 to public meetings and the press. Again, the political context was changed decisively. The more blatant forms of administrative intervention in elections were now recognised as counterproductive. Acts of political opposition had become far less risky than previously. There was an immediate and spectacular revival of newspapers and political meetings, most of them hostile to the government. The circulation of Parisian newspapers, which had been around 50,000 in 1830, rose to over 700,000 in 1869, reflecting rising literacy and falling production and distribution costs as well as the political situation. Interest in politics was being renewed at municipal as well as national level, bringing to an end the widespread indifference of the previous two decades. The outcome of the 1869 election was a severe blow to the regime, and if compared with previous elections made the rise of opposition clear.

It was the results in Paris that particularly impressed contemporaries, with only 77,000 votes for government candidates, compared with 234,000 for opponents and 76,500 abstentions. Moreover, the campaign was marked by the emergence of Léon Gambetta – famous for his speeches for the defence in political trials – as the leading figure on the left. His espousal of a programme that included vague promises of social reform was accompanied by large anti-regime demonstrations, with crowds singing the *Marseillaise* and struggling with police and troops. Together with a teleological view of history, this has led many historians to exaggerate the strength of republican opposition. If it reveals the development of support for avowed republicans, the 1869 election also suggests that there were definite limits to this. Thus, of the seventy-eight declared opponents of the regime who were elected, only twenty-nine were republicans and the remaining forty-nine liberals. Furthermore, although it was the more extreme, indeed revolutionary, meetings and newspapers that made the greatest impression on the public, most leading republicans were moderates desperate to avoid violence. These bourgeois republicans were as committed as government supporters to private property and a liberal economic system. Moderates such as Jules Favre, Jules Simon and Ernest Picard were determined to employ strictly legal forms of political action and, in effect, to postpone the establishment of the republic to the indefinite future. Even the 'radical' Gambetta maintained that 'for us the victory of democracy…means security and prosperity for material interests, everybody's rights guaranteed, respect for property, protection of the legitimate and basic rights of labour, the raising up morally and materially of the lower classes, but without compromising the position of those favoured by wealth and talent… Our single goal is to bring forth justice and social peace.' His was a commitment to 'progress without revolution'. He was afraid that socialist agitation would reawaken fear of the 'red menace' and, as in 1848, frighten the mass of small property owners, and provoke a repressive government reaction.

Support for the republicans cannot be easily characterised. It existed in all social groups, but was predominantly urban and often the product of the continuing competition for local status between established and up-and-coming bourgeois groups. Even if every manifestation of discontent by workers should not be taken to represent opposition, industrial conflict – particularly the strike waves of 1869/70, when troops were deployed against strikers – certainly increased tension. Although real living standards had improved since the late 1850s most workers continued to live in cramped and often squalid conditions and suffered from chronic insecurity. In contrast, with some regional exceptions, the rural population was much more likely to support the regime, and for positive reasons,

Plate 5.7 The Schneider works at Le Creusot, a major metallurgical centre during the Second Empire, with fifteen furnaces, 160 coke ovens and eighty-five steam engines. Watercolour by I. F. Bonhommé. Photo: DEA/G. DAGLI ORTI/De Agostini/Getty Images.

though opposition leaders generally claimed that the Empire's survival was entirely due to administrative manipulation of an ignorant peasantry. This led the liberal Lucien-Anatole Prévost-Paradol to describe the regime as *la campagnocratie impériale*, based upon 'rural imbecility and provincial brutishness' – an expression of Parisian intellectual arrogance repeated in the republican Henri Allain-Targé's claim that the future republic would need to re-educate the '[t]hirty-five million brutes who compose the Nation to the rank of active citizens'.

Whatever the limits to opposition, the 1869 election results certainly caused considerable concern amongst supporters of the regime. Amongst the newly elected deputies at least ninety-eight erstwhile government supporters were liberals whose views differed little from those of opposition deputies. Many of these supported an immediate demand for a government responsible to the Corps législatif. It was clear that concessions would have to be made to maintain the allegiance of the social élites. These took the form of closer parliamentary control over both ministers and the budget. In practice, ministers in future would need to ensure support in the assembly, although constitutionally they remained responsible to the emperor alone. As one republican newspaper recorded with glee, 'The Empire of 2 December no longer exists.' These concessions were followed by a lengthy effort to form a government likely to enjoy both the confidence of the emperor and majority support in the chamber. This culminated in the appointment on 2 January 1870 of a ministry headed by a former moderate republican, Emile Ollivier. Although opposition liberals such as Thiers remained dissatisfied because of the emperor's retention of considerable personal power, most deputies were prepared to accept this as necessary for the preservation of order in a situation of growing social tension and political unrest.

The early measures of the new government reinforced this conservative support. They included the final abandonment of the system of official candidature; the dismissal of Haussmann, in order to satisfy orthodox financial interests; the removal of the secularist education minister Victor Duruy to pacify clericals; the announcement of an enquiry into customs legislation, which was seen as the prelude to a return to economic protectionism; and determined efforts, involving the use of troops, to restore a social order threatened by strikers in the major industrial centre of Le Creusot and by republican demonstrations in Paris. Indeed, for many liberals liberalisation had gone far enough. They had been anxious to restore parliamentary controls over the government as well as greater freedom for the press, but increasingly had come to fear that liberty might be abused. The call for revolution made in some sections of the republican press and at the public meetings that had mushroomed in Paris, together with the grossly exaggerated reports found in the conservative press, contributed to the creation of a 'red scare' just like that of 1848. A similar process of political polarisation was also under way, as the clerical and liberal critics of the Empire increasingly came to participate in a broad conservative alliance. There seemed to be no alternative to supporting the regime as the most effective guarantor of social order and Christian civilisation – a point repeatedly made in official propaganda.

On 8 May 1870 a plebiscite was held. The electorate was asked to decide whether it 'approves the liberal reforms introduced since 1860'. The advocates of a 'Yes' vote seem to have stressed the danger of revolution rather than the achievements of the regime. Typically, a clerical newspaper in Alsace affirmed: 'Our *Yes* is to strengthen the emperor against the reds.' The results were an overwhelming success for the regime: 7,350,000 voters registered their approval, 1,538,000 voted 'No' and a further 1,900,000 abstained. To one senior official it represented 'a new baptism of the Napoleonic dynasty'. It had escaped from the threat of political isolation. The liberal Empire offered greater political liberty but also order and renewed prosperity. It had considerable appeal. Opposition remained strong in the cities. In Paris, 59 per cent of the votes cast were negative, and this rose to over 70 per cent in the predominantly working-class *arrondissements* in the north-east. In comparison with the 1869 election, however, opposition appeared to be waning. Republicans were bitterly disappointed. Gambetta felt bound to admit that 'the Empire is stronger than ever'. The only viable prospect seemed to be a long campaign to persuade the middle classes and peasants that a republic did not mean revolution.

In this situation, the Empire's final collapse was a consequence of the incompetent management of foreign affairs. The Prussian triumph over Austria in 1866 had altered the European balance of power, and since then many commentators had believed in the inevitability of a war between France and Prussia, by means of which France could reassert its authority. When war came in 1870, however, it was due to a series of errors by a government operating under pressure from conservative opinion. The hysterical response of the right-wing press to the news of a Hohenzollern candidature for the Spanish throne, and the prospect of 'encirclement', was a major factor in the creation of a bellicose atmosphere. Although the emperor and Ollivier might both have been willing to accept a simple withdrawal of this candidature, conservative deputies demanded guarantees that, in the infamous Ems telegram, Otto von Bismarck, the Prussian minister president, refused – in deliberately insulting terms. To have accepted this would have meant another humiliating foreign policy reversal and risked parliamentary disapproval, which could have thrown into doubt the bases of the recently revised constitution and, in particular, the emperor's personal power. In this situation, although he was aware that the military preparations were seriously defective, Napoleon, his health rapidly deteriorating, succumbed to pressure from the empress and other authoritarian Bonapartists and accepted the advice proffered by overconfident professional experts: the foreign minister, the Duc de Gramont, and the war minister, Marshal Le Boeuf. He hoped that victory would further consolidate the regime. Internal politics were clearly displaced onto foreign policy.

The initial public response was indeed overwhelmingly positive. With the exception of a very small minority of revolutionary militants even republicans felt bound to rally to the national cause. Huge crowds singing patriotic songs gathered in the streets to see the troops off. The first defeats brought panic. The emperor's response to the developing military crisis was to replace the Ollivier government with one made up of authoritarian Bonapartists under General Cousin-Montauban. This could not alter the fact that, in terms of organisation, training and materiel, the army was better prepared for dealing with internal security problems and colonial conflicts than waging a major European war. In comparison with Prussia and its German allies, French mobilisation was chaotic. The army lacked adequate trained reserves. Its manoeuvres in the field suffered from poor staff work and a lack of effective coordination, which the emperor's indecision only made worse. *Elan*, the spirit of improvisation and the ability to muddle through, on which its leaders prided themselves, cost it dearly. Only the concentration of forces might have compensated for numerical inferiority. The high command's inability to achieve this probably made disaster inevitable.

News of the defeat at Sedan and the capitulation of the emperor and one major army was received in Paris on the evening of 2 September and became public knowledge the following day. This catastrophe utterly discredited the regime. In demanding its replacement, the small group of twenty-seven republican deputies were supported by large crowds. On 4 September these invaded the Palais Bourbon and drove out the imperial Corps législatif. In such an uncertain political situation the troops and police responsible for the assembly's security were unwilling to use their weapons. Inspired as much by the desire to prevent a takeover by revolutionaries as by the opportunity to replace the imperial administration, a group of Parisian deputies proclaimed the republic, and established a Provisional Government of National Defence presided over by the military governor of Paris, General Trochu. They were determined to continue the war. In the provinces the news of defeat and revolution usually came as a great surprise, but there appeared to be no immediate alternative to acceptance of the Parisian initiative. In its various manifestations, the Empire had attracted widespread support. Together with its clear commitment to law and order, liberalisation had seemed likely to reinforce this. In spite of their initial fears, the government and the élites had learnt to live with manhood suffrage. Whether as a means of expressing support or else a sense of grievance, voting had been institutionalised. 'Democracy' appeared to have rendered Revolution irrelevant. Military defeat represented governmental failure on a scale sufficient to destroy the regime's legitimacy, however. It would have a massive and long-term impact on the European balance of power. The industrial, demographic and military might of the German Empire would represent a permanent challenge to successive French governments.

Plate 5.8 Paris, 4 September 1870. Following news of the defeat and capture of the emperor at Sedan, crowds gather in front of the Corps législatif. Republican deputies declare 'the fatherland in danger' and proclaim the overthrow of the Bonaparte dynasty. Painting by J. Guiaud. Musée Carnavalet. © Musée Carnavalet/Roger-Viollet/TopFoto.

THE THIRD REPUBLIC, 1870-1914

Once the republic had been proclaimed, its survival seemed to depend on a successful outcome of the war. There were major obstacles to this, however, in particular the shortages of trained troops and equipment resulting from the defeat and capitulation of the imperial armies at Sedan and Metz. Public morale never really recovered. Conservatives, in particular, questioned the wisdom of fighting a lost war particularly because they feared that, just as in 1791, this would lead to political radicalisation. This made the task of inexperienced republican administrators all the more difficult. Their appeals to the Jacobin tradition in order to justify new levies of men and increased taxes only intensified tension. In this desperate situation, with Paris under siege, the government was obliged to request an armistice, and in February 1871 held an election essentially on the issue of whether or not to continue the war. The widespread desire for peace and social order, and the discrediting of both the Bonapartist and republican advocates of war, resulted in a massive majority, especially in rural areas, for the mainly monarchist *notables* who stood as peace candidates. This defeat for the republicans was to result in further serious difficulties.

In the capital, besieged by the Prussians from 19 September 1870 to 28 January 1871, those adult males who chose or had no alternative but to remain, overwhelmingly from the poorer classes, had been armed and incorporated into a National Guard. The political radicalisation already evident in the closing years of the Empire was accelerated by the sense of betrayal resulting from the government's acceptance of a 'humiliating' peace. This would result in a German victory parade through the city that they and regular troops had successfully defended, as well as the loss of the provinces of Alsace and Lorraine. There was also concern that the newly elected National Assembly, meeting in Bordeaux on 12 February, with its monarchist majority, would destroy the Republic and with it all hope of further democratic and social reform. Certainly, the nomination of a government made up of the most moderate of republicans and led by the arch-conservative Thiers did little to calm these fears. Indeed, the crisis deepened as a result of the government's insensitivity in deciding to end the payment of National Guards. For many families

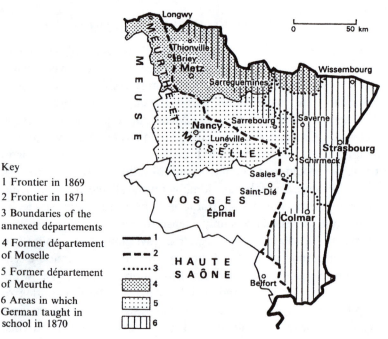

Key

1 Frontier in 1869

2 Frontier in 1871

3 Boundaries of the annexed départements

4 Former département of Moselle

5 Former département of Meurthe

6 Areas in which German taught in school in 1870

Figure 5.3 The loss of Alsace-Lorraine. (Source: Dupeux *et al.*, *Atlas historique*.)

this represented the only source of income until economic activity was restored. The existence of many small businesses was also threatened by the requirement for the immediate payment of rents and commercial debts. Nevertheless, the revolt that began on 18 March was largely unpremeditated. Initially it took the form of popular resistance to a tactless and incompetently managed effort to seize National Guard cannons parked on the heights of Montmartre. Signs of disaffection amongst the troops involved caused a panic, with Thiers ordering a withdrawal to Versailles to await military reinforcements. The resulting power vacuum undoubtedly stimulated the wider insurrection he had feared. Two rival political authorities came into existence, the central committee of the federation of National Guard battalions in the city and the national government at Versailles, each controlling its own armed force. On 26 March, following the failure of confused negotiations, insurrection turned into revolution with the election in Paris of the Commune, committed

Plate 5.9 The burning of Paris in an effort to obstruct the advance of government troops into the city, May 1871. Amongst the buildings destroyed were the Tuileries Palace and the Hôtel-de-Ville. Musée Carnavalet. Photo: Musées de la Ville de Paris. © SPADEM.

to democratic and egalitarian reforms. Fighting between the two bodies began on 2 April. In retrospect it seems clear that, enjoying little provincial support and isolated by a military *cordon sanitaire*, the Parisian movement was doomed. It was suppressed with extreme brutality by the troops of the imperial army, largely freed from German prison camps for the purpose. Ill-disciplined and poorly led National Guards were incapable of defending the city. Already, in 1848, military commanders, easily reinforced by rail, had developed effective street-fighting tactics. The struggle turned into an increasingly desperate defence of isolated *quartiers* throughout an appropriately named 'bloody week' (21–28 May). In fierce street fighting the army lost 500 dead and 1,100 seriously wounded. No one really knows the number of insurgent casualties. Estimates vary between 6,000 and an improbable 30,000, with many of them summarily executed after surrendering. In the following days and weeks more than 38,000 others were arrested. Clearly, for generals, as well as for monarchist deputies and moderate republican ministers, this represented an opportunity for a final settling of accounts. Those political radicals whose calls for reform and revolutionary rhetoric had appeared to pose a threat to the established social order were associated in the fevered imagination of conservative discourse with the criminal, rootless horde, the 'dangerous class', in a plot to destroy 'civilised society'. The execution of hostages, including the Archbishop of Paris and twenty-three priests, by desperate communards only confirmed this perception and served to justify state violence. As Jules Simon, the education minister, so revealingly put it: 'June 1848, March 1871 – the same struggle.' On the other side of the political divide, the Commune created a Socialist myth of revolutionary heroism. This was to be the last of the great nineteenth-century revolutions, however. Emerging out of the particular circumstances of war and defeat, in the long term it represented little more than an interlude in the process whereby political protest was being institutionalised.

It remained to settle the precise character of the new regime. The struggle between the 'party of order' – committed to a hierarchical society, to the decentralisation of government and to a monarchical regime and determined on *résistance* to change – and those favouring *mouvement*, in the shape of representative government and 'greater social justice', was to continue. Once the threat from the extreme left had been dissipated, at least for the moment, moderate republicans were once again able to distance themselves from their temporary monarchist allies. The essential reference points, the bases of two opposing political cultures, were once again the great myths of 1789. The election held in February 1871 had returned an assembly, a majority of whose members (about 400 of 645) favoured the establishment of some kind of constitutional monarchy. They made some progress. Thus in May 1873 Thiers, whose government had crushed the Commune, and secured the withdrawal of German occupying forces through the payment of an indemnity of F5 billion, as well as beginning the urgent task of reorganising the army, was replaced by more committed royalists, with Marshal MacMahon as president and the Duc de Broglie as prime minister. Thiers' fault had been to appear increasingly sympathetic to the notion of a conservative republic as 'the regime which divides us the least'. Once again, though, as in 1850, the royalists were to waste their opportunity and fail to achieve a restoration.

The obvious candidate for the throne, Charles X's grandson, the Comte de Chambord, in exile in Austria and out of touch with conditions in France, continued to insist on the replacement of the tricolour, 'the emblem of revolution', by the white flag and *fleur de lys* of the old monarchy. This refusal to compromise was supported in the National Assembly by around 100 Legitimist deputies, but opposed by the two hundred Orléanists, who were undoubtedly committed to a conservative politics but uncomfortable with the more extreme forms of Legitimist devotion to throne and altar. Faced with this intransigence, the monarchist leaders were forced to postpone a constitutional settlement and decided to wait until the death of the childless Chambord. The succession would then legitimately pass to the House of Orléans, securing, it was hoped, the natural fusion of the warring monarchist groups. In the meantime, with the assistance of the Church, they were determined to establish a regime devoted to re-establishing moral order. France needed to expiate the sins that had caused God to inflict military defeat on her armies. Religious revival, symbolised by the construction of a basilica dedicated to the Sacré Coeur and dominating the Parisian skyline, also offered the means of persuading people to accept the place in society that God had ordained for them. It was increasingly the defence of religion rather than monarchism that supplied cohesion and a sense of purpose to conservatives during these early years of the Third Republic.

In contrast, for many of the 150 republicans elected in 1871, together with their fundamental determination to defend the Republic, anticlericalism provided a basic sense of unity. Significantly, there was no return to clandestine activity, even in the repressive circumstances of the early 1870s. The institutionalisation of political protest, interrupted by the Commune, continued. Republican spokesmen insisted upon their own commitment to legal political activity and made every effort to dissociate the Republic from revolution. Furthermore, they asserted that it was the conservatives who threatened social order, by planning not only restoration of the monarchy but also re-establishment of noble privilege and the tithe. It was claimed additionally that the monarchists would lead France into another disastrous war, designed to restore the temporal power of the Pope. It followed that it was the republicans who were the true defenders of social order. Even the radicals played down the question of social reform. The more prosperous circumstances of the 1870s encouraged them to replace their previous appeal to the *Petits* (the little people) against the *Gros* (the bigwigs) with concern for the interests of those whom Gambetta now labelled the *couches nouvelles*: the property-owning lower middle classes and peasants. These policies were to enjoy growing electoral success. By-elections meant that the composition of the Assembly changed quite rapidly. As early as July 1871, when elections were held in 114 constituencies, a further 100 republicans had been elected, indicating both how peculiar the circumstances of the February election had been and also the real appeal of Thiers' conservative republic, which had after all smashed the Paris Commune. By January 1875 a conservative Catholic, Henri Wallon, was able to obtain sufficient support for a constitutional amendment in favour of the definitive establishment of the Republic.

The constitution of that year sought to avoid the mistake of 1848 by ensuring that the president was elected by parliament and denied the authority accorded by a popular vote. In the aftermath of the Commune he was certainly granted substantial executive power, but in practice the Chamber of Deputies, increasingly dominated by republicans, would insist upon its own predominance. The key role in government was assumed by the *président du conseil* (prime minister), who was dependent upon parliament. The 1876 general election brought 340 republicans, elected especially in the east and south-east, into the Chamber of Deputies, alongside 155 monarchists from rural areas of the west and north-west. Around a half of these were Bonapartists, elected mainly in the south-west and representing a revival that had begun in 1873 and would end only with the Prince Imperial's futile death in 1879, serving with the British army in the Zulu War. In these circumstances a final showdown between the increasingly confident republican deputies and the monarchist president of the Republic could be postponed no longer. In May 1877, following a vote of no confidence, MacMahon dissolved the Chamber. The following October, and in spite of a return to a Bonapartist system of administrative pressure, the electorate returned 321 republican and only 208 monarchist deputies. MacMahon was obliged to invite the moderate republican Jules Dufaure to form a government. Cohabitation was to fail, however, and, when in January 1879 the delegates of the communes elected a republican majority in the senate, MacMahon finally accepted that his position was untenable.

This triumphant republican victory cannot be explained in simple sociological terms. Ideological divisions cut across those of class. Certainly, it appeared to represent '*la fin des notables*' (D. Halévy), a defeat for the traditional social élite, which was made up primarily of noble and non-noble landowners but which had also come to include many wealthy business and professional men, as well as those with mixed interests, such as the Duc Decazes, involved in finance and mining, or the Duc de Broglie, chairman of the Saint-Gobain glass and chemicals company. Nevertheless, a substantial portion of the economic élite, including financiers such as Henri Germain or iron-masters such as Jacques Dorian and Pierre Magnin, deputies from the Loire and Côte d'Or, respectively, had come to favour a conservative republic. So too had the much larger numbers of business and professional men with local standing and influence, in relatively close touch with a mass electorate (the '*couche sociale nouvelle*' to which Gambetta had appealed in 1872 in a speech at Auxerre) that had already attained a significant level of political consciousness and had increasingly come to believe that its material and social aspirations would best be served by a republic.

The resignation of MacMahon was followed by a long period of conservative republican rule, lasting until 1898. The rapidly shifting parliamentary alliances and repeated ministerial crises of this era, though reflecting a fragmentation of authority, should not be allowed to obscure this basic reality. At the outset, a programme designed to firmly establish a liberal democratic political system was introduced, representing, whatever its shortcomings, a major affirmation of individual liberty. In the absence of a modern party organisation, unity and a sense of purpose were conferred on moderate republicans by informal networks, electoral committees and newspapers presenting a simple ideology, which associated the Republic with indefinite progress towards liberty and material well-being. Restrictions on the press and public meetings and on the right to create associations, including trades unions, were eased (laws of 29 January and 30 June 1881 and 28 March 1884, respectively) and less repressive policies adopted towards strikes. Just like their predecessors, once in power the republicans abandoned plans for governmental decentralisation, and, indeed, the administration was purged of politically suspect figures who might otherwise obstruct the application of republican laws. Several anticlerical measures were introduced, including repeal of the 1814 ban on Sunday work and the re-establishment of divorce, although the status of the Roman Catholic Church as the established state Church was not threatened. The Concordat had its advantages.

More important for the republicans was the establishment of a secular education system as the means of combating clerical 'obscurantism', securing the emancipation of the individual and safeguarding the principles of 1789. For Jules Ferry, the law of 28 March 1882, by which he established free and obligatory primary education and removed religious instruction from the curriculum, was 'the greatest social reform and...the most durable political reform'. He appreciated that education was an important source of power. To establish lay education was to provide the means for securing the *bourgeois* Republic against both its clerical and monarchist enemies on the right and the threat of social revolution from the left. It provided the means of inculcating fundamental notions of civic responsibility, patriotism and respect for the law, property and the established social order. In 1886 further legislation provided for the gradual replacement of clerics by lay personnel in all public schools.

Plate 5.10 Peasants travelling by rail. Photo: Popperfoto.

The new Republic was also very active in the economic sphere. It attempted to conciliate diverse interest groups by recognising their very real difficulties following the onset of economic depression in the late 1870s. Thus in 1878 Charles Freycinet introduced a counter-cyclical public works programme designed to improve communications through the construction of branch railway lines and local roads. Criticised for its cost, it proved very attractive to the host of rural and small-town voters. The reintroduction of protective customs tariffs by Jules Méline between 1881 and 1892 similarly consolidated support for a regime that promised *progrès* and *bonheur* (good fortune). His policy represented a philosophical commitment to preserve the 'eternal', rural France against the corrupting impact of capitalism and urbanisation. Although it was combined with a populist attack on the monopoly powers of the banks and railway companies, in practice government policy provided for the fullest possible protection of the rights and vested interests of property owners, combined with a laissez-faire attitude towards social reform. Very little was done, for example, to improve appalling housing conditions.

Moderate republicans were committed to a form of consensus politics, which protected the status quo whilst enlarging individual opportunities for advancement. Together with the enhanced role of government as a provider of services, this encouraged a growing interest in politics. Clearly, more than ever deputies were expected to do their utmost to cultivate ministers and obtain favours for their constituents. In spite of the creation of a stable political system, criticism nevertheless grew. In part this reflected a major political realignment, as many solid middle-class and conservative republicans, having ousted the traditional élites, found that they had achieved their essential political objectives and now struggled to defend their own privileged positions against more radical groups. As early as 1887 Maurice Rouvier, closely associated with big business, sought to establish a right-of-centre parliamentary majority. Although this failed, because of differences over religious matters, it made evident the renewed interest of many moderate republicans in a broad conservative alliance in defence of social order. The electoral success of these *opportunistes* in 1893 allowed them to risk a breach with republicans to their left and resume the search for more congenial allies on the right. Younger men such as

Raymond Poincaré, Louis Barthou and Théophile Delcassé, with
fewer emotional attachments to the past, were more concerned
about the rise of socialism than continuing the struggle against the
clericals. A rash of anarchist outrages in the 1890s, which included
the assassination of President Carnot, only encouraged this outlook.
In the event, the hoped-for realignment was not to occur.

For one thing, the loss of electoral support in the 1898 legislative
election suggested that many voters would reject a move to the right.
Mutual suspicion between conservative republicans and those further to the right over religious issues also survived. It was intensified
by the Dreyfus Affair, as well as by the threat to the Republic posed
by the increasingly rabid nationalism of the extreme right. This was
evinced in February 1899 by Paul Déroulède's farcical attempt to
persuade soldiers to participate in a coup, and by a hostile crowd
that in June insulted the president of the Republic, Emile Loubet,
at the Auteuil races. Together with the evident moderation of many
so-called Radicals, these developments promoted instead a realignment towards the centre-left and in defence of the Republic, which
resulted in the formation of the *bloc des gauches* for the 1902 election
to include most conservative republicans, including Poincaré and
Pierre Waldeck-Rousseau, together with Radicals and even reformist
Socialists such as Alexandre Millerand.

The evolution of the Radicals bears examination. Initially, they had
posed as the protagonists of the *Petits* against the *Gros*, proclaiming
their fidelity to Gambetta's 1869 Belleville programme and demanding
constitutional reform to abolish such remnants of monarchy as the
presidency and senate. Radicals had proposed administrative decentralisation; the election of judges; the separation of Church and state;
and social reform, to include a shorter working day and pensions
for the aged and sick, to be financed by an income tax. They had
condemned the *opportunistes* for their cautious religious policies and
for their close links with big business. In practice, however, the absence
of disciplined parties meant that a deputy's first loyalty was assumed to
be towards his constituents. His primary responsibility was to obtain a
fair share of new roads, schools and jobs. This was also the means of
securing re-election. The boundaries between 'parties' were always
fluid, and ministerial instability the inevitable result. In such circumstances, and most notably perhaps in the aftermath of the 1885

election, when the Radicals actually held the political balance, their own internal divisions and indiscipline prevented them from making effective use of their opportunity. Additionally, during periods of crisis for the republican regime such as that precipitated by the neo-Bonapartist agitation linked to General Boulanger in 1889, or when, following the first ballot in the 1895 election, a victory for clerical conservatives seemed possible, Radicals were prepared to cooperate with more conservative republicans and to respect *discipline républicaine*. In similar circumstances they participated in the Waldeck-Rousseau government of *défense républicaine* in June 1899. Their role was thus essentially a secondary, supportive one, except when Léon Bourgeois was able to form a government in October 1895, only to lose parliamentary support in the following April as a result of his rather modest income tax proposals, which most deputies feared would create a dangerous precedent. These limited successes did suggest, however, that an effort to improve Radical organisation in time for the 1902 election might pay a handsome political dividend.

Plate 5.11 The threshing machine: by far the most common machine introduced onto French farms in the nineteenth century. Painting by A. Rigolot. Musée des beaux-arts, Rouen. Photo: Giraudon/the Bridgeman Art Library.

The Radical Party had remained a *parti des cadres* based on informal groupings of professional politicians and local *notables*, who created autonomous power bases by dispensing patronage to their communities, rather than a mass party. Its parliamentary deputies would remain resistant to ministerial control. Nevertheless, something akin to a modern party electoral organisation was created in the rue de Valois in Paris. This was one factor contributing to the election of 233 Radical deputies in 1902, a victory that inaugurated the great period of Radical administration, in alliance with the forty-three Socialists and the *républicains de gauche* – in fact moderates who refused to accept the logic of Méline's *progressiste* position that the defence of social order required an alliance with the right. This survived until 1909, with governments led successively by Emile Combes, Ferdinand Sarrien and Georges Clemenceau. It saw the first timid efforts to introduce old-age pensions but was above all characterised by a further assault on the Church, in large part in response to the Dreyfus Affair and the renewed threat to the Republic from the extreme right.

The affair had been caused by the court martial of a Jewish army officer for spying. It had become a *cause célèbre* in 1898 when the great novelist Emile Zola challenged the verdict in an open letter to the president of the Republic, and was then himself found guilty of slandering the army. The evidence against Dreyfus was always dubious but, for conservatives, upholding it came to be synonymous with defending the honour of the army, the institution that for them represented authority and order at home and patriotic endeavour abroad. Regarding themselves as the only true patriots, they were hostile towards all those 'bad' French who questioned their chauvinism, and in particular condemned Socialists, trades unionists, Jews, and those Radicals such as Joseph Caillaux who supported horrifying proposals for an income tax to finance social reform. The intellectual leaders of the extreme right, Paul Déroulède, Maurice Barrès and, especially, Charles Maurras, through the newspaper (and political movement) *L'Action française*, rejected the egalitarian values of the Republic in favour of a mystical Catholicism, an authoritarian monarchism and a visceral anti-Semitism, together with a glorification of violence and war. The cult of Joan of Arc came to

Plate 5.12 'A family dinner'. Cartoon by Caran d'Ache, illustrating the furious disputes engendered by the Dreyfus Affair. Bibliothèque nationale, Cabinet des Estampes.

symbolise the spiritual union of *Religion* and *Patrie*, whilst the right also appropriated former symbols of the revolutionary republic, such as the *Marseillaise*, the tricolour and, of course, the army. Largely incorporating the personnel and ideals of traditional conservatism, this new right created a more potent political force than conservatism had known since the 1870s – one that was fundamentally anti-democratic and anti-parliamentarian in its demands for a strong executive power to overcome political and social 'factionalism'. Certainly, the mixture enjoyed some spectacular successes, including victory in forty-five of the eighty seats contested in the Paris municipal elections in May 1900, and gained considerable support amongst those groups that felt threatened by the evolution of modern society, including clericals – represented by the leading Catholic newspaper *La Croix*, members of traditional élites and small businessmen. The latent strength of their anti-Semitism was revealed by the activities of right-wing leagues and the widespread incidence of verbal and even physical violence.

The response on the left was to denounce clericalism as the enemy, and to attack its roots, the Catholic schools, whose particularistic teaching was seen as a threat to national unity and republican institutions. Thus a series of measures was introduced, culminating in July 1904 in the suppression of the Catholic teaching orders and the closure of their schools, and in December 1905 in the disestablishment of the Church. This terminated the Napoleonic Concordat, which had recognised the special place of the Catholic Church in French life and compensated it for the losses endured during the Revolution by paying the stipends of its clergy. Official inventories of Church property stimulated an intense but short-lived resistance. It was clear, however, that the extreme right enjoyed only limited mass support. The violently xenophobic and anti-Semitic tone of its leading representatives even alienated many potential conservative and clerical supporters. The primary achievement of the extreme right was to place nationalism and a supposedly growing German threat at the centre of the political agenda. A major political realignment was already well under way, as support grew not only for 'patriotic' policies but in opposition to what was seen to be the growing 'social peril'.

Plate 5.13 Strike in the Nord coalfield: the use of troops as strike breakers.
Engraving from *L'Illustration*.

Once the Radicals had achieved their 'final' victory over the *ancien régime*, their main preoccupation became the growth of unrest amongst industrial workers demanding an eight-hour day, and particularly miners shocked by the 1,200 deaths in an explosion at Courrières in the Pas-de-Calais on 10 March 1906, as well as amongst peasants in wine-producing areas in the south, who in 1907 protested about the collapse in prices. Clemenceau, who as minister of the interior had already inaugurated a repressive policy, became *président du conseil* in 1906. Soon the government's former Socialist allies were denouncing him as the *premier flic* [cop] *de France*. His coercive policy represented a fundamental commitment to the ethos and institutions of a *bourgeois* property-owning society and to social order. If the Radical conception of the role of the state was influenced by the egalitarian ideals of the Revolution, so equally was it inspired by a belief in the rights of the individual in a property-owning democracy. Radical calls for social justice had long had an empty ring about them. Access to power and the improved material situation of many of their supporters had transformed the Radicals into an anti-revolutionary force.

How real was this social threat that so exercised both Radicals and more obvious conservatives? The Socialists had taken some time to recover from the repression that had followed the Paris Commune. They remained ambivalent about the Republic when it promised social reform but then deployed troops against strikers. Nevertheless, the election of a deputy in Marseille in 1881 was followed by steady growth in support. In 1886 a parliamentary group distinct from the Radicals was formed, which by 1913 had 102 members and attracted 1,413,000 votes. Conservative fears were exaggerated nonetheless. In April 1905 the creation of the Unified Socialist Party – the Parti socialiste unifié, known as the SFIO after its idealistic subtitle Section française de l'Internationale ouvrière, in a deliberate effort to establish a clear socialist and revolutionary alternative – could not resolve the many ideological and tactical differences within the movement. Bitter sectarian squabbling continued amongst politicians as well as with members of the Confédération générale du travail (CGT), the trades union organisation created ten years beforehand.

Even more decisive in the realignment of internal politics than the supposed rise of socialism was the impact of deteriorating relationships with an increasingly assertive imperial Germany. International affairs took pride of place amongst politicians' concerns, and resulted in the nomination of the conservative republican Poincaré as head of government in January 1912 and to the presidency in May. His efforts to form a 'national' government foundered on Radical hostility to the proposed presence in government of conservatives such as Méline or of Catholic spokesmen. Subject to the baneful influence of intensely patriotic and Germanophobe Foreign Ministry officials, and with support from the right, Poincaré nevertheless continued to prepare for a war he believed to be inevitable. Abroad, this involved efforts to reinforce links with Britain and especially Russia – the only power that seemed likely to provide substantial military support in a continental war; at home, measures designed to increase both the status and strength of the army and to develop a greater sense of national unity. The Empire, acquired as a result of the ruthless expansionism favoured by military, commercial and missionary interests, had also become a token of the nation's great power status as well as of its civilising mission. In case of war, its myriad peoples would compensate for the shortage of military manpower in the *métropole*. The conservative press and mass circulation dailies such as *Le Petit Parisien* contributed to the creation of an increasingly chauvinistic mood. Intellectuals such as Charles Péguy eagerly anticipated a 'just war', which would restore 'heroism' and the spirit of 'sacrifice', as well as respect for God and the army to a society corrupted by the materialistic Republic. Inevitably, the debate on military organisation was shaped as much by internal political considerations as real military needs. The Socialists and many Radicals continued to resist the nationalistic xenophobia that threatened to restore the right to power, and made up the minority of 204 deputies who in August 1913 opposed the extension of military service from two to three years. The majority, however, made up of 358 deputies, was determined that France should make an effort to match German military strength. Indeed, growing international tension was promoting a more favourable attitude towards the army even on the left.

The April/May 1914 general election was fought on this conscription issue as well as the question of how to finance the growing military budget. Caillaux, the new Radical leader, who was suspect to conservatives because of his desire to improve relations with Germany, increased their already venomous hostility by again proposing recourse to income tax. Whilst insisting on the need for sacrifices, the wealthy were clearly unwilling to dip into their pockets to provide for national security. The electoral victory of the left with 342 successful candidates, including 102 Socialists, many of whom had stressed the need to mobilise international working-class opposition to an imperialist war, was evidence of the strength of hostility to extended military service. In the last resort, though, the new government, headed by the independent Socialist René Viviani but dominated by Radicals, would prove unwilling to risk weakening the army by repealing the three-year law.

During the international crisis in July 1914 following the Austrian archduke Franz Ferdinand's assassination at Sarajevo, the essential foreign policy decisions were taken by a small group of politicians, most of them lawyers, together with aristocratic and *haute-bourgeois* career diplomats – mainly graduates of the private Ecole libre des sciences politiques – and soldiers, influenced by their perceptions of the intentions and strength of their opponents and allies, and of their own internal political support. The most forceful single influence on foreign policy in the immediate pre-war period had been Poincaré, first as prime minister and then in the supposedly decorative post of president during the crucial days of July 1914, partly because of the incompetence and inexperience of Viviani and the foreign ministers Stéphen Pichon and Gaston Doumergue and partly because of his own forceful and intransigent personality. On a previously arranged official visit to Saint Petersburg, although not wanting war, Poincaré did little to encourage caution, insisting upon the need to support Russia and respect the alliance upon which French security appeared to depend. Abandonment of Russia would have decisively shifted the balance of power in Europe in favour of the Triple Alliance (Germany, Austria–Hungary and Italy). Even if war was not inevitable, with a certain fatalism Republican France had bound itself to accepting the consequences of policy initiatives defined by the Russian autocracy and a sense of urgency determined by military imperatives. Russian mobilisation on 31 July was followed by a German declaration of war on the tsarist empire the next day and on France on 3 August.

The ease with which French mobilisation would occur was evidence of the degree to which, in spite of social and political divisions, a sense of national community had been created. A broad consensus on basic social values, presented as eternal truths, had been established. These included the commitment to private property, possession of which the wealthy élites shared with much broader sections of the middle and lower middle classes and the rural population. An overwhelming consensus, employing the language of 1789, also existed in favour of manhood suffrage and parliamentary democracy. Moreover, over the centuries, but with increasing effect during the nineteenth century, a shared linguistic and mental universe had been created, combining an elemental love of France, a belief in the innate superiority of French civilisation and a sense of moral responsibility to defend the homeland. Coercive action was thus not normally needed to maintain the social and political subordination of the mass of the population. Although the declining minority of dissidents were subjected to increasingly effective state repression, order was maintained largely by the adverse reaction of most people against those who appeared to be breaking the rules. Political conflict was restrained. These sentiments were inculcated through a combination of education, universal military service (introduced in 1874), the mass media and integration into a democratic political system. As the influential historian and educationalist Ernest Lavisse has insisted: 'If the schoolboy does not become a citizen fully aware of his duties, and a soldier who loves his gun, the teacher will have wasted his time.'

6

A time of crisis: 1914–1945

The outbreak of the First World War was a seminal historical event, the beginning of a catastrophic era of conflict that would redefine the global situation of Europe as well as the place of France within the Continent. The war came as a great surprise to the vast majority of French people. The population seems to have reacted more from a sense of resigned acceptance than with any great enthusiasm. Overwhelmed by the speed with which events succeeded each other, individuals felt helpless, unable to influence the situation. Nevertheless, reservists reported to their regimental depots and were sent off by cheering crowds, convinced that France had been the victim of unprovoked aggression and that the war would be brief. The newspapers were virtually unanimous in publicising in the most condemnatory terms the crimes committed by the 'Teutonic barbarians' and in insisting upon the superiority of French arms and the power of the Russian 'steamroller'. The critics of the republican regime, both to the right and the left, rallied to the cause, the nationalists with their confidence enhanced by the feeling that their warnings had been confirmed, the clericals confident that in this moment of crisis the population would turn to the Church for hope and consolation. The Socialist press, which had so recently adopted a pacifist, anti-militaristic stance, warned its readers that 'the Fatherland, home of all great revolutions, land of liberty and freedom, is in danger' and called for commitment to a just war in defence of the relatively progressive French Republic against an autocratic and aggressive German Empire. Minor demonstrations against mobilisation occurred in thirty-six departments, mainly involving Socialist and trades union militants, but the vast majority of activists were unwilling to contemplate action that might assist an enemy.

Social and political differences seem to have been set aside and replaced by a common patriotism, the *union sacrée* for which Poincaré had appealed. The genuine consensus that appeared to have been created was also recognised by the inclusion in the government in late August of two Socialists, Marcel Sembat and the veteran Marxist Jules Guesde, and two representatives of the right, Delcassé and Millerand. Resignation rapidly turned into resolution; a patriotic *élan* became the dominant emotion during the following two weeks as mobilised reservists left their home communities. Overwhelmingly nationalistic sentiments predominated in spite of the anxiety caused by the departure of menfolk and breadwinners for the front. The strength of this initial consensus was evident from the very small proportion of men (about 1.75 per cent) who failed to report for duty. Given the strength of anti-militarism on the left, the government had expected that as many as 13 per cent might try to evade service. Indeed, since 1905 the police had been required to maintain a list of those, mostly syndicalist members of the CGT trades union federation, and especially railwaymen, coal miners and workers in the docks and shipping, in the electricity industry and in the postal and telegraphic services, who might disorganise troop movements or cause economic chaos. They were to be subject to preventative arrest in case of war – a measure that rapidly seemed unnecessary given the weakness of the trades union movement, the lack of rank-and-file support for revolutionary action and the absence of concrete plans to interfere with the process of mobilisation, which itself removed many potential troublemakers. The imposition of martial law restrained others, as did the sense of isolation in a nation committed to defending itself.

Leaderless and threatened with arrest, the small minority of opponents of the war felt unable to resist the immense patriotic fervour. The Catholic concept of the 'just war' and invocation of the spirit of Joan of Arc were accepted widely, far more so than the clerical conception of this time of trial as an opportunity for the expiation of sins. The apparent religious revival that accompanied the outbreak of war was short-lived but the role of the clergy in helping to maintain patriotic commitment should not be underestimated. Nor should the importance of religious faith, as a source of hope and consolation, manifesting itself in prayers, religious medals and images, and votive offerings. Even more important was the culture of heroic patriotism, developed in the schools and by the pre-war processes of socialisation they had promoted, which were now being put to the test.

This unique *union* was nonetheless to be severely strained in the following years. Intended, by the various political groups, to be a truce for the duration of what was expected to be a short war, its strength was greatly exaggerated. In practice the various political and confessional groups retained their pre-war objectives and hoped to take advantage of hostilities to achieve them. Not unnaturally, they disagreed about the nature and objectives of the war itself. Was it a defensive battle against a predatory and militaristic German Empire and in defence of the universal values enshrined in the Declaration of the Rights of Man, as much of the left supposed, or a struggle for survival between peoples in which France sought to defend itself against 'the instinctive savagery of German flesh and blood' (Maurras), as the right tended to claim?

Nevertheless, and although mutual suspicion rapidly re-emerged, the need to drive the enemy from French soil continued to provide a basis for cooperation. The evolving war culture would be characterised by the ferocity of its rhetoric in support of a moral crusade justified by reports of German atrocities. Official propaganda and censorship were less important than the outpouring of emotion in newspapers, music and film.

Even so, sustaining the military effort against the background of repeated failure and the continuous attrition of trench warfare, which was so destructive of morale, was to impose a considerable stress on the social and political systems. Preparations for war had long been under way, and military mobilisation took place without much difficulty. The superior tactics and training of the German army soon took their toll, however. In comparison with their opponents, the French suffered from shortages of junior officers and non-

Plate 6.1 The offensive tactics of 1914/15: massive casualties for minimal gains.

commissioned officers (NCOs), from a relative lack of essential equipment, particularly of heavy artillery, and from training better suited to the parade ground and strike breaking than to modern warfare. Inspired by the Schlieffen Plan, on 3 August German forces began their rapid advance through Belgium with the objective of encircling the major French armies in the north and taking Paris. Having misread German intentions, the French high command ordered an advance into the 'lost' provinces of Alsace and Lorraine, leaving the armies in the north to face vastly superior forces. Convinced of the military and moral superiority of the offensive, the generals were committed to tactics that resulted in the slaughter of the early encounter battles. Some 329,000 men died in August and September, and around a half of the French soldiers killed in the war met their end between August 1914 and the end of 1915. In spite of these sacrifices, the French armies were forced to retreat until General Joseph Joffre finally managed to save the

situation by mounting a counter-attack against the exposed flank of
the tired enemy forces on the Marne in September, forcing them to
adopt a defensive strategem and, through a process of 'leapfrogging',
leading to the establishment of an unbroken line of trenches from
Switzerland to the sea.

Symptomatic of mutual exhaustion, these defensive dispositions,
constantly strengthened, were intended to provide a breathing space
for reorganisation and reinforcement. In practice, they created the
conditions for stalemate and a long war of attrition. By means of the
'miracle of the Marne', Joffre, chief of the General Staff since 1911
and already enjoying immense power within a centralised command
system, succeeded in securing primacy over the politicians in strategic
decision making. As the symbol of national endeavour, he would
give full rein to the contempt for politicians so characteristic of
military leaders, hardly bothering to keep the government informed
of his plans. Millerand, the war minister, was self-effacing before the
military 'experts'.

Initial confidence in the high command would inevitably be sap-
ped, however, by its inability to live up to its promises. The wasting
effect of a succession of ill-conceived offensives in 1915 weakened
military self-assurance. The scale of the trench warfare, with its
barbed wire, machine guns and increasingly intense artillery bom-
bardments, and the advantages enjoyed by defending forces, challenged existing conceptions of waging war. Methodical preparation
for battles of attrition appeared to be the way forward. Long periods
of low-intensity conflict were interspersed with bloody frontal
assaults during which machine guns and artillery turned the front
line into a place of mass death accompanied by unprecedented
brutality, frequently culminating in the slaughter of prisoners.
Eventually, the massive losses suffered during the desperate defence
of Verdun would lead to the replacement of Joffre at the end of 1916,
as a first step in the reimposition of civilian authority. Even then such
problems as the nature of parliamentary control over ministers and
the activities of an increasingly interventionist state, as well as the
means of safeguarding civil liberties in time of war, were never to be
satisfactorily resolved.

Joffre's successor, General Robert Nivelle, was selected in part
because, as a Protestant and unlike most senior generals, he was

Plate 6.2 Trench warfare: the aftermath of hand-to-hand fighting in the Meuse region. © Roger-Viollet/TopFoto.

not suspected of hostility towards the Republic, in part because he managed to persuade politicians that he was the man of providence who would finally breach the German trench system. The new commander was an artillery specialist who had successfully employed the rolling barrage at Verdun as a means of reducing the level of casualties. The bloody failure over which he presided on the Chemin des Dames almost broke the army.

It led to the mutinies of the spring and summer 1917, when elements of forty-nine divisions refused to take part in further attacks, although they remained willing to defend their positions. The cumulative strain imposed by bombardment, fear of death, the constant loss of comrades, and a miserable existence led to the development of a strong sense of grievance focused on incompetent and arrogant officers, poor-quality rations and inadequate leave. Political motives seem to have been largely absent, although paranoid and self-excusatory generals tended to blame everything on subversives. Military discipline was quickly reimposed. The harsh punishment of suspected 'leaders', resulting in the court martial of 3,427 soldiers, 554 death sentences and forty-nine executions, was combined with improvements in conditions. The soldiers' confidence in their commanders was restored, at least partially, by means of a number of carefully prepared offensives with limited objectives and consequently relatively few casualties. It was by such means that Nivelle's successor, General Philippe Pétain, the hero of Verdun, made his reputation as a caring general. As a result the French army was able to hang on during the desperate crisis caused by Russian withdrawal from the war and the reinforcement of the German armies on the western front. In spite of the horrors visited upon them, soldiers fought on, partly as a result of the military discipline imposed on them, but especially out of loyalty to their immediate comrades and a sense of duty, of patriotic responsibility to families and homeland, combined with hatred of the invader. They wanted peace but, after so much sacrifice, were determined not to lose the war.

The deterioration of the military situation was, however, to have significant political consequences. The weariness evident at the front, together with the demands the war made on civilians, inevitably influenced morale. From as early as 1915 a minority amongst the Socialists, led by Karl Marx's son-in-law Jean Longuet, had begun to question not the commitment to national defence but the unwillingness of the government even to consider the possibility of a negotiated peace, and its evident determination to fight to the bitter end (*jusqu'au bout*). In response, the authorities forbade Socialist delegates to attend a conference of the Workers' International to be held on neutral territory in Stockholm in August 1917. Together with rising working-class discontent with living and working conditions, this gradually pushed the Socialists into opposition and led to the withdrawal of their ministers from government in September. November saw the installation in power of Clemenceau, however, the incarnation of the Jacobin republic, motivated by an intransigent patriotism and a determination both to wage 'total war' and to restore the authority of the civilian leadership over the military. A parliamentary majority equally determined to secure the more effective prosecution of the war supported him. Although even their perception of a negotiated peace required the return of Alsace and Lorraine, the arrest for defeatism of the former interior minister Louis Malvy and of the Radical leader Caillaux in January 1918

Plate 6.3 Senior officers planning in 1916 – in isolation from front-line realities. Drawing by G. B. Scott. © Paris – Musée de l'Armée, Dist. RMN–Grand Palais.

represented the culmination of a gradual shift of government towards the right, together with a loss of identity on the part of Radicals as they came increasingly to accept an intransigent nationalism. Indeed, for most of the population there appeared to be little alternative to fighting a war, in which so many sacrifices had already been made, to the finish. A negotiated peace would hardly be possible with German forces entrenched on French soil whilst an undefeated Germany would have required further and utterly unacceptable territorial concessions to add to those of 1871.

In the meantime, the unprecedented needs of the armies had to be met and the war financed. It was paid for from the receipts of indirect taxation, through the floating of enormous loans and the printing of money. Of an estimated F157 billion gold (1913) of government expenditure between August 1914 and October 1919, it has been calculated that F45 billion came from tax revenue, F60 billion from defence bonds and the remaining F52 billion from various other forms of borrowing. The introduction of an income tax was resisted successfully by parliamentarians until 1916, and would make a substantial contribution to government revenues only after the war. The middle classes appear to have been more willing to contribute their sons than their wealth to the war effort. Inevitably, the impact was inflationary. The massive civilian effort was made especially difficult by the loss to the enemy of major industrial regions in the north and north-east that had previously supplied 48 per cent of coal production and 58 per cent of steel. The economic achievement becomes all the more impressive if it is remembered that the 'short-war illusion' meant that mobilisation plans had taken virtually no account of munitions production. There had been immediate man-power and raw materials shortages. Some 63 per cent of male indus-trial workers had been called up for military service, including many with skills essential to war production. Priorities had needed to be urgently established, resulting, for example, in the release from mili-tary service of around 500,000 key workers by the end of 1915. This had all called for the progressive extension of state intervention in the economy on an unprecedented scale, to fix prices, distribute raw materials and organise production and transport. A haphazard struc-ture of old and new administrative organisations had been created, frequently in close cooperation with the employers' organisations. Indeed, in an effort to maximise production, businessmen were offered large capital advances and the inducement of substantial profits. Even though these networks of control were to be demolished rapidly after the armistice, the experience promoted a certain amount of rethinking about the economic role of the state and the means of promoting greater efficiency. The war did not simply result in a waste of resources. In some sectors, most notably steel, engineering, elec-tricity and chemicals, the war effort and the high profits it offered promoted expansion and technical innovation that would be suffi-cient to re-equip the massively expanded French army, as well as that of the United States, with tanks, artillery and aeroplanes. Nevertheless, the losses caused by military action and the destruc-tiveness of the occupation in northern France, as well as the distort-ing impact of the diversion of resources to satisfying military needs, must be emphasised.

The occupation of the north, shortages of fertiliser and machinery and, above all, the requisitioning of draught animals and the con-scription of manpower resulted in a sharp decline in agricultural

Plate 6.4 Mobilisation for 'total war': female munitions workers. Photo: P. Lorette.

production. The 1917 grain harvest, the worst of the wartime period, was about 40 per cent below pre-war levels. Although imports covered much of the shortfall, food prices inevitably rose, finally forcing state intervention and the introduction of rationing. In the meantime, the incentive of high prices encouraged superhuman efforts on the part of the women, children and old men left in the rural areas. The producers of meat, vegetables and fruit in particular benefited, and many peasants were able to pay off debts, acquire land and perhaps enjoy a somewhat more comfortable existence. The separation allowances paid to servicemen's dependants seem to have represented a welcome supplement to the incomes of many poor rural families. More than any other social group, however, it was the rural population that paid for the war with its blood, accounting for almost half the total casualties. This did not protect farmers from criticism. The urban consumers who faced the full impact of rising prices condemned their 'greed'. High food prices were clearly a major cause of discontent, especially amongst industrial workers. The constant efforts of employers to increase productivity and lengthen the working day, justifiable in terms of the war effort, of course had the additional effect of increasing profits substantially and were resented bitterly by workers, who claimed that wages were rising far too slowly in comparison with prices and that as a result their diets were increasingly inadequate for hard physical labour. Established male workers were also concerned by the employment of a growing proportion of unskilled labour. This threatened not just their existing status and remuneration but also their future prospects. Many of these newcomers were women, attracted to the ordnance factories by the prospect of higher wages, and often forced to supplement separation allowances insufficient for the needs of urban life.

In spite of these problems and inevitable social tension, for some time the expression of anything other than unqualified support for the war effort remained exceptional. By the end of 1916, even if little enthusiasm remained, people on the home front at least seem to have adapted to the war. It had become routine. Although families must have endured considerable anxiety and suffered intense stress as they waited for letters from loved ones, once the original patriotic fervour had declined people got on with living, accepting even bereavement with a surprising degree of stoicism. A popular and patriotic war culture was diffused, on an unprecedented scale, through the press, in patriotic songs, in the schoolroom and from the pulpit, and in the carefully controlled images of the cinema newsreels, so avidly watched in even the most isolated rural communities. As the war was prolonged, whilst soldiers developed an utter contempt for this *bourrage de crâne* (brainwashing), civilians still sought reassurance in the confident optimism of the media.

The failure of the spring 1917 offensive seems finally to have destroyed any lingering hopes that the war might soon end. Pessimism spread, together with the daunting prospect of endless war. The letters read by the postal censors revealed a definite sense of strain and of war weariness. The middle classes, perhaps the most stridently patriotic, alongside the peasants, perhaps the most resigned, appear nevertheless to have accepted the situation. In spite of the particularly high casualties amongst young officers and the material difficulties of families living on fixed incomes, the former had endured too much to draw back. Disaffection was most clearly evident amongst the working classes. The widespread sense of grievance concerning both working and living conditions was intensified by the impotence of the trades unions, bound as they were initially by the *union sacrée* and then, from January 1917, by compulsory arbitration procedures. This discontent only slowly took on political form. Many Socialists and trades union militants had been called up for military service, and those who remained were at first reconciled to inactivity for the duration of what, after all, was expected to be a short war. The first serious strike waves occurred in the Paris region in January and May/ June 1917, mainly before the public became aware of Nivelle's disastrous offensive, and were essentially spontaneous, involving around 100,000 chiefly women workers in the clothing trades and munitions. They were frequently condemned by union officials, many of whom as reservists risked being recalled to the front if they incurred the authorities' displeasure, and were brought to an end easily by the imposition of compulsory arbitration together with wage increases. Similarly, strikes in the Toulouse munitions factories and in the Loire basin were short-lived. In spite of the stir caused by an unofficial May Day parade by 5,000 to 10,000 people along the Grands Boulevards in Paris during which shouts of 'Down with the war' were proffered, the vast majority of workers were not opposed to the war effort, even though they were determined to protect their vital interests. Although desire for a compromise peace was not uncommon, there were still very few advocates of peace at any price. With the Germans remaining on French soil, and after so much sacrifice, there seemed to be little alternative to fighting on until final victory. Prefects' reports blamed unrest mainly on 'social problems' and seemed confident that minor concessions to workers' demands would calm the situation. Anxiety about the impact of the Russian Revolution on working-class opinion soon eased as it became evident that initial enthusiasm had turned to hostility when workers had become aware of its potential impact on the military situation.

A second strike wave hit munitions factories in the Paris region in May 1918, involving well over 100,000 workers, although the better-organised strikes of miners and engineering workers in the Saint-Etienne area were potentially more damaging for the war effort. Again, though, there were few signs of support for revolutionary action. The obvious determination of the Clemenceau government to prosecute the war to a victorious conclusion had a positive impact on morale, whilst the enormous German offensive in March had encouraged a renewed rallying to the national cause. General Ludendorff gambled on employing troops transferred from the east following the Russian collapse and committed his armies to a final convulsive effort to gain victory. It was to be a close-run thing. In spite of initial successes by the Germans, dogged resistance, heavy casualties and their lack of reserves of men and material halted the assault. This last great attack decisively broke the imperial army. The counter-attack that followed, for the first time involving large numbers of fresh American troops, as well as massed tanks and aircraft, was coordinated effectively by General Ferdinand Foch, the supreme commander finally accepted by the Allies in the moment of ultimate crisis. Nevertheless, the accelerating collapse of the Central Powers came as a great surprise. In spite of heavy losses, victory at last seemed possible. The desire to drive the enemy out of France and to impose a salutary lesson on the invader by utterly smashing his armies and invading his territory was, however, soon tempered by a desire to save lives and bring the war to an end as soon as possible. The armistice, which came into force on 11 November 1918, was cele-brated with unrestrained joy. Its terms made it virtually impossible for the Germans to renew the war. The following year the Treaty of Versailles imposed an admission of guilt for causing the war, as well as substantial reparations, but the terms fell far short of those demanded by the victorious generalissimo, the newly promoted Marshal Foch, who warned that Versailles represented merely a twenty-year truce after which Germany would seek revenge.

THE INTER-WAR YEARS

The war was over. Its victorious outcome seemed to represent a triumph for republican institutions. It left France, in appearance at least, as the major continental European power. The humiliation of 1870 was finally effaced and the lost territories of Alsace-Lorraine, previously subjected to an intense and increasingly successful cam-paign of Germanisation, had been recovered. Disillusionment would soon set in, however, as the long-term implications of participation in such a brutal and bloody conflict became evident. This was indeed a Pyrrhic victory. The human cost was enormous. Almost 8 million men had been mobilised and 1,322,100 (16.8 per cent) of them killed, a proportion rising to 25 per cent amongst the infantry and even higher for junior officers and NCOs. Many others (some 3 million) had been maimed in combat or were debilitated as a result of disease or trauma. Frequently, readapting to civilian life was difficult. The soldiers and their families would never forget their experience. Virtually the entire nation had been plunged into mourning. The memorials to the dead erected in every community recorded their loss and kept the memory alive. Moreover, over 1 million were to receive invalidity pensions. The demographic impact was particularly severe in France, which had mobilised 168 out of every 1,000 inhabitants and lost thirty-four of them, whilst Britain had mobilised 125 and lost sixteen, and Germany had mobilised 154 and lost thirty. The effect, on a country already experiencing demographic stagnation, of the loss of so many young men (27 per cent of those in the eighteen to twenty-seven age group) and of the resultant decline in the numbers of marriages and births would be felt in the 1930s, as the size of the active labour force and of the cohort of men of military age fell.

The war also had a significant long-term impact upon the economy. In spite of the progress made in the early part of the century, France had gone to war in a state of relative backwardness in comparison with both Britain and Germany. Whilst the economic balance was not entirely negative – much useful investment had occurred – it remained decisively in the red. In 1919 levels of agricultural and industrial production were around 45 per cent below those of 1913. Resources had been destroyed or diverted to military use. Large areas of the most productive farmland had been devastated by battle, livestock driven off, towns and villages smashed. In the German zone of occupation, over-exploitation and systematic destruction had reduced massively the productive capacity of mines and factories and the carrying capacity of the railway network. Disruption on this scale, and the harsh treatment of the population of occupied areas, deprived of adequate supplies of food and fuel and subject to a reign of terror, deportation and forced labour, would be a major cause of the mass exodus of refugees from the north in 1940. Clearly, they were not anxious to repeat the experience of German rule.

Plate 6.5 The cost of reconstruction: the ruins of Montdidier (Somme), June 1919. Photo: Collection Albert Kahn.

The demobilisation of the massive military forces, the disposal of surplus armaments, the reallocation of resources, and reconstruction would take time and money. Even so, the process was achieved with surprising rapidity. The war had encouraged many large-scale enterprises to modernise their equipment and make more efficient use of labour. Industrial production was restored to pre-war levels by 1924, and by 1929 was 40 per cent above the 1913 level. This was due to a combination of factors, including the stimulus of reconstruction, the release of pent-up consumer demand and the rising exports made possible by the depreciation of the franc in world currency markets. It began to appear as if the war would represent only a brief interlude in a long-term process of economic growth. The process of growth and the concentration of production would remain insufficient to eliminate the major structural weaknesses of the French economy, however. These resulted from a combination of demographic and demand stagnation, the survival of a large and inefficient agricultural sector and the presence of numerous small and medium-sized and – more to the point – poorly equipped industrial and commercial businesses. The existence of modern large-scale enterprises within such sectors of industry as chemicals, electrical engineering or automobiles, growing through the reinvestment of their massive wartime profits, contrasted markedly with the cautious reluctance to invest on the part of most entrepreneurs. As a result, the average industrial machine in the 1930s was to be twenty years old, compared with seven in Germany. The cost of production remained relatively high and the employers (*patronat*) obsessed with the need to ensure continued protection against foreign competitors. Potential investors tended to prefer the relative security of government loans. Nevertheless, patchy efforts to increase productivity were stimulated both by the relative prosperity of the 1920s and by the depression of the following decade, when rationalisation came to the fore. Table 6.1 suggests some idea of the scale of structural change.

The continuing movement of labour away from agriculture, the decline of artisanal production and indeed the shift away from industry towards the services so characteristic of a modernising economy can be observed in the figures in Table 6.2. These reflect

Table 6.1 *Distribution of active industrial population (per cent)*

	1913	1938	Variation
Energy	4.0	6.2	+ 2.2
Building and construction materials	18.6	16.9	– 1.7
Metallurgical industry and engineering	14.7	22.6	+ 7.9
Chemicals	1.6	3.9	+ 2.3
Textiles, clothing and leather	42.4	29.7	– 12.7
Agriculture and food-processing industries	7.8	9.6	+ 1.8

Source: J.-C. Asselain, *Histoire économique de la France du XVIIIe siècle à nos jours*, vol. II, *Le blocage de la croissance pendant l'entre-deux-guerres* (Editions du Seuil, 1984), 74.

Table 6.2 *Structure of the active population (per cent)*

	1913	1938
Agriculture	37.4	31.4
Industry	33.8	32.3
Services	28.8	36.3

both the growth of a 'modern' bureaucracy, of the financial and banking sector and chain stores and also the burgeoning numbers of small shops and bars. Another characteristic of the period was the concentration of so much of this activity in and around Paris, a city increasingly 'swollen' with people, and the corresponding under-development of the west, centre and south-west.

Technological stagnation was even more evident in farming than in industry. Mechanisation made slow progress. There were only 35,000 tractors in use in 1938. They were expensive, and peasants, often still committed to the ideal of self-sufficiency, were reluctant to borrow. In any event, most small farms generated an income inadequate to support debt repayment. Farmers were insufficiently aware of their markets or of the potentially beneficial effects of investment. Cost accounting was a complex mystery. Costs were high and productivity gains primarily the result of the removal of surplus labour through migration. Afraid that this might both increase the cost and reduce the submissiveness of labour, typically conservative land-owners condemned its morally corrosive effects. By 1929–31 cereal yields had risen to 14.2 quintals per hectare, only slightly above the pre-war figure of 13.3 and well below the British and German averages (21.9 and 20.5, respectively). Although productivity was much higher on the large capitalistic farms of the Paris basin and the north, it remained the case that the one-third of the labour force employed in farming contributed only one-quarter of the country's national income. Nevertheless, the 1920s were a decade of rising food prices, creating a sense of well-being within the rural population. Easier access to local towns by train or motor transport, and the beginning of rural electrification (from 1928), reinforced the mind-broadening effect of the wartime experience. These developments stimulated improvements in diet, changes in dress and the decline of local customs, although most peasants continued to put up with miserable housing conditions.

The war still had to be paid for. International debts incurred during its course, especially to the Americans and British, would need to be honoured. This was rendered all the more difficult by the wartime outflow of gold and foreign currency, the sale of overseas assets and the substantial losses on investments as a result of the Russian Revolution. Prices had more than tripled during the war, and this had heralded a massive depreciation of the franc once wartime exchange controls had been removed and public confidence in a post-war return to 'normality' had been disabused. Faced with problems of such severity, it is hardly surprising that French politicians looked to the peace treaty not only to provide long-term military security but to force Germany to make proper and adequate financial reparations for a war for which there was universal agreement it was to blame. The slogan 'Germany will pay' won near-unanimous support. Disagreement with the Allies about how much Germany should pay was to cause considerable resentment amongst people who felt that they had borne the highest cost in human sacrifice, as did evident German 'bad will' when presented with the bill. In the end, France would receive the substantial sum of F10 billion (1913 value) before payments were suspended in 1931, enough to burden Germany without satisfying the French.

Thus France emerged from the war victorious but seriously damaged, her long-term security gravely weakened by the collapse of her former Russian ally, growing American isolationism and British unwillingness to enter into formal military commitments, as well as German determination to secure revenge for what was perceived to be the unjust humiliation imposed by the Versailles treaty. The effectiveness of social and political systems that had endured the military threat triumphantly was soon to be further tested, moreover. The global economic crisis that began in 1929 would reveal an overwhelming sense of caution, and an inability to adapt, in all sectors of society. Together with increasingly bitter social and political relations, these attitudes owed much to the experience of war and to disappointment with its outcome.

Whatever else had changed, French society remained profoundly inegalitarian. Information on inheritance suggests that half the wealth passed on from one generation to the next belonged to only 1 per cent of the deceased. It remained the case that, in a society made up of roughly 14 million peasants, 13 million workers and 14 million members of the even more disparate middle classes, only the *grande bourgeoisie*, a fraction of the bourgeoisie as a whole, enjoyed real power. The need for professional and cultural qualifications, together with correctness in dress and manners, comfortable accommodation and the ability to entertain and mix socially, continued to put severe restrictions on entry to important decision-making positions in government, administration and private enterprise. These attributes combined to protect position and to distance the less fortunate. Birth, culture and – ultimately – wealth determined access to education: the great divider. The vast majority of children attended primary school until the age of fourteen, a small minority received instruction in the primary classes attached to fee-paying *lycées*. Women too continued to be discriminated against. Although the Chamber of Deputies agreed, in 1919, on female enfranchisement, the proposal was overturned in the Senate, and subsequently was not an issue to which politicians accorded high priority.

The small number of upwardly mobile people succeeded because of ability, luck and a willingness to conform. The real threat to established order came, on the one hand, from structural change in the economy and, on the other, from the activities of political 'renegades', the largely middle-class and lower middle-class politicians on the left, who from a genuine commitment to a more egalitarian society, or else as a means of enjoying electoral success, were prepared to propose reforms that might destabilise the social system. Nevertheless, established élites could count at least on the conservative instincts of most of those, whether peasants, shopkeepers, clerks or business and professional men, who prided themselves on the possession of property, however small, or of professional qualifications; on those who were determined to 'improve themselves' either directly or vicariously through their children, and who in various ways emulated their 'betters' and sought to distinguish themselves from the property-less and uneducated. Thus many of the skilled and better-rewarded workers dreamt less of revolution than of social promotion. They were encouraged by a mass-circulation press and radio network, which claimed to be non-partisan whilst diffusing an essentially conservative ideology.

The war had encouraged a rallying to nationalistic values, and the 1919 election brought overwhelming conservative success. A new electoral system, which benefited those parties capable of organising alliances, had disastrous consequences for the left. Isolated by its break with the *union sacrée* in 1917, and divided internally over its response to the Bolshevik revolution, the Socialist Party rejected any sort of compromise with the 'bourgeois' parties. This forced the

Radicals to negotiate agreements with conservatives and to form part of a Bloc national, whose most notable figures, Clemenceau and Millerand, stressed the need to continue the wartime *union*. In effect, part of the political centre, which in 1914 had allied with the left, had now moved to the right. The creation of the Bloc signified both a greater willingness on the part of conservatives to accept the republican regime and the belief of many Radicals that the real threat to the established order came now from the left. Their rapprochement was symbolised by the emergence of an acceptable modus vivendi between Church and state. Although the Socialists' share of the vote rose from 17 to 21 per cent, under the new electoral system the number of seats they gained fell from 102 to sixty-eight. Furthermore, many of those Radicals who had rejected an electoral alliance with the right were defeated. As a result, the parties of the centre-right gained 450 of the 616 seats in parliament.

The outcome was the formation of a government led by Millerand, and from 1922 by Poincaré. Clemenceau had become impossible because of the accumulated hostility aroused by his anticlericalism, insistence on the need for continued austerity and increased taxes, and desire to establish a strong interventionist presidency. The government's aggressive foreign policy was marked by efforts to secure reparations and to weaken Germany by encouraging separatist movements in the Rhineland. It culminated, in 1923, in the occupation of the Ruhr, a decision that alarmed public opinion to such a degree as to stimulate a move to the left, which resulted in the electoral victory of the centre-left alliance, the Cartel des gauches. Again, the campaign revealed wide divisions amongst the Radicals – that is, the fundamental instability of the key group in the political centre upon whose support governments depended for survival. If they continued to differ on questions of social reform, however, they could at least generally agree in 1924 on the need to work for a perpetual peace through collective security and the League of Nations, an approach that would come to be associated with the pragmatic foreign minister Aristide Briand and that led in 1925 to the Locarno Pact, by which Germany recognised, and the British and Italians guaranteed, the eastern frontiers of France. This settlement was reinforced by the negotiation of defensive treaties between France and her Czech and Polish allies in a feeble effort to fill the power vacuum left by the collapse of the Austro–Hungarian and Russian Empires. The idea of a European federation was also floated. It was perceived to be a means of exercising some control over a Germany whose economic potential and population appeared to dwarf those of France. Nevertheless, government by the centre-left was only an interlude in a long period of conservative ascendancy that lasted until 1932, in which the dominant figure (until 1929) was to be Poincaré. His primary objectives were to ensure military security whilst at the same time eliminating inflation, balancing the budget and limiting the burden of taxation. These policies were combined with a visceral anti-socialism and a determination to associate it with the terrible menace of Bolshevism.

The formation of the Union nationale government in 1926 (presided over first by Poincaré and then, after illness forced his resignation, by André Tardieu and Pierre Laval) brought the final acceptance, in 1928, of a law requiring compulsory protection against sickness. This had first been introduced in 1921, when, following the war, it had represented a widespread sense of social obligation. Subsequent insistence on financing the measure through assurance revealed continuing middle-class opposition to any hint of social reform financed through taxation. Egoism was concealed by an appeal to the defence of 'moral order' and warnings about welfare dependence. The left's self-inflicted wounds made the success of this approach all the more likely. In the aftermath of the war membership of both the Socialist Party and the trades unions had increased initially, reflecting both a hatred of the regime that had involved the nation in a bloodbath and belief in the imminence of revolution. Since 1917 the Socialists had been faced with the need to work out their attitudes towards Bolshevism. In the event, the party split. At its Tours congress in December 1920, 67.3 per cent of delegates voted to adhere to the Communist International, ignoring Léon Blum's warnings about leftist extremism, and reducing the Socialist Party to 30,000 members. Their action was inspired by anti-war sentiment, by enthusiasm at the apparent success of the Soviets in establishing a new form of popular government and by disillusionment resulting from the repeated failure of the parliamentary approach to securing far-reaching social reform, as well as by the evident 'careerism' of so many Socialist deputies. The spread of disquiet at the brutality of the Soviet regime, in addition to its demands for subservience on the part

comment voter
contre le
bolchevisme?

0.50 EN VENTE DANS
TOUTES LES LIBRAIRIES

Édité par le GROUPEMENT ÉCONOMIQUE
des Arrondissements de SCEAUX & SAINT-DENIS

Plate 6.6 The widespread fear caused by major strikes, in the aftermath of the Bolshevik revolution, allowed conservatives to develop the theme of the man with a knife between his teeth during the November 1919 electoral campaign. Bibliothèque nationale, Cabinet des Estampes.

of foreign communists, however, soon encouraged many of these errant comrades to return to the fold. This would re-establish the Socialist Party as the major proponent of social reform.

Nonetheless, the party would remain profoundly divided on tactics, between, on the one hand, those favouring a rapprochement with the Communists and, on the other, a right wing closer to the Radicals. The impact of these divisions was increased when, following the failure of the general strike called in May 1921, the CGT also split, with a Communist minority forming a CGT unitaire in January 1922. Overall union membership collapsed from around 2 million in 1919 to 600,000 in 1921. As the left tore itself apart, electoral support declined, with Socialist candidates obtaining about one-fifth of votes cast in elections in the 1920s and the Communists one-tenth. The latter succeeded in establishing a well-organised movement, with its bastions in the grim industrial suburbs of Paris and parts of the Cher and central France amongst workers who, if they largely enjoyed rising real incomes in the 1920s, continued to endure often appalling housing conditions and the rigorous and insensitive imposition of discipline in their workplaces. Nevertheless, party membership declined from 110,000 in 1921 to only 30,000 ten years later. Internal unity was achieved at the cost of isolation from the rest of the political nation. The leadership pursued a policy of class-based opposition towards both the 'bourgeois' parties and its main competitor for working-class votes, the Socialist Party, repeatedly described as a nest of 'social traitors'. Meanwhile, whilst not repudiating revolutionary ideals and language, and refusing to participate in government, the Socialists pursued an essentially reformist policy that involved electoral pacts with a Radical Party unwilling to contemplate substantial measures of economic and social reform. This tactical flexibility at least allowed it to benefit from the decline of support for the Communists in the towns and for the Radicals in the countryside.

For many contemporaries, however, the most threatening problems seemed to be posed by inflation and the inability of successive governments to balance their budgets. The former was due primarily to the massive increase in government borrowing and in the volume of money in circulation (from F6,000 million in 1914 to F37,000 million by December 1920) as a result of war and reconstruction. For almost eight years after the war internal prices had risen sharply whilst governments had repeatedly failed to come to an understanding of, much less to solve, the problem. Furthermore, this had resulted in a collapse in the value of the franc. The currency had lost half its real value during the war, and the decline accelerated sharply following the withdrawal of British and American support in March 1919. The growing lack of confidence only encouraged speculation and the flight of capital abroad. The failure of the French occupation of the Ruhr in 1923 to secure the payment of reparations added to the gloom.

Plate 6.7 More conservative electoral propaganda, blaming the Cartel des gauches government for budget deficits and inflation. Poster by Jack. Bibliothèque nationale, Cabinet des Estampes.

Between 1922 and 1926 prices again doubled. The international devaluation was even more marked with the pound sterling, worth F25 in 1914, rising to F243 by June 1926. In this situation the real losers were the large numbers of *rentiers*, in a country still lacking a general system of old-age pensions. By 1926 the fixed-income bonds they had favoured traditionally had lost five-sixths of their pre-war value. Otherwise, the immediate effect of inflation and the consequent easing of the debt burden, together with the stimulus afforded by devaluation to external trade, was to promote prosperity. Most social groups seem to have enjoyed rising real incomes, in the case of workers, for example, by something between 9 and 26 per cent, but this did little to diminish the general air of pessimism caused by the constant rise in prices. The German hyperinflation of 1923 seemed to lend credibility to the most nightmarish visions.

Only with the formation of the Poincaré government in June 1926 did financial stabilisation occur. Its conservative composition and the support it enjoyed from the self-proclaimed Union nationale, made up of Radicals and right-wing deputies, helped to reassure orthodox financial opinion, which had had little confidence in the previous Cartel des gauches administrations led by Edouard Herriot. A combination of cosmetic and real measures followed, including tax increases, higher interest rates and reductions in government expenditure, together with, in June 1928, a partial return to the gold standard but with the franc at one-fifth of its pre-war value – realistic enough to avoid the loss of competitiveness in international markets that had resulted from the overvaluation of the British currency in 1925. Efforts were even made by Tardieu to reduce social tension by sharing some of the benefits of prosperity by means of legislation on social insurance and family allowances. Inevitably, the prospect of being required to make contributions alarmed employers, and in any case the renewal of prosperity would be short-lived.

The Wall Street crash in October 1929 saw the onset of the most serious crisis ever to hit the capitalist world. During the following decade France would experience a depression severe enough to shatter many illusions about both the nation's internal stability and its great power status. Nevertheless, the crisis affected the country later than the other industrialised nations. The year 1930 was thus a prosperous one. Poincaré's 'stabilisation', in effect devaluation, had made French goods competitive on international markets – at least, until the British devaluation in September 1931. The relative backwardness of the economy and the limits to its integration into world markets further delayed the impact. Even when the crisis came, in terms of bankruptcies, falling production and unemployment, it did not appear to be as severe in France as elsewhere. Complacently, many French commentators took pride in the supposedly more balanced character of the national economy, which retained so much of the population on the land. Agriculture was experiencing its own crisis, however, also marked by falling prices and attributable essentially to the oversupply of both domestic and international markets. The price of vegetable products fell by 34 per cent between 1930 and 1935, that of wine by 60 per cent and that of meat by 40 per cent. Landowners' rental income, farmers' profits and labourers' wages all experienced substantial decline. The purchasing power of the rural population collapsed. The crisis in France was to be more prolonged than elsewhere. The 1930s were to be a decade of perpetual crisis.

Poincaré's much-vaunted currency 'stabilisation' was to be a brief interlude in a lengthy period of disequilibrium. Subsequently, budgetary deficits, now caused by falling tax receipts, led to depreciation of the currency on international markets. Despite such notable exceptions as the Socialist Blum and the conservative Paul Reynaud, however, most political leaders were to oppose bitterly planned currency devaluations of the kind used by Britain in 1931 and the United States in 1933 to stimulate trade. The passionate strength of opposition to devaluation as a 'swindle' that threatened the value of savings meant that it was an option politicians proposed at their peril. There was much more political mileage in denouncing it in the most apocalyptic terms possible. When, in 1934, Reynaud spoke in favour of devaluation, Action française, the organ of the extreme right, with its habitually delicate turn of phrase, denounced him as 'vermin' with the 'mind and morals of a termite' and called for his imprisonment. As a result of this determination to preserve the international value, status and purchasing power of the currency and to avoid a return to the inflation of the 1920s, French products became increasingly uncompetitive in world markets. Between 1929 and 1935 exports fell by 44 per cent in volume and a staggering 82 per cent in value. The country's share in an anyway sharply reduced volume of international trade in manufactured goods declined from 11.2 per cent in 1929 to 5.8 per cent by 1937. Efforts to stimulate trade within the protected markets of the Empire enjoyed some success, accounting for 25 to 30 per cent of exports by 1936–8. The centenary of the conquest of Algeria and the creation of a 'greater France' was celebrated in 1931 with a major and much-publicised colonial exhibition. Imperial trade could not compensate adequately for the loss of markets in the major industrial countries, however, or prevent a growing reliance on imports of both foodstuffs and oil.

Even in 1938 levels of industrial production were little higher than they had been in 1913. For this reason it might be said that France was the most seriously affected amongst the leading economic powers. Gross prices fell 46 per cent between 1929 and the cyclical low in spring 1935, whilst share values declined by 60 per cent. Industrial production was reduced by around a quarter, with such key sectors of heavy industry as steel making experiencing a 40 per cent decline, whilst consumer goods producers, with the notable exception of textiles, suffered far less. Declining sales and falling profits were an evident disincentive to industrial investment. The unwillingness of manufacturers to replace old machinery reduced productivity and caused a 37 per cent decline in the production of industrial equipment. Certainly, in terms of unemployment, France suffered far less than Britain, Germany and the United States. Even if it is accepted that the official figure of registered unemployment needed to be doubled and that real unemployment was around 1 million, concentrated especially in the Paris region, this constituted only about 2.6 per cent of the population, compared with maxima of 7.6, 9.4 and 12.75 per cent, respectively, in the three leading industrial nations. Of course, these statistics all conceal withdrawals from the labour force, especially by older workers and women, the repatriation of immigrants and substantial underemployment due to reductions in working hours. Nevertheless, as prices fell, many of those who remained in work enjoyed substantial improvements in their real incomes. Levels of personal consumption remained surprisingly high, largely because the nominal fall in national income of around one-third between 1929 and the depths of the crisis in 1935 was partly compensated for by a 20 per cent decline in retail prices.

This could not prevent the development of an intense sense of insecurity, however, as employers constantly tried to reduce their costs. Moreover, the impact of the crisis obviously varied between social groups. Most adversely affected were the mass of small-scale peasant farmers, as real incomes from agriculture fell by 32 per cent. Many industrial workers enjoyed an increase in real incomes, though they were more aware of declining wage rates and the threat of unemployment. Business profits fell by around 18 per cent, affecting most notably the mass of small manufacturers and shopkeepers, whilst the real incomes of landlords and *rentiers* with fixed incomes tended to rise. In general, the wealthy retained their privileged position, but in a society characterised by growing social and political tension. At least the cinema and popular music offered relatively cheap distraction from the problems of daily life. Major successes included the songs of Edith Piaf and Charles Trenet and films directed by René Clair and Marcel Pagnol. These appealed to a taste for drama and romance, whilst the comedian Fernandel offered humour. Imported American films were generally condemned as puerile by intellectuals. Such supremely escapist movies as *42nd Street* (1933), *Broadway Melody* (1936) and *Snow White* (1938) nevertheless enjoyed much greater commercial success than the bulk of unimaginative home-grown products.

A constant feature of the decade was governmental weakness. Politicians and economists – and not just in France – felt helpless, simply reacting to problems as they occurred. Although renewed budgetary deficits were a consequence rather than a cause of the depression, governments continued to be obsessed with the need to achieve balance and engaged in deflationary policies, which further reduced demand. The multiplicity of parties and weak party discipline ensured that they were at the mercy of shifting parliamentary coalitions and that ministers spent most of their time trying to manipulate deputies. There were to be forty-two administrations in the inter-war period, each averaging only six months in power and clearly unable to adopt a long-term perspective. The electoral system gave disproportionate power to the rural and small-town electorate generally opposed to social reform – perceived as most likely to benefit the urban worker – and to the taxation necessary to fund such measures. Voters tended to favour the Radicals, whose deputies, if they did not always lead, played a crucial role in the formation of every government. Although the party posed as being of the left, its members were unalterably conservative on economic and social questions. Parliamentary deputies, drawn overwhelmingly from the liberal professions, made considerable efforts to secure their constituencies by concentrating on local issues and seeking favours from ministers for their constituents.

Certainly, governmental instability was partly offset by bureaucratic stability, but the effect of this was to ensure a dominant role in policy formulation for senior officials drawn from the upper classes and inhibited by caution and respect for routine. This was a system of government peculiarly unsuited to coping with major crises and unable to contemplate, much less accept, the proposals for planning and a mixed economy coming from apolitical or even conservative technocrats such as Auguste Detoeuf, president of the electrical engineering company Thomson, or economists such as Alfred Sauvy, inspired by a mixture of moral and scientific ideas, as well as from reformist trades unionists such as Léon Jouhaux, secretary

general of the CGT. A right committed to the free market and a left
that conceived of the state as simply the agent of oppression both
rejected such reformist ideas. As a result, the 1930s would see a
growing loss of confidence in the regime.

The incoherence of government policy was undoubtedly evident in
the case of agriculture. Initially, as prices fell, protection was offered to
domestic producers through increased tariffs. The response to the
bountiful harvests of 1932 and 1933 was simply to falsify the statistics
to avoid alarming the market. Nevertheless, prices continued to fall,
and by June 1933 wheat, at F85 a quintal, was half its 1929 price. The
next step, in July 1933, was to impose a minimum price of F115. The
funds provided were inadequate, as were the facilities available to
stock surpluses. This short-lived policy therefore only encouraged
the development of an unofficial market on which wheat could be
purchased for as little as F60 to F70. An effort was also made to reduce
the supply of wine by means of restrictions on planting and an obligatory reduction in acreage, but with little effect on prices. Measures
were also taken to protect small shopkeepers against competition from
chain stores. In the case of the trade deficit, rather than taking measures to stimulate exports – that is, act against the causes – governments
sought to limit the effects by reinforcing protectionism from the summer of 1931. The sense of insecurity was so great that even habitual
free traders, including the representatives of the woollen and silk
industries, were attracted by the prospect of autarky.

In May 1932 a desperate electorate turned towards the left for a
solution. The result was its greatest success since before the war, with
334 deputies returned, including 157 Radicals and 129 Socialists,
compared with 230 on the right. In spite of their rhetoric, however,
Radical ministers, led by Herriot, retained their commitment to
financial orthodoxy. As obsessed as more obvious conservatives by
the need to balance the budget and restore business confidence, they
were determined to reduce government expenditure. They remained
bitterly opposed to increases in taxation, which would, moreover,
have had a negative impact on their small business and peasant
supporters. This was an approach unacceptable to their Socialist
parliamentary allies. Successive ministerial combinations failed to
secure agreement. As the economic crisis deepened, ministers
appeared helpless. The weak-willed resignation of a government

led by Edouard Daladier following serious rioting in Paris on 6 February 1934 allowed the accession to power of an *Union nationale* that included Radicals but was dominated by conservatives and led successively by Gaston Doumergue, Pierre-Etienne Flandin and then Laval. This was even more determined than its predecessors to reduce inflation by means of tough, deflationary measures. It was vested by parliament with 'exceptional powers to ensure the defence of the franc and the struggle against speculation'. Its basic policy was to restore the competitiveness of French producers by reducing their costs. In seeking to achieve this, it brutally cut civil service salaries by 10 per cent, reduced the interest payable on government debt and even decreed reductions in rents and the prices of bread, coal and electricity. Between 1932 and 1935 there were to be eleven governments and fourteen plans for economic recovery, all based upon a combination of deflationary and protectionist measures intended to secure the economic and social status quo. The value of the franc was to be defended at all costs. Unfortunately, the measures taken had the effect of reinforcing economic stagnation. Influence in favour of continuity was also exerted by such representatives of the social élite as senior civil servants, directors of the Bank of France (still privately owned in spite of its central bank functions) and leading industrialists such as the Peugeots, Wendels and Schneiders.

Change was made all the more difficult by political instability, which reflected the fragmentary character of the political system, and the particular weakness of the Radicals, who occupied the crucial centre position, as well as the ease with which undisciplined deputies could abandon governments that had in some way incurred their displeasure. In this situation, politicians were reluctant to propose the substantial economic and social reforms that, in retrospect at least, the crisis would seem to have demanded. Nor were they willing to contemplate a move towards presidentialism in order to strengthen the executive vis-à-vis parliament. At most, they might accept the need to grant temporary decree powers, as during the 1935 financial crisis, in this case to a government led by Laval. To add to their difficulties, governments were also faced with an alarming deterioration in the international situation. At Lausanne in July 1932 the great powers had recognised both Germany's inability to continue to pay reparations and her right to rearm. In January 1933

Adolf Hitler became German chancellor, and in October he with-drew from the Geneva disarmament conference. By June 1934, as French military expenditure reached an all-time low, the government began to feel the need to increase arms procurement.

Amongst the middle classes, and especially the more wealthy and influential, this continuing air of crisis and mounting anxiety con-cerning income and status, together with an awareness of the dete-rioration of the country's global standing, resulted in a growing conviction that democracy had failed. Strong authoritarian govern-ment appeared to many to be the answer to the nation's problems. Once again the call for 'moral order' came from the right, uniting nationalism, clericalism, economic liberalism and anti-Bolshevism. Anti-parliamentary feeling was rekindled by every electoral success the left enjoyed. The élite, those with economic power and substan-tial influence over governments, the civil service and the media, found it hard to accept that people whose objectives conflicted with their own might hold political power. In 1924 this sort of outlook had led to the formation of the Jeunesses patriotes by Pierre Taittinger, organised on a military basis, uniformed and committed to street action. The analogy with fascism can easily be overdrawn, but it should not be ignored, particularly in terms of organisation, objectives and forms of action. Such leagues were to attract growing support during the following decade. The most notable was to be the Croix de feu, initially an old soldiers' organ-isation, but which developed a much broader appeal to the middle classes and at its peak had over 300,000 members. Joining in the rank-and-file revolt against ineffective conservative politicians, it was characterised by a fervent anti-communism and anti-socialism and, whilst expressing support for the established social hierarchy, its spokesmen denounced the political parties as 'lying, parasitical, corrupt, outdated'. From 1928 Henri Dorgères and his Chemises vertes expressed the anguish of many peasants: their desire for lower taxes, for an end to imports, and protection of the values and traditions of rural society. These leagues were the heirs of the extreme nationalistic organisations of the 1880s, and like them were committed to the establishment of authoritarian government to replace the decadent, dishonest and ineffective Republic. They were supported by influential personalities, including the surviving

Plate 6.8 Members of the Croix de feu parade in front of their leader, Lieutenant-Colonel de la Rocque. Founded in 1927 as an ex-soldiers' organisation, from 1933 it recruited more widely and developed para-military structures. © Roger-Viollet/TopFoto.

Marshals of France, and amply provided with funds by the employ-ers' organisations and such leading businessmen as the perfume manufacturer François Coty and the industrialists Ernest Mercier and François Wendel, whose objectives in the early 1930s seem to have included rallying support for Pétain as a potential saviour. Of course, not all ex-soldiers were attracted by the right. Many sub-scribed to the pacifism more typical of the left. Nevertheless, there was a widespread and visceral hatred of politicians and a desire for some kind of a rebirth of the *union sacrée*. The sense of disenchant-ment with the regime was never to be as intense in France as in Germany, however. The economic depression was less severe, and the country had not suffered a catastrophic military defeat.

There were nevertheless certainly moments of intense crisis. Early in 1934 the Stavisky Affair, in which the fraudulent financial activity of a naturalised Ukrainian Jew appeared to involve leading political

Plate 6.9 Members of extreme right-wing organisations clash with police protecting the approaches to the Chamber of Deputies in the Place de la Concorde, 6 February 1934. Around fifteen were killed and over 2,000 injured.

figures, provided an excuse for a campaign by the extreme right that combined all its habitual themes: xenophobia, anti-Semitism, anti-parliamentarianism and hatred of the Republic. The deportation of immigrants was presented as the simple solution to unemployment. A literature of hate attracted growing numbers of readers. On 7 January Action française inaugurated a series of demonstrations, which was to culminate on 6 February in a gathering of the various right-wing leagues in Paris. On that occasion, when groups in the crowd attempted to break through the cordon protecting the approaches to the Chamber of Deputies, police panicked and opened fire, killing fifteen demonstrators. Over 2,000 were injured in the mêlée.

Deserted by the leaders of his own party, the Radical prime minister, Daladier, resigned, creating a dangerous precedent by giving way to pressure from the streets. His replacement, Doumergue, was brought out of retirement to restore order and additionally to reform the political system. Pétain would briefly serve as war minister.

Instead of pressing for the strengthening of executive authority in the immediate aftermath of 6 February, however, when such proposals would have gained widespread support, Doumergue allowed himself to be deflected by squabbles between the Radical and conservative members of his administration. The former were suspicious of a so-called 'Bonapartist' solution to the crisis. The latter included most notably Tardieu, who as a member of previous governments actually appears to have channelled funds to the *ligues*. The Senate too, with its habitual irresponsibility, made known its opposition to proposals that would have reduced its ability to bring down governments. Doumergue and his successor Laval, as a short-term measure, could only attempt to restore business confidence by balancing the budget. In 1935 they reduced government expenditure by measures that included cutting pensions, employing emergency decree powers to avoid parliamentary debate. The crisis of the liberal state was becoming ever more intense.

In the slightly longer term, however, the most important consequence of 6 February was to be the formation of the Front populaire, as those parties most committed to the democratic Republic, or frightened by what they saw as an attempted fascist coup, rallied to its defence. There were, of course, major obstacles to the formation of a broad alliance of the left. In the immediate aftermath of 6 February, and with Radical ministers in the Doumergue government, the various groups continued to hurl abuse at each other. In the past efforts to collaborate had always ended in a rancorous atmosphere of mutual recrimination. The Socialists were extremely suspicious of new proposals to cooperate, whilst the Radicals and Communists were poles apart. Committed to class conflict and convinced that the Great Depression was the last major crisis of the capitalist system, the Communists were particularly hostile to the Socialist 'traitors', who, they claimed, were attempting, through reformism, to divert the working class from its true revolutionary goal. Only at the end of June did the Communist leader Maurice Thorez, following instructions from Stalin – increasingly alarmed by the growing fascist threat – open the way for the formation of the Popular Front by calling for an alliance of all democrats. Together with a super-patriotic Jacobin dedication to national defence, which lasted until the signature of the Nazi–Soviet Pact in August 1939, this was the means by which his party could escape from the isolation and ineffectiveness that had resulted from its class-war tactics. In July an agreement was negotiated with the Socialists for mutual support in the struggle against fascism, war and the deflationary policies of the Doumergue government. Much to the surprise of the Socialists, and the discomfort of the Radicals, this was followed by a call from Thorez for an alliance between the working and middle classes. With unity against the international menace of fascism as the essential objective, the Communists were determined not to frighten the Radicals and were prepared to tone down their distinctive revolutionary programme.

The decision by the Radicals to enter the Popular Front depended on the outcome of an internal struggle between the followers of Herriot, an opponent of cooperation, and the so-called 'Young Turks' of the party, including Jean Zay, Jacques Kayser, Pierre Cot and Pierre Mendès-France, supported by Daladier and strengthened by growing disenchantment with the existing alliance with the parties of the right. Agreement to cooperate was finally reached in June 1935, and on 14 July the three parties of the left celebrated the anniversary of the taking of the Bastille by uniting in a mass demonstration in Paris. Furthermore, they established a committee to organise collaboration for the April/May 1936 electoral campaign. The main obstacles to agreement appear to have been the formulation of an economic policy dealing with the means of financing social reforms, the scale of nationalisation and the question of devaluation. The moderation of the compromise that emerged made it obvious that the essential objective of the Popular Front was the defence of republican institutions. It was profoundly disappointing for all those who had seen the unity of the left as opening the way for fundamental economic and social change, but little more could really have been expected when the parties to the agreement were so suspicious of each other.

The electoral campaign opened in April 1936 and was notable for the use made by party spokesmen of the radio to increase public awareness of the issues. For the first ballot each of the parties belonging to the Popular Front retained its own candidates and programme, much of which was in flagrant disagreement with aspects of the joint programme the parties had agreed to present for the second ballot. Thus the Socialists promised substantial nationalisation and abolition of the Senate, both of which were anathema to most Radicals.

Plate 6.10 Léon Blum with members of his new Popular Front government outside the Elysée Palace in 1936. Hulton Archive. Photo: Keystone/ Getty Images.

Internally the party was divided both over tactics, for which, as always, there was a glaring contradiction between the party's revolutionary rhetoric and reformist proposals, and on such fundamental questions as whether it should drop its policy of non-participation in coalition governments if the alliance succeeded at the polls. The Communists offered the only reasonably coherent explanation of the economic crisis and could point to the Soviet experiment in planned growth as an apparent solution to the world's ills. Whilst recognising the strength of the rank-and-file working-class desire for unity, and in March agreeing to a merger between the two rival trade union federations, they nevertheless accorded absolute priority to the unity of the anti-fascist movement, for which it was essential to attract middle-class support.

The mutually agreed programme of the left would include proposals to protect republican institutions by means of suppression of the *ligues* and the defence of lay education and of trade union rights.

It attacked the deflationary policies previously pursued and presented measures designed to reduce unemployment and to improve the quality of working-class life. These included a public works programme, higher unemployment relief payments and a reduction in the length of the working day. Together with tax reforms, it was assumed that these policies would help to restore purchasing power and stimulate economic recovery. It was also proposed to assist the rural population by means of official intervention in agricultural markets to secure higher price levels. The foreign policy of a Popular Front government would seek to promote disarmament and collective security through the League of Nations.

In sum, this was a programme inspired by the American New Deal rather than by socialism. It represented a determination to make capitalism work, to humanise social relations and to modernise the state. The only nationalisations proposed, those of the armaments industry and the Bank of France, were inspired by the desire to accelerate the pace of rearmament and to curb the power and influence of key conservative pressure groups. It was a moderate programme, which offered genuine social reform whilst seeking to reassure the small property-owning supporters of the Radical Party. Even so, any hint of measures designed to reduce the power of conservative élites was bound to create a storm of protest, and to stimulate a political mobilisation inspired by arrogance and anxiety. The employment by conservatives of 'the politics of fear' (Jackson) combined the themes found in the manifesto of a Parisian candidate of the Fédération républicaine:

If the Popular Front is victorious;
There will be a flight of capital;
There will be a devaluation leading to total bankruptcy;
There will be anarchy;
There will be war;
For behind the Popular Front lurks the shadow of Moscow.

Initially, the election results were disappointing for the left. On the first ballot the Popular Front parties attracted 5,420,000 votes, only 300,000 more than they had obtained in 1932. The decisive factor was to be the disciplined way in which these voters rallied to the single candidate most likely to succeed in the second ballot, on

3 May. This had the effect of giving the Front a clear majority of 376 seats, compared with 222 for the parties of the right. In addition to solid working-class support the left had also gained voters amongst the lower middle classes and, especially in the south, the rural population. Although a clear swing of the electorate to the left had increased substantially the representation of both the Communists and Socialists in the Chamber, from ten to seventy-two and ninety-seven to 146, respectively, this had occurred partly at the expense of their Radical partners, however, who were reduced from 159 to 116. The survival of Popular Front governments would nevertheless depend on this nervous Radical rump.

On 4 May 1936, as leader of the largest single party, Blum laid claim to leadership of a Popular Front government to be composed essentially of Socialists and Radicals, with the Communists deciding to remain outside on the pretext that their participation might cause panic. Instead, they committed themselves to loyal support, and, as the most radical element in the alliance, enjoyed a tenfold expansion in membership to 300,000 in 1937. In contrast, Blum's basic assumption was that in the absence of a Socialist parliamentary majority he lacked a mandate to introduce fundamental social reform. Together with the realities of an alliance with the Radicals, this allowed for only limited reformist measures. The formation of the government – which for the first time included three women as junior ministers – had created a widespread sense of expectancy, however, evident especially in an unprecedented wave of strikes and factory occupations involving around 2 million workers. The movement was essentially spontaneous and localised. These were euphoric outbursts by workers for whom suddenly everything seemed possible. They were assertions of the dignity of labour, protests against harsh factory discipline, and a demand for better working and living conditions and enhanced security.

Compared with the hopes and fears the government had inspired, the measures actually introduced in the summer of 1936 were nonetheless moderate and dictated by circumstances, especially by the need to bring the strikes to an end. On the night of 7/8 June representatives of the employers and of the CGT met and signed the Matignon agreements. Both sides were frightened by their inability to control the workers' movements. They agreed on wage increases of 7 to 15 per cent, partly as a means of increasing purchasing power and stimulating economic recovery, and on recognition of trades unions' negotiating rights. These measures were to be supplemented by legislation providing, for the first time, the right to two weeks' paid holiday a year and a forty-hour week, intended both to improve the quality of working-class life and to contribute to the reduction of unemployment. To extend the benefits of the new regime to the rural population, an official marketing agency (the Office national du blé) was to be created as a mechanism to stabilise and raise cereal prices. Less effective measures were taken to ensure that the Bank of France placed the national interest before that of its shareholders, whilst nationalisation of the armaments factories only added to the state of disorganisation in which they existed under private control. Blum had succeeded in provoking feelings of intense anxiety within the ranks of industrialists and financiers without increasing the government's ability to control their activities effectively.

The probably inevitable result was to disappoint many of the Communist and Socialist supporters of the Popular Front, who condemned what they saw as Blum's excessive legalism. At the same time, Radicals were disturbed by what had already been achieved. To operate within a basically liberal economic framework and yet to introduce measures that threatened business confidence was to court disaster. In the absence of exchange controls, unacceptable to the Radicals, there was a massive outflow of capital abroad. Employers' efforts to minimise the impact of the Matignon agreements led to heightened social tension, whilst the measures themselves increased costs significantly, reducing international competitiveness and provoking internal inflation. By September the devaluation of the franc (by 30 per cent), which the government had promised to reject, had become unavoidable. In the event it did little to increase the competitiveness of French firms, suffering as they were from sustained underinvestment. In January 1937, in an effort to restore business confidence and to reduce the strains with his Radical allies, Blum announced a 'pause' in the government's programme of social reform. This would do little to head off the growing conservative backlash. Further tensions within the alliance were to be caused by the decision to commit substantial resources to rearmament in response to German remilitarisation of the Rhineland and over the question of whether to support the embattled Spanish Republic. When Blum asked for emergency powers to deal with the continued deterioration in the financial situation, these were voted by the Chamber of Deputies but rejected by the Senate. Blum resigned on 20 June 1937.

From then until the autumn of 1938 the Popular Front underwent a process of gradual disintegration as relationships between its constituent parts deteriorated. Initially, as its parliamentary majority had survived the departure of Blum, the president of the Republic felt obliged to call upon the Radical Camille Chautemps to form a government, which would include Blum and other Socialists until their final withdrawal in January 1938. Unable either to reverse or proceed with reforms, Chautemps did little more than preside helplessly over new strike waves, a worsening in the balance of payments and the growth of budget deficits, due to the combined effect of increased military expenditure and falling tax receipts. Nationalisation of the railway companies to create the Société nationale des chemins de fer français (SNCF) was simply a means of rescuing them from bankruptcy and on terms extremely favourable to their shareholders. In March Hitler annexed Austria, as French politicians grappled with the internal political crisis caused by the Socialists' unwillingness to support Chautemps' request for decree powers to deal with the country's financial problems, and his subsequent resignation.

The rules of the parliamentary game required the Socialists to attempt to form another administration. Blum called for a government of national unity to prepare for a war that was beginning to seem inevitable. Determined to finish finally with the Popular Front, conservatives rejected this immediately. The second Popular Front government formed by Blum was doomed from birth, and its leader's proposals to introduce exchange controls and a capital tax only hastened its demise. President Albert Lebrun called on the Radical leader Daladier to form a government in which the Socialists were not represented, although, in the hope of keeping the anti-fascist front alive, the parties of the left combined to pass a vote of confidence in the new ministry. Dissension over the Munich agreement, bitterly condemned by the Communists, would finally bring a formal end to an already insubstantial Popular Front.

Daladier's term of office was to be dominated by the deteriorating
international situation, and by efforts to restore internal order. He
relied upon liberal economic mechanisms to promote economic
recovery. Determined action was taken against strikers, however,
both by the police and by employers anxious to root out 'troublemakers'. It soon became clear that this was a government that
depended on parliamentary support from the right, and that its
strongest card was its much-trumpeted anti-communism. On 1
November 1938 the newspaper *L'Ere nouvelle* could emphasise
with delight that 'the revolution of June '36 is well and truly over'.
The language used is indicative of the degree to which the Popular
Front had both reflected and, above all, stimulated a process of
political polarisation. The hopes aroused on the left and amongst
workers had created an apocalyptic vision of revolutionary anarchy
on the right and amongst the property-owning classes, feeding on
resentment of a government whose policies seemed to favour the
workers at the expense of the middle class. Parallels were drawn
between Blum and Aleksandr Kerensky, their actions preparing the
way for Bolshevism. The Popular Front was denounced as both a
Jewish and a Communist plot. A group of extremist army officers
organised as the Comité secret d'action révolutionnaire, but better
known as the Cagoule, even planned a coup d'état. Although this
was uncovered by the police in November 1937, it is significant that
such military eminences as the retired marshals Pétain and Louis
Franchet d'Esperey, aware of what was happening, did not see it as
their duty to report matters to the authorities. Another feature of this
movement of resistance to communism was the creation of new
parties on the extreme right. Banned along with the other *ligues* in
June 1936, the Croix de feu transformed itself into the Parti social
français and attracted between 600,000 and 800,000 members with
its demands for strong, authoritarian government. More clearly
fascist in character was the Parti populaire français, with briefly
some 200,000 members, created by the former communist Jacques
Doriot. The political atmosphere was poisoned by a wave of verbal
and occasionally physical violence. Anti-Semitism was once again
becoming part of normal political discourse, particularly in conservative and Catholic circles, with even mainstream politicians such as
Tardieu and Laval echoing the sentiments of the extreme right. To its

credit, in April 1939 the government introduced legislation – later repealed by the Vichy regime – making incitement to racial or religious hatred in the press an offence.

It was against this background of bitter internal disunity that the Daladier government sought to cope with the crisis caused by continuing economic depression, and by a deteriorating international situation. Industrial production continued to fall in the early months of 1938. In September the British and French prime ministers, Neville Chamberlain and Daladier, abandoned Czechoslovakia to its fate, as the price, they hoped, of securing peace. On their return from humiliation at Munich the vast majority of their fellow citizens had greeted the two prime ministers as heroes. Whilst believing that the time had come to stand up to Germany, even Blum felt what he described as 'cowardly relief'. There was a desperate desire not to repeat the slaughter of 1914. As well as anti-communists on the left, conservatives continued to associate war with revolution. Traumatised by 1936, many conservatives also saw Nazi Germany as a welcome barrier to the bolshevisation of Europe. Daladier, concerned about French military inferiority and unable to act independently of the British or to ignore the overwhelming weight of public opinion, nevertheless appears to have had few illusions. Moreover, in the aftermath of Munich the British were finally prepared to face up to the possibility of a renewed Continental commitment and to commence high-level military discussions with the French. Internally, and in the interests of national defence, governmental authority was reasserted. Numerous exceptions to the forty-hour working week were allowed and compulsory overtime introduced. Furthermore, the Senate was prepared to grant to Daladier the emergency powers it had refused to Blum. In supporting employers against strikers, the government participated in the counter-attack against workers who had briefly challenged their exclusive right to manage their enterprises. This victory over the forces of the Popular Front, together with the stimulus afforded by rearmament, undoubtedly contributed to the restoration of business confidence and to the beginnings of economic recovery evident from the autumn of 1938.

The German occupation of what remained of Czechoslovakia in March 1939 finally provoked a major shift in public opinion. In July an opinion poll claimed that 70 per cent of the population was opposed to further concessions to Germany. Previous weakness in response to Hitler's claims, beginning with acceptance of German rearmament in 1935, had only encouraged further demands. A new strategy seemed essential. It was agreed to guarantee the territorial integrity of Poland as a means of discouraging further German expansion. British suspicion of the Russians, however, prevented the creation of an alliance, which alone might have made the guarantee militarily effective. Tired of Western procrastination, and suspicious of their motives, Stalin signed an agreement with the Germans on 23 August 1939, which sealed the fate of Poland. It also, of course, meant that, in comparison with the situation in 1914, France would enter this war as part of a considerably weaker military alliance.

THE SECOND WORLD WAR

When war came on 3 September, following the German invasion of Poland, there were few signs of enthusiasm. Memories of the previous carnage were only too fresh. The additional prospect of aerial bombardment terrified many, including Daladier. Conservatives in particular resigned themselves reluctantly to a conflict that, by weakening Britain, France and Germany, threatened to serve the interests of the Soviet Union. Their concern was intensified when the French Communist Party, belatedly receiving new instructions from Moscow, turned on 20 September from being the most active supporter of the anti-fascist cause into an outright opponent of a war that, it was now claimed, was the outcome of imperialist rivalry and of no concern to the working class. The Party was proscribed for its pains and its parliamentary representatives imprisoned. The declaration of war was followed by a lengthy period of relative inaction, the 'phoney war'. Solidly entrenched behind the fortifications of the Maginot Line, the French, with their British allies, remained on the defensive whilst the Poles, in whose interests they were supposedly fighting, were crushed. They appear to have avoided offensive action, which might, irrevocably, have committed them to war. Strategic thinking was based on the assumption that a long war would permit an accumulation of military strength, drawing once again on the industrial resources of the United States, at the same time as Germany was weakened by a maritime blockade.

The apparent absence of danger only encouraged internal political dissent, in marked contrast to the *union sacrée* of 1914. On 19 March 1940 Daladier was forced to resign by a parliamentary vote of no confidence. He was blamed for the lack of military action, and by the right for the failure to rush to the defence of Finland against the Red Army. This possibility had been actively considered by the Allies and would have involved them, of course, in a war of almost inconceivable danger with both Nazi Germany and Soviet Russia. An apparently more dynamic figure, Reynaud, took Daladier's place. Nevertheless, the former prime minister continued to serve as defence minister in a Cabinet enlarged to include the representatives of as many political opinions as possible. The French war effort was to be beset by personal rivalries between ministers and military leaders, and by the absence of clear objectives. Whilst the Allies plotted peripheral operations against Soviet oil installations and Scandinavian iron ore supplies to Germany in order to deprive it of the means of waging war, they were taken by surprise by the German invasions of Denmark and Norway, and then by the opening of the Wehrmacht's offensive in the west on 10 May 1940.

The French high command, in spite of the apparent confidence of General Gamelin, was singularly ill-prepared to meet a German assault spearheaded by concentrations of aircraft and tanks. It was those senior officers, including Pétain, who had exercised considerable influence on military planning throughout the inter-war years who bore the heaviest responsibility for the defeat of 1940. The experience of the previous war had convinced them that modern weapons offered the advantage to the defence. Subsequently, they would lay the blame for defeat on the politicians, who had in fact from 1934 onwards sanctioned large increases in military expenditure. The Maginot Line, to which substantial portions of the defence budget had been committed between 1930 and 1936, was designed to maximise the advantages of entrenched armies. It was not extended to cover the northern frontier even after the Belgian decision to opt for neutrality in 1936, and little else was done to prepare defensive positions along either the route taken by the invading German armies in 1914 or in front of the hills and forests of the Belgian Ardennes, assumed to be impenetrable to large masses of troops. In the event of a second German failure to respect Belgian neutrality it was assumed that the relatively light

Plate 6.11 Paul Reynaud leaving a Cabinet meeting, 21 May 1940. Within two weeks his companions Marshal Pétain, the deputy prime minister, and General Weygand, the commander-in-chief, would be pressing for an armistice. Photo: Keystone/Hulton Archive/Getty Images.

manning of the Maginot Line would allow a concentration of man-power for the defence of Belgium and northern France.

   In practice, the Allied forces that advanced into Belgium to meet the invasion were outflanked by German divisions, which passed through the Ardennnes and on 10 May launched an offensive that, in three days, broke the weakly held French line at Dinant and Sedan. From the French point of view, the Germans had attacked in the wrong place! The crisis that ensued showed up the deficiencies of the high command, as well as the lack of effective coordination of the activities of the French and the relatively small British army. The successive commanders-in-chief, Maurice Gamelin and Maxime Weygand, and General Georges command-ing the crucial north-eastern front, were old and tired, and out of touch with the realities of modern warfare. Nothing appeared to have been learnt from the *blitzkrieg*, which had so rapidly smashed the Polish army the previous September, or, indeed, from the brilliantly successful counter-attack that had rolled back the German assault in March 1918. The French air force was both ill-equipped, partly due to the inefficiency of the aircraft industry, and poorly led. British aircraft were present only in small numbers. There was little appreciation of the offensive potential of concen-trations of tanks, and the substantial numbers available were largely dispersed in support of the infantry. Attempts to halt the German advance by means of the piecemeal commitment of inad-equate reserves were doomed to failure. In spite of serious deficien-cies in the air it was indecision at the top, incoherent command structures, ineffective communications, inappropriate tactics and poor training rather than inferior numbers or materials that led to rapid and total collapse and that lost the Battle of France. Orthodox operational planning and the commitment to method-ical preparation and a continuous front meant that senior French officers were intellectually unprepared to cope with a fluid and fast-moving encounter battle. They were rapidly overwhelmed by events. The evacuation of 329,000 British and French troops from Dunkirk signalled the final disintegration of the Allies' most effec-tive fighting force. Subsequent efforts by Weygand to establish new defensive lines on the rivers Aisne and Somme, deploying greatly outnumbered forces, were, as he realised, destined for failure.

In five weeks the Germans took 1,850,000 prisoners, who would mostly remain in prisoner of war camps, in effect as hostages, for the next five years. Some 92,000 servicemen were killed, a figure that testifies to the intensity of fighting in some sectors, but that was low in comparison with the murderous battles of the previous war. The roads towards the south were blocked by hordes of miserable refugees, as perhaps between 6 and 7 million people left their homes and tried to escape from the expanding war zone, inspired in part by bitter memories of the previous German occupation. Essential services collapsed as officials left their posts and joined in the exodus. To prevent its destruction, Paris was declared to be an 'open city'. The Government first moved to Tours and eventually to Bordeaux. In desperation, Reynaud sacked generals and reshuffled his Cabinet. The appointment of a virtually unknown protégé of his, one General Charles de Gaulle, an expert on armoured warfare, as a junior defence minister was of little immediate significance. Far more important was the inclusion of the revered Marshal Pétain as deputy prime minister. By 12 June, and supported by Weygand the new commander-in-chief, the Anglophobic Marshal of France was demanding an armistice. Weygand, a traditionalist Catholic, contemptuous of politicians, appears to have been obsessed by the need to safeguard the honour of the army, and, as in 1871, to preserve it intact as the means of securing social order and preventing a communist takeover. With the peculiar arrogance of the soldier posing as the guardian of the nation's soul, he vigorously opposed Reynaud's proposal that the defeated army should capitulate to avoid further useless sacrifice. This would have left the government with 'freedom of action'. Amongst the possibilities mooted were the creation of a Breton redoubt and continuing the war from north Africa. Symptomatic of the final collapse of civilian authority, Weygand announced that he would simply refuse to obey orders to this effect. Even as the struggle continued, blame for its outcome was being apportioned. Pétain condemned the Popular Front as the symbol and cause of national decadence. There can be little real doubt, however, that the main reason for defeat was the generals' own incompetence.

On 16 June an exhausted and rather browbeaten Reynaud resigned in favour of Pétain. The following day the Marshal

announced his intention to seek an armistice. His decision undoubtedly reflected a widespread belief that there was no alternative.
A fight to the last, which would have devastated France, could hardly
be contemplated. In this calamitous hour the old hero of Verdun,
around whom a potent myth had been created, appeared to his
compatriots as a potential saviour. His offer of 'the gift of my person,
to attenuate her suffering', made to the nation during the broadcast
announcing the armistice request, was received with deep emotion
and gratitude. Although the ceasefire was not to take effect until 25
June organised resistance effectively came to an end. The war
appeared lost beyond all hope. It was generally assumed that, if the
mighty French army could not resist the Germans, then, and in the
very near future, the British would also be forced to sue for peace.
Even Winston Churchill, the British prime minister, still dependent
on the appeasers in his government, and aware of David Lloyd
George positioning himself as a focus for discontented defeatists,
considered this possibility. In this situation, it was hardly surprising
that the departure of an obscure general, de Gaulle, the undersecre-
tary at the War Office, from Bordeaux to London on 17 June and his
establishment of a French National Committee pledged to act as 'the
provisional guardian of the national patrimony' went almost unno-
ticed. The vast majority of officials and those army officers not
demobilised or in prisoner of war camps remained loyally at their
posts in France itself and throughout the Empire. Those servicemen
who found themselves on British territory when France surrendered
almost all decided on repatriation rather than continuing the struggle. The British attack on the French fleet at Mers-el-Kebir on 3/4 July
1940, designed to ensure that it would never come under German
control, and which caused 1,297 deaths, aroused considerable hostility towards the former ally.

The armistice terms were certainly harsh. They were alleviated
only by the German concern to prevent continued French participation in the war. For this reason, it was clearly in their interests that the
French government should retain an appearance of sovereignty and
that it should remain in France rather than seek refuge in Britain or
the Empire. Furthermore, by means of a quasi-colonial system of
indirect rule, employing the French administration and police, the
demands made upon German manpower would be decreased

Figure 6.1 The division of France in 1940. (Source: J.-P. Azema, *From Munich to the Liberation, 1938–44.* Cambridge University Press, 1984.)

substantially. The French army was to be reduced to 100,000 men, equipped only to safeguard internal order. That portion of the fleet in home ports was to be demobilised. A substantial part of France, the most densely populated and productive, was to be occupied and an enormous levy imposed to meet the costs of the occupiers.

The subordinate position of the French government was made clear immediately when in August 1940, and in apparent contradiction of the armistice agreement, Alsace and Lorraine were once more annexed to the Reich and subjected to conscription – affecting some 130,000 young men – and an intense programme of Germanisation. German settlers were also to be introduced into the contiguous reserved zone, whilst the industrial areas of the Nord and Pas-de-Calais were to be

Plate 6.12 The (re-)Germanisation of Alsace: a Nazi parade in Strasbourg in October 1941. Young men became liable for conscription into the German armed forces. Photo: Taillandier.

controlled by the military command in Brussels. In the years that followed, German demands were to become ever more exorbitant and to involve the systematic exploitation of the French economy. The return to 'normal', which so many desperately desired, was not to occur. The obvious reason for this was that the war did not end. Unexpectedly, the British kept on fighting. Unable to win air superiority, the Germans failed to launch a cross-channel invasion and were eventually to turn east in search of *lebensraum*. If, in the short term, the essential concern of the occupying power was to make use of French resources and maintain a secure base for military action, in the longer term, and once final victory had been secured, France was to become the market garden and playground of Europe. In the meantime, it seemed better to keep the French in ignorance of these intentions and to encourage them to bargain in an effort to improve their position within a German-dominated Europe.

The defeat was blamed on national decadence by many French people, particularly, but not exclusively, those on the political right.

It did provide a historic opportunity for change, however. The man to whom the nation now looked for leadership, Marshal Pétain, was attracted by the notion of strong, authoritarian government, like so many military men. He had nothing but contempt for politicians and parliamentary politics. His government established itself, from 1 July, in the cramped and unsuitable hotel rooms of the spa town of Vichy. It expected to return to Paris soon, and most civil servants remained in the capital. On 10 July Pétain was charged to draft a new constitution by a demoralised National Assembly, and had been granted in the meantime, by 569 votes to eighty, 'full executive and legislative powers...without restriction'. He and his advisors began to plan a 'national revolution'. The 'constitutional acts' promulgated in July concentrated in the person of the Marshal the powers of both president and prime minister, with the right to designate his own successor and, in the absence of an elected assembly, the ability to exercise legislative powers through a Council of Ministers made up of his own nominees. Immensely flattered by the popular adulation he was receiving, Pétain was determined to rule in spite of his advanced years (he was eighty-four in 1940). He would remain politically alert. His close collaborators, mostly military men or senior civil servants, would compete for influence, much like royal courtiers. This was to cause considerable frustration amongst his younger associates, many of them technocrats, such as Pierre Pucheu and François Lehideux, successively ministers of industrial production, attracted by the prospect of employing the potential of an *authoritarian* regime in order to achieve economic modernisation. As his deputy he selected Laval, the archetypal Third Republic political manipulator and four times prime minister. Laval had little time for high-flown notions of national regeneration. He was a pragmatist, determined to establish better relations with Germany, whilst at the same time preserving as much as possible of French sovereignty. His ambition led to his dismissal in December 1940, but after April 1942, with German support, he was to become the dominant figure in the Vichy regime, although there is no doubt that major policy decisions still required support from the Marshal.

Pétain's own outlook can be summed up by the formula 'Work, family, homeland' (*Travail, famille, patrie*), which replaced the familiar republican device *Liberté, fraternité, égalité*. His dream was to restore the virtues of hard work, honesty, a sense of family loyalty and community, and respect for one's social superiors, which he imagined had previously existed. Rather than fascism, the dominant note in government statements was the traditionalism associated with right-wing movements such as Action française and paternalistic social Catholicism. In many respects it echoed the Moral Order regime of the 1870s, which had also been established after a humiliating defeat. Even such anti-German nationalists as General Weygand could support what they believed were measures essential to national regeneration whilst condemning the sort of indiscipline typified by de Gaulle's defiance of the legitimate French government.

Out of a mass of confused and often contradictory designs, the intentions of the more dedicated adherents of the regime can be discerned. They had been granted the opportunity to implement an often long-held political agenda. Above all, there was a continuing conservative desire for strong government as an answer to the threat of social revolution, of which the Popular Front had been only the most recent manifestation. The social élite wanted the protection of private property, social harmony and order. They were united in their hostility to those blamed for the national humiliation, including Jews, freemasons, and 'Bolsheviks'. These were to be excluded from the national community and stripped of positions in the civil service (some 35,000 dismissals) and professions. A cultural revolution was ordained in which the proper instruction of the young was regarded as being of central importance. Through this, the standing of existing élites, as well as their 'natural' leadership roles, would be secured by restricting the already limited entry to secondary education and by a reaffirmation of its exclusive classical basis. Other social groups would receive an instruction that did not excite unrealisable ambitions. Teachers who wished to retain their positions were obliged to preach the virtues of the regime. Parental responsibilities were also emphasised and efforts made to reduce the number of women working outside the home and to glorify the roles of housewife and mother. Only growing labour shortages halted the dismissal of married women from the public service.

Initially at least, the Vichy regime enjoyed widespread support from a public traumatised by the speed and scale of defeat. There was no real alternative. Pétain's government was, furthermore, the legitimate successor to the discredited Third Republic. More than this, though, the Marshal assumed near mystical qualities as the father and saviour of his people, in the 'appalling situation' resulting from the fact that 'the fate of France no longer depends on the French' (Bloch). He alone promised protection from the invader. A personality cult was manufactured and sustained through posters and songs, in the controlled spheres of the press, radio and newsreel, in all manner of mementos, by means of Pétain's provincial tours, in the schools and youth groups, and in public festivals such as the one – its meaning, to say the least, ambiguous – that glorified Joan of Arc. By means of the interception of letters and the tapping of telephone lines, the regime was also determined to ensure that it was informed about the state of public opinion.

The combination of what appeared to be complete and utter defeat with the desire to preserve some semblance of normality seems to have persuaded most of the population to take refuge in the privacy of home and work, and to seek to make the best of things. Some groups appear to have been more supportive of the regime than others. These included big business, traditional landowning élites, senior civil servants and many of the local notables, who as mayors continued to play an important role in local administration. In particular, Catholics welcomed the regime's adoption of the Church's teaching on morality, the family and the importance of spiritual values, and its benevolent attitude towards religious education. Defeat appeared to represent divine punishment. This was the moment for the people to prove themselves worthy of forgiveness and to turn away from a selfish materialism and towards God. Cardinal Gerlier, Archbishop of Lyon, affirmed that 'if we had remained victorious, we would possibly have remained the prisoners of our errors. Through being secularised, France was in danger of death.' Although individual priests would censure Vichy and German policies, and especially the treatment of the Jews, the hierarchy would, in the opportunistic manner so typical of the Church, generally remain loyal to the regime, offering consolation but only rarely moral leadership. As late as February 1944 the bishops would denounce resistance as 'terrorism'.

Plate 6.13 Marshal Pétain and Pierre Laval at Vichy in November 1942 accompanied by Cardinals Suhard and Gerlier. As in the 1870s following a previous catastrophic defeat, Church and state sought to collaborate in the re-establishment of 'moral order'. © Roger-Viollet/TopFoto.

Nevertheless, there was to be a continuous tension between the regime's traditionalist ideology and the practical problems involved in meeting the organisational and material needs of a modern urban society, as well as satisfying the insatiable demands of the occupier. The economy was to be increasingly subordinated to German interests. By 1943 15 per cent of agricultural and 40 per cent of industrial output was exported to Germany and largely paid for by the French themselves in the form of occupation costs, made all the more burdensome by the overvaluation of the mark for exchange purposes. In that year French payments to Germany are estimated to have accounted for 36.6 per cent of the country's national income and to have amounted to the equivalent of one-quarter of Germany's pre-war gross national product, a figure that does not include the contribution made by the large numbers of French workers employed in Germany or the goods and services consumed by German troops in France. Indeed, taking account of demand from the occupying forces, perhaps one-third of the French labour force was employed in meeting German needs. In effect, France was making a massive contribution to the German war effort. In order to achieve this, the government, whilst promoting the virtues of rural society, and encouraging the revival of folklore and the 'return to the soil' as the essential bulwarks against the advance of materialism, was obliged to promote *remembrement* – that is, the consolidation of small farms – in order to increase productivity. The peasant *corporation* created in December 1940 as a means of producer self-regulation rapidly turned into a bureaucratic machine for official intervention in the market, to establish production quotas and set prices – at levels that peasants were determined to ignore.

In industry, too, insatiable German demands called for a degree of planning, particularly of the distribution of raw materials, that required much closer cooperation between the state and big business. The economic planning that some economists had previously declared might be a remedy for the pre-war crisis had become a necessity, and was to be reinforced substantially after the liberation to meet the equally pressing needs of reconstruction. The paternalistic rhetoric, and the corporatist structures enshrined in the Labour Charter, which were supposed to unite master and man and overcome class conflict, became effectively a cover for policies overwhelmingly favourable to employers. Trades union federations were banned in August 1940, and the few strikes that did occur – such as that in the Nord in May 1941, through which miners protested about the sharp deterioration in their living conditions and the pronounced intensification of workplace discipline – were brutally repressed. Many employers welcomed what they saw as revenge for the Popular Front and the restoration of their freedom to manage. For those with scarce commodities to sell, whether foodstuffs to the French, or champagne, shoes, aircraft, locomotives, motor vehicles or cement to the Germans, this was a time of rare opportunity. In an otherwise depressed economy, frequently the inducements to work for the occupier were irresistible. Productivity nonetheless fell substantially, as a result of labour shortages and the demoralisation of a poorly nourished workforce.

The return of Laval to government in April 1942 symbolised the victory of the pragmatists over the traditionalists and the practical abandonment of the dream. Although, until the end, the regime continued to benefit enormously from the personal prestige of

Marshal Pétain, the motive force behind its activities increasingly changed from that of the restoration of France to participation in an increasingly desperate German-led crusade against the Bolshevik menace to Europe. At the outset only a small number of extreme right-wing politicians, such as Marcel Déat and Doriot, and avowedly fascist intellectuals, such as Robert Brasillach, Pierre Drieu La Rochelle and Louis-Ferdinand Céline, had openly welcomed German victory. They were as contemptuous of the traditional conservative values that the new government espoused as they had been of the former liberal democratic regime, and were to be kept at arm's length by Vichy until towards the end. They constituted the hard core of committed 'collaborationists'. For the Germans they were a useful threat, the basis for a possible alternative government, which could be used to put pressure on Vichy.

Initially, Paris, with its German subsidised newspapers, had provided the main focus of collaborationist activity. Former outsiders appear to have relished suddenly being invited to share the charms of Parisian high society. Doriot's Parti populaire français helped to organise the Anti-Bolshevik Legion of some 12,500 French volunteers, who were to fight, in German uniform, against the Russians. Amongst these French fascists, however, only Déat and Joseph Darnand were ultimately to achieve ministerial office in December 1943, as, respectively, minister of labour and secretary general for the maintenance of order, although some sympathisers, including Pucheu (minister of industry and then interior), Jacques Benoist-Méchin (responsible for relations with Germany) and Ferdinand Marion (propaganda minister), also held key governmental positions. They came into their own only as the traditionalist conservatives began to appreciate that the war was likely to end in defeat for Germany and started to desert.

Of course, collaboration was not simply a matter for politicians. The entire population had to adapt to German rule. Life is full of ambiguities. Collaboration might represent an ideologically informed pattern of behaviour, or the simple assertion of self-interest. An individual might collaborate in the workplace, whilst remaining bitterly hostile to the occupier. Frequently the nature of a person's employment, as a government official or in an engineering works, on the railways, in a café, as an artist or performer, made contacts with the

Plate 6.14 French miners working under German supervision. © Roger-Viollet/TopFoto.

occupier unavoidable. At all levels, most officials simply continued doing the jobs they had held before the war. Understandably, they were concerned to safeguard their salaries and pension rights, and the habit of obedience was difficult to break. The lack of alternative employment, but also professional loyalty and a determination to preserve an ordered society, kept them at their posts.

An effort was additionally made to create a popular organisation committed to Vichy by appealing, in the Marshal's name, to First World War veterans formed into a Légion française des combattants, which by early 1941 had 590,000 members, a newspaper and a daily radio programme. The various squabbling collaborationist groups also attracted around 220,000 members towards their peak late in 1942, largely from amongst the urban lower middle classes. Their extreme views appear to have limited their appeal, however. In practice, it would be the inflated civil service that would serve as the dominant link between the government and the masses. The increasingly difficult economic situation and growing shortages, and the need to play a mediating role between the German authorities and the civilian population, necessitated greater administrative intervention. Departmental prefects also depended a great deal on the more or less willing compliance of local notables. Mayors were appointed rather than elected, and councils purged. Thus, under Vichy, an unelected social and administrative élite was able to hold sway, imposing its control through the civil service, the judicial system and the police, together with the institutions of local government and the corporations. In the absence of an electorate to win over, it was especially well placed to forward its own sectional interests. This was an assertion of the primacy of public administration over politics, which delighted many officials even as it disturbed the traditionalist proponents of regionalism and decentralised administration.

In the early post-armistice period in particular, considerable scope for initiative was left to the Vichy authorities, although even then, and in spite of the armistice agreement, effective recognition of Vichy's sovereignty in the occupied zone would always depend on the whims of the occupier. Thus the German authorities prevented the extension of the youth organisation to which Vichy attached so much importance as an agent of moral regeneration. Increasingly, however, collaboration appeared to be the necessary means of purchasing membership, and on relatively favourable terms, of the new Europe that the Germans seemed to be constructing. On 24 October 1940 Pétain met Hitler at Montoire. The discussions were inconclusive but the widely diffused photograph of the Marshal shaking hands with Hitler was of considerable symbolic importance. The message was reinforced by a speech on 31 October in which he proclaimed: 'It is with honour, and in order to maintain French unity..., that in the framework of an activity which will create the European new order I today enter the road of collaboration.' Moreover, anger at the British attack on Mers-el-Kebir and the Free French takeover in French Equatorial Africa, and the resolve to preserve the Empire, increased interest in an accommodation with the Germans. Even so, the determination to resist these incursions by force, revealed in the successful defence of Dakar in September 1940 and the bitter struggle in Syria in June/July 1941, did not develop into a burning desire to go to war with Britain as an ally of Germany, although the most significant reason for this was Hitler's own preference for the neutralisation of France and avoidance of the extension of the war to new fronts that would have followed French intervention.

In return for collaboration, Vichy expected concessions on the armistice terms, the release of the nearly 2 million prisoners of war held by the Germans and, eventually, a favourable peace treaty. The Germans were not prepared to respond to Laval's insistence on the need to prove that collaboration brought benefits, however. His failure in this respect, and Pétain's concern that he was accumulating too much power, led to his temporary removal from office in December 1940. This served only to confirm Hitler's suspicion of the sincerity of French intentions. The desperate search for a general settlement of Franco-German relations continued nevertheless. François Darlan, who by February 1941 had emerged as the dominant Vichy minister, was an admiral, a devious opportunist inspired by the dream that France might assume the maritime and colonial role of a weakened Britain. The return of Laval, the French politician Hitler distrusted least, to power, together with his growing independence of Pétain, was based on his continued commitment to Franco-German reconciliation. Addressing a meeting on 30 May 1942 he insisted that 'France's salvation, at a moment when Germany is preparing its final offensive against Russia, is in total obedience, without mental reservations. France can seize, in playing an economic role in the victory, a historic chance to modify her destiny. From being a defeated country she can become a nation integrated into the new European order.' To achieve this objective he called on support not only from his political cronies but from men with a reputation for efficiency, such as Jean Bichelonne, as minister of industrial production, and René Bousquet, secretary general at the Interior Ministry. Laval hoped to secure German concessions in return for 'intensive economic aid' and even broached the possibility of a military alliance 'to save our civilisation from sinking into communism' (13 December 1942). Negotiating from a position of extreme weakness, he enjoyed little success. Nevertheless, not even the clear breach of the armistice terms occasioned by the Allied landings in north Africa and the subsequent German move into the unoccupied zone on 11 November 1942 deflected Vichy from the path of collaboration. The Germans were able to dissolve the armistice army virtually without resistance. In north Africa itself, however, Pétain's order to resist the Allies was countermanded by Darlan, who happened to be visiting the area. The army, thus saved from destruction, was to re-enter the war on the Allied side, albeit still commanded by mainly Pétainist officers.

In France itself the credibility of the regime was diminishing rapidly. It became increasingly evident that it had been reduced to a state of complete dependence and ever-increasing subservience. Satisfying the demands of the German war economy and protecting the security of its military forces became of paramount importance. It was also becoming evident that Vichy had chosen to support the losing side in the war. It might have been otherwise if Britain had sued for peace, as had been confidently expected. Even then, however, the best that France could have expected would have been the status of a favoured client state in a Europe subordinated to German needs. As the situation evolved, the Vichy regime committed itself more fully to a reactionary politics that favoured existing élites and the Catholic Church, largely at the expense of the poorer classes, which were to be subject to the paternalist and authoritarian controls favoured by the right. In practice, they were to experience little more than shortages of necessities, harsh labour discipline, the loss of democratic rights and police repression. Increasingly, the regime's only hope – and it became ever more unlikely – was some sort of a compromise peace. In the meantime, it sought to defend itself against mounting internal opposition.

Following the war it was to be claimed that Vichy had served as a 'shield' protecting France from even worse excesses, perhaps on the scale of those inflicted on Poland. The 'National Revolution', the anti-masonic legislation and the Statute on Jews of 3 October 1940 were essentially French initiatives, however, with Pétain himself playing an active role in their elaboration. The Statute debarred French Jews from elective office, the civil service, teaching and journalism. Grateful for the enhancement of their career prospects, former colleagues eagerly filled the positions vacated. The measure pre-dated by two years German pressure to contribute to the 'final solution' of the Jewish question. Vichy's anti-Semitism thus tended to be nationalistic and Catholic rather than racialist. It reflected the prejudices held by much of the population. The economic depression, followed by defeat, had reinforced xenophobia. Foreigners and Jews proved to be useful scapegoats. The armistice had furthermore obliged the French government to repatriate Jewish refugees of German origin who had sought sanctuary in France. As a perverse means of preserving its tattered sovereignty, the Vichy regime implemented the policies of the occupier as its own. From the summer of 1941 foreign Jews were rounded up and deported. More than any other group they were seen as expendable, their sacrifice a useful means of improving relations with the occupier. On 16/17 July 1942 12,884 Jews, including 4,051 children, were arrested by French police in Paris, and many of them were held in appalling conditions at the 'Vel'd'hiv' cycle arena whilst awaiting deportation. These policies were then extended to the unoccupied territory as part of a policy of standardising legislation over the entire country and in the hope that this spirit of cooperation would facilitate the extension of the civil authority of the Vichy state in the German zone. Vichy officials even complained bitterly about efforts by the occupation authorities in the Italian zone to offer some protection to the Jewish population. Jewish property in the occupied zone was subsequently seized by a regime anxious to share in the profits expected from the confiscation and sale of assets. This affected some 40,000 Jewish businesses – corner shops as well as large enterprises – depriving their owners of their livelihoods.

Apologists for Vichy have pointed out that 'only' 26 per cent of the 350,000 Jews resident in France were deported to German death camps and that this included 'only' around 24,000 French citizens. It must be borne in mind, though, that, in spite of honourable exceptions, the action taken against Jews occurred with the active cooperation of the French government, and with the assistance of its police, even after it had been warned by its own diplomats of the impending fate of the deportees. At considerable personal risk French families hid many Jews, and in August 1942 Archbishop Saliège of Toulouse and four other Catholic prelates protested. Public sympathy was only gradually mobilised, however.

Far more unpopular than the regime's anti-Semitic policies was the introduction of labour service in Germany, initially on a voluntary basis in May 1942, and, when this failed to prove attractive, from September, through compulsion. All men aged between eighteen and fifty, as well as unmarried women between twenty-one and thirty-five, were liable. Only those workers engaged in vital war work were to be exempted. In all, some 40,000 mainly unemployed volunteers and 650,000 conscripts of the Service du travail obligatoire (STO) were sent to Germany – whilst in France itself close to 4 million people must at some time have worked for the occupiers. Nothing did as much to provoke hostility to Vichy and the Germans alike as this deportation of labour to the Reich. Caught between the occupying power and their fellow citizens, local officials were placed in an impossible situation. Resignations, absenteeism and passive resistance intensified. Many of those who had previously supported the Marshal were alienated. The efforts of many young men to escape from the STO substantially reinforced hostility, and even active resistance, to both the increasingly discredited French government and the German occupation regime. Severe measures were employed in response. German control was tightened, and terror was increasingly used in an effort to prevent the expression of opposition. Although perceived by its proponents to be a further means of exerting the sovereignty of the French state, the war against its internal enemies would do much to finally destroy its legitimacy. In this, the French administration and its police, supported by the

Plate 6.15 Execution of young members of the Resistance by German troops. © Roger-Viollet/TopFoto.

45,000 volunteers of the *milice* formed in January 1943 to help maintain 'order', served as the agents of the occupiers, and engaged in increasingly bitter civil strife. They were assisted by an immense wave of anonymous denunciations from people anxious to settle old scores – a development indicative of a deep sense of demoralisation.

Rapidly transformed into a police state, the Vichy regime cooperated closely with the Germans as a means of preserving some autonomy, but also from a positive desire to participate in the struggle against communism and other forms of 'terrorism', and increasingly in the interests of simple self-preservation. Liberation by the Allies threatened to turn France once again into a battlefield and bring with it the prospect of civil war. The growing success of the Red Army only reinforced this anxiety. It is likely that as many French men and women, as magistrates and in the police and groups such as the *milice*, participated in the defence of 'law and order' against 'brigands' in 1943/4 as were involved in active resistance. These collaborators were increasingly marginalised, however, as well as radicalised. With the appointment of Joseph Darnand as chief of security in December 1943, police action became more brutal as well as ever more subservient to German control. Torture and the execution of hostages were increasingly common. The imminence of the Allied landings only intensified the viciousness of repression, which achieved new paroxysms following D-Day as, in the panic of retreat, German forces only too frequently slaughtered innocent civilians as well as resistants. In all, some 40,000 resistants or hostages were murdered, and 60,000 deported to concentration camps for 'Gaullism, Marxism, or hostility to the regime'.

Resistance had been slow to develop. In the aftermath of defeat there had appeared little alternative to 'accommodation' (Burrin) and making the best of the situation. People were absorbed increasingly by the struggle to make ends meet and keep out of trouble. The cinema, and in many cases religion, provided means of escape from an often harsh reality, and from the loneliness experienced by the numerous women whose husbands were prisoners of war. Most of the population had initially supported the Vichy government's efforts to conciliate the invader and at first had been pleasantly surprised by the unusually disciplined behaviour of the occupying forces. Nevertheless, there was a general desire to see them gone and thus to look forward to an Allied victory. Graffiti, the slashing of official posters, booing newsreels, minor acts of sabotage and listening to the BBC were all symptomatic of widespread resentment. The profound demoralisation of much of the population, together with the anxiety caused by the growing brutality of the occupiers, did not easily translate into active opposition, however. As it slowly developed, resistance activity was to be characterised by its diverse origins and forms. Early landmarks included the clandestine publication in November and December 1940 of the army officer Henry Frenay's newspaper *Combat* and the trade unionists Robert Lacoste and Christian Pineau's *Libération*. These did something to counter the otherwise paralysing feeling of isolation amongst potential resisters. The learning process in establishing opposition from scratch was to prove costly, however. This was the lesson of such rare public confrontations as the demonstration by students in Paris on Armistice Day, 11 November 1940. The miners' strike in the north-east in May 1941, although occasioned mainly by food shortages, was blamed on Communist agitation by both the Vichy prefect and the Germans. It was not until June–August 1941, however, following Hitler's invasion of Russia, that the occupiers began to show real concern. This marked the commencement of a vicious upward cycle in which acts of resistance were followed by savage repression, including the execution of hostages. Hostility towards the occupiers increased, although defiance was also frequently condemned because of the violent German response it provoked. The deterioration in living standards, the unopposed entry of German forces into the unoccupied zone and the conscription of labour for work in Germany were to mark further stages in the process of confrontation, whilst growing Allied military successes helped to establish a new climate of hope.

The diverse forms of resistance were inspired by a variety of motives. Initially, they took the form of a series of disconnected initiatives in particular, especially urban, localities by small groups of like-minded people related by kinship, friendship, profession, religious or political attitudes. These included patriotic and politically conservative officers serving in the Vichy army, civil servants or intellectuals meeting in the Musée de l'Homme in Paris. Workers, subject to both German repression and exploitation and Vichy authoritarianism, were also prominent, profiting from the relative impenetrability to the police of city *quartiers* such as the *faubourg* Montmartre, les Halles or Belleville in Paris. Activity was more evident in the occupied zone, where the enemy presence was obvious, rather than in the south, where the existence of Vichy clouded the issue. Loyalty to the Marshal and anti-Bolshevism both limited conservative involvement. In many areas, especially in the countryside, it was possible to live in peace with very little contact with the occupiers, although official food requisitioning would increasingly alienate peasants. Nevertheless, if, with notable exceptions, members of the traditional élites preferred refined coexistence, the role of the middle classes should not be underestimated. As both Vichy and the Germans placed growing demands upon them, civil servants and the police became less convinced of the virtue of collaboration, less reliable and, particularly as the prospect of Allied victory increased, more determined to avoid compromising themselves. Gradually, the machinery of state began to disintegrate. The future Socialist president, François Mitterrand, a pre-war adherent of the extreme right, would turn from being a loyal and highly decorated

Vichy civil servant into an active member of the Resistance, although he would never cease to venerate Marshal Pétain.

Attitudes and allegiances changed over time. Support within all social groups would grow in reaction to the increasingly obvious subordination of Vichy and in response to German racism and brutality. Previous political convictions, together with local variations in the experience of occupation, also influenced decisions. Initially the Socialists, reacting to the repression of the trades unions and the loss of civil and political rights, were probably the most active political grouping. The official Communist approach, inspired by the Nazi–Soviet Pact, was to avoid conflict with the occupying power whilst condemning the 'traitors' at Vichy. Even before the invasion of the Soviet Union, however, the clandestinely published *L'Humanité* was adopting a more hostile tone, industrial sabotage was increasing and arms were being stockpiled. The final entry of the Communist Party into active resistance would have a substantial impact on both its numerical strength and combativeness. It would also establish the Party as a major political force. Although resisters were recruited from all social groups, their activity could often be seen as a means of continuing the class struggle.

A mood of protest and hostility towards the better off was created amongst the poorer social groups by shortage and deprivation. Reinforcement of the authority of employers, the persecution of trades unionists and the extension of the working day were bitterly resented. Food shortages on a scale not experienced since the late eighteenth century were the result of sharply reduced levels of production, lack of access to overseas suppliers, German purchasing, transport difficulties and the reluctance of farmers to sell their produce at low fixed prices. Bread rationing was introduced in September 1940 and most necessities were rationed by the end of 1941. By 1943 the official ration amounted to only 1,200 calories a day, well below the 1,700 usually considered as the minimum necessary for good health. In the following year the crude death rate reached 19.1 per thousand compared with 15.3 before the war. The burden on women anxious to provide for their families and spending long hours standing in queues was especially desperate. There was a growing obsession with meeting physical needs, and, inevitably, those who could afford the cost resorted to an increasingly pervasive and corrupting black market. The gulf between town and country, rich and poor, widened. Power cuts and acute shortages of heating fuel added to the widespread misery, whilst the intensification of police round-ups, deportation for labour service and the toll taken by inaccurate Allied air raids, which eventually accounted for around 60,000 deaths, all added to the general feeling of intense anxiety.

Increasingly, the various Resistance groups and networks created by local effort would respond to the external influence of the Free French and British and perform a range of functions, including the collection of intelligence on troop movements, at which railwaymen were particularly adept; the distribution of tracts and newspapers; the establishment of hiding places and escape routes for political suspects, Jewish refugees and Allied servicemen; and sabotage and assassinations, of collaborators and Germans alike. From 1943, in sparsely populated areas of the centre and south, guerrilla activity would develop, involving large armed groups made up of young men avoiding labour service in Germany, stiffened by those rare army officers sympathetic towards the Resistance and by experienced Spanish Republican refugees. By the beginning of 1944 perhaps 30,000 were involved in this *maquis*. All these activities were, of course, extremely dangerous. The various groups were penetrated frequently by informers, and their members subjected to torture and a miserable death if captured. They shared the added moral burden of knowing that the German authorities were also likely to visit retribution on their families and innocent hostages.

Cooperation between the various local groups was slow to develop, due both to the added risk of exposure this would inevitably involve and to mutual political suspicion. The London-based Free French had, at first, little impact. The British and especially the Americans continued to keep open the possibility of negotiations with Vichy. Although Churchill had at first supported de Gaulle only because alternative and more illustrious leaders failed to materialise, the general's consistent denial of the legitimacy of the Vichy regime, his total intransigence in defence of what he believed to be the vital interests of France and the gradual strengthening of his military power, as parts of the Empire were liberated, slowly improved his position vis-à-vis the Allies. It did little to reduce what he regarded as a humiliating dependence, however. The Free French were excluded from the Allied landings in north Africa in November 1942, following which the Americans made every effort to negotiate with the Pétainist Admiral Darlan and, following his assassination, with the ineffectual General Giraud. Although Churchill conceded that there was no real alternative to de Gaulle, US president Franklin Roosevelt continued, even during the liberation, to resist recognition of an administration led by someone he perceived to be an unelected and obstreperous general.

The situation of the Free French leader was transformed, however, when in May 1943 a Conseil national de la Résistance (CNR), made up of representatives of political groups, trades unions and Resistance organisations, was established as a means of coordinating internal activity. One of its leading figures, the former prefect Jean Moulin, a member of the Lyon-based and largely Catholic-inspired group Combat, who had made the hazardous journey to London to meet de Gaulle in October 1941, persuaded its members to declare their support for the general. They preferred to appeal to the Free French for the external assistance, and especially the weaponry, they so desperately needed, rather than go cap in hand to the Allies. Contacts proliferated. Moreover, whatever his own political views, de Gaulle was prepared to make the compromises necessary to increase his authority within France and particularly to commit himself to the re-establishment of democracy. This, together with his apparent determination to prevent a communist takeover in post-war France, and the manifest incompetence of potential rivals, finally persuaded the Allies to accept the general's pre-eminent position and to recognise the status of the Comité français de Libération nationale. Formed in June 1943 from a mixture of Resistance leaders and former Third Republic politicians such as Vincent Auriol and Mendès-France, this group increasingly took on the character of a provisional government able to count on the allegiance of a regular army of 500,000 men, formed in north Africa and equipped by the Allies.

Powerful internal political tensions would survive, however, as well as differences over both tactics and objectives. The arrest, torture and death of Moulin in June 1943 was symptomatic of the dangers of resistance, the repeated fragmentation of its structures as a result of repression, and the constant efforts to reconsolidate its activities.

Growing Communist influence within France caused particular concern. Undoubtedly, many Communists thought in terms of a future mass struggle not only against the German enemy but also the treasonable ruling classes as a prelude to social revolution. This was in marked contrast with the more conservative and cautious approach of other groups, concerned essentially to prepare for action to support the Allied armies on some still distant day of liberation. As a result, the Communist Front national and Francs-tireurs et Partisans français tended to be starved of weapons and money in comparison with the resources sent by both the Free French and the British Special Operations Executive to the non-communist Mouvements Unis de la Résistance and its Armée secrète. The struggle for power in the post-war world was already under way before the Allied landings.

Assisted by overwhelming air superiority, Allied troops were able to land on the coast of Normandy on 6 June 1944, and achieve a rapid military build-up, although it took seven weeks to break out from their bridgeheads. Paris was liberated on 25 August. In the meantime, Allied forces, including a substantial French element, had landed in the south – on 15 August – liberated Marseille on 28 August and moved swiftly up the Rhône valley. They received substantial assistance from Resistance groups both during this operation and in the liberation of Brittany and subsequent containment of German garrisons in the port of Saint-Nazaire and other pockets, which continued to hold out until the end of the war. By the end of the year most of the country was free of German troops. The contribution of regular French forces to the initial landings had been limited, much to de Gaulle's disgust. Nor had there been a call for a mass rising by Resistance groups. Premature risings were only too likely to end in carnage. Their essential role in the Allied grand strategy was the extremely important one of delaying the arrival on the Normandy front of German reinforcements. Although the plans of Communist and non-Communist groups alike had been coordinated quite successfully, within the overall command structure of the Forces françaises de l'Intérieure (FFI), controlling events on the ground was always going to be difficult. Nevertheless, and in spite of a lack of military equipment, Resistance forces were able to play a major role particularly in the liberation of Paris, as the Germans withdrew to the east.

Dwight Eisenhower, the Supreme Allied Commander, had planned to bypass the capital rather than risk involvement in a costly house-to-house conflict, but this was to ignore the determination of Resistance leaders, particularly the Communists, to play a more active role. Tension had grown in the city. Even the police went on strike. The rising began on 18 August, and the following morning the Prefecture of Police was occupied, largely by rebellious policemen. A succession of ministries and other key buildings were also taken over and representatives of the Free French authorities installed. Barricades went up throughout the city and especially in the working-class districts of the north and east. In response, Eisenhower felt obliged to rush the Second French Armoured Division towards Paris, and on 25 August the German commander, ignoring Hitler's order to fight on in the ruins, surrendered. Liberation of the capital had cost the lives of some 3,000 members of the Resistance and civilians. De Gaulle arrived in the city late in the afternoon. His speech at the Hôtel-de-Ville displayed his habitual genius for myth making: 'Paris! Paris humiliated! Paris broken! Paris martyrised! But now Paris liberated! Liberated by herself, by her own people with the help of the armies of France, with the support and aid of France as a whole, of fighting France, of eternal France.' As well as re-establishing the legitimacy of the state, he was determined to recreate a sense of national unity around the legend of heroic resistance. The decisive role played by the Communists in the liberation of Paris, and even that of the Allies, was conveniently ignored. Although the Resistance played an essentially subordinate and secondary role in the liberation, the contribution of French forces, including most notably the 24,000 members of the FFI who lost their lives, would do much to restore national self-confidence.

In the face of the onslaught, the Vichy regime disintegrated rapidly. The government itself was forced by the German authorities to move first to eastern France and finally, as virtual captives, into Germany itself. At local level the administration simply tended to collapse, with only small numbers of the more ideologically motivated officials and *milice* assisting in a last, often ferocious, round of persecution. Pétain's call on Frenchmen to remain neutral in the struggle was meaningless. His primary concern appears to have been to ensure an orderly transfer of authority, and to avoid internal strife, whilst somehow protecting his own situation. There remained a very real danger after so many years of misery and oppression that, as Pétain feared, the liberation would degenerate into a massive settling of accounts and into civil war. Indeed, amongst members of the Resistance and also the mass of more passive citizens who had associated themselves at the last minute with the anti-Nazi crusade, the prospect of liberation had created an immense sense of expectancy. In this situation the political left, strengthened by its association with the struggle, appeared representative of the national interest. In part this had been fostered by the CNR's programme, which, as well as affirming a commitment to democracy, promised to dismantle and to nationalise the 'feudal' economic empires, to involve workers themselves in planning for a greater and more fairly shared prosperity and to create a social security system. This implied a rejection of the self-centred individualism of the property-owning classes. As the coalfields in the Gard and in northern France were liberated, miners rejected the authority of the owners and carried out de facto nationalisation. Once more, an almost millenarian sense of anticipation built up in some sections of the community, at the same time as social fear encouraged conservatives, in whatever political guise, to prepare for the struggle against communism.

Although members of every social group had participated in resistance, the traditional political and social élites, as well as major employers, could not escape blame entirely for the moral and practical failings of the Third Republic or those of Vichy. Now, former supporters of the Pétainist regime faced what appeared to them to be the nightmare prospect of a Communist-inspired social revolution. In practice, the dangerous period in which a power vacuum existed, following the collapse of one regime and the imposition of control by its successor, was to be short-lived. During it, nonetheless, perhaps as many as 10,000 supposed collaborators were summarily executed – a high enough figure, but far lower than subsequent conservative estimates, which seem to have represented an attempt to tarnish the reputation of the Resistance. As the rule of law was re-established, another 7,037 death sentences were pronounced by legally constituted courts, although only 1,500 were carried out. Over 40,000 people received prison sentences and a further 50,000 suffered the loss of civil rights. Many others, notably women who had associated with German boyfriends, were humiliated and paraded through the streets with shaven heads. Following an initial phase of violent reaction, those punished tended to be the makers of policy under Vichy rather than the executors, unless the latter had been overly zealous in their duties.

Gradually, passions calmed. Even Xavier Vallat, one of the architects of Vichy's anti-Semitic legislation as head of the Commissariat général aux questions juives, was sentenced to only ten years' imprisonment. He would be freed in 1949 and amnestied five years later. Pétain and Laval were to endure extremely partisan trials. Even so, their lawyers were able to offer a defence in terms of the two men's success in providing at least partial protection from the occupier. Another conservative myth was in the making. Nevertheless, both were sentenced to death. Laval was shot, but Pétain was to be reprieved because of his age and advancing senility. High-profile groups such as intellectuals and journalists suffered much more than the officials and businessmen who had been so essential to the workings of collaboration and who had often managed to turn it into a very profitable proposition. Over 20,000 civil servants were dismissed as part of a purge, especially severe on the police. Most of them were to be reinstated by 1950, however; the machinery of government survived virtually intact. Continuity appeared essential to the smooth operation of the new regime and to the reaffirmation of centralised republican democracy over local initiative. Senior officials were too useful to suffer the sanctions they might have deserved, and sufficiently well connected to be able to conceal their previous actions. Moreover, too many people felt guilty about collaboration in all its forms, large and small, for there to be sustained support for a massive enquiry. In many rural areas and small towns traditional ruling groups rapidly reasserted themselves, often to dominate local liberation committees in order, they claimed, to protect 'the integrity of local communities' (Gildea) and prevent a Communist takeover. In practice, the determination to prosecute the war to final victory and then the work of reconstruction would take priority over either retribution or social reform. In order to establish a sense of unity and national purpose, de Gaulle would insist that the vast majority of the population had supported, or at least sympathised with, the Resistance. This myth

Plate 6.16 Execution of members of the *milice* in Grenoble in August 1944.

would survive, largely unchallenged, until the 1970s, when Marcel
Ophuls' powerful documentary *Le chagrin et la pitié* and the work
of the American historian Robert Paxton reawakened memories of
the compromises that were part of everyday life under Vichy.

As an Allied victory had come to look increasingly likely people
had begun to think of the post-war world. Within the Resistance,
many activists, inspired by socialism or Catholic humanitarianism,
were determined to avoid a simple restoration of the pre-war social
and political systems and to establish a more egalitarian society.
Amongst those close to de Gaulle, as well as the former Pétainist
officers of the north African army, there was considerable anxiety
about the intentions of the many Communist-dominated groups
making up the largest and most dynamic segment of the Resistance.
Establishing the authority of a new government was going to be
fraught with danger. The intention of the Allies had been to secure
the rear areas of the advancing armies by means of the establishment of their own military government. In the event, a new institutional framework had already been prepared by the Comité français
de Libération nationale. The transfer of power had been prepared
carefully. Early in 1944 secret administrative and military hierarchies had been established in parallel with those of the Vichy state.
Alexandre Parodi was appointed de Gaulle's delegate general in

France, with Jacques Chaban-Delmas as national military delegate and General Koenig as commander of the FFI. Commissaires had also been nominated to replace Vichy's prefects. Generally they were drawn from the established social and political élite – men such as Michel Debré, graduate of the prestigious Sciences-Po and of the cavalry school at Saumur, who took over at Angers – but belonging to a different, younger generation than their predecessors. On 2 June the Comité had declared itself to be the Provisional Government, with its members drawn from a variety of political horizons, including the Communists, in recognition of the balance of power within the Resistance movement and from a desire to establish a working political consensus.

De Gaulle's triumphant reception in a succession of liberated towns, but above all in Paris, had moreover legitimised his role as the embodiment of a resurrected French state. The Provisional Government's authority over the internal Resistance was also reaffirmed by the incorporation of its fighters into the regular army and, from October, by the disarmament of civilians. With what must have appeared to many members of the Resistance as almost indecent haste, they were thrust aside. This restoration of the state's monopoly of armed force substantially reduced the left's capacity for independent action. For their part, and in the interests of both France and the Soviet Union, the Communists were too committed to furthering the war effort to risk civil war. Moderation on their part also offered the prospect of mass support after the final victory.

In the meantime, there was still much to do before the enemy was driven out finally. Somehow, too, people had to be fed and prevented from freezing during the extremely harsh winter of 1944/5, and this in the midst of the devastation caused by war. Communications networks had been targeted by friend and foe alike. Fuel was in short supply. The distribution of necessities was difficult and the black market continued to thrive. Even when victory had been gained some 2 million former prisoners of war and deportees had to be returned to their homes, and soldiers demobilised. Jewish survivors would still encounter anti-Semitism and often insurmountable difficulties in securing the restitution of their property. There was widespread misery and disappointment.

Plate 6.17 Liberation: General de Gaulle walking down the Champs-Elysées on 26 August 1944. Photo: Robert DOISNEAU/Gamma-Rapho/ Getty Images.

In spite of these massive problems, the scale of de Gaulle's achievement was nevertheless evident in the Allied decision to treat France not as a collaborationist state but as a co-belligerent. In contrast, the regime that most French people had welcomed in 1940 had to be accounted a disastrous failure. In effect, Vichy had constituted another round in the long civil war inaugurated in 1789. This particular conflict could be said to have started in the 1930s with the economic crisis and establishment of the Popular Front and to have climaxed with the Pétainist regime. It was the last in the series of crises between 1914 and 1945 that gave the period its fundamental unity. With it, a long period of economic and social stagnation came to an end. In marked contrast, the following three decades – the *trente glorieuses* – would bring sustained economic growth and a transformation of French society.

7

Reconstruction and renewal: the *trente glorieuses*

INTRODUCTION

Like most transformative events, the Liberation aroused substantial expectations of political and social reform, and at the same time considerable anxiety, particularly within established élites. The right had been discredited as a result of its association with Vichy. Committed to social justice and economic modernisation, the left was in the ascendancy. In the following years France would experience a sustained upward cycle of growth – the *trente glorieuses*, as the economist Jean Fourastié would label them. A massive stimulus would be afforded by reconstruction and then by the liberalisation of international trade and increased domestic prosperity. Greater state engagement and high levels of both public and private investment would promote sustained demand. This development of a mixed economy established a framework for the renewal and expansion of capitalistic enterprise, initially drawing on previously underused resources and labour and increasingly on improved technology. It was the scale and pace of change, in contrast with the periods both beforehand and afterwards, that defined these three decades. The statistics on gross domestic product (GDP) growth provide the clearest indicator of change (see Table 7.1).

Such rapid growth, and the structural change in the economy and society that accompanied it, inevitably provoked repeated *crises d'adaptation*. In addition, the opportunity was taken to substantially increase social welfare spending, with significant redistributive

Table 7.1 *GDP growth, 1896–1996*
(annual average percentage increase)

1896–1913	1.9	1959–69	5.7
1913–29	1.5	1969–73	5.6
1929–38	−0.3	1973–9	3.0
1945–51	8.7	1980–91	2.1
1952–9	4.2	1991–6	1.1

Source: K. Mouré, 'The French economy since 1930', in
M. Alexander (ed.), *French History since Napoleon*
(Arnold Publishers, 1999), 374.

effects. This helped to promote a social consensus in favour of modernisation. Nevertheless, there was considerable resentment of reform on the part of the propertied classes, whilst the intensification of competitive pressures threatened the vital interests of many farmers, workers in uncompetitive industries, and small businessmen. In a remarkably short time the promise of a new era of social justice was to be followed by a restoration of the social and political relationships of the pre-war period. Many former *résistants* were to endure the sour taste of betrayal. More realistically, it is hardly surprising that the heterogeneous coalition that came together in the struggle against the occupiers fell to squabbling once it was a question of determining the shape of reconstruction and the locus of political power. The collapse of the left–centre political consensus, which had emerged from the resistance, and the inevitable recovery of the right would rapidly threaten to destabilise and, increasingly, to discredit the Fourth Republic.

A system of government based, like that of the Third Republic, on rapidly shifting alliances within a class of political notables, and election by proportional representation, was inherently unstable. Governments with impermanent majorities were not best suited to dealing with the problems of reconstruction and the rapid expansion of the state's responsibilities, with colonial wars, repeated financial crises and the social tension caused by unequal access to the rewards of economic growth. In contrast with the Third Republic, however, when the state had appeared as the helpless spectator of economic and social change, the result was no longer stalemate. Economic and social forces, in particular the internationalisation of economic activity resulting from the US ascendancy and moves towards European integration, were too strong. Moreover, an increasingly self-confident and assertive bureaucracy provided guidance and continuity. In this respect, one of the regime's weaknesses – the disassociation between political and administrative and economic power – facilitated reconstruction and the establishment of a welfare state, and inaugurated an unprecedented period of sustained economic growth and improvement in the standard of living. In many respects, the regime revealed a firmer grasp of the economic and political realities than did British governments of the same period.

ECONOMY

The most obvious indicator of the scale and pace of economic and social change in the years following the end of the Second World War was the transformation of the everyday environment. In 1945 the rural landscape was little different from that of the late Middle Ages, and the urban scene similar to that of the Second Empire, complete with overcrowded, run-down housing and nineteenth-century industrial landscapes. Between 1946 and 1975 the population grew from 40.3 million to 52.6 million. Life expectancy for men rose from sixty-two to sixty-nine, and for women from sixty-seven to seventy-seven. The proportion of the labour force employed in agriculture fell from 36 per cent in 1946 to 8.6 per cent by 1979 and, whilst that employed in industry slowly rose from 32 per cent to 35.3 per cent, employment in the service sector increased far more dramatically, from 32 per cent to 56 per cent. The large-scale construction of offices and housing changed the appearance of most towns. Many of the old factories were demolished. People lived in much greater comfort, and most worked in less oppressive conditions. Symbolic of this new age of mass production and greater personal mobility, the automobile was everywhere. Of course, not everything had changed. Old and new coexisted, but the scale and pace of transformation were far more substantial than anything previously experienced. A decisive shift had occurred in the balance between continuity and change, beginning with post-war reconstruction, the renewal of infrastructure and heavy industry and the creation of full employment for men, and then, from the 1960s, involving more decisive steps towards modernity through technological innovation and structural transformation, new patterns of consumption and changing mentalities, and the acceptance of substantially enlarged responsibilities on the part of the state. This all added up to a massive social revolution.

At least initially, there was an important degree of consensus amongst the various political groups and within the reconstituted trades unions concerning reconstruction. Although it could not be sustained indefinitely, speeches, newsreels and press articles praising miners, steelworkers and railwaymen boosted popular enthusiasm. The shortage of labour was made good by working longer hours and raising productivity. The task seemed enormous, far greater than after the First World War. According to an estimate by the Ministry of Reconstruction, the return to 'normality' would cost F4,900 milliard, or the equivalent of three years' pre-war national income. Other sources suggest that over one-quarter of the nation's wealth had been destroyed, compared with one-tenth during the earlier war. The depredations of war and German requisitioning and the neglect, since the onset of the Great Depression, of maintenance and investment in capital goods resulted in shortages of such basic necessities as food and fuel. In 1944 industrial production stood at 38 per cent of its 1938 level. First priority had to be given to the reconstruction of the transportation infrastructure, which had been a prime target of Allied bombing and resistance activity. At the end of the war only 18,000 kilometres (in disconnected sections) of the 40,000 kilometres of railway lines were serviceable and only one in five lorries had survived the conflict. The other major campaign to be fought was the 'battle for coal'. This remained the basic source of industrial and domestic fuel, and in 1945 only 40 million tonnes were available (including imports), compared with 67 million in 1937. Although the shift to alternative energy sources was already under way, in 1950 solid fuels still provided for 74 per cent of energy consumption (90 per cent in 1913), with hydroelectricity supplying 7.5 per cent and oil 18 per cent. The restoration and modernisation of the steel and engineering industries were other pressing objectives.

In this situation a high degree of state intervention in the economy was to be expected. The intensity of anti-capitalist feeling at the time of the Liberation made this inevitable. The *patronat* was blamed by

Plate 7.1 Reconstruction: the Communist Party calls for a further effort.
Photo: Taillandier-D.R.

much of the population for the defeat of 1940 and for collaboration, and was thus 'disqualified' (de Gaulle) from its previous pre-eminence. It had become necessary for the state to assume control of the 'levers of command' and direct investment, not simply into reconstruction but also into a programme of economic and social modernisation impelled by a now widely shared perception of France as a backward, archaic society. A 'Malthusian' capitalist class, which had given ample proof of its shortcomings already, could not be trusted to ensure that the country kept pace with other Western societies. Nationalisation occupied a central place in the programme adopted by the Conseil national de la Résistance in March 1944, and this reflected a broad consensus created not only by the war but also in reaction to the pre-war economic crisis. Between December 1945 and May 1946 the major banking and insurance companies, gas and electricity utilities, and the coal mines were added to firms such as Renault, which had been taken into state ownership because of its directors' collaboration. Compensation was paid to shareholders but generally at the prevailing, and very depressed, stock market valuation. By 1948 around 25 per cent of the non-agricultural labour force was employed by state enterprises. In spite of their great hopes and whilst benefiting from a greater security of employment, the employees of these enterprises saw little change otherwise in their relationship with their employers. Although state intervention in long-term planning was frequent, on a day-to-day basis the nationalised companies operated in much the same way as other enterprises.

Another feature of the period of reconstruction was the adoption of successive Plans, a move that had been contemplated during the inter-war years but that now, in such difficult circumstances, seemed essential. A team led by Jean Monnet prepared the first Plan, published in January 1947. It sought to define priorities, circulate information (collected by a massively extended statistical service), provide economic forecasts and develop contacts between businessmen, trades unionists and civil servants in order to create a dynamic climate for investment. This was 'indicative planning'; not the Soviet-style planning that the French Communist Party favoured, but a form of technocracy by means of which officials who had received their professional training in the most élitist sector of higher education, the *grandes écoles*, attempted to ensure the more effective working of the capitalist system. In retrospect, the establishment of direct links between government and particular sectors of the economy was far more important. Although the orthodox financial views of the Finance Ministry and governmental concern to restore business confidence as a means of promoting recovery would reassume predominance rapidly, this would be within the new intellectual climate imposed by the widespread acceptance of Keynsian economic ideas, and which insisted upon the necessity of state intervention to promote growth and full employment. As a proportion of GDP, government (including local authority) spending rose from 26.5 per cent in 1938 to over 50 per cent during the 1960s. Initially too, in the aftermath of war, there had been little alternative to running up large trade deficits in order to secure the import of essential foodstuffs, raw materials and capital equipment. Only the introduction in 1948 of the Marshall Plan, and the provision of aid on a massive scale by a United States anxious to promote European recovery, would ease the strains. This act of altruism combined with self-interest helped confirm the growing fascination, sometimes combined with revulsion, for all things American, including the cultural manifestations of Hollywood as well as advanced industrial technology.

By 1947–9 the key economic sectors had been restored to at least pre-war levels of activity. To a large degree reconstruction was achieved at the expense of consumption. Resources were concentrated on the production of coal, steel, electricity, cement and agricultural machinery, and on transport. The result of the effort to restore industrial supplies meant that domestic consumers of coal, gas and electricity suffered repeated shortages. Bread rationing continued until 1949, although it was already becoming clear that domestic recovery combined with imports threatened the return of pre-war problems of agricultural overproduction. The first Plan, with its 'productivist' concerns, sought to encourage an agricultural revolution by means of the tractor (20,000 in 1946, 558,000 by 1958, 1 million by 1965) and chemical inputs, inaugurating a cycle of technical innovation largely financed by borrowing, which would create an immense debt burden for farmers. Increasingly, reliance on banks and on contracts to supply cooperative and food-processing companies placed farmers in a dependent position. At the same time as the exodus of population from the countryside revived, due both to mechanisation and the growing attractiveness of urban life, considerable gains in productivity were achieved, at an annual rate of 6.4 per cent between 1949 and 1962, in part as a result of growing specialisation and the shift from cereals cultivation into higher-value produce such as fruit, vegetables, meat and dairy products. The technical gulf between large-scale capitalist farmers in the Paris basin and the north and small farmers in the uplands, producing for local markets, also became wider than ever.

The phase of reconstruction was completed by 1949/50, by which time the maximum pre-war levels of production, those of 1929, had been exceeded. The success of reconstruction was such that it provided a firm base for a unique period of sustained and accumulative economic growth marked by substantial gains in productivity, real incomes and mass purchasing power and by major changes in economic and social structures. In western Europe only the Federal Republic of Germany would surpass the French achievement. Subsequently the role of the state continued to be of considerable importance, both in terms of direct investment and through the creation, partly by means of the Plan, of an encouraging climate for business activity. Prior to the establishment of the European Economic Community (EEC) governments remained resolutely protectionist, using an arsenal of monetary controls to facilitate industrial expansion based upon a protected internal market, and employing deficit financing to maintain high levels of infrastructure investment as well as to stabilise the capitalist system.

Inflation was to be a constant problem. Deficit financing, repeated currency devaluations as a means of maintaining international competitiveness, expansion of the money supply both during and after the war, shortages and the early abandonment of many wartime controls generated substantial price rises, fuelled by major wage increases as employees sought to protect their already diminishing living standards. When, in 1948/9, stabilisation appeared possible as a result of increasing production and more effective limits on money supply, the effects of the Korean War on world raw material prices set off a new inflationary round. Inflation certainly contributed to the revival of economic activity by widening profit margins and reducing the burden of indebtedness, but it also revealed something of the fragility of the economic recovery and the ineffectiveness of the political system, as well as contributing to rising social tension. Only with the action inaugurated by Antoine Pinay, the prime minister, in 1952/3, which combined persuasion with fiscal controls and a successful loan to soak up excess capital, was inflation temporarily curbed. Greater financial stability stimulated a second cycle of economic growth, which was brought to an end from 1956 by renewed inflation caused by the rising costs of the war in Algeria, the impact of the Suez Affair on the cost of oil and other raw materials, and the spending of a left-wing government committed to social reform. These factors combined to reduce French competitiveness in international markets and to dent business confidence severely.

In spite of these setbacks the conditions for largely self-sustained economic growth were being established, as rising productivity pushed up both company and personal incomes and stimulated growing investment and consumer spending. The greater mobility of labour and its transfer from the less dynamic parts of the economy such as agriculture and textiles into such sectors as chemicals, electrical goods, engineering and construction, in which per capita productivity was higher, constituted an essential part of this process, helping to ease the severe labour shortages evident until the entry into employment of the large post-war generations. Increasingly, too, France was integrated into the west European and Atlantic economies, initially through the General Agreement on Tariffs and Trade (GATT, 1947). Then, alongside the ill-advised efforts to hang on to Empire, major moves were also taken towards Franco-German reconciliation and greater European unity within the Organisation for European Economic Co-operation (1948, created to coordinate the disbursement of Marshall Aid), the Council of Europe and the North Atlantic Treaty Organization (NATO, 1949), the European Coal and Steel Community (1951) and finally, with the Treaty of Rome in 1957, the EEC.

The signing of the Treaty of Rome, against the advice of many businessmen, might appear something of a paradox, given the protectionist policies of post-war governments. It did represent a further stage in the commitment to modernisation, however, by providing access to new markets and through the intensification of competitive pressures. Furthermore, the treaty, partly inspired by 'geopolitical imperatives', sought to bind West Germany into a union that, according to Robert Schuman, the foreign minister, would make another war 'not only unthinkable, but materially impossible'.

In a situation of rapidly rising prices and with a growing deficit in external trade it was widely assumed that France would be unable to fulfil its engagements under the Treaty of Rome. Not only were tariffs within the Community to be eliminated within twelve to fifteen years (in practice by 1968) but the common tariffs levied on imports from outside the Community were to be reduced to the average prevailing in 1958, which tended to be below French levels. In compensation, the Common Agricultural Policy (CAP), finally agreed in 1962, provided for price guarantees and income supports and, thanks to tough negotiating by the French government, was extremely favourable to its farming constituency. Combined with the enlargement of the potential market, these measures were especially beneficial for large-scale farmers, the 10 per cent who already by 1968 produced 60 per cent of total output. They also provided a margin for survival for many small farmers, however, slowing the process of structural change necessary to enhance the international competitiveness of French agriculture. In 1973 60 per cent of farms still had fewer than 20 hectares. Especially in the uplands, in the south-west and in the Breton interior, many families remained impoverished, and the situation was only gradually eased by migration and measures such as the Pisani law of 1960, which encouraged farmers to retire. Peasant farmers (and small shopkeepers) were to be consistently protected from the full impact of the free market, although their incomes remained subject to the vagaries of the climate, fluctuating interest rates and changes in the CAP.

France proved able to meet its EEC obligations because of the combination of a series of deflationary financial measures, including an end to the indexation of prices and wages, with a relaxation of administrative controls and a partial restoration of market mechanisms. With the return of de Gaulle, the establishment of strong political leadership with clearer objectives and prepared to encourage, even to enforce, industrial restructuring and modernisation by means of investment in improved communications, cheap loans, export credits and tax concessions was another vital factor. The overall effect of the establishment of the Community was to promote a rapid increase in trade between its six member states. Although, undoubtedly, farmers and businessmen experienced considerable problems of adaptation in increasingly homogeneous and competitive markets, the benefits of integration were soon evident, and increasingly the process came to be seen as irreversible. The results surpassed expectations, with sustained economic growth at an annual rate of 5.5 per cent during the first fifteen years of EEC membership, higher even than that of West Germany (5 per cent), and levels of profitability that encouraged high rates of investment. The French economy underwent a major process of structural change, with industrial growth promoting the modernisation of such services as banking and advertising. Comparative advantage also had an effect. Thus the stimulus to change was particularly effective in agriculture and food processing and in the automobile and aircraft industries, whilst manufacturing benefited from imports of German machine tools and consumers from Italian refrigerators and washing machines. The relatively low price of raw materials and energy on world markets, and high levels of foreign, especially American, investment, further assisted the process of growth. At the same time this orientation towards a dynamic market for advanced high-quality goods meant a shift away from the far less demanding Third World markets represented by the former Empire, with the franc area taking over one-quarter of exports in the late 1950s but only 5 per cent twenty years later.

As the economic (and, indeed, the political) context changed it became inevitable that the role of the state, exercised through the Plan, direct investment, price controls, subsidies and manipulation of the tax system, would be criticised from a liberal standpoint as inefficient and wasteful. The emphasis shifted towards the creation of a climate favourable to private sector investment. The share of the state and public enterprise in total investment, which had been 38.4 per cent in the period 1949–53, fell to 28.5 per cent by 1969–73. This policy was partly contradicted, however, by investment in a series of prestigious projects regarded as being of strategic national importance. In aerospace these included both military aircraft and the Caravelle airliner in the 1950s and subsequently the supersonic Concorde and the Airbus family. The Ariane series of rockets, designed to take satellites into space, maintained a major French presence in one area of advanced technology, as did massive investment in the nuclear power programme, information technology, transport and armaments. This represented a determination, shared by all governments, to stimulate continuous technological modernisation. The cost-effectiveness of these programmes is difficult to estimate, not only due to the complexity of their impact but because so many inefficiencies were concealed by government support and the lack of genuine cost accounting. In the case of the nuclear industry, secrecy has further inhibited discussion of such crucial matters as safety and the disposal of waste.

Inflation would continue to be a problem throughout the 1960s, fuelled as it was by the massive extension of bank credits necessary to finance major investment programmes. Nevertheless, from around 20 per cent of GDP in the 1950s the investment rate rose to 23.5 per cent per annum between 1965 and 1973, peaking at 24.7 per cent in 1974, a level unsurpassed in Europe. The result was the rapid introduction of more efficient methods of production, which allowed the mass production of such consumer durables as the motor car, a former luxury that now became the most potent symbol of the new consumer society. In 1960 30 per cent of households already possessed a car; by 1973 this had risen to 62 per cent. Especially in chemicals and electronics, scientific advances created a continually expanding range of new products, which, from packet soups to refrigerators and televisions, were made available at prices the mass of the population could afford, with payment often deferred on credit terms.

The period from 1958 to 1973 saw the most rapid economic growth in French history. Its effects were cumulative. Per capita income almost doubled between 1960 and 1975, and, significantly, it has been estimated that almost 60 per cent of this was due to technical innovation. Structural change in the economy occurred in response both to new opportunities and to growing competitive pressures. Frequently, adaptation was difficult. One reaction to heightened competition was the growing size of enterprises, a response to financial as well as to technical pressures and encouraged by the state. Amongst the most spectacular were the takeover of Citroën by Peugeot and the development of conglomerates such as Péchiney-Ugine-Kuhlman in metal production and chemicals. The proportion of the industrial labour force employed in establishments with more than 500 workers (but excluding those with fewer than ten) rose from 37 per cent to 45 per cent between 1962 and 1974. With the release of a pent-up consumer boom, the 1960s saw the beginnings of the transformation of commerce and daily life with the development first of super- and then hypermarkets by enterprises such as Carrefour, Radar and Euromarché, and more specialised chains such as FNAC in photographic equipment and books, Darty in household electrical goods, or the butchers, Bernard. All were increasingly accessible to the growing numbers of motorists and operated according to the same basic principles of low profit margins on each item, rapid rotation of stocks, bulk purchases and delayed payments to suppliers to allow the use of receipts for operations on the financial markets. In spite of restrictive legislation, in the 1960s in the Paris suburbs alone the number of supermarkets grew from ten to 253 – a development sufficient to create unsustainable competition for many small shopkeepers. Supermarkets accounted for 8 per cent of foodstuff sales in 1965 and 45 per cent by 1985. Many niches remained, however, in which small businessmen prospered by providing a personal service or guaranteed quality or by means of specialisation.

SOCIETY

Such massive economic change, involving increasingly rapid technological innovation, was accompanied by the transformation of living standards, of mentalities and of social relationships, but also, of course, by continuities. At any single point in time the perceptions each generation possesses of society and events are greatly influenced by the experience of its formative years. The historian needs to set generation alongside class or place of origin as a basic determinant of attitude and behaviour. Of the three generations alive in the 1960s, the oldest had been formed by the experience of the First World War. Most had direct links with the rural world. Their children, born in the 1920s and 1930s, and relatively few in number, had been marked by the experience of the Second World War and post-war austerity. Nevertheless, this was the generation that broke with tradition, with the 'eternal France'. Their children, those of the 'baby boom', were far more numerous, and grew up in a world of plenty. These were the first children of the consumer society, their values profoundly different from those of either their parents or grandparents. The 1960s were to be the 'years of rupture' (Borne). Economic growth facilitated both geographical and social mobility. The towns recovered their dynamism, and the exodus from the countryside accelerated. Traditional religious and moral values were questioned as part of a revolution in 'taste and expectations' (Rioux). The clearest indicators of the scale of change are the statistics on socio-professional structures, revealing as they do a rapid decline in the population employed in agriculture, stability in the number of industrial workers, growth in that of office workers, and a decline in the number of employers offset by a substantial growth in the professional and managerial categories, contributing to a strengthening of the middle classes.

An early indicator of change was the rise in birth rate evident from 1943, symptomatic of an alteration of mood in a period of acute crisis

Table 7.2 *Evolution of socio-professional groups,*
1954–75 (percentage of active population)

	1954	1962	1968	1975
Farmers	20.7	15.8	12.0	7.7
Agricultural labourers	6.0	4.3	2.9	1.8
Businessmen	12.0	10.6	9.6	8.7
Liberal professions and upper management	2.9	4.0	4.9	6.9
Middle management	5.8	7.8	9.9	13.8
Office workers	10.8	12.5	14.8	16.6
Workers	33.8	36.7	37.7	37.0
Others	8.0	8.3	8.3	7.5

Source: J.-L. Monneron and A. Rowley, *Les 25 ans qui ont transformé la France* (Nouvelle Librairie de France, 1986), 133.

and difficult to explain, particularly given the absence of so many men in German prisoner of war and labour camps. This increase proved to be more substantial and sustained than the one that had followed the previous war. The average birth rate of 21 per thousand for 1945–50 was the highest for fifty years, and, although subsequently it fell, it remained at an average of 17 per thousand as late as 1966–73, encouraged by generous family allowances, the provision of childcare facilities and a growing confidence in the future. Combined with falling mortality and rising life expectancy in all social groups, this resulted in the most rapid rate of natural demographic growth in French history, of 0.8 per cent per annum between 1946 and 1962.

The presence of large numbers of young people, and a reduction in the age of retirement, initially placed a considerable burden on the relatively small active generation born in the inter-war period. The problem of the shortage of labour was eased, however, by the eventual repatriation of over 1 million French citizens from north Africa (*pieds noirs*), by the greater employment of women, by the movement from low-productivity agricultural to more productive urban employment and by large-scale immigration from the poorer regions of Europe and from the former African colonies. The number of resident foreigners rose from 1.7 million in 1954 to 4.1 million by 1975 (6.5 per cent of the population). According to official figures the number of resident Algerians rose from 211,000 in 1954 to 884,000 by the end of 1975. Population growth both reflected and stimulated economic expansion, eventually resulting in a substantial increase in the labour force, by 2.5 million between the census of 1962 and that of 1975.

A new demographic phase became evident from the 1970s, however. In spite of the apparent enhancement of their status by enfranchisement in 1944, in the immediate post-war decades women appear largely to have accepted the ideals of home, motherhood and femininity signified by the baby boom and proclaimed in the media. Gradually, and regardless of class, a greater sense of personal autonomy developed. To meet the growing material needs of their families, women were more likely to find work outside the home, and for longer periods of their lives. The size of the average family again declined. Women's status in law also changed. The influence of both legislation and religion on sexual activity was increasingly marginalised. The provisions of the Napoleonic Code, which subordinated them to their fathers or husbands, were abrogated in 1965. An older generation despaired as moral standards appeared to be transformed. The 1975 law legalising abortion probably did nothing more than displace a widespread practice from the back streets into the more sanitary conditions of the hospital. The contraceptive pill would have a massive impact on women's lives, accompanied as it was by a sharp decline in marriage and birth rates and a further rise in labour market participation. Although the family remained the fundamental social unit, the growing popularity of cohabitation outside marriage and of divorce was further indicative of a greater sense of individual autonomy. In spite of this, and of the 1975 law on equal pay, women would nevertheless remain in an inferior position. At work they were still concentrated in particular poorly rewarded professions, providing in 1975 97.6 per cent of secretaries, 83.9 per cent of nurses and 67.2 per cent of primary school teachers. In a male-dominated society the progressive feminisation of shop and clerical work as the tasks involved were transformed by new technologies, from the typewriter to the computer, is especially revealing.

To a substantial extent, economic recovery immediately after the war had been at the expense of current consumption. The improved living standards that many had expected following the defeat of

Germany were slow to appear. Although all political parties agreed on the priority given to increasing industrial production, the CNR had nonetheless also committed itself to measures of social reform. Together with immediate wage increases, awarded to compensate for a reduction in real incomes of the order of 30 to 40 per cent during the war, these were important means of encouraging the productive effort. In a major statement of principle, the preamble to the 1946 constitution recognised the right to social security. Decrees of 4 and 19 October 1945 substantially extended protection against sickness, old age and accidents at work. Measures were also introduced that increased the rights of tenant farmers and, to the intense irritation of employers, created enterprise committees as a means of involving workers in the management of their workplaces. Through the Plan, by means of direct intervention in the economy, and through its guarantees of social welfare, the state had taken steps that represented a transition from a liberal to a mixed economic and social system. Important though these major changes were, continuities should also be stressed. Measures such as those establishing enterprise committees were to be largely ineffective in practice, and governments anxious above all to increase production were unwilling to press radical initiatives. For much the same reason, little effort was made to implement such measures in the CNR charter as the confiscation of black-market profits or those made on contracts with the German occupiers. Although most conservative politicians and businessmen were maintaining a low profile and had little choice but to accept reform, their time would come again. Little had happened to alter the basically inegalitarian character of French society or to enlarge the small circle of key decision makers.

In these circumstances, discontent was rife. Poverty and hunger were widespread. Queues were endless. Bitterness intensified. Shortages were blamed on speculators and the greed of the rich. Real incomes were slow to recover. In spring 1947 wages were worth only 64 per cent of their 1938 level. Working hours were long – an average of forty-five hours a week in 1948. At least unemployment was minimal, but inflation rapidly eroded the value of wage increases. Even when food supplies improved, consumer goods were in short supply. There were few rewards for considerable effort. Political agitation intensified unrest and the widespread sense of insecurity and injustice. Strikes were endemic. The property-owning classes complained about what they saw as the privileged treatment of the workers, and denounced rent controls, trades unions and wage increases. They were concerned about the impact of inflation on their incomes and worried about their future social status. Nevertheless, operating in a sellers' market, many farmers, manufacturers, merchants and shopkeepers did very well, in contrast with wage earners, who appear to have been considerably disadvantaged.

Much of the population continued to live in overcrowded and insanitary accommodation little changed since the nineteenth century. Desperately needed improvements in the housing stock, made all the more urgent by neglect since the onset of the depression in the 1930s, as well as wartime destruction, had been postponed in the face of the more pressing investment needs of the basic industries. At its most extreme the shortage of housing was represented by the *bidonvilles*, the shanty towns found on the outskirts of many urban areas. From around 1954, however, the housing stock was increased by means of an emergency construction programme, although many of the standardised, low-cost, high-rise suburban estates (*grands ensembles*) built for factory and office workers in the 1960s were isolated and poorly constructed and rapidly degenerated into new slums. Whilst preserving historic city centres, just like Haussmann's clearances a century earlier, the effect was to destroy the fabric and vibrant culture of many working-class *quartiers*. Even so, higher incomes and government subsidies ensured that standards of accommodation were improved considerably. By 1975 one family in two lived in recently constructed buildings. In 1954 more than one-third of households lacked running water. Only 17.5 per cent had a bathroom or shower. By 1975 70 per cent possessed these facilities. Central heating also spread rapidly, with 19 per cent of households enjoying its benefits in 1962 and 67 per cent in 1982. Greater spaciousness and physical comfort were accompanied by changing lifestyles. The television replaced the dining table as the focus of family life. The improvement of housing was combined with efforts to modernise and rejuvenate urban centres. Thus Paris saw the removal of the meat market from the city centre at Les Halles to Rungis and its replacement by a subterranean shopping complex topped with a park. Efforts were also made from the 1960s to promote economic decentralisation and encourage regional development, though, inevitably, with varying degrees of success.

The economic growth and increasing labour productivity of the 1950s allowed a substantial rise in real incomes and in purchasing power, which virtually doubled between 1949 and 1957. The following decade saw a veritable explosion of pent-up consumer demand and the diffusion of the four products, now increasingly purchased on credit, that symbolised the new age: the refrigerator (present in only 7.5 per cent of households in 1959), the washing machine (10 per cent), the television (26 per cent) and the motor car (21 per cent); the number of cars increased from 5 to 15 million between 1960 and 1975. To these would be added in the 1970s the telephone, found in only 15 per cent of homes in 1968 and 74 per cent by 1982 – a new means of communication to replace letter writing. Equally symbolic, the proportion of incomes spent on food fell from 34 to 27 per cent during the 1960s, whilst that spent on housing, health and leisure grew. The less well off revealed a great determination to catch up with the prosperous middle classes and acquire consumer durables. Amongst forty-year-olds, 50 per cent owned their accommodation in 1978, compared with only 20 per cent in 1955. By the 1970s too they were searching for a greater autonomy and expressing a preference for the little house with its own garden rather than the apartment. One of the paradoxes of the period was the greater uniformity in consumption combined with a multiplication of the opportunities to express individuality in terms of dress or culture. Intellectuals frequently expressed their contempt for the values of this consumer society, and especially for the immensely popular invasion of American pop music and films and the widespread use of words borrowed from the English language. Similarly, the wealthy resented the extension to the many of the privileges previously reserved for the few. Nevertheless, although most of the population enjoyed a security and comfort they had previously only dreamt about, income disparities between – and, indeed, within – social groups remained substantial.

The development of a welfare state contributed to the reduction of perceived inequality, however. Social security was substantially reinforced by the decrees of 1945 and law of May 1946, which sought to improve the partial protection previously available against illness, invalidity, childbirth and old age and to extend it to all wage earners and progressively to the entire population. Assurance against unemployment was generalised in the 1950s. The trades unions' role in the administration of benefits, alongside the representatives of employers and the state, would enhance their status considerably. At the same time, and largely as a pro-natalist measure, existing family allowances were increased substantially. In 1947 a national minimum wage was introduced (known since 1970 as the SMIC: *salaire minimum interprofessionel de croissance*), although in practice governments generally allowed its levels to lag behind those of wages in general in order to limit its inflationary impact.

Improvements in healthcare, seen most notably in the disappearance of the scourge of tuberculosis, and the possibility – through a combination of social security payments (reimbursing 80 per cent of the cost) and assurance – of gaining virtually free access to medical care, increased public expenditure substantially. Growing longevity and rising numbers of old people intensified this trend. The old, together with the handicapped, were for long neglected by a social security system concerned essentially with improving the situation of children and workers. Minimal pensions were extended to most of the population between 1946 and 1952, but as growing social mobility reduced familial solidarities it gradually became clear that more needed to be done. Thus increases in the real value of pensions were combined with initiatives by municipalities and parishes and, above all, self-help to provide a wide range of assistance and entertainment, which significantly improved the situation of the older age groups.

In these various ways social security played a crucial role in protecting family living standards. Its significance as a component of average household revenue rose from 2.9 per cent in 1929 to 16.6 per cent in 1950, 25 per cent in 1970 and then, largely under the impact of rising unemployment, 35.2 per cent in 1980. Funded by insurance, employer contributions and taxation, the system involved transfer payments from the better off to the poorer members of society, and as such inevitably faced considerable criticism, voiced in particular by special interest groups such as doctors, anxious to protect their independence and earnings, and businessmen, critical of a contributions system which added to their costs. The better off, in their self-interested – and, indeed, selfish – condemnation of the so-called 'dependency culture', tended to ignore the inequities of a taxation structure that, heavily based on indirect taxes, imposed a major burden on the poor. They also often forgot the inherently conservative impact of a system that reduced discontent.

Combined with that of the educational system, one major consequence of economic expansion was to increase the opportunities for geographical and social mobility. Between 1954 and 1962 12 million people are calculated to have changed their commune of residence. In spite of substantial upward movement, however, the acquisition by the less well off of the educational qualifications necessary for mobility continued to be obstructed by social and self-imposed handicaps alike. Moreover, even as the numbers of skilled, supervisory, managerial and professional positions expanded, the space created for newcomers was inevitably restricted, both by the rates of economic growth and by the ability of the already relatively privileged to maintain their positions within the overlapping professional, wealth and status hierarchies. It would be the generation reaching maturity in the 1960s that would be in the best position to take advantage of the expansion of opportunity.

The structure inherited in 1945 provided for compulsory primary instruction until fourteen. Secondary education was reserved for a small minority (about 200,000 at any one time). Most received a humanistic teaching in which the classics retained a dominant position. Only some 3 per cent of each age group took the final examination, the *baccalauréat*. The system largely reflected the prevailing social hierarchy, with a fundamental segregation between the primary and secondary levels and between the sexes. With the exception of a very small group of 'deserving' and often intellectually outstanding working-class and peasant children, secondary education was reserved for the middle classes. The dominance of the state was unchallenged, with a uniform curriculum designed to ensure the diffusion of a common culture and sense of civic virtue, although, especially in the west, private Catholic schools were tolerated and, controversially, from 1959 were to receive substantial state funding. Their continuing popularity amongst parents was based not only on the religious instruction they offered but also on their reputation for firmer discipline and their 'snob' value. The educational system in general was increasingly criticised both for its élitism and for its neglect of scientific and technical instruction.

The arrival of the baby boom generation, urbanisation and the commitment of post-war governments to raise the school leaving age from fourteen to sixteen (in 1959), as well as to increasing access to secondary education, created a pressing need for an increase in and a redistribution of resources. A substantial rise in demand should in any case have been anticipated. It had already affected nursery schools from 1949/50 and primary education from 1951/2, and would hit secondary schools in 1957/8 and, finally, higher education from 1964. Successive governments failed to appreciate that the growing population and the modernisation of French society would result in substantial increases in participation rates and in demand for secondary and higher education, however, and their response was rarely adequate. The number of pupils attending secondary schools rose from around 1 million in 1950/1 to 5 million by 1979/80. Over one-third of these obtained the *baccalauréat*, turning what had been the means by which a small minority qualified for entry into the élite into a mass qualification. The problems of expansion were enormous. Schools had to be constructed and equipped, teachers trained and teaching programmes adapted. Reform followed reform, adding to the confusion, with the most far-reaching probably being the final imposition of the comprehensive principle by Valéry Giscard d'Estaing's education minister, René Haby, in 1975. Access was massively widened, although élitism survived through the selection processes of particular prestigious *lycées* or private schools. Concerned overwhelmingly with the protection of their own vested interests, the powerful teaching unions contributed little of any value to an increasingly bitter debate on the objectives and methods of education. Nevertheless, and in line with the development of less overtly authoritarian relationships in society as a whole, teaching methods changed. A new generation of teachers was concerned less with the transmission of knowledge and more with the development of the pupils' curiosity and critical faculties. An idealistic pedagogy designed for enthusiastic and competent teachers and intelligent and highly motivated children was difficult to sustain, however, and often inappropriate for pupils who were intellectually less well endowed or lacked parental support.

Higher education also faced the problems of expansion, with, by 1980, a tenfold growth from the 100,000 students of 1950, as governments made determined efforts to widen access. In this sphere, élitism was preserved by the selection procedures of the most prestigious institutions of higher education, the *grandes écoles*, which offered access to the most powerful and highly remunerated positions in the public service and private enterprise, and through the process of *pantouflage* – established networks of graduates sharing a commitment to modernisation (and mutual advancement) and circulating between the civil service, business and politics.

Did economic growth and social reform reduce social inequality? Certainly, living standards improved considerably, and social mobility increased as high levels of demand for well-qualified employees were created by the expansion of public and private sector companies such as France Télécom and Airbus, in the motor industry, electronics and energy production, in healthcare and in the universities. New opportunities also reflected the growing complexity and tertiarisation of the economy and expansion of public services. The numbers of doctors and teachers and of managerial, clerical and technical staff in both public and private employment grew considerably. These were the groups that particularly benefited from the development of educational opportunity and of the welfare state. The barriers crossed, however, were essentially those between peasants and workers and the lower clerical and managerial grades. Access to political office, higher managerial and bureaucratic posts, the professions and employment in the media remained extremely restricted. Moreover, the relationship between status, wealth and power was complex. A family-based *patronat* survived in such major enterprises as Michelin, Dassault and Schlumberger, but most large companies were run by managers and owned by a diverse group of individual or institutional shareholders. Whilst one should certainly avoid the mistake of thinking about social and political élites in monolithic terms, and pay careful attention to sometimes bitter personal, generational, professional and ideological rivalries, what this 'untidy reality' (Wright) added up to was the existence of a group holding public and private power that was recruited primarily amongst the Parisian bourgeoisie and given a sense of unity by linkages based on shared social origins,

Table 7.3 *Middle-class professions, 1954–75*

	1954	1975
Industrialists	86,000	61,600
Wholesale merchants	183,700	190,200
Artisans	734,700	535,344
Shopkeepers	1,274,000	921,000
Liberal professions	163,160	249,440

Source: D. Borne, *Histoire de la société française depuis 1945* (Armand Colin, 1988), 112.

inherited wealth, graduation from the élite *écoles*, intermarriage, acceptance of common norms of behaviour and of a Parisian location, and shared goals, including the effective management of a pluralistic society and a capitalistic economy and the safeguarding of the established social order. Greater upward mobility into an expanding and increasingly technocratic civil service and managerial class did not profoundly alter this situation. Normally, success remained the result of accumulated effort, often spread over two or three generations, and its translation into wealth and cultural capital. The minority of newcomers succeeded because of both ability and effort and their willingness to conform to established expectations. As so often in the past, in post-war France, old and new élites coalesced. Shared objectives even persuaded many Catholics to finally accept the permanence of republican institutions.

Whatever the limits, economic expansion certainly facilitated upward social mobility on a substantial scale, renewing the middle classes and ensuring that they remained as determined as ever to emphasise the social and cultural gulf that separated them from the working classes. In contrast, technological change and economic concentration had their most marked adverse effects on artisans and shopkeepers, who declined from 13 per cent to 8 per cent of the working population between 1954 and 1975, with their insecurity being translated into political terms through Poujadism in the 1950s and later by the Front national. Even so, for many workers and immigrants a small business still represented the possibility of social promotion.

The reduced significance of agriculture was evident both in its declining contribution to GDP and in the reduction of the active farming population from 7.4 million in 1946 to 2 million by 1975. Together with government encouragement of restructuring, the rural exodus, involving most notably the young and landless, facilitated an increase in the average size of farms. When combined with technical innovation and price supports, this resulted in a substantial growth in farm incomes. Nevertheless, with the exception of the large capitalistic farms of the north and the Paris basin, these remained relatively low. The improvement in communications, greater awareness of the wider society, and the desire for better living standards this promoted increased rural discontent and support for pressure group activity. Moreover, dependence on traditional social élites was replaced by subordination to the banks (especially the Crédit agricole) that financed the technical revolution, as well as to the cooperative and processing companies to which most farmers were tied by long-term contracts. The decline in rural population was also accompanied by the deterioration of public services as churches, schools, post offices and shops closed due to lack of custom. Formerly vital social networks withered. The collapse of peasant farming and the sense of desperation evident in many rural communities provoked repeated disorderly protest.

In contrast, the industrial working class initially expanded in the post-war decades. From the 1950s many workers began to enjoy a rapid improvement in their living standards. A new lifestyle and a more materialistic and individualistic culture emerged with the provision of subsidised housing by the state and the possession of a car (by nearly 75 per cent of working class families by 1975) and television (88 per cent). Nevertheless, many workers remained dissatisfied, more aware of the threat posed to their nominal wages by inflation than of the gradual rise in their real incomes. This 'unique generation', a relatively homogeneous and class-conscious proletariat forged in the struggles of the 1930s, war and reconstruction, and symbolised above all by the heroic figures of the coal miner and steelworker, was to be overwhelmed rapidly by technological innovation and structural change in the economy. Widespread urban renewal resulted, furthermore, in the physical destruction of many formally vibrant – if appallingly housed – working-class communities.

From the 1960s employment declined in the old staple industries such as coal, steel and textiles. Green-field sites were developed for the manufacture of cars and other consumer products, particularly in the west, around Rennes and Caen, by governments anxious to spread prosperity and employers looking for less militant and cheaper labour. The development of assembly line work for largely unskilled labour in automated plants offered employment to migrants from the countryside, southern Europe and overseas, as well as to growing numbers of women. In large factories mass-producing consumer goods, as well as in the smaller enterprises of the clothing or building industries, increasingly the aim of management was to take on a cheap and relatively undemanding labour force, whose members could be dismissed easily in case of recession and replaced when conditions improved. Flexibility and restructuring for the businessman represented increased insecurity for the worker, though. Opportunities for social promotion remained extremely limited and workers shared a resentment of authoritarian management, of the petty tyranny and stopwatch mentality of managers and foremen. Wage differentials also widened to reflect shortages, particularly in sectors of industry with a high proportion of skilled labour such as aeronautics, chemicals and electronics. A more stable, high-wage employment was also provided by many small and medium-sized family enterprises in sectors such as engineering. Whilst the better rewarded, together with workers in the public sector, were able to maintain the protection of trades union membership, other groups lacked effective representation and risked marginalisation. Overall, these diverse developments represented a greater fragmentation of the labour market and of the working class as working conditions and lifestyles grew more diverse.

Workers at least shared in the expansion of leisure time that is such a feature of contemporary society, both in terms of time gained from work and by means of the decline of traditional pursuits such as Sunday churchgoing. Whilst surviving as a formative cultural phenomenon, for most of the population religion declined almost to insignificance as a feature of daily life. The participation of the Christian democrat Mouvement républicain populaire (MRP) in the Cold War struggle against communism encouraged morally bankrupt, conservative elements in the Vatican hierarchy, close to Pope Pius XII, to reassert the absolute authority of the papacy. The collapse of religious vocations in the 1950s and the resultant ageing of and sharp decline in the numbers of priests were nevertheless clear signs of a crisis and of an inability to combat secularisation. The liberalisation of the Church's teaching apparently promised by the election of John XXIII (1958–63) as Pope and as a result of the second Vatican Council was reversed by his successors. The Church appeared increasingly out of touch, especially on such crucial moral questions as abortion and contraception, the role of women in society and the celibacy of the clergy, and this in spite of the development of a less rigorist moral theology. A new Sunday, for a new society, and a mass culture emerged in the 1960s. The decade saw the emergence of a relatively classless 'pop' culture devoted to such idols as Johnny Hallyday and Sylvie Vartan. Symptomatic, according to its critics, of the 'Americanisation' of French culture, Bob Dylan encouraged the young to believe that 'les temps changent'. In spite of stultifying government controls and censorship of news, radio and television, as well as gambling and sport, boomed, as did expenditure on holidays.

POLITICAL LIFE

The Fourth Republic

The Third Republic was finally declared dead by a large popular majority in a referendum on 21 October 1945. A Constituent Assembly with a mission to prepare a new constitution was elected on the same day. For the first time women were allowed to vote, although the various parties would select only a tiny number of women as candidates. Politics continued to be overwhelmingly male-dominated. Conducted using a system of proportional representation, this election revealed an overwhelming shift to the left. The old political class appeared to have been swept away, and replaced by newcomers to parliament (85 per cent), the vast majority of whom (80 per cent) had been involved in resistance. Indeed, three-quarters of the electorate supported the parties most clearly identified with the Liberation: the Communists (Parti communiste français: PCF),

Plate 7.2 Brigitte Bardot on the set of *Vie privée*, 1 January 1961. Photo:
Loomis Dean/Time & Life Pictures/Getty Images.

Socialists (Section française de l'internationale ouvrière: SFIO) and
Christian Democrats (MRP). The divisions between these groups
would soon become evident, however, as they jockeyed for power.
So too would the tensions between these elected politicians and

Table 7.4 *Results of Constituent Assembly election,*
21 October 1945

	Votes	Share (percentage of votes)	Seats
Communists	5,024,174	26.12	159
Socialists	4,491,152	23.35	146
Radicals, UDSR[a] and others	2,018,665	10.49	60
MRP	4,580,222	23.81	150
Conservatives, independents and others	3,001,063	15.60	64
Abstentions	4,965,256	20.1[b]	

Notes: [a] Union démocratique et socialiste de la Résistance.
[b] Percentage of registered voters.

General de Gaulle. The general was convinced that the political system of the Third Republic, which had reinforced the authority of parliament and its squabbling parties at the expense of a relatively weak executive, had been a primary cause of catastrophe in 1940. He insisted on the need to establish a strong presidential regime. His unique position as head of state was initially recognised by the assembly. There were nonetheless widespread suspicions of his authoritarian, 'Bonapartist' intentions. On 20 January 1946, following a disagreement with ministers over the military budget, de Gaulle resigned, recognising that with the restoration of the party system his authority was increasingly likely to be challenged, and assuming that public opinion would soon demand his recall. He would have to wait until 1958.

The surviving idealism of the resistance and the initially secure majority of the three parties committed to a cooperative *tripartisme*, together with suspicion of authoritarian government, ensured the rapid re-establishment of a parliamentary system, with a largely decorative presidency, although it does seem likely that, given the difficult circumstances in which the country found itself, much of the electorate would have welcomed a strong executive power. The initial proposals emerging from the Constituent Assembly, and supported especially by the Socialists and Communists, provided for a unicameral system with an omnipotent Chamber of Deputies. Surprisingly, this was rejected in a referendum held on 5 May 1946, by 10.5 million votes to 9.4 million, largely it seems because of anxiety about possible Communist dominance of such an assembly. During the campaign for the election of a second Constituent Assembly in June, the MRP, which had called for rejection, significantly increased its support at the expense of the Socialists. It was clear that the parties of the left (Communists and Socialists) no longer commanded an absolute majority. Although *tripartisme* survived, an alternative majority made up of the centre-left (MRP) and the re-emerging centre-right began to appear a real possibility, particularly with the return of de Gaulle to the political scene.

In a speech made in Bayeux on 16 June 1946 the general had called for the establishment of a presidential regime, with a head of state independent of party, although responsible to parliament. On 13 October, however, another referendum accepted the second Constituent Assembly's proposals for the establishment of a Fourth Republic with a bicameral Assembly. Although the Socialist Auriol, elected president (1947–54) by a joint meeting of both houses of the legislature, would come to play an influential role in the formation of governments, both the Senate and the president were to enjoy only very limited power. Authority would rest with the elected representatives in the Chamber of Deputies. This was hardly an auspicious beginning. The prolonged constitutional debate had been greeted with widespread public apathy – partly reflecting disillusionment caused by economic hardship – and a revealing lack of commitment on the part of many leading political figures.

Politically, the Fourth Republic can be divided into four phases, defined by the predominance of one or other political coalition. First came *tripartisme*, with government based on an alliance of Socialists, Communists and Christian Democrats. This was a fruitful period of economic and social reform, brought to an end in May 1947 when, as a consequence of the emerging Cold War, the Communists were forced into opposition. They were replaced by a combination of Radicals and other centrists, who helped constitute a 'Third Force' opposed to both the Communists and the Gaullists on the right. Subsequently, after the 1951 election, the predominant groups in government were to be Radicals and conservatives, until in 1956 a majority made up of Socialists and their allies was returned to deal with mounting financial problems and the colonial war in Algeria.

The initial desire of the three main political groups within the resistance to work together represented a commitment to implementing the reform measures included in the CNR charter. The strength of popular support for these parties had been made clear in the election of the Constituent Assembly in October 1945. Perhaps inevitably, unity was short-lived. The defeat of the common enemy was followed by a reconstitution of political life, much along pre-war lines. Tension rapidly grew between the partners in this uneasy alliance. Distrust of the Communists was evident from the start. Events in eastern Europe kindled considerable suspicion. The PCF's strong electoral showing raised the unappealing prospect, particularly for the Socialists, of serving as the junior partners in a Communist-dominated coalition. Neither the Socialists nor the MRP would accept the Communist leader Thorez as prime minister, however, whilst de Gaulle ensured that Communist ministers were excluded from the key ministries controlling the police and army. The initial willingness of the Communists to at least temporarily postpone realisation of the revolutionary dreams of many of their supporters reflected not just Stalin's reluctance to challenge the Western powers at a time when his main concern was to secure Soviet control over eastern Europe but also the commitment of the French Communist leaders to reconstruction. They were convinced that the moral credit derived from a brilliant war record would ensure continued mass support. The prospect of assuming power, perhaps with Socialist collaboration, must have seemed very real. At the end of 1946, with 800,000 mainly working-class members, the PCF was the largest political party, well organised, with an effective propaganda machine, the sympathy of influential artists and intellectuals such as Pablo Picasso and Jean-Paul Sartre and a predominating influence within the trades unions, its sense of identity nowhere more evident than at the annual Fête de l'Humanité.

The MRP had been founded in November 1944 as a means of reconciling the working classes with the Church, and the Church with the Republic. Its potential influence had been reinforced substantially by the enfranchisement of women. Discredited by its close links with Vichy, initially the Catholic hierarchy was prepared to accept a more liberal politics as the price of preserving its influence over the new regime, a significant proportion of whose ministers were known to be practising Catholics. Even in 1945/6, however, the left-wing idealism of the party's founders was giving way before the more conservative outlook of many of its supporters. A substantial proportion of these were simply refugees from more overtly conservative groups discredited by their association with Vichy's collaborationist policies. They viewed the MRP primarily as a bulwark against Marxism, and, with increasingly enthusiastic support from the Vatican, they were able to ensure that, more than ever, political behaviour came to reflect the map of religious beliefs.

It was the emergence of the Cold War that increasingly determined the political situation within France. Initially most politicians, including the Communists, shared a determination to restore the country to its pre-war position as a leading military and imperial power. Coming to terms with being a second-rank state was always going to be difficult. The struggle for hegemony between the two superpowers, together with the agonies of decolonisation, made it all the more painful. De Gaulle's sensibilities had been offended greatly by the absence of an invitation to attend the great power discussions at Yalta and Potsdam in 1945. Dependence upon US aid made it difficult to adopt a tough, independent line, however. Concessions had to be made on such key issues as the creation of a centralised administration in West Germany, West German rearmament and free access to the French market for American products. Furthermore, the US government required the implementation of policies designed to secure a balanced budget and reduce inflation. Tax increases, reductions in government spending and price and wage controls were unpleasant remedies in a period of extreme austerity. The American administration also made clear its growing unhappiness about the presence of Communists in the French government, with Dean Acheson, the US Secretary of State, warning President Truman in February 1947 that a Communist takeover in France was a very real possibility. The Marshall Plan, announced in June and providing for a massive programme of free aid (between April 1948 and January 1952 France received $2,629 million, of which $2,122 million were non-repayable), was conceived both as a way of providing markets for American goods by assisting European

Table 7.5 *Results of National Assembly election,*
10 November 1946

	Votes	Share (percentage of votes)	Seats
Communists	5,430,593	28.2	182
Socialists	3,433,901	17.8	102
Radicals, UDSR and others	2,136,152	11.1	69
MRP	4,988,609	25.9	173
Conservatives, independents and others	3,072,743	15.9	76
Abstentions	5,504,913		

recovery and as a means of reducing the likelihood of unemployment and misery and thus of Communist-inspired political disorder. It was to be a major stage in the reinforcement of the Western alliance.

The elections to the National Assembly held on 10 November 1946 made it clear that a process of left–right polarisation was under way and that the left was in a minority. The tripartite alliance was riven by dissension, and a renewal of the governing coalition had become impossible. The efforts of a minority Socialist administration under Blum to control inflation and stimulate economic recovery were short-lived. The Socialists themselves were bitterly divided. At their July 1946 congress they had elected Guy Mollet as party secretary on a platform that, whilst rejecting the Soviet model, reaffirmed the party's commitment to Marxist ideology, warned against collaboration with the bourgeois parties and recommended closer links with the Communists. This was not the moment. As the international situation deteriorated, the Communists denounced the Marshall Plan, the subservient position of French governments and all those who supported this manifestation of American imperialism. The brutal imposition of Soviet rule in eastern Europe persuaded the Socialists, however, that communism posed a far greater threat than liberal, capitalistic democracy. Rumours of an imminent Communist coup led Paul Ramadier, another Socialist, who had succeeded Blum in January 1947 as the head of a government that now included Radicals and other representatives of the centre, to alert reliable military units. In this situation the dismissal of Communist ministers from the government, in May 1947, was inevitable. It was occasioned by Thorez's denunciation of wage and price controls and the refusal of Communist ministers to vote credits for the war in Indo-China. Tactically, the PCF was determined to win the support of workers disappointed by the slowness of social reform and of improvement in living standards, and who were resorting to strikes and violent protest. At this stage the eventual return of its ministers to government was certainly expected. The takeover by the Communist Party of Czechoslovakia in Prague in February 1948, welcomed by the PCF as a 'great victory of Czech democracy', would generate an increasingly hysterical, but also very understandable, anti-communism, however.

Internal political tension grew all the more bitter as fear of a global nuclear conflict reached its peak between 1948 and 1958 due to events in Prague, the Berlin blockade, war in Korea and the invasion of Hungary. Signed in March 1947 by France and Britain, the Treaty of Dunkirk had been directed primarily against a potentially resurgent Germany. The establishment of NATO in 1949 reflected the efforts of the foreign minister, Georges Bidault, and his British counterpart, Ernest Bevin, to secure American military support against the Russian menace. Although this was the prelude to an eventual and much-resented rearmament of West Germany, these treaties at least provided the security guarantees that France had failed to obtain following the First World War. In these circumstances, the PCF developed as a party of permanent opposition. In a period of intense political debate and of engaged militancy, enjoying the prestige it and the Soviet Union had won in the liberation of Europe, the party and its various front organisations were able to create a dynamic counter-culture and to offer a spiritual refuge to those members of an increasingly exhausted and demoralised working class still prepared to continue the struggle against low wages and social injustice. In spite of the ineffectiveness of its political and industrial tactics, a quarter of the electorate voted for the party in 1951. Subsequently, gradually but almost continually, support would drain away. Increasingly inward-looking, concerned to preserve its Stalinist purity and to purge dissenters, the PCF welcomed Soviet suppression of the 1956 Hungarian revolt as yet another famous victory for Leninism. Although it was able to retain much of its working-class

Plate 7.3 Troops, employed by Socialist ministers as strike breakers in October 1947 and early 1948, guarding pitheads in the Saint-Etienne region.

support, even when anti-communists split the trades union federation (the Confédération générale du travail: CGT) to form the CGT-FO (Force ouvrière) in April 1948, the party was unable to escape from its isolation. It became patently unable to come to terms with economic and social developments that resulted in the improvement of living standards. Moreover, changes in the structure of the workforce resulted in a continuous decline in the size and economic importance of its working-class constituency, which was becoming more diverse and more fully integrated into the national society.

In November 1947 Ramadier's fragile coalition gave way to a government led by Schuman of the MRP, the composition of which marked a clear shift to the right. Within it even the Socialist interior minister, Jules Moch, was committed to repressive action against strikers and demonstrators. In the interests of 'Republican defence' he mobilised 60,000 riot police and troops against 15,000 miners in the northern coalfields during November and December, a move that left six dead and many injured. However uncomfortably, the SFIO, a

Table 7.6 *Results of National Assembly election, 17 June 1951*
(metropolitan France only)

	Votes	Share (percentage of votes)	Seats (including overseas)
Communists	4,910,547	25.67	101
Socialists	2,744,842	14.35	107
Radicals	1,887,583	9.87	95
MRP	2,369,778	12.39	96
Conservatives, independents and others	2,656,995	13.88	108
Gaullists	4,125,492	21.56	120
Abstentions	4,859,968		

party with a revolutionary ideology, was to remain within a series of increasingly conservative 'Third Force' governments, skilfully presided over by the Radical Henri Queuille, all of them committed to the Atlantic alliance, to colonial wars, to the rejection of further social reform and to the repression of the working-class movement. Although they brought down a whole series of governments on questions of economic and social reform between 1947 and 1951, the Socialists were unable to combat effectively the MRP's growing adherence to liberalism or the essential conservatism of a reviving Radical Party still led by such stalwarts of the Third Republic as Herriot and Daladier. As a result of this situation and of the internal differences it provoked, the Socialist Party was to lose much of its credibility. Membership collapsed from 280,000 in 1947 to 130,000 in 1951 and was increasingly confined to the old strongholds in the north and Midi. This weakening was revealed clearly by the results of the 1951 election, in spite of changes in the electoral system designed to disadvantage the critics of the regime on both left (Communists) and right (Gaullists). In future, governments would be drawn from the centre-right, with only occasional Socialist participation.

Although it divided the left, the Cold War helped to ensure mass support for the right under the anti-communist banner. It facilitated the return to political life of many former Vichy sympathisers. The fear of social revolution, which in the nineteenth century had led to the bloody massacres of 1848 and 1871, remained a potent political force. This was a theme that could be stressed by the Catholic MRP, as well as by de Gaulle in founding his Rassemblement du peuple français (RPF) in April 1947. Apparently convinced that a global war against communism was close, the general called for the association of capital and labour within the free enterprise system, for the rejection of confrontational party politics, for a strong and independent France within the Western alliance and for firm and effective internal government. This declaration of war on the Fourth Republic appealed especially to the possessing classes, but in a fashion reminiscent of Bonapartism it won adherents in all social groups. By the end of the year the movement had perhaps 1 million members, many of them attracted from the MRP. Such a dynamic organisation clearly posed a threat to the regime. It proved impossible to sustain the commitment of the disparate groups, however, which had looked on it as yet another new beginning. The years 1950 and 1951 saw a substantial loss of enthusiasm and a collapse of membership.

The recovery of the right was nevertheless evident. Whilst supported by the MRP, the governments that emerged from the Assembly elected in 1951 were essentially representative of the centre-right. This was clear during the 1952 Pinay administration, which sought to promote economic liberalisation, limit state expenditure and reduce taxation. These were policies well suited to the times, helping to moderate and to sustain economic growth and to ease the transition from austerity to consumerism. In the shorter term, however, they could do little to reduce the budget deficit, caused – in spite of massive American assistance – in large part by the destructive colonial wars fought to preserve France's 'civilising' influence in Madagascar and especially Indo-China. The latter might well have been avoided if the colonial lobby and military commanders on the spot had not been so determined to restore an imperial system that still appeared of central importance in the re-establishment of French power and pride. They were not prepared to respect the agreement reached in 1946 between the Communist leader Ho Chi Minh and de Gaulle's emissary Jean Sainteny. As a result, an overextended and poorly equipped army would be committed for seven years to an increasingly hopeless struggle. 'Selling out' on the Empire would remain a position most politicians did not dare adopt.

The unfavourable balance of payments situation was another persistent problem. Ministerial instability, together with widespread discontent caused by the impact of regressive tax structures and inflation on incomes, and amongst farmers because of falling agricultural prices, added to the impression of chaos. Governments could be overturned suddenly on all manner of issues. They rarely lasted more than six months, and, whilst in practice the establishment of a new government involved little more than a reshuffling of ministerial personnel, it became clear that political stability was impossible on the basis of the Assembly elected in 1951. There were too many fissures within as well as between parties.

Perhaps the last chance for the Fourth Republic came in the immediate aftermath of the humiliating military disaster at Dien Bien Phu. On 17 June 1954 Mendès-France, a severe critic of the political system and proponent of strong, coherent and reforming government, became prime minister with apparently broad parliamentary and public support. His objectives were to negotiate a withdrawal from Indo-China and to accelerate the pace of economic and social modernisation. The new prime minister's energy and refusal to play the usual political games inevitably aroused considerable suspicion. In place of the usual sharing of ministries between the governing parties, Mendès-France insisted upon the appointment of relatively youthful and independent figures of proven competence. They included Mitterrand from the centre-left as interior minister, and the left-Gaullist Jacques Chaban-Delmas as minister of public works, as well as the more experienced Edgar Faure, who took the key Finance Ministry. The radio broadcasts in which he seemed to be appealing to the nation, over the heads of the political establishment, aroused particular hostility, and nowhere more than within the ranks of his own Radical Party.

The most pressing problem, that of Indo-China, was solved by an armistice signed on 21 July, which provided for partition along the seventeenth parallel and the withdrawal of the French expeditionary force. This had already lost some 92,000 men. The agreement left its leaders with a deep sense of humiliation. Blaming the politicians for their failure, they were determined to make no further concessions in what many of them saw as a crusade against international communism. In spite of its short life, the Mendès-France government was

Plate 7.4 The government of Pierre Mendès-France, 19 June 1954. François Mitterrand is on his right. © Roger-Viollet/TopFoto.

able to introduce a series of measures intended to improve the competitiveness of the French economy. These included agricultural price supports and cheap loans and assistance for industrial restructuring and training. Surprisingly little public interest was shown in a social policy that promised increased investment in housing and education. In contrast, the government's campaign against alcoholism drew venomous attacks from both the home distillers and the commercial alcohol lobby, much of it anti-Semitic in character and intended to throw doubt on the patriotic credentials of a prime minister who seemed to prefer milk to more 'manly' national beverages.

Although initially opinion polls suggested that Mendès-France had secured the enthusiastic support of most of the population, the prime minister was soon under attack from the right for his supposed betrayal of Empire. Doubt was thrown on his determination to defend vital French interests. The possible creation of a European army within the remit of the proposed European Defence Community – conceived of as a means of controlling West Germany – and its implications for national sovereignty enflamed a bitter debate amongst government supporters. Mitterrand, victim of a secret service plot to discredit the government it was supposed to serve, was accused of leaking defence secrets to the Communists. On the left, Mollet, the Socialist leader, was more concerned with preserving the unity of his own party than with supporting the government. It was hardly surprising that, although there was a widespread public desire for the curtailment of an increasingly sterile political conflict, Mendès-France's proposals for constitutional reform, designed to strengthen the executive, enjoyed limited parliamentary support.

It was events in north Africa that led to the final showdown. The government had reacted firmly to the outbreak of intercommunal violence in Algeria, in May 1945 and again in November 1954, as well as to the foundation of the nationalist Front de libération nationale (FLN). Although disturbed by reports of military atrocities, Mitterrand had unequivocally declared that Algeria would remain part of France and supported this by sanctioning troop reinforcements and widespread arrests. Mendès-France's willingness to end the protectorate over Tunisia and to improve the situation of Algerian Muslims had nevertheless thrown doubt upon this commitment. On 5 February 1955 conservative politicians concerned about Mendès-France's modernisation programme were joined by MRP deputies, who saw the prospect of reform in Algeria as a sign of weakness, and by the Communists, consistent opponents of any 'neo-capitalist' administration. The Radical Party itself was irremediably split. Faure challenged Mendès-France for the party leadership, and on 23 February was able to form a centre-right government. Although unable to survive a debate on electoral reform on 29 November, this master of political compromise proved able to use some of the more complicated articles of the constitution to secure the dissolution of parliament before the end of its full term – the first time this had happened since 1877.

The campaign that preceded the general election, held on 2 January 1956, revealed growing political fragmentation. Mendès-France was able to form a Front républicain with support from the Socialists and from a diverse centre-left, which included Mitterrand and members of the UDSR as well as Chaban-Delmas and some Gaullists. Their inevitably vague programme supported a negotiated peace in Algeria and the continuation of economic modernisation and social reform at home. In an unpleasant campaign, moderate conservatives were anxious about the prospect of being outflanked on the right by candidates of the Poujadist movement (after the name of its leader) the Union de

Table 7.7 *Results of National Assembly election, 2 January 1956 (metropolitan France only)*

	Votes	Share (percentage of votes)	Seats (including overseas)
Communists	5,514,403	25.36	150
Socialists	3,247,431	14.93	95
Radicals, UDSR and others	3,227,484	14.84	91
MRP	2,366,321	10.88	83
Conservatives, independents and others	3,259,782	14.99	95
Poujadists, extreme right	2,744,562	12.62	52
Gaullists	842,351	3.87	22
Abstentions	4,602,942		

défense des commerçants et artisans. Beginning as an anti-tax protest movement, this was supported by small businessmen and farmers from the economically underdeveloped centre and south-west, attracted by its opposition to modernisation and to the 'vampire' state. The movement also enjoyed the backing of the defenders of the cause of French Algeria (Algérie française), including such luminaries as the thuggish ex-paratrooper Jean-Marie Le Pen. They shared a contempt for parliament, an extreme xenophobia, anti-Semitism and a visceral anti-communism.

Once again the elections failed to provide a clear parliamentary majority. Whether of the centre-left or right, the Gaullists in particular lost heavily. The president, René Coty, decided that the Socialist Mollet rather than Mendès-France stood the better chance of forming a government. This would be based on a very uncertain centre-left parliamentary combination, constantly imperilled by the lack of party discipline and divisions between its constituent parts. Although the Mendès-France government is often represented as the last real opportunity to preserve the Fourth Republic by means of reform, and in spite of the usual incensed opposition on the part of conservatives to tax increases, the Mollet administration was able to secure substantial improvements in welfare provision for the aged and sick, as well as to increase funding for housing and regional aid. Ominously, however, the war in Algeria was beginning to absorb capital and manpower on a scale that seemed to threaten financial stability and economic growth. It also further embittered political life.

Mollet acted on the mistaken assumption that the FLN would settle for something less than full independence and that Europeans in Algeria would accept a diminution of their privileged position. He was to be rapidly disabused. Revenge killings by French soldiers and civilians, following the FLN-inspired massacre of 123 Europeans in the Constantine region in August 1955, probably destroyed any lingering hope of a compromise based upon the integration of Algeria into France with full rights of citizenship for all its inhabitants. The concessions previously made to the Muslim population had often not been implemented, by a colonial administration that was more responsive to the racism of a French settler population of around 1 million and that had done little to counter the growing unwillingness of the majority population to tolerate social and racial inferiority. The mistakes of Indo-China were about to be repeated. Successive governments were to accept the self-interested advice of colonial administrators and military commanders, and to succumb to pressure from settler opinion and conservative politicians. Now 'pacification' became a precondition for reform. In the search for a military solution Mollet would find himself increasingly in the paradoxical position of being condemned by the left and winning support from the right.

The army would enjoy considerable success. Its officers had developed a new sense of purpose as a result of their harsh experience in Indo-China. They believed they had a mission to integrate Algeria into the national community and to continue the crusade against the Communist-inspired subversion that alone, in their eyes, prevented the achievement of this aim. Once again, in assuming ever closer control over Algeria, the officer corps could pose as the incarnation of France. Their patriotism was exceeded only by their arrogance and by their contempt for the politicians, who they believed had betrayed them in the earlier war and might do so again. Some 400,000 men were eventually committed to an increasingly ruthless campaign. General Massu's paratroopers fought and won the 'Battle of Algiers' against the FLN's urban networks. The construction of the electrified Morice Line made it impossible for independence

Plate 7.5 Military operations in Algeria: on guard in the casbah. Photo: Central Press/Getty Images.

fighters to cross the frontier from their havens in Tunisia without suffering heavy casualties. The recruitment of Muslim auxiliaries (*harkis*) reinforced divisions within the indigenous population at the same time as strengthening the French military position.

Politically the campaign was a disaster, however. In November 1956, in cooperation with Britain and Israel, France launched an attack on President Nasser's Egypt, believed to be both the inspiration and armourer of Algerian insurgents. The bombing of the Tunisian village of Sakhiet in February 1958, and particularly the systematic use of torture to obtain information, added to the sense of international outrage. Within France itself the initial broad support for preserving French Algeria was dissipating. In spite of censorship, criticism of government policy was voiced especially by Communists, some Catholic activists and members of Socialist youth groups. They were supported by leading newspapers and, most notably, *Le Monde* and the weekly *L'Express*, although this was little enough in comparison with the patriotic, pro-war sentiments of the mass-circulation right-wing press and the government-controlled radio and television. Even official Communist criticism was restrained from fear of alienating a working-class constituency that was, initially at least, committed to a war being waged largely by its own sons. Nevertheless, public opinion, which had been relatively indifferent to the distant Indo-Chinese war fought mainly by regular and colonial troops, was much more concerned about a conflict waged in an area that was, nominally at least, part of France and that drew in rising numbers of young conscripts. A majority of the respondents to an opinion poll in autumn 1957 already doubted whether Algeria would remain French. The rise of opposition was based on moral and political objections and doubts as to whether the rising costs of the war in terms of men and money could be maintained, in spite of the willingness of the United States to absorb some of the material burden as part of the worldwide struggle against communism. The resignation of Mendès-France, minister without portfolio in the Mollet government, and the criticism voiced by Mitterrand, too ambitious to actually resign, were signs of a loss of confidence within the political élite itself.

The subsequent replacement of Mollet, successively by the Radicals Maurice Bourgès-Maunoury and Félix Gaillard, represented a reshuffling of ministries between Socialists, members of the MRP and Radicals, in the absence of new initiatives towards Algeria or solutions for the escalating financial problems caused by the war. In May 1958, however, the Socialists finally decided that coalitions with parties of the right in efforts to solve the Algerian problem were

leading nowhere. Their withdrawal made the formation of a government all the more difficult. After almost a month President Coty
called on Pierre Pflimlin of the MRP to form an administration.
The real significance of this action was that the new prime minister
had previously called for negotiations with the FLN. Demonstrations
in Paris and an open rejection of the government's authority by
civilians and the army in Algeria greeted his appointment. The final
crisis of the regime had begun.

In Algeria European extremists had called for resistance, and on this
occasion they received support from senior military commanders. On
13 May a Committee of Public Safety, including General Massu,
assumed power. In response, Pflimlin took an apparently tough line,
calling on all parties to join him in defence of the Republic. In a
parliamentary vote of confidence he obtained the support of 274
deputies, but a significant 129 rejected his policy. The Socialists at
least were prepared to re-enter the government. The prime minister
was clearly unwilling to risk civil war in an effort to assert his authority, however. His desire for compromise encouraged the rebel generals, as did the manoeuvres of leading Gaullists such as Chaban-Delmas
and Michel Debré. On 15 May General Salan, the commander-in-
chief in Algeria, was heard to shout 'Vive de Gaulle' to crowds
gathered in front of the Government-General building in Algiers.
Later that day de Gaulle himself announced that he was prepared to
reassume power – a move that the government failed to condemn.

Civil war remained a real possibility, with generals in Algeria planning parachute drops in the Paris region to link up with potentially
rebellious troops already there, and de Gaulle saying nothing to dis-
courage this planned military coup. As the days passed it became more
and more evident that the authority of the government was disinte-
grating, with ministers paralysed by fear of provoking a conflict in
which their staunchest supporters would be the despised Communists.
Pflimlin, his deputy Mollet, and even President Coty were all in touch
with de Gaulle. Corsica was taken over by the rebels on 24/5 May,
without resistance. On 27 May, with complete contempt for the
constitution, de Gaulle announced that he intended to form a government. Pflimlin resigned, aware of his growing isolation. As they
appeared to President Coty, the alternatives were now military dictatorship or the appointment of de Gaulle. He preferred the latter, and

Plate 7.6 Demonstrators in Algiers, 1958. Photo: Meagher/Getty Images.

the general was duly invited to become the last prime minister of the Fourth Republic. Although he had refused to condemn the military *putchistes* and had clearly manipulated the crisis to his own advantage in the hope of being called upon once more as the saviour of his country, de Gaulle's promise to respect republican institutions at least seemed to offer escape from the crisis without total humiliation.

On 28 May a mass demonstration in Paris, with Mendès-France and Mitterrand at its head, rejected the prospect. On 1 June, however, de Gaulle appeared before the National Assembly and was granted emergency powers for six months. Some 329 deputies supported this move and 224, including the Communists and half the Socialists, opposed. De Gaulle's administration reflected the widespread desire for compromise. The situation seemed to demand a government of national unity. It would be composed of leading parliamentary figures from all parties save the Communists, with most notably his predecessor Pflimlin, together with Pinay at the Finance Ministry. Reassuringly, it included few committed Gaullists. One of its first tasks was to prepare a new constitution and bring down the curtain on the despised Fourth Republic.

The Fifth Republic

The style of political authority and the structures of political institutions were now to undergo major changes. De Gaulle's objective remained that defined in his 1946 Bayeux speech – that is, to reinforce the power of the president of the Republic and his ability to secure the common interest against the particularism of political parties, trades unions, business and other private interests, whilst preserving a parliamentary system. Another urgent priority was to bring the Algerian war to an end, and with it the continual drain on French manpower and money. These objectives were to be the means of achieving a greater goal: the modernisation of the French economy and society, and of its defences, in order to establish internal unity and order, and to restore the country to its rightful place amongst the great powers. Thus de Gaulle's frequent references to the eternal values of France concealed a determination to adapt to the realities of a rapidly changing world.

The new constitution was prepared by a committee of experts advising one of ministers chaired by de Gaulle's henchman Debré and including such eminent representatives of the old regime as Pflimlin and Mollet. The result very much reflected the general's views. It provided for a president, elected for a seven-year term by a restricted electoral college, who would select his own prime minister and assume responsibility for the conduct of government. His position was reinforced by the right to appeal to the nation through referenda – the old Bonapartist tactic, with results so unpredictable that it was rarely employed; through dissolution of the National Assembly – a useful means of putting pressure on its members; and by means of the assumption of emergency powers. Governments remained responsible to the National Assembly and could be forced to resign by a vote of no confidence, although this would require the support of an absolute majority of deputies, and, to make it all the more difficult to achieve, abstentions would be counted as rejections of the censure motion. The Assembly was to be diminished further by restrictions on the rights of deputies to ask questions or to amend legislation, as well as a reduction in the length of its sessions and in its overall legislative responsibilities. The proposals thus sought, very deliberately, to achieve a weakening of parliament and a considerable enhancement of the executive power. In future it was intended that deputies would be able to influence government but not to control it. Moreover, the many ambiguities contained in the constitutional document would be resolved by de Gaulle himself during a long period of office lasting until April 1969, whilst presidential authority would be further reinforced by the failure of deputies to develop the potential powers of parliament.

Presented to the nation in the Place de la République on 4 September – the anniversary of the proclamation of the Third Republic in 1870 – the new constitution allowed de Gaulle to pose once again as the 'saviour' of the nation, and, as the referendum of 28 September would overwhelmingly confirm, he enjoyed the support of most of the population. People were impatient with the seeming incompetence, the constant squabbling and the indecisiveness of the parliamentary regime, and anxious for the restoration of the authority of the state. The parties of the right were strongly in favour, those of the left divided. The main opposition came from the Communists, together with prominent but isolated figures such as Mendès-France and Mitterrand. The latter would describe this new manifestation of charismatic authority as 'a permanent coup d'état'.

A new electoral system for legislative elections was introduced by decree, and deliberately constructed to favour candidates from the right and to prejudice the chances of their Socialist and particularly Communist opponents. In the general election that followed, on 23 and 30 November 1958, major changes in voting behaviour were nevertheless evident with massive gains for the Gaullists and other conservatives, united in the Union pour la Nouvelle République (UNR), whilst the left lost heavily because of its confused or hostile attitudes towards de Gaulle. Some 70 per cent of the deputies elected supported the general. Such eminent opponents of the new regime as

Table 7.8 *Results of National Assembly election, 23 and 30 November 1958 (metropolitan France)*

	Percentage of first ballot votes	Seats after two ballots	Percentage of seats
Communists	18.9	10 (including overseas)	2.1
Socialists	15.7	40 (including overseas 47)	8.6
Radicals and others	8.2	37 (including overseas 40)	8.0
MRP	10.8	55 (including overseas 64)	11.8
Gaullists	20.3	196 (including overseas 206)	42.2
Conservatives, independents and others	24.2	127 (including overseas 129)	27.3
Others		81 overseas deputies	

Mendès-France and Mitterrand were defeated. This was to be an Assembly very much made up of newcomers. Only around one-quarter of the new deputies had sat in the previous parliament.

In the presidential election held on 21 December, 78.5 per cent of the local councillors and deputies who made up the electoral college (80,000 people in all) voted for de Gaulle. On 10 January 1959 the general asked Debré, a committed Gaullist and passionate advocate of the retention of French control over Algeria, to form a government. It soon became clear that the president regarded ministers, including the prime minister, as very much his subordinates. The strict separation of powers, which made membership of parliament incompatible with ministerial office, sought to ensure – if only with limited success – that ministers were deprived of an independent power base. Moreover, the authority of the president would be reinforced considerably by the outcome of the September 1962 referendum, which determined that the head of state should be elected by universal suffrage. Following the near-success of an assassination attempt by Algérie française extremists at Petit-Clamart on 22 August, de Gaulle was determined to ensure that, as the elect of the people, his successor would enjoy sufficient legitimacy to provide strong leadership. Hostile commentators reminded their readers that the last president elected by universal

Table 7.9 *Results of National Assembly election, 18 and 25 November 1962*

	First ballot votes	Percentage of votes	Seats after two ballots
Communists	3,992,431	21.7	41
Socialists	2,319,662	12.6	66
Radicals and others	1,384,498	7.5	42
MRP	1,635,452	8.9	38
Gaullist UNR and others	5,847,403	31.9	233
Conservatives, independents and others	2,540,615	14.3	52

suffrage had been Louis-Napoleon Bonaparte and that his success had been followed by dictatorship. Even Debré felt obliged to resign in protest, whilst parliamentary opposition was sufficient to bring down the government, now led by Georges Pompidou, the former director of the general's private office.

De Gaulle's response was to dissolve the Assembly and hold a further referendum (28 October), followed by elections to a new Assembly (18 and 25 November). In both votes he was successful. In the referendum, 61.7 per cent of the electorate voted in favour of constitutional reform; in the election, the UNR gained record levels of support for a French political party. In neither ballot was victory as overwhelming as the general might have wished, however. The centre was crushed, but the left achieved a respectable showing. Nevertheless, these successes saw the completion of the process of constitutional reform that established the presidential system of the Fifth Republic. The process of institutional change, and the more gradual development of constitutional conventions, were to create a new political culture. Perhaps de Gaulle's greatest achievement, during what was to be an extremely constructive period of government, was to be the creation of a political system acceptable to almost the entire population. For the first time since the Revolution there appeared to be a general consensus in favour of republican institutions.

The political system that emerged after 1958 was thus clearly presidential. De Gaulle reserved for himself the spheres of defence and foreign policy and the Algerian question. Whatever his constitutional position, the prime minister was in practice very much the president's man. Ministers were executants, drawn increasingly from the bureaucracy and replaceable at will, rather than from parliament, which was treated in disdainful fashion as a useful debating chamber but incapable of decision taking. The replacement of the faithful Debré with Pompidou in April 1962 was symptomatic of the general's assertiveness, as was the immediate reappointment of the latter in October after a parliamentary motion of no confidence had forced him to resign.

Another major trend evident from the elections was the beginning of a process of 'bipolarisation', a political restructuring in which the various parties tended to coalesce into Gaullist and opposition groups, with the parties of the centre such as the Radicals and MRP largely absorbed into the presidential coalition. Christian Democrats had become increasingly conservative during the Cold War. The provision of substantial state subsidies for private Catholic schools in December 1959 was the final concession necessary to secure their commitment to de Gaulle. In any case, this process of adjustment to new institutions was largely imposed on politicians by an electoral system that required alliances for success. This forced de Gaulle himself to adopt the role of party leader in order to secure a parliamentary majority for the UNR and its allies. He recognised that even a president elected by universal suffrage depended on the institutionalised support of a political party during his lengthy (seven-year) period of office. A further factor promoting bipolarisation was of course the presidential system itself, which focused attention on the need to support the personalities capable of capturing that key office in a final ballot that allowed for only two candidates. From the point of view of the voter, the reduction in competition between parties, whilst reducing freedom of choice, at least provided more clearly defined alternatives.

Whatever the rhetoric of national unity, this was essentially government from the right, its economic and social policies acceptable to a broad coalition of centrist and conservative opinion. Additionally, and for as long as de Gaulle himself remained head of state, the regime benefited from the unique status enjoyed by the former leader of Free France. The great advantage the Gaullist state would provide was the political stability necessary to sustain economic and social modernisation. First, however, the last great legacy of colonialism had to be eliminated.

Concerted rebellion by Muslims in Algeria, in protest against the European ascendancy, had begun on 1 November 1954. After at least 300,000 deaths and numerous atrocities on both sides, in July 1962 the outcome would be French withdrawal. De Gaulle's policy was essentially pragmatic. It evolved from an initial determination to maintain close ties between France and Algeria and commitment to the established combination of military repression with social and political reform, to a reluctant acceptance (possibly as early as September 1959) that 'self determination' for Algeria was unavoidable. Disengagement had come to be seen not only as necessary to avoid the waste of material and human resources needed for national rejuvenation (although probably the economic costs were exaggerated at the time), but also as the means of ending the sustained crisis that had brought the army into politics and that continued to threaten both internal political stability and the country's international moral standing.

The referendum of 8 January 1961 made it clear that a large majority of war-weary voters agreed (75.2 per cent). Those who voted against de Gaulle's proposals for withdrawal included the Communists – who, with typically false logic, strongly favoured independence for Algeria but opposed the government on principle – as well as the extreme right, which wanted to impose a military solution whatever the cost. It had been the army's distrust of the political leadership that had led to de Gaulle's return. The general's own apparent betrayal of the cause of Algérie française now led many of these soldiers into a second attempted coup in April. Most army officers remained loyal to the general, however, whilst, listening on their transistor radios, the mass of weary conscripts responded positively to his brilliant broadcast appeals. The murderous campaign subsequently waged in both France and Algeria by rebel officers and civilians linked to the Organisation de l'armée secrète (OAS) failed to change government policy, only widening the already enormous gulf between the two communities in Algeria and ensuring that there would be no place in an independent Algeria for its 1 million European residents or for the Muslim auxiliaries of the French army, 150,000 of whom – with their families – were forced to join the exodus of Europeans. Shamefully, many more were abandoned to a gruesome fate.

Racial tension in France itself had also been intensified by the war. Paris, with its 180,000 Algerians – mostly immigrant workers – had served as a recruitment base and major source of funds for the FLN as well as the theatre for deadly rivalries and intimidation within the nationalist movement. Even as the government negotiated with the representatives of the Algerian Front de libération nationale at Evian, on 17 October 1961 police in Paris launched a ferocious assault on a peaceful but nonetheless provocative crowd of over 20,000 people protesting against the imposition of a curfew on north Africans. Some 11,000 were arrested and at least 200 killed by the defenders of law and order. Ever since his appointment in 1958, the prefect of police, Maurice Papon, had encouraged them to engage in ruthless repression. The disappearance of a large number of people, together with the discovery of bodies floating down the Seine, could always be blamed on internecine conflict between rival nationalist factions. Subsequent police violence in February 1962, this time directed at left-wing anti-OAS demonstrators, would cause the deaths of nine people, crushed as they sought to escape through the Charonne metro station.

In foreign policy too the advent of de Gaulle meant not only a change of perspective but also a greater determination to secure what were believed to be vital national interests. Resentment of what was perceived to be the American failure to provide sufficient support for French forces during the Dien Bien Phu campaign, and of the pressure exercised to bring the Anglo-French assault on Egypt to a premature end, had already encouraged French politicians to dream of exercising a more independent role. Successive governments, and most notably that led by Mendès-France in 1954, had committed themselves to developing the military potential of nuclear power. The cooling of the Cold War made it safer to engage in a more autonomous and assertive foreign policy. Disengagement from Empire shifted the focus of strategic planning. Having benefited substantially from multilateral defence, France increasingly distanced itself from a Western alliance perceived to be excessively subordinate to US foreign policy objectives. The decision by de Gaulle to withdraw from the NATO command structure took effect in March 1966, although France would remain within the alliance. Whilst recognising the continued importance of American nuclear protection, the regime poured much more in the way of resources than had previous governments into the development of an independent nuclear force. A first device was exploded in the Algerian desert in February 1960, and enormous sums were to be expended on its development as well as on that of delivery systems. It was hoped that this would safeguard France from nuclear blackmail by the Soviet Union or any other state in situations like that prevailing during the Suez campaign, in which the United States might be reluctant to risk all-out nuclear war to protect one of its allies. Suspicion of America's hegemonic intentions was one reason for de Gaulle's refusal to agree to British membership of the European Community. It was assumed that the British would too closely represent American interests. In contrast, the French president and the West German chancellor, Konrad Adenauer, both energetically pursued Franco-German reconciliation.

The development of a broad popular consensus in support of these policies provided an important political underpinning for governments of the right throughout the following decades. France appeared to have been restored to its 'true' position as a major power. In spite of efforts to secure a rapprochement with the Soviet Union, the reality was a continued anti-communist commitment and a dependence on the Western alliance, particularly evident during such moments of heightened international tension as the Czech crisis of August 1968.

Of course, enhanced military strength was closely dependent upon economic modernisation. Whilst the foundations had already been laid, economic growth and restructuring were to continue at a rapid pace. This was greatly facilitated by the political stability, combined with greater governmental financial rigour and a more effective anti-inflationary policy, that characterised the de Gaulle presidency. The Treaty of Rome, committing France to membership of the European Economic Community, had been signed in 1957, and took effect from 1 January 1959. Besides its potential economic advantages, the Community offered a means of satisfying the desire to contain

Plate 7.7 General Charles de Gaulle speaks to the nation on television, 23 April 1961. Condemning the military putsch in Algeria, he concludes with the appeal 'Français, Françaises, aidez moi'. Photo: Keystone/Hulton Archive/Getty Images.

Plate 7.8 Reconciliation and the construction of a new Europe. President de Gaulle with Chancellor Konrad Adenauer during his visit to West Germany in September 1962. Photo: Camera Press (UK) Ltd.

German ambitions, and afforded France the opportunity of exercising a predominant role in a resuscitated western Europe – and, indeed, greater influence on wider international affairs. There were limits to the French commitment, however. Thus, in May 1962 the general declared his opposition to further integration, favouring instead cooperation within a much looser 'Europe of the nations'. He assumed that the nation state was, and would remain, the fundamental reality in international affairs.

The progressive opening of frontiers within the EEC reflected the deliberate intention of forcing French enterprises to become internationally competitive, and of securing markets through the Common Agricultural Policy, framed very much with French needs in mind. Businessmen and farmers alike were assisted by massive subsidies and tax incentives and the rapid growth (especially before 1975) of both the west European and world economies. Additionally, economic growth facilitated the improvement of living standards, with per capita incomes rising by an annual

A L'AUBE DU MARCHÉ COMMUN
VENDRE EST AUSSI IMPORTANT QUE PRODUIRE

IPEAC   INSTITUT POUR LA PROMOTION ECONOMIQUE PAR L'ACTION COMMERCIALE

Plate 7.9 The establishment of the Common Market by the Treaty of Rome, signed on 25 March 1957 and taking effect from 1 January 1959, provided both an opportunity and a challenge to French enterprises. This 1957 poster by Savignac encourages industrial modernisation to ensure competitiveness. Photo: Larousse.

average of 4.5 per cent between 1959 and 1973. Certainly, the regime took much of the credit for this greater prosperity. Widespread discontent persisted, nevertheless. In part this was because rising aspirations made gross inequalities in the distribution of wealth all the harder to bear, in part because government policies designed to limit the inflationary consequences of continuous growth led to the neglect of social investment in housing, schools and hospitals, and to wage controls, periodic rises in unemployment and greater insecurity. The revival of political opposition was one symptom of a sense of malaise.

The emergence of the Fifth Republic had created a potentially disastrous situation for the left. In the 1958 election only ten Communists, forty-seven Socialists and forty Radical deputies had been returned. The Communists set out on what was to be a

Table 7.10 *Results of National Assembly election, 5 and 12 March 1967*

	First ballot votes	Share (percentage of votes)	Seats after second ballot
Communists	5,039,032	22.51	73
FGDS[a]	4,231,173	18.90	121
Centre démocrate	3,153,367	14.09	41
UDR[b] (Gaullists and allies)	8,608,959	38.45	244

Note: [a] Fédération de la gauche démocrate et socialiste.
[b] Union pour la défense de la République.

prolonged, though for long concealed, decline. The Socialists, like the Radicals, remained closely associated in the public mind with the failures of the Fourth Republic. Moreover, cooperation between these parties was made all the more unlikely by the Communists' rigidly Stalinist and pro-Soviet stance. The 1962 legislative election, with de Gaulle enjoying the credit for the solution of the Algerian affair, only reinforced this picture of apparently terminal decline. Increasingly, however, as the 1960s progressed, the left took a stand against the excessive 'personal' power of the president and condemned social injustice. The presidential election of December 1965, when de Gaulle failed to win an overall majority in the first round and was forced into a humiliating run-off with Mitterrand – who now claimed to espouse socialist values – finally obtaining 55.2 per cent of the votes cast, as well as the general election in March 1967, revealed a growing audience for the left's point of view.

The improved showing of the opposition was a result of the more cooperative spirit of the Communists and the emergence of a credible alternative to de Gaulle in the person of Mitterrand. He had succeeded in persuading the mainstream Socialists and various splinter groups, as well as the Radicals, to collaborate in the new Fédération de la gauche démocrate et socialiste. His longer-term strategy would be to alter the political balance on the left and, by reducing the Communists to a clearly subordinate position, to broaden the opposition's electoral appeal.

Plate 7.10 Police chasing demonstrators, 6 May 1968. Photo: Caron.

The widespread and utterly unexpected disorders of 1968 were to provide further proof of discontent. Suddenly, all manner of smouldering resentments surfaced – against authoritarianism in the family as well as in government and in the workplace; against élitism in society and its manifestations in secondary and higher education; against overcrowded and inadequately resourced teaching facilities; against inequality, injustice and the insecurity bred by rapid social change. The movement began in March in the grim new university campus at Nanterre on the outskirts of Paris, as students protested about both the shortcomings of the educational system and the workings of an international capitalist order whose moral bankruptcy had been made evident by American policy in Vietnam. It was engineered by small and normally marginal groups of Trotskyists, anarchists and Maoists. It spread because of the ineptitude of the university administration and police brutality. The night of 10/11 May saw the first barricades and rioting in the centre of the capital. Subsequently demonstrations spread into the provinces. There were massive strikes, as well as factory occupations involving 10 million workers and resulting in the loss of 150 million workdays. This all helped to create the euphoric sense of a new beginning, especially amongst the young, gathering in the faculties, theatres, cafés and streets of Paris. Taken completely by surprise, the government improvised a programme based on the vague project of *participation*, which would involve students and employees in decision taking, and offered bribes in the form of wage increases. It was largely ignored. So too was Mitterrand's declaration that it was necessary to establish a provisional government under Mendès-France. His further announcement that he intended to present himself as a candidate for the presidency seemed to be redolent of the worst kind of political opportunism. To student demonstrators, all this manoeuvring amongst the old political élite was irrelevant.

These events had shown up some of the disadvantages of an excessively centralised political system, dependent on decision making by an ageing head of state and virtually incapable of rapid response to an unexpected crisis. They revealed a widespread loss of confidence in existing institutions. To terrified conservatives, including the prime minister, Pompidou, France appeared to be on the verge of another revolution, almost in the style of those of the nineteenth century. This was not to be, however. De Gaulle, who on 29 May had flown to Baden-Baden to consult General Massu, regained his self-confidence and recaptured the initiative

Plate 7.11 A Gaullist demonstration in the Champs-Elysées, 30 May 1968 (50,000 were expected, 300,000 to 400,000 turned up). Photo: Le Campion/ANA.

through a mixture of concessions and repression. With the benefit of hindsight, this seems not to have been a difficult task. The decision of the Communist Party, the major organised force on the left, to remain within the bounds of legality and avoid a possible bloodbath was especially significant. The government was greatly assisted by the lack of unity amongst its critics. Similarly, the leaders of the weak and fragmented trades union movement set themselves the limited objectives of securing improvements in wages and working conditions. They were anxious both to control and to restrain the protest movement. This was in marked contrast with those denounced by the Communist leader, Georges Marchais, as 'counterfeit revolutionaries': the more utopian student leaders and members of extreme left splinter groups, inspired by the flood of words and the sheer theatricality of events. There was no group willing or able to take the final step and attempt to seize power, however. The government itself was determined to avoid the escalation of violence so typical of the revolutions of the previous century. In a very effective broadcast on 30 May, de Gaulle announced the dissolution of the National Assembly and called for unity in defence of the Republic against the threat of anarchy and communism. A massive and carefully orchestrated Gaullist demonstration along the Champs-Elysées lent weight to his demand. In the legislative election that followed, on 23 and 30 June, the regime, fighting on a law and order platform, was able to go a long way to restoring its legitimacy. The 'silent majority' most certainly did not want a revolution. The old values remained vibrant. The extreme left was isolated. A gradual return to work occurred and with it the renewed marginalisation of revolutionary protest.

Above all, the election result revealed the strength of political conservatism. To a large degree it was an instinctive reaction based on fear of social upheaval. In spite of this victory, it was clear nevertheless that the 'événements de Mai' had considerably weakened the authority of the president of the Republic. Only Pompidou, who had seemed better able to cope with the crisis, emerged with his reputation enhanced. His subsequent dismissal appeared to be a petty-minded attempt by the general to remove a former subordinate who had been transformed by events into a potential successor.

Table 7.11 *Results of National Assembly election, 23 and 30 June 1968*

	First ballot votes	Share (percentage of votes)	Seats after second ballot
Communists	4,435,357	20.03	34
FGDS	3,654,003	16.50	57
Centre (PDM[a])	2,290,165	10.34	33
UDR (Gaullists)	9,663,605	43.65	293
RI[b]	917,533	4.14	61

Notes: [a] Progrès et démocratie moderne.
[b] Républicains indépendants.

Plate 7.12 Georges Pompidou, as prime minister, with a youthful Jacques Chirac on his left. Photo: AFP/Getty Images.

This was also the moment when de Gaulle chose to renew his search for a 'third way' between capitalism and communism as a means of relaunching the regime. In April 1969 he presented, for the electorate's approval, a series of proposals designed to enhance *participation*. These would have resulted in greater employee involvement in enterprise management and in a limited decentralisation of government by means of regional devolution. This measure would have been balanced by a reduction in the powers of the Senate, however, which previously had served as a sounding board for opposition. The proposals were a major misjudgement. They attracted little public interest. Such eminent representatives of the conservative majority as Giscard d'Estaing, personally embittered at being used as a scapegoat for unpopular measures and then dismissed from the Finance Ministry in 1966, called for their rejection. Of even greater significance, Pompidou announced his intention of standing as a candidate at the next presidential election. This assured conservatives that a dependable successor to de Gaulle stood in the wings. The general had threatened to resign in the event of defeat, and he returned to private life on hearing that 53 per cent of voters had rejected his proposals. He died eighteen months later, on 9 November 1970.

The demise of its leader might have been expected to cause major problems for the Gaullist party. It had possessed little in the way of a distinctive programme and had owed its unity to loyalty to de Gaulle, together with a desire to share in the spoils of office. Pompidou, the son of a socialist schoolteacher from the impoverished Cantal who had reached the top through the Ecole normale supérieure and the banking world, had been virtually unknown to the public until thrust into the office of prime minister by de Gaulle. He had proved his ability as a political leader in the following six years, however, and it had been his emergence as heir apparent in 1968 that had led to his removal from office. He was the obvious candidate for the right in the presidential election called for June 1969. His success would owe much to the evident disarray of the Socialists, for whom, on a joint ticket, Gaston Defferre and Mendès-France obtained only 5 per cent of the first-round vote – in comparison with the Communist candidate's 21 per cent. In the run-off, against the centrist Alain Poher, Pompidou was elected with a substantial majority (58.21 per cent of votes). Significantly, much of the popular support that de Gaulle had enjoyed melted away, leaving Pompidou much more dependent on the loyalty of traditional conservatives. This outcome would not result in a return to the political situation existing prior to de Gaulle's comeback in 1958, however. Pompidou was determined to exercise his constitutional authority to the full – as well as to enjoy the pleasures offered by high society – and possessed all the status of a president elected by universal suffrage. This resulted in the 'normalisation' of a system that, in its origins, had owed so much to the 'charismatic' leadership of de Gaulle.

For organised political support Pompidou would continue to depend on the Gaullist UNR, a group initially constructed around the mystique of the liberation and on de Gaulle's claims to be above the traditional party conflict, but which had rapidly taken on the attributes of a party of the right. As the party in power, the UNR had attracted support from other, non-Gaullist groups from the centre and right of the political spectrum, and most notably the Républicains indépendants led by Giscard d'Estaing. A powerful federation of the right had been created, united by the desire to retain power and face the threat posed by the slow recovery of the parties of the left. Rival leadership claims were not far from the surface, however. Chaban-Delmas, the prime minister appointed by the new president, combined an impeccable record of loyalty to de Gaulle with an image of respect for parliament. He rapidly attempted to enhance the authority of his own office at the expense of that of the president. In so doing, he was able to appeal to the resentment amongst Gaullists of a president who had played no part in the heroic days of their movement during the resistance, in the RPF immediately after the war or, indeed, in the return to power in 1958. Influenced by the Christian trades unionism of Jacques Delors, Chaban-Delmas was also anxious to rebuild relations between government, employers and labour and to appeal to workers by increasing the minimum wage. Although the reforms he actually introduced were essentially cosmetic, his talk of a 'contractual politics' and of the need to create a 'new society' irritated Pompidou profoundly. In 1972 Pierre Messmer, clearly the president's man, replaced Chaban-Delmas. His selection represented a restatement of the presidential character of the regime and of its commitment to financial orthodoxy and economic growth. A particular favourite of the president, Jacques Chirac, an upper middle-class graduate of the Ecole nationale d'administration, who had been parachuted into a rural constituency in

Table 7.12 *Results of National Assembly election, 4 and 11 March 1973*

	First ballot votes	Share (percentage of votes)	Seats after second ballot
Communists	5,084,824	21.40	73
Socialists and allies	4,919,426	20.71	102
Réformateurs (centre)	3,048,520	12.88	34
UDR and allies	9,009,432	37.32	183
Independent Republicans			55

the Corrèze (to which, typically, he adapted with great enthusiasm), was appointed minister of agriculture. With a legislative election due in 1973, conservatives rallied to the government and gained a surprisingly comfortable victory.

This was the reward for the restoration of social order in 1968 and for the success of economic policies designed to combat inflation, balance the budget, restore business confidence and encourage continued economic modernisation. For Pompidou, this was the means of securing his place in history. As part of this policy of encouraging growth he also tolerated some of the uglier physical manifestations of property development and continued to commit vast funds to such prestige projects as Concorde, the Airbus family of airliners, the creation of the immense steelworks at Fos, near Marseille, and the ultimately far more fruitful programme of investment in telecommunications. To a large degree, these policies were a continuation of those inaugurated by de Gaulle. The same was to be true in foreign policy, although Pompidou's greater commitment to the European Community was revealed by his acceptance of its enlargement to include Britain, Ireland and Denmark in 1972. At the same time he sought to ease the strains of modernisation, and to protect the conservative vote through guaranteed prices for farmers and restraints on supermarket development in the interests of small shopkeepers.

Pompidou enjoyed considerable success in the difficult task of following de Gaulle. At the end of 1973, however, he was to face

Plate 7.13 The urban landscape transformed by the construction, on an unprecedented scale, of new offices and apartments. Photo: Sappa/CEDRI.

new problems, caused by the sudden, fourfold, increase in the price of oil as a result of the Arab–Israeli war and the onset of a major international crisis. One of the central technological innovations of the post-war period had been the rapid replacement of coal by oil as the main source of energy. By 1973 oil provided for 75 per cent of French energy needs. It was relatively inexpensive and easier to use.

Inevitably, the balance of trade deteriorated sharply as the cost of oil imports increased. By February 1974 inflation had risen to 15.6 per cent, whilst the rate of economic growth was halved (to a still not inconsiderable 3 per cent). Unemployment rose rapidly, and so too did social tension and the general feeling of malaise. In a period when strong government was necessary, the president was increasingly incapacitated by illness. He died of leukaemia on 2 April 1974. Finally, the *trente glorieuses* had come to an end.

8

A society under stress

INTRODUCTION

The *trente glorieuses* – a period of unprecedented prosperity, social mobility and job security (particularly between 1955 and 1975) – were to be followed by a prolonged *crise d'adaptation* as successive governments attempted to come to terms not only with the problems caused by the oil crises of the 1970s but with the more fundamental and multifaceted impact of globalisation and of a 'third' industrial revolution. The markets for goods and services, and those for capital and labour, were transformed by technological innovations, which resulted in massive reductions in the cost of communication and transport. The market-integrating impact was reinforced considerably through the further development of the European Union as well as the outcome of wider international agreements to reduce barriers to trade. The growth of global capitalism offered new economic opportunities, but within a much more competitive environment. Change was constant and had a massive impact on culture as well as material goods. The development of a consumer society and of a commitment to personal fulfilment thus proceeded apace. Moreover, whilst the state continued to possess a substantial capacity for intervention, multinational corporations, market forces and the imperative need to promote competitiveness in the developing global economy challenged its capacity for autonomous action and even its ability to safeguard the welfare of its citizens. Together with shorter-term crises, structural change caused high levels of unemployment, especially amongst the young and ethnic minorities, and intensified the difficulty of funding social relief as well as the pensions and healthcare of an ageing population. Social inequality was especially evident in the shortcomings of the educational system. As a result of these factors, national sovereignty, the welfare state and even the distinctiveness of French culture appeared to be menaced.

ECONOMY AND SOCIETY

Although in the twenty years after 1967 economic growth continued at a rate of 3.3 per cent per annum (Germany 2.8 per cent, Britain 2.6 per cent), a marked slowing became evident following the peak of 5.9 per cent in 1973. By the 1980s growth rates had fallen to around 2 per cent. This deceleration was blamed by the more optimistic economists on the oil crises of 1973 and 1979. Previously, like the other industrial economies, France had benefited substantially from cheap imports. By 1973 75 per cent of energy needs were supplied by imported oil. Inevitably, the quadrupling of prices between September 1973 and January 1974 had a substantial impact both on the balance of payments and on business costs. Furthermore, the increased price of fuel provoked a severe depression by reducing demand for other products. At the end of the decade a second oil crisis would result from the war between Iraq and Iran. By 1979/80, however, more efficient energy use and continued investment in nuclear power – which produced 75 per cent of domestic electricity by 2002 – had reduced dependence on imported energy; the last coal mine was closed in 2004.

Instead of focusing on the temporary effects of higher energy costs, however, the more pessimistic economists sought to explain the slowing of growth in terms of the structural problems caused by insufficient investment in new technologies, together with the maldistribution of resources induced by welfarism at a time when the rapid internationalisation of trade was intensifying competition. The National Statistical Institute (INSEE) appeared to confirm this view, estimating that the rate of growth of labour productivity, which had averaged 5.1 per cent per annum between 1953 and 1973, had by 1979 to 1984 fallen to 2.4 per cent. It seems clear that there would have been a recession in the early 1970s without the oil crisis, though it did substantially intensify the difficulties. Nevertheless, national income grew by an annual 3 per cent between 1973 and 1979. Levels of capital investment and productivity growth remained sufficient to allow the continuous increase in real incomes and to ensure a high level of demand for consumer products. Unlike the 1930s, world trade also continued to expand. Whereas widespread protectionism had caused a reduction in exports of 44 per cent between 1929 and 1935, between 1973 and 1979 they actually rose by 50 per cent. Furthermore, the French share of world industrial exports increased from 7.9 per cent in 1973 to 8.6 per cent in 1978, so that the balance of payments, thrown into disequilibrium by the rise in oil prices, had been restored on the eve of the second oil crisis. The widespread pessimism that prevailed in spite of these successes was due to rising inflation, which governments appeared unable to control, to the growth of unemployment and to the disconcerting effect of a long period of relative stagnation.

Unemployment, which had affected less than 3 per cent of the active population before 1973, rose rapidly, subsequently levelling out at around 10 to 12 per cent by the late 1980s. The young, unskilled and immigrants were especially likely to be out of work. The complex of causes rendered a solution difficult. These included the increasing numbers of young people entering the labour market; the adverse impact of the oil crisis on international demand for some products, especially industrial equipment; and rising wage costs, which encouraged efforts to maintain profitability through capital investment to replace labour. Most seriously affected were the traditional staple industries of the north and east – coal, steel and textiles – which faced the disruption of their markets by the use of alternative energy sources and materials. The regional policies designed in the 1960s to assist declining or underdeveloped areas and limit congestion in the Paris region were of limited effectiveness. In the main, they provided poorly paid part-time and unskilled employment, mostly for women, except where combined, as in Grenoble and Toulouse, with substantial investment in infrastructure, in technical and scientific education and research, and in state-assisted projects. Quite clearly, some regions are more suitable for economic development than others, due to the availability of specialised labour, capital, entrepreneurial skills and efficient communications, as well as their attractiveness as markets.

The other unique feature of the crisis was that it was accompanied by a return to high rates of inflation, rather than the deflation that economic theory and experience might have suggested. The annual inflation rate had already risen from 3.3 per cent between 1965 and 1968 to 6.3 per cent in the period 1970 to 1973. In 1974 it reached 15.2 per cent, and remained at around 10 to 12 per cent for the remainder of the decade. Higher oil prices contributed only 2 per cent of this further increase. The major causes were wage increases because of skill shortages, growing company and state indebtedness, rising levels of bank credit in spite of high interest rates, the declining exchange value of the franc and the growing disequilibrium of the international financial system. Solving these problems called for competent political leadership. Faced with unprecedented difficulties, which the Keynsian solutions previously favoured proved incapable of solving, governments adopted policies that were often contradictory.

Nevertheless, during the 1980s and 1990s the French economy grew by 1.9 per cent per annum, compared with 1.3 per cent in Germany and 2.3 per cent in Britain. World-ranking companies included AXA (insurance), Carrefour (retailing), L'Oréal (cosmetics) and Danone (foodstuffs) – the last even so dwarfed by Kraft or Nestlé. Peugeot/Citroën (PSA – still controlled after 220 years by the family of its founders) briefly became Europe's most successful car maker, designing a flow of attractive vehicles and maintaining high levels of plant utilisation and profitability. Michelin, one of the world's leading tyre makers, sold some 80 per cent of its production outside France. Toulouse became the main centre for the production of Airbus aircraft by the European enterprise EADS. Substantial US and Japanese investment was also attracted by skilled labour and an efficient infrastructure.

The internationalisation of production often followed that of sales, however. Thus, in order to be closer to customers and reduce labour costs, in 1999 Michelin caused a major shock by cutting some 7,500 jobs in Clermont-Ferrand, its home town. Apparently it cost €50,000 per annum to employ a worker in France, €10,000 in the Czech Republic and €3,000 in Morocco. This was a sign of things to come throughout the motor industry, particularly for mass-market car makers and their suppliers, finding it difficult to compete in the more lucrative high end of the market with the likes of BMW and Mercedes, and struggling with European-wide overcapacity. By 2012 PSA – which in February 2013 recorded a massive annual loss of €5 billion – retained only 41 per cent of its production in France, and Renault (though strengthened by its alliance with Nissan) only 30 to 35 per cent. A leader in the development of electric cars, for reasons of cost, Renault was forced to look to Asian suppliers of batteries. From 2012 the end of car production at Aulnay, one of the few surviving manufacturing plants in the Paris region, reinforced the pessimistic outlook.

Signs of declining international competitiveness were clearly evident. Although by 2010 France still had thirty-nine entries in *Fortune*'s list of the top 500 global companies ranked by total revenue, compared with thirty-seven German enterprises, during the previous decade the country's share of European merchandise exports had fallen from 15.7 to 13.1 per cent – reflecting, particularly in comparison with Germany and the United States, a failure to control labour costs and invest sufficiently in training and research and development. Thus between 1998 and 2010 the cost of labour is estimated to have risen by 25.5 per cent in France compared with 5.4 per cent in Germany.

The pressure on major companies to increase their profitability sometimes encouraged problematic international acquisitions. Through sometimes reckless, and generally expensive purchases, Jean-Marie Messier turned the water supply and waste management specialist Générale des Eaux into Vivendi, the transatlantic telecommunications and entertainment conglomerate. The accumulation of a mountain of debt was finally terminated by the collapse of investor confidence. By the time Messier finally overreached himself, massive losses had been incurred (reaching €13.6 billion by 2001). At the beginning of the new century other major companies were also experiencing difficulties. The engineering group Alstom and the telecoms equipment producer Alcatel were close to bankruptcy and, to the despair of the European Commission, required state assistance to achieve restructuring. The remains of domestic steel production were threatened by cyclical shifts in demand and efforts by the

Anglo-Indian company Arcelor Mittal to concentrate activity on the coast at Dunkirk at the expense of Florange in Lorraine. France-Télécom also suffered from massive debts, incurred by acquisitions at home and abroad and through the purchase of mobile phone licences. In the important and profitable export-led luxury goods sector, which employed some 200,000 people and contributed 5 per cent of total industrial production, LVMH and Pinault-Printemps-Redoute were not without their problems, partly due to excessive diversity and a failure to focus sufficiently on core business.

The overambitious efforts of the state-owned company EDF to acquire British and US energy businesses led to neglect by management of the fifty-nine ageing nuclear power stations built in France between 1971 and 1991, which still generate around 78 per cent of French electricity, as well as to a weakening of the leading role of another Franco-German company, Areva, in the design and construction of nuclear plants. Entry into the rapidly growing Chinese market by Areva and EDF represented a response to opportunity at the risk of transferring technology to local partners likely soon to become competitors in global markets. In spite of concern about construction costs, the disposal of nuclear waste and potential environmental damage, particularly following the catastrophe at Fukushima in Japan in 2011, considerable support survives for an industry that retains substantial strategic importance and engages in effective – state-supported – pressure group activity.

All this, and the occasional disastrous outcome, might serve as a warning about the shortcomings of the management culture prevalent within the largest French companies. Business leaders are still largely drawn from the graduates of such world-class meritocratic institutions as the Ecole Polytechnique and the Ecole nationale d'administration (ENA), from relatively closed, almost exclusively French and overwhelmingly male social circles. Those associated with this intimate and immensely rewarding world of interlocking company directorates make up an economic élite, closely linked, on a mutually profitable basis, with leading politicians and civil servants. Moreover, faced with top-down autocratic management, lesser mortals as well as shareholders retain limited influence. In order to promote more transparent procedures, the reforms of company management proposed by the 1995 Vienot Report have nevertheless gradually been implemented. This also represents a response to the globalisation of capital markets. By 2000 some 40 per cent of the shares traded on the Paris Bourse were foreign-owned. Companies such as Aventis, Suez and TotalFinaElf were increasingly forced by major American or British institutional investors to adopt a wider perspective, as well as Anglo-Saxon approaches to management.

Of course, this is not the whole picture. In addition to the top forty companies (the CAC 40), heavily engaged in international markets, and to the 2,000 companies listed on the stock exchange, which depend on national or even regional markets, there are currently some 2,000,000 small and medium-sized enterprises. The failure to replicate the successes of the German *Mittelstand* – medium-sized firms with an output of high-quality, particularly engineering, products sold at a premium – appears to result from inferior management, short-termism, skills shortages and underinvestment, due largely to the reluctance of banks to extend loans, as well as the slowness with which major companies recompense subcontractors. In sectors as diverse as textiles, shoemaking, household electrical goods and toys, only a small minority of high-quality, luxury producers have survived. Although numerous opportunities remain open to small businessmen, particularly in the provision of services, such enterprises invariably face considerable competitive pressure. In the ten years from 1986, in Paris alone, over 3,000 shops closed (one in ten). These were mainly food shops in working-class areas and in the suburbs, facing competition from hyper- and supermarkets, most notably Carrefour; cafés unable to combat the spread of fast food outlets – symbolised by McDonald's; and specialised retailers incapable of competing either on price or with the range of products offered by FNAC for books, CDs, DVDs and cameras, by Castorama to DIY enthusiasts, or by Go Sport. As ever, the small business world is in a state of constant flux. The growing importance of sales over the internet once again provides new opportunities, together with intense competition from enterprises such as Amazon-France.

In the financial sector, the ending in 1971 of the financial discipline imposed by the Bretton Woods agreement had facilitated an increasingly unregulated expansion of public and private credit and reinforced the dependence of governments on financial institutions. The ideology of market efficiency and the potential for enormous rewards encouraged bankers to neglect the management of risk and to promote the sale of ever more complicated financial instruments. In August 2007 the near-collapse of a major French bank – BNP Paribas – as a result of its exposure to sub-prime mortgage investments might have been seen as a harbinger of future problems. Nevertheless, the onset of an intense global financial crisis in September 2008 came as a shock. In poorly regulated markets, governments and consumers, as well as financial institutions, had accumulated unsustainable debts in an effort to maintain investment and consumption through access to 'cheap' money. Although probably better regulated than their US and British counterparts, and certainly not as carried away by mortgage lending, inevitably French banks would be affected. Public indebtedness and the exposure of banks such as the Société Générale to the American sub-prime debacle and the Greek financial crisis were potent causes for concern.

Moreover, the cost of funding debt, as well as rising labour costs, pointed to a growing lack of competitiveness. By 2010 hourly wages, which in 2000 had been 8 per cent lower than in Germany, would be 10 per cent higher. The difference was marked by much higher levels of unemployment and an accelerating process of deindustrialisation, with the contribution made by industry to national income declining to 14 per cent by 2010, compared with 25 per cent in Germany, where substantial labour market reforms in the early 2000s had reduced costs and helped to generate an export-led dynamism. French political leaders were slow to accept that similarly radical – and unpopular – austerity measures were necessary. A reduction of government expenditure – which had exceeded income since the early 1970s, and which would have required reform of the pensions and welfare systems – would inevitably have provoked widespread protest.

The countryside too has undergone massive change, leading to the virtual disappearance of the traditional peasant farm. In the immediate aftermath of the Second World War, and with considerable success, government policy was directed towards modernising farming, maximising outputs and improving rural living standards. The Common Market provided protected markets and guaranteed prices, and, although the enormous subsidies benefited particularly the big farmers – most notably the highly efficient cereals and sugar beet producers of the north and the intensive pork and poultry producers of the west – productivity throughout the sector rose substantially as a result of mechanisation and the intensive use of chemicals. The Crédit Agricole bank loaned the capital. Increasingly, however, farmers came to be dominated by the large agri-business enterprises that controlled the supply of inputs and the processing and marketing of foodstuffs. Moreover, by the 1980s it had become impossible for governments to ignore the growing crisis in farming resulting from overproduction and falling prices.

The rural population was demoralised and in decline. Integrated into an urban world by the car, popular music and television, many young people were unwilling to eke out a living on a family farm. Indeed, by the end of the twentieth century agriculture provided employment for only 4 per cent of the labour force (compared with one-third in 1945) and contributed just over 3 per cent of GDP. Since 1970 the number of farms had fallen from 1.6 million to 700,000 as a result of the creation of larger holdings, and half of these were operated on a part-time basis. In the following decade the number fell to 490,000 as small dairy farmers largely disappeared. The marginalisation of agriculture within the economy also made it increasingly difficult to resist proposals for reform of the European Union's Common Agricultural Policy. In 2001 France was in receipt of 22 per cent of CAP subsidies. These were estimated to add 15 to 20 per cent to the cost of food. French ministers could be relied upon, however, to wage a stubborn rearguard action against both the more consumer-orientated British proposals to reduce price guarantees and efforts to reduce the export subsidies that had a devastating impact on the agriculture of developing countries – disputes that often merely disguised competition for market share between France and the United States, the world's two largest agri-food exporters.

Consumer confidence has also suffered as a result of the environmental impact of large-scale capital-intensive farming. In response, the Confédération Paysanne and its colourful leader, José Bové, sought to create an alliance between small farmers, environmentalists and consumers to defend food quality, public health and sound ecological practices against market forces, as well as the genetic engineering of plants and animals. Widely held romantic urban perceptions of 'the eternal order of the fields' enhanced the ability of such groups to attract support and to persuade the public to accept motorway blockades and the dumping of manure on Parisian boulevards as methods of putting pressure on governments. In December 1993, although he was mayor of Paris, Chirac felt obliged to associate himself with the interests of his rural constituency in the Corrèze by opposing the globalising accords presented during the GATT trade liberalisation negotiations. He insisted that the countryside was held in trust as a unique feature of the national heritage.

It appears likely that in future farmers will be subsidised according to whether their primary role is food production in competitive markets or, alternatively, the preservation of an idealised and static landscape, as part of the 'rural heritage'. Continued diversification will also be encouraged, with tourism creating a market for rented accommodation and the sale of distinctive, relatively high-value products – wine, cheese and crafts – at farm gates. Indeed, and in spite of the sharp decline in the number of farmers, in many areas the long decline in rural population has been reversed as urban dwellers searching for a rural idyll or else desperate to escape from an increasingly degraded environment, and unable to afford expensive city property, have acquired homes within – often long – commuting distance of Paris and the major provincial cities. Many families, including large numbers from other countries, have also acquired second, holiday homes in the more picturesque and accessible areas. Rural society has thus been progressively urbanised. As a result, house prices have often been pushed up beyond the levels that local people can afford. Additionally, holiday homes have failed to prevent the gradual ageing of the permanent population, the closure of schools and shops, and the general decline in services.

Overall, the impact of sustained economic growth has been especially evident in the rapid decline of industrial and agricultural employment and the growing importance and dynamism of the service sector of the economy, in a process of tertiarisation common to all the advanced economies – and in the transformation of the world of labour. By the 1980s over 60 per cent of the active labour force already worked within the tertiary sector, including some of the most highly rewarded and the most poorly paid. Indeed, the development of the tertiary sector has taken varied forms, including the provision of personal services, from plumbers and hairdressers to lawyers, and the growth of the public sector, including civil

Table 8.1 *Structure of the active population (per cent)*

	1973	1985
Primary sector	10.9	7.5
Secondary sector	37.8	30.6
Tertiary sector	51.3	61.9

servants and teachers; of transport and tourism; banking and assurance; and advertising and the retail–wholesale systems. Further developments, associated with the spectacular development of information technology, promise enhanced opportunities for increasing economic productivity and wealth creation, but also even more intense global competition and greater social inequality. If most of the population continues to enjoy material prosperity, a sense of crisis has been induced by rampant consumerism and rising stress levels, by working in a more competitive and less secure job market and by living in congested and polluted cities, in which crime and racial tension are perceived to represent growing threats. Greater affluence is not without its costs.

SOCIAL PROBLEMS

The definition, and solution, of these problems is largely the responsibility of a relatively small socio-political élite, whose control of government and the media allows it to exercise considerable influence on wider public attitudes. Unequal inheritance and income inequality, together with differential access to social and cultural capital, invariably lead to massive disparities in the possession of power. A predominant role thus continues to be played by former pupils of a small number of prestigious Parisian *lycées*, the best qualified and most ambitious of whom subsequently graduate from university-level institutions or the Ecole libre des sciences politiques, and around 5 per cent of whom go on to study at such *grandes écoles* as Polytechnique, Mines, normale supérieure and, more recently Hautes études commerciales, its rise reflecting both the changing needs of the economy and effective networking. Especially important is the Ecole Nationale d'Administration, established in 1945 to produce a meritocratic administrative élite, and which selects around 120 students each year on the basis of fiercely competitive written and oral examinations. Subsequently, appointments to the three most prestigious administrative bodies, the Inspection générale des finances, Conseil d'Etat and Cour des comptes, open the road to the top in both the civil service and private enterprise. In 1999 two-thirds of the chairmen of the top forty listed companies were graduates of Polytechnique or ENA. This is symptomatic of the interpenetration of economic, social and political power. Leadership roles in the leading political parties on left and right are also generally occupied by *grandes écoles* graduates with a common professional training and similar values.

The 'establishment' thus created is supposedly selected on a meritocratic basis through the public examinations that allow university entry to everyone obtaining the *baccalauréat* at the end of his or her secondary education. In addition to the well-funded *grandes écoles*, there are over eighty far less prestigious universities and a further hundred technological institutions. In practice, prosopographical data suggests that the children of members of the existing élite enjoy considerable advantages. Inherited wealth matters. Family background and kinship links remain of central importance in determining ambition and attainment, and in the accumulation of cultural capital, and thus indirectly govern admission to the most prestigious schools and institutions of higher education. As a result, the system is as élitist as its British, Oxbridge-based equivalent. Subsequently, the tight social networks constituted around kinship, friendship, intermarriage and shared educational experience are the crucial determinants of career prospects. Not surprisingly, successive governments have been persuaded to largely exempt the *grandes écoles*, so important in the process of élite formation, from supposedly egalitarian reforms of higher education.

Nevertheless, growing concern has been expressed concerning the competence and even the integrity of these élites. It has been suggested that the basis for their recruitment is too restricted, their training too narrowly conceived and the end products too inflexible. Change has been slow, however. Affirmative action to support students from less privileged backgrounds has had only a marginal impact. If President Nicolas Sarkozy – a man with a definite chip on his shoulder – was trained as a lawyer, his predecessor and his successor were both products of ENA, the latter a member of the 1980 *promotion Voltaire* that currently dominates France. The widespread resentment of the self-satisfaction and arrogant air of superiority believed to typify members of the élite has been reinforced, furthermore, by accusations of corruption. *Pantouflage*, the process through which politicians and civil servants have traditionally moved between public service employment and jobs in the private sector, has helped to create cosy networks based upon the mutual exchange of favours. At its most extreme, during the 1990s, this kind of situation made it possible for the nationalised Crédit lyonnais bank to engage in an aggressive and reckless lending policy, funding property development in France and Asia, and concealing its mounting losses by means of creative accounting. The taxpayer met the bill. Supervision, by the bank's own directors, the Finance Ministry and the Bank of France, proved notably deficient. Significantly, the company chairman, Jean-Yves Haberer, had served previously as an inspecteur des finances and as the senior civil servant in the Finance Ministry. Magistrates investigating such murky activity complained about a culture of secrecy as well as about political interference with investigations. Such transgressions reveal the determination of members of the political élite to preserve their privileges and inevitably throw doubt on the legitimacy of the political system.

The air of distrust has been increased by the opening up of a gulf between the élite's understanding of the implications of globalisation and the concerns expressed by many French citizens. As if to illustrate the confusion, on 4 October 1996, whilst affirming that the social security system was the 'last rampart against what could be a dramatic decline of civilisation', President Chirac insisted nevertheless that the government deficit, and particularly that of the public health service, had become 'unbearable'. Conservative politicians, as well as the representatives of Medef, the leading employers' organisation, are particularly concerned that relatively high rates of personal and corporate tax, as well as social security charges and the legal obstacles to and costs of dismissing employees, have reduced productivity and competitiveness. For most key decision makers the need to liberalise the markets for capital and labour and to reduce state expenditure (which accounted for 52 per cent of GDP in 2007) and regulation appears self-evident and unavoidable if France is to retain its place in the world. In a period of economic recession, however, public resentment of the incomes and lifestyles enjoyed by directors of the major enterprises listed in the CAC 40, whose mutually supportive remuneration committees supposedly reward 'success', has become increasingly evident. The efforts of businessmen and representatives of the entertainment world to minimise their tax liabilities whilst loudly condemning 'social security fraud', as well as their much-publicised threats to leave France, have provoked additional anger.

Demographic factors add complexity to the situation. The rising costs of healthcare are due to the ageing and growing obesity of the population, the impact of AIDS, the recrudescence of diseases associated with poverty, and the effects of accelerating social change on stress levels, as well as the development of a more costly medical technology. There is also considerable wastage. Patients, 75 per cent of whose costs are normally reimbursed by the public health insurance fund, and the remainder through private or mutual insurance or, in the case of the very poor, by the state, are able to pay repeated visits to doctors and consume vast quantities of often useless drugs. Rationalisation is intended both to meet the changing needs of healthcare and to impose greater control over spending, as well as higher charges for users. Reform will continue to be resisted, however, not only by patients' groups concerned about such matters as hospital closures but also by doctors and health service workers anxious to protect salaries, job security, early retirement and generous pensions and to prevent a deterioration in what is an extremely high-quality system of healthcare.

Although the decline in the popularity of marriage and the growing likelihood of divorce has increased the number of single-parent families and of isolated individuals substantially, the traditional family remains of central importance to social cohesion. Increasingly it has become based on more affective and less paternalistic and authoritarian relations. Whilst women still accept more than their share of domestic responsibilities, gradually marriage – or, indeed, cohabitation – seems to have become a more equal partnership. In recognition of changing social *mores*, in 1999 legislation allowed 'cohabiting couples, whatever their sex', to register a civil union. Moreover, the provision of state-funded childcare facilities has made it easier for women to work outside the home. The impact on attitudes and behaviour of liberalising legislation on contraception (1967), abortion (1974) and divorce by mutual consent (1975), as well as against sexual harassment in the workplace, should also be emphasised. The stresses imposed on family life by the need for both parents to work to maintain living standards should not be ignored, however.

Together with generous family allowances, these developments have done something to ensure that – at 1.89 children per woman between 2005 and 2010 – fertility is higher than in other west European countries. Nevertheless, the long-term decline in fertility rates, and rising life expectancy (78.2 years for men and 85.3 for women in 2010), have already created a population with a high ratio of pensioners to workers. By 2040 the proportion of the population aged over sixty is likely to rise from one-fifth to one-third. Inevitably, an ageing population will increase the costs of pensions and healthcare substantially. Not surprisingly, reform of the pensions system and the postponement of retirement from sixty to sixty-two has become an emotive political issue, particularly for those groups such as railway workers and the police whose 'special regimes' allowed for early retirement in compensation for difficult working conditions.

Moreover, as the numbers out of work rose in the 1970s, the spiralling cost of providing assistance became a matter of grave concern, leading to restrictions on entitlement in 1984, particularly harsh in their consequences for the young and long-term unemployed. Subsequently, the need to reduce government expenditure to enhance French economic competitiveness and to satisfy the Maastricht criteria for European Monetary Union exacerbated the problem. Budget deficits needed to be reduced from 6 per cent to 3 per cent of GDP by January 1999. Achieving this, rather than reducing unemployment, rapidly became the government's new 'priority of priorities', with the change of emphasis being heralded as the most effective means of cutting unemployment in the long term, as reduced government borrowing led to falling interest rates, and this in turn stimulated investment and job creation.

Between the beginning of 1997 and December 2000 an estimated 1.6 million new jobs were created. This was due partly to prosperous economic conditions and the creation and growth of small high-tech computer-based companies and, to some extent, to the Socialist government's reduction in the length of the working week. The thirty-five-hour week, together with high social security costs, frequently led large companies to reorganise work practices, however, in order to increase productivity and avoid the need to employ additional labour. New problems emerged. As a result of the erosion of industrial employment the number of industrial workers continued to decline, to around 13 per cent of the adult population, with an additional 44 per cent employed in the service sector, often in poorly rewarded part-time and temporary work. The focus by successive governments on expensive short-term and low-productivity job creation measures for the young did little to boost skill levels whilst labour force participation by women and older men was sharply reduced by early retirement, so that only an exceptionally low 39 per cent of those in the fifty-five to sixty-four age group were left in productive employment by 2010. Unemployment levels also remained stubbornly high amongst the young, women and the unskilled and in depressed regions.

Gradually, governments have come to accept the employers' case for more flexible labour markets and an easing of the regulations designed to protect workers' rights. Trades union membership has collapsed (to around 8 per cent of the labour force), and with it the class consciousness of much of an increasingly fragmented working class. Nevertheless, employment remains a major electoral issue, reflecting the growing sense of vulnerability amongst the self-employed, as well as employees in every sector of the economy and every social class, as the application of information technology, together with the restructuring of business activity, has had a substantial impact on the labour market. Typically, in banking, when the Crédit agricole assumed control of the Crédit lyonnais in 2002, a major reduction in costs was achieved through a substantial cutback in the numbers of back-room staff. In contrast, with the explosion of opportunity and the expansion of the middle classes in the 1960s, the space available for upward social mobility has sharply contracted. Social demotion has become more common. Differences in the experience of age cohorts – a *fracture générationnelle* – have become evident. In comparison with their predecessors – who were particularly burdened by poverty in old age – and successors – entering the labour market as the economy slowed down – the generations born between 1950 and 1975, and particularly senior managers and civil servants, have enjoyed relatively well recompensed and secure careers and generous pensions. Currently, for the mass of ordinary citizens, the 'dominated classes', employment, prosperity and security all appear to be threatened by apocalyptic visions of unrestrained global change and of the destabilisation associated with post-industrial capitalism, as well as by the unrestrained greed of social élites. As a result of the severe financial crisis beginning in 2008, unemployment increased to 3 million in May 2011. The number of people defined as 'poor' by official statisticians rose from 7.83 to 8.17 million within a year.

In contrast with the prosperity still enjoyed by much of the population, a substantial minority, including many members of ethnic minorities, is experiencing real, or at least relative, deprivation. To some extent difficulties are concentrated in the regions that attracted most immigrants during the *trente glorieuses*. Thus, outside the *boulevard périphérique* that defines the boundaries of the city of Paris with its 2 million inhabitants, a further 8 million people live in the often isolated and deprived housing complexes forming part of a greater Paris. The collapse of employment in formally vibrant coalmining and steel communities in such places as Lens and Valenciennes in the north and Longwy in Lorraine, or in textiles centres such as Roubaix and Tourcoing, has also had extremely damaging consequences. Many, particularly amongst the long-term unemployed, as well as members of their families, have suffered from a sense of social exclusion and have frequently sought solace in drugs and alcohol. Grants made by the state to encourage the establishment of new businesses and the renovation of housing have had only a limited impact. The situation is probably at its worst in deprived inner-city areas and in the suburbs created in the 1960s and 1970s, characterised by brutalist tower blocks and a lack of collective services. These were constructed by well-meaning politicians and planners anxious to improve a housing stock dilapidated by long neglect and wartime devastation, and are grossly overcrowded as a result of population growth and massive immigration. Today's political leaders similarly promise improvements to ever more degraded physical environments and deteriorating living conditions, but change is slow, perhaps because there are few votes to be gained amongst the disaffected. In spite of efforts to improve low-cost public housing (*habitation à loyer modéré*) and to encourage the construction of private housing, high rents and the difficulty of obtaining loans ensures that around 8 million people inhabit 'defective' dwellings. At least mobility and access to employment in the Paris region should be improved by the construction of a 130-kilometre-long super-metro by 2017.

In the meantime, the sense of deprivation and resentment felt by inhabitants of run-down high-rise estates is palpable, whether in La Corneuve in the Paris suburbs, Chanteloup-les-Vignes (where the film *La Haine*, with its realistic portrayals of gang violence and clashes with the police, was shot) or Val-Fourré outside Mantes, to the west of the capital – the largest estate, with 25,000 inhabitants. Similar situations prevail in Les Minguettes outside Lyon or La Concorde on the edge of Lille. Deindustrialisation has resulted in loss of employment, welfare dependence and feelings of worthlessness. Complex reactions are provoked. On the one hand, unemployment and deprivation exacerbate gender, generational and ethno-cultural tensions. White people, in older suburbs, as well as those who feel they have been left behind as the ethnic character of estates has been transformed by immigration, complain bitterly about different cultures and customs and at what they perceive to be the preferential treatment of blacks and Arabs by the local authorities. Those who could afford to have already left. On the other hand, a shared sense of exclusion and of resentment at the stigma attached to living in a notorious neighbourhood unites unemployed young men in racially mixed street gangs and in a common hostility towards those they believe to be responsible for their predicament. Graffiti makes the sense of frustration and its targets all too obvious. The most common is probably 'Fuck the police'. Pop groups such as *Nique ta mère* ('Screw your mother') won support with lyrics such as 'We've got nothing to lose because we've never had a thing. If I were you, I wouldn't sleep soundly; the bourgeoisie should tremble, the rabble is in town.' The resentment of the young is also expressed through widespread vandalism and crime – mainly small-scale drug dealing, muggings and petty theft, but additionally through rapes, which reveal a disturbingly negative perception of women, and attacks on the police, themselves frequently accused of harassment – and with some justice, given the much greater likelihood of identity checks on non-whites. The major disorders, lasting three weeks, that occurred in November 2005 in Clichy-sur-Bois, near Paris, following the accidental electrocution of two young men being chased by the police might be represented as an expression of accumulated resentment. The dismissal by interior minister Sarkozy of the rioters as *racaille* (scum) who ought to be cleaned out with a power hose only inflamed the situation, although a tough stance on law and order certainly helped promote his 2007 presidential campaign.

Throughout France, the police have identified more than 700 *quartiers difficiles* in which arrests are only too likely to trigger riots, car burning and looting, increasingly involving groups rapidly mobilised by the ubiquitous mobile phone and social networking. Inevitably, this has created a climate of insecurity and fear, particularly in the more run-down estates, and, together with the far more widespread sense of panic aroused by the popular press, has ensured that the issue of law and order is kept towards the top of the political agenda. This is certainly where the police unions would like it to be, to support their case for increasing the numbers and salaries of their members, and opposition to reform of their own working practices. What is really needed, though, is not additional policemen (there are already 146,000 national police controlled by the Interior Ministry, 101,000 gendarmes answering to the Defence Ministry, and 13,000 municipal police) but more effective deployment and, especially, cooperation rather than rivalry between police forces. Incompetent management is a greater problem than numerical insufficiency, and certainly makes an often extremely stressful job all the more difficult.

In 2002 Sarkozy, insisting that the police were not social workers, scrapped the neighbourhood policing (*police de proximité*) first introduced during the Second Empire and re-established by Lionel Jospin, the prime minister, in 1998 as a means of building local confidence and security. Funding for community projects (sport, music, culture) and for social workers was reduced at the same time. A repressive, interventionist role was preferred: investigating crimes, checking identities and 'taking back neighbourhoods'.

Proposed reforms of the judicial system during the Sarkozy presidency that would have reduced the investigative powers of the *juge d'instruction*, whilst strengthening the authority of public prosecutors, were widely perceived to be a means of reinforcing government control, and as a politicisation of the legal system.

The tensions inevitable in any society when immigrants with different customs enter the space of a settled population and compete for work and accommodation have become only too evident, most recently in the case of popular and official hostility towards the Roma. France is undoubtedly a racist society. Thus, according to a 1999 Harris poll, 68 per cent of a representative sample of the population believed themselves to have racist tendencies, with 61 per cent insisting that there were already too many foreigners in France. Since 1983 28 per cent had voted, at least once, for the Front national. Particular hostility towards individuals perceived to be of north African extraction was revealed, typically on the grounds that they preferred to rely on welfare benefits rather than work – an accusation thrown at most immigrants, but additionally at

Plate 8.1 Protest against reform of the pension system, Marseille, 13 May 2003. Photo: Gerard Julien/AFP/Getty Images.

north Africans because it was assumed that they were unable or unwilling to assimilate into French society. Significantly, blacks, especially those from the *départements d'outre-mer* in the Caribbean, are less likely to encounter prejudice than people of north African origin, although more so than white immigrants. These attitudes are partly the result of the deep scars on the collective memory left by the Algerian War of Independence.

The substantial contribution made by north African troops to the French military effort in two world wars and in Indo-China seems to have been forgotten, as does that of the first migrant generations to post-war prosperity. Encouraged to move to France by major companies such as Renault in search of cheap labour, and to work as unskilled labourers in building and mining, they and their children were faced with reduced employment opportunities as a result of robotics and down-sizing. Many had fled rural poverty and

Plate 8.2 Dependence on immigrant labour to sustain economic growth: typically accommodated in low-cost housing, as here at Gennevilliers in the 1980s. Photo: Chollet-Rapho.

the horrific violence of the colonial war and the bloody civil conflict fought in Algeria in the 1990s. Typically, once men had found work, their families followed. The growing number of mosques, with imams generally recruited in the Maghreb, of halal butchers and of satellite dishes turned towards Arab television stations was evidence of their presence and of continued commitments to their communities of origin as well as to those in which they had settled.

The official objective remains the assimilation of immigrants, which does indeed appear to have done much to promote integration and even to encourage upward social mobility. The British model of multiculturalism is rejected by the French authorities as divisive and segregationist. Moreover, hostility towards any form of cultural distinctiveness is institutionalised by a deep-rooted official and public commitment to the universalist, secular and egalitarian values of *La République une et indivisible,* coupled with the insistence that ethnic, racial, religious, regional and corporate groups should have no distinctive rights or privileges. In line with this, published official statistics reject distinctions based on race or religion. Thus the number of Muslims in France can only be estimated, at around 5 to 6 million, of whom around 3 million are of north African origin or descent, including 1.5 million with Algerian links. The presence of unknown numbers of illegal immigrants ensures that these figures are grossly inflated by public opinion.

Traditionally, the schools have played a vital part in this integrative process. For this reason alone, the insistence in 1989 by three schoolgirls from Creil near Paris, and in 2003 by two students from Aubervilliers in the Parisian suburbs, on their religious duty to wear headscarves whilst attending secular public schools was bound to court controversy. In 2004 legislation was introduced to reinforce the secularising provisions of the 1905 education law. It was determined that the law that forbids the 'ostentatious' display of religious symbols, which was interpreted as not applying to 'discreet' crucifixes or stars of David, prohibited the wearing of headscarves as likely to 'constitute an act of pressure, provocation, proselytism or propaganda'. It was maintained by the education authorities that the students' behaviour served to suggest that the Muslim sharia, sacred law, should be given precedence over the civil law. Supported by President Chirac and most parliamentary deputies, the official ban ran the risk, however, of reinforcing the influence of Islamist groups that claimed that Muslims were being treated unfairly. Many young representatives of a second or third generation, French citizens but caught between two cultures, seem increasingly determined to assert their Islamic identity, in the case of young women by adopting the headscarf that many of their mothers had rejected, and, more generally, accepting the label *beur* ('Arab' in Parisian slang) and adopting a culture based on reggae, rap and Arabic raï, whilst expressing themselves in an impenetrable slang. They fast during Ramadan and demand religiously correct food in school canteens. A report by the Council on Integration in 2004 estimated that 31 per cent were high school dropouts. Once they would have wanted to become French. Feeling rejected, but with nowhere else to go, many have become increasingly assertive.

The hyper-sensitivity of French political leaders of whatever political hue (but particularly those on the right) to this situation can be illustrated further by the response to the events of 6 October 2001, when French and Algerian football teams met for the first time in Paris: French-born Muslims whistled during the French national anthem and subsequently invaded the pitch, forcing the abandonment of the game. This was in very sharp contrast with the mass celebration of the victory of a multiracial French team in the 1998 World Cup final. Typically, the forceful conservative interior minister, Sarkozy, overreacted by introducing legislation that made it a criminal offence to dishonour the principal symbols of the Republic – the *Marseillaise* and the tricolour. There is a clear danger that Muslim fundamentalism and the threat from terrorism, with which it is frequently associated, will further reinforce racial stereotypes and tension and that it might promote an ultra-nationalist backlash. Nevertheless, there are also more positive signs. Most young Muslims, especially those living in ethnically mixed areas and committed to education, still favour integration. The growing number of mixed marriages is one sign of this. Predictions that the young would increasingly distance themselves from Islam have not been confirmed, however. Whilst, overall, only around 15 per cent of Muslims are estimated to worship on a regular basis, recent surveys (*Le Monde*, 1 November 2012) suggest that 90 per cent of eighteen- to twenty-five-year-olds respect the dietary prescriptions of

Ramadan and 30 per cent of the twenty-one to twenty-five age group attend prayers. Many of them, living in the *quartiers immigrés* in the suburbs, feeling rejected, have increasingly abandoned their parents' dreams and determined to reject European culture. There might only be around 12,000 dedicated Salafists in France but many more who favour a traditionalist Islamism – homophobic and imposing a subordinate role on women, sympathetic towards the Palestinian campaign against Israeli occupation and calling on their websites for a holy war against Jews and 'crusaders'.

There are some 2,000 mosques and prayer rooms in France supporting a process of re-Islamisation. On occasion, as at the Al-Fath mosque in a deprived part of the eighteenth *arrondissement* of Paris, worshippers overflow into the surrounding streets. In this case, and rather than make concessions to outraged conservatives, the response of city hall has been pragmatic and conciliatory, with the construction of a new Islamic cultural centre. Elsewhere, obstacles have frequently been posed and building permits refused. The inauguration of the grande mosque in Strasbourg on 28 September 2012 – attended by Manuel Valls, the Socialist interior minister – was the culmination of twenty years' effort.

In spite of well-meaning gestures, there remains a very real danger that Islamic fundamentalists, as well as representatives of the extreme right and centre-right in French politics, might seek to exacerbate differences. In 2011, following heated debate, the burqa, providing head-to-toe covering for women, was banned in public places on both security grounds and to prevent what President Sarkozy referred to as the 'subjugation' and 'debasement' of women. The danger implicit in the strict official insistence on assimilation is that it will interfere with the complex, difficult and ongoing process by which Muslims adapt to the broader cultural environment in which they live and non-Muslims themselves adapt to the Muslims in their midst.

Christianity also serves as a central feature of contending systems of identity, although often only a vague adherence to the basic tenets of the faith has survived the challenges of secularisation. Thus, whilst around 90 per cent of French children were baptised by Catholic priests in 1945, by 2000 this had fallen to 50 per cent. Whilst 80 per cent of the French population claimed to be Roman Catholic in 1966, the same was true of only 51 per cent in 2007, with only 5 per cent – drawn mainly from the older generations – regularly attending Mass. In addition, 2.1 per cent described themselves as Protestants and 0.6 per cent as Jews. According to a survey in 2012, 35 per cent of the population, and 63 per cent amongst the eighteen to twenty-four age group, were 'sans religion'.

As well as being symptomatic, this decline reinforces the severe crisis the Catholic Church is undergoing at an institutional level. In an age of growing prosperity, when self-gratification increasingly appears to be the norm, less heed is paid to the moral teachings of the clergy. The advent of a relatively liberal Pope, John XXIII (1958–63), aroused hope that the Church would reach out and attempt to communicate more effectively with the population. The reaffirmation of traditionalist teaching by his successors, Paul IV (1963–78) and especially John-Paul II (1978–2005) and Benedict XVI (2005–13), and particularly their re-endorsement of the Catholic condemnation of contraception, resulted in a considerable loss of authority. Whilst 20 per cent of practising adult Catholics made their monthly confession in the 1950s, by the early 1990s the figure had fallen to 1 per cent, and, although women were still more likely to attend Mass than men, over 80 per cent of those who did so regularly were prepared to ignore the Vatican's instructions on birth control.

The number of priests also shrank, due both to a fall in vocations and resignations, frequently resulting from an unwillingness to respect the need for celibacy. In two decades, between the mid-1960s and mid-1980s, the secular clergy declined from 40,000 to 27,000. The situation has continued to deteriorate, and membership of the religious orders has also collapsed. Parishes have been amalgamated, and a rapidly ageing clergy forced to rely more on the commitment of a pious laity. As an institution, the Church has never found it easy to admit to mistakes, or to sanction reform. Plagued by revelations of sexual transgressions and abuse of children by priests, the charismatic Polish Pope, and his equally authoritarian successor, have thus presided over unprecedented religious decline, although every gathering of young believers, for example those at Taizé, renews hope of recovery.

The influence of the Church on political behaviour has diminished at the same time. Nevertheless, in the sphere of education, traditionally a major battleground between the Church and the secular

Republic, disputes have continued. When, in June 1984, the Socialist government introduced plans for a limited increase in state control over the private Catholic schools, for which it provided substantial subsidies, it was forced to desist in the face of a massive demonstration by enraged parents, inspired by middle-class snobbery as well as religious convictions. Although, prior to the 2012 legislative election, both the conservative Union pour un mouvement populaire (UMP) and the Socialists reaffirmed their commitment to the 1905 law on the separation of Church and state and to religious liberty, in its aftermath the issue of homosexual marriage could still provoke major demonstrations.

Education remains central to shared ideals of republican egalitarianism, and of a united, secular society. In practice, of course, whilst facilitating social mobility, schools also play a vital role in the reproduction of social élites and in the perpetuation of inequality. In the developing knowledge society, retaining a competitive educational advantage for children, whether within the better-resourced, more disciplined environment of a private school, or at a reputable state *lycée*, can easily become a matter of vital import for parents anxious to open pathways to the *grandes écoles* and glittering professional careers for their offspring. Three-quarters of pupils now stay on, and often struggle, to complete the broadly based *baccalauréat*, which opens the way to a university education. The educational system, designed to assimilate the poorer classes to an élite culture, or at least to prepare them for a labour market dominated by the service sector, in all its diversity, has nevertheless been criticised frequently for failing to develop apprenticeship training on the German model, and turning out an 'underclass', lacking basic literacy and numeracy skills as well as the cultural competence necessary for success. The numbers involved and the frequent lack of motivation amongst students place considerable pressure on state schools. For poorly rewarded and frequently demoralised teachers, the great difficulty is motivating often unruly pupils, suffering from low self-esteem and overwhelmingly representative of the *classes populaires* isolated from the cultural values of the educational system. Invariably, however, efforts to ensure better training of teachers and closer monitoring of 'failing' students are limited by financial priorities and opposed by the powerful teachers' unions, which are torn between the desire to encourage pupil creativity and pressure for a return to a more structured and disciplined system of instruction, as favoured recently by President Sarkozy and typified by his determination to abandon the currently fashionable thematic and universalistic approach to the teaching of history and revert to the nationalistic and strictly chronological methods of the Third Republic.

The universities themselves, mainly committed to the provision of free tuition, are often overcrowded, underequipped, suffering from a shortage of staff and able to function only thanks to a massive dropout rate – often over 50 per cent – in the first year. Awareness of their low international standing has promoted reforms, introduced in 2009 and taking effect in 2012, designed to grant greater autonomy to institutions and allow for some selection of students on the basis of ability. In all likelihood, those universities most successful in attracting private as well as public funding, and increasingly committed to research, will gradually draw apart from the others, still concentrating on the mass production of social science graduates. In a less expansive and more competitive labour market, the development of mass instruction has contributed to a devaluation of formerly prized educational qualifications, as well as to widespread disillusionment amongst young aspirants to secure well-rewarded middle-class professions.

The nation's sense of identity and international status have also appeared threatened by 'Americanisation'. The position of English as the international language of business, of science, of advertising, of the internet and, to a large degree, of popular music, and as the second language chosen by most school pupils, nevertheless appears irreversible. Considerable emotional energy and large subsidies have been focused on the French cinema, which has been in a permanent state of crisis since the expansion of the television audience brought the immensely popular post-war cinema craze to an end. The number of households with a television set rose from 15 per cent to 70 per cent during the 1960s and then to 95 per cent by 1990. The output of films has fluctuated with the level of state support, increasing. For example. from ninety-five in 1995 to 181 in 1999. Audiences have tended to prefer American films, however, presumably because of their production values as well as the massive sums invested in their creation and marketing. In 1999 the success of *Astérix* (an emblem of French assertiveness and guile) *and Obélix against Caesar* was still dwarfed by that of the American epic *Titanic*, a film saved from its awful banality only by the special effects. The development of satellite and cable television and increasingly massive DVD sales and digital streaming are only likely to increase further US dominance of the film market. Nonetheless, in 2010 ticket sales at F215 million – the best for forty-five years – and the opening of multiplexes in every commercial centre, together with the production of 271 French films, encouraged a renewed sense of optimism.

The culinary dimension of globalisation has also caused great concern. Writing in *Le Monde* (9 September 1999), and only partly tongue in cheek, Alain Rollat claimed: 'Resistance to the hegemonic pretensions of hamburgers is, above all, a cultural imperative.' Nevertheless, McDonald's has continued to increase the number of its outlets, adapting to the peculiarities of the local market, whilst the number of traditional cafés has declined sharply. This is also symptomatic of a broadening in the range of leisure activities. Already by 1983 30 million people took at least one holiday a year. EuroDisney was established near Paris in 1992, in spite of everything it symbolised, because it promised jobs and massive tourist revenues.

Pessimism reigns, but French culture, whether élitist or popular, remains vibrant. The vastly expensive assertion of *grandeur* engaged in by Mitterrand might be taken to represent an assertive self-confidence, a determination both to make a cultural statement and, along Bonapartist lines, to transform and revivify the capital city. Construction, almost without counting the cost, of such monuments as the Grande Arche, the Bastille Opera, the Louvre Pyramid, the new Finance Ministry (the transfer of which to Bercy allowed renovation of the Louvre and Tuileries Palaces) and, above all, the Bibliothèque François Mitterrand, followed by Chirac's Musée du quai Branly (a post-colonial evocation of 'primitive' art), could hardly fail to have a major impact. The inauguration of the Centre Pompidou at Metz in May 2010 and of a branch of the Louvre at Lens in December 2012 represented collaborative efforts by local and central government to share cultural assets and stimulate depressed areas. At the level of high culture, substantial investment has raised the standards of classical music and opera and provided impressive venues. Intellectually, the hugely influential philosophical concepts of structuralism and postmodernism – the search for underlying realities – was developed by a succession of French academics, including Roland Barthes, Jacques Lacan, Jacques Derrida, Michel Foucault and Jean Baudrillard.

Social differences survive, of course. Unequal access to cultural capital is evident in attendance at orchestral concerts, the opera, theatre and major exhibitions, and in the purchase of specialised books and journals. The Socialist governments of the 1980s, like post-Liberation regimes, were to be disappointed in their dream of the democratisation of culture. The audience remains overwhelmingly middle-aged and middle class. In terms of popular culture, although television companies find American programmes both cheap to purchase and often extremely popular with audiences, home-grown products, especially 'soaps' and game shows, attract large audiences in spite of their often abysmal quality. Within the media, politically committed newspapers increasingly gave way from the 1960s to periodicals such as *Paris-Match* or *L'Express* or to the *Figaro Magazine*, targeted especially at managers and professionals too busy to read a daily newspaper. Special interest, and especially women's, magazines have encouraged a fascination with lifestyle, sport and the lives of media personalities. Events such as the Tour de France attract massive audiences. Horse racing retains its popularity mainly because it provides an opportunity to gamble. The most threatening trend is probably the growing control over the media by a small number of powerful financial groups as a means of furthering their business interests and of setting the terms of political debate. This process, inevitable in a market increasingly unfettered since liberalisation in the 1980s, has allowed the two major defence contractors, Lagardère and Dassault, to assume control of as much as 70 per cent of the press, with serious implications for the country's political life. A further threat is posed by the collapse in readership, to around 8 million for national newspapers and 17 million for their regional counterparts, with *Ouest France* (circulation 2.2 million) the most successful, thanks to its 'human interest' stories and regional focus. Although the regional dailies play a key role in local politics and in the struggle against corruption, the disappearance of the weaker titles and concentration of ownership reduced their number from 170 to fewer than sixty between 1944 and 2010. Even the centre-left *Le Monde*, the most prestigious of national newspapers, with a circulation of 1,223,000 in 2010, succumbed when faced with bankruptcy to a takeover by a small group of financiers determined to humble its unions, and reduce its high editorial and printing costs. Online publication, e-books and competition for advertising revenue are additional features of a communications revolution that poses a challenge to the traditional media and to commerce in general.

That the social problems outlined above are faced by every European society has not spared successive French governments, regardless of their political complexion, from criticism for an inability to provide solutions. This perceived failure has fuelled an almost instinctive distrust of politicians' motives and competence. This, then, is the place to consider the evolving political life of a society under stress.

POLITICAL LIFE

The death of President Pompidou in April 1974 was followed by a vicious electoral contest in which the two leading protagonists were the conservative politicians Chaban-Delmas and Giscard d'Estaing. The former's apparent strength as a resistance hero and former prime minister, and his position as the nominee of the Gaullist Union des démocrates pour la République (the UDR's name from 1967 to 1976), was undermined by the desertion of a group of Gaullist notables, led by the ambitious Chirac. Personal rivalries combined with the disquiet caused by Chaban-Delmas's evident commitment to social reform. Furthermore, police polls had made it clear to Chirac, who had been appointed interior minister just before Pompidou's death, that Chaban would probably lose in a run-off against Mitterrand, the leading contender on the left. In the event, Chaban was forced to withdraw after the first ballot, in which he received only 15 per cent of the vote. His support had been dented further by accusations of tax evasion and indifferent television performances compared with those of Mitterrand (43 per cent), and the RI leader, Giscard d'Estaing (32 per cent). As a result, the latter, a non-Gaullist, would serve as the single conservative candidate for the second ballot. This was indicative of a shift in the balance of power within the conservative coalition and of a return to a more straightforward left–right competition. Giscard – youthful, elegant and so obviously extremely intelligent – obtained 13,396,203 votes (50.8 per cent). This meant that, for the first time during the Fifth Republic, the president was not to be the leader of the largest party in parliament – a factor bound to cause problems of political management. The continuing revival of the left, with Mitterrand obtaining 12,971,604 votes (49.2 per cent), would, however, impose a degree of unity on conservative politicians.

The new president was an extremely well connected member of the traditional social élite and a graduate of both the Ecole Polytechnique and Ecole nationale d'administration. Like his predecessors, he was committed to economic and social modernisation, and additionally to the creation of an 'advanced liberal society'. Previously he had served as a very orthodox finance minister. His essential objectives were now to be the re-establishment of the conditions for a return to rapid economic growth, which had widely come to be perceived as the norm rather than an exceptional state of affairs, and a reduction in the potential for social conflict. The overall result was excessive state expenditure and substantial increases in wages and social benefits. The men appointed to prime ministerial office, first Chirac and then Raymond Barre, searched desperately for an effective economic policy. Efforts were made to identify leading sectors likely to be competitive in world markets and whose success would provide a vital stimulus to French enterprise. Armaments producers, the aeronautical industry – which with its European partners developed Airbus – the space programme, as well as telecommunications and information technology, were stimulated by massive state contracts and subsidy. In an effort to balance the books, however, the Chirac government (May 1974–August 1976) also introduced credit restrictions, which resulted in a deepening recession, and were abandoned in favour of reflationary policies that only stimulated higher inflation. Tension between the president and his prime minister grew over these matters. Almost inevitably, too, there was disagreement over the balance of authority between them. Eventually, Chirac was forced into resignation on 25 August 1976, and he was replaced by Barre, a professional economist who, lacking a political base of his own, was far more dependent on the president.

Subsequently, Barre (1976–81) sought to implement a more cautious economic policy in response to the problems caused by the oil crisis, seeking to restore business confidence by means of an economic liberalisation that involved a reduction in direct government intervention in the economy and greater reliance on market forces to restore international competitiveness. The government's austerity programme, which included increases in social security contributions and a price and wage freeze, was hardly popular but it did contribute to stabilising inflation, although at a high rate (9 per cent in 1977). This took precedence over curbing unemployment, which had risen to 1.3 million by the end of 1978, and, indeed, proved to be a useful means of curbing inflationary wage increases.

Initially Giscard was instrumental in the introduction of important libertarian reforms designed to update the law and ensure that it conformed better to a changing morality. The age of consent and of voting was reduced to eighteen (law of 5 July 1974), abortion was legalised (17 January 1975), divorce procedures were simplified and chemists were authorised to sell contraceptives (July 1975). Social security provisions were made more generous and efforts made to improve access to secondary education (*loi Haby*, 11 July 1975). An attempt was also made to desacralise the office of president. Giscard spoke on television in an informal, relaxed manner, in marked contrast to the almost regal style he developed later. In spite of efforts to conciliate Gaullists, and to reward Chirac with the office of prime minister, the president's early legislative programme nevertheless caused considerable disquiet and tension within the conservative coalition. Most conservatives were unwilling to support proposals to reinforce workers' rights or to increase the taxation of capital gains as a means of easing the burden that indirect taxation imposed on the poor.

These divisions became increasingly evident as Chirac reorganised the Gaullists into the more aggressively populist Rassemblement pour la République (RPR), a mechanism for assisting his increasingly obvious presidential ambitions. He further increased the pressure by presenting himself as a candidate for the office of mayor of Paris, newly created by Giscard as a major step towards decentralisation, and, on 25 March 1977, defeated the president's own hand-picked candidate. Giscard's response was to organise the groups of non-Gaullist conservatives into the Union pour la démocratie française (UDF), in the hope of widening his appeal in the centre, to political moderates. In the short term, in spite of recurrent tensions, the broad conservative alliance survived. A self-interested determination to hang on to power ensured cooperation for the second ballot in the legislative election of March 1978. Victory was made all the easier by the revival of internecine conflict on the left.

In the remaining years of his presidency Giscard focused his attention on international affairs, with little impact except in Europe, where as a result of a joint Franco-German initiative it was agreed that the European parliament should be elected by universal suffrage. This was in spite of Gaullist distaste for any reinforcement of the principle of supranationality. Otherwise, French 'mediation' in the increasingly tense relationship between the superpowers was clearly ignored. Indeed, growing domestic problems inevitably reduced the government's international prestige. The second oil crisis brought a further tripling of prices in 1979/80, renewed balance of payments difficulties, increased inflation (11.8 per cent in 1978, 13.4 per cent in 1979) and unemployment.

The general sense of disquiet and of insecurity was intensified by the threat of terrorism, exemplified by an explosion at a synagogue in the rue Copernic in Paris. According to an Institut français d'opinion publique (IFOP) poll in September 1979, only 26 per cent of respondents were satisfied with the president's performance. Criticism was stimulated further when the satirical weekly *Le canard enchaîné* exposed the strange affair of the 'emperor's' diamonds, the gift made to Giscard by the unsavoury Emperor Bokassa, ruler of the Central African Empire (as he had renamed the Central African Republic). Together with his growing *hauteur*, this increasingly made Giscard a figure of fun. Even so, opinion polls throughout 1980 continued to suggest that he would beat any likely left-wing challenger in the 1981 presidential election. In spite of the economic 'crisis', most of the population was continuing to enjoy a very real prosperity.

Nevertheless, the slow recovery of the left from the profound divisions and weakness of the early years of the Fifth Republic posed a growing threat to conservative dominance. Serious efforts to ensure closer cooperation had begun in 1964 on the initiative of the Communist Party, then the largest group on the left and anxious to escape from its political isolation. This had borne fruit in the candidature of Mitterrand in the 1965 presidential election. The events of 1968 and the splintering of the decrepit Socialist Party had hindered further progress. It took the disastrous showing of the left in the 1969 presidential election, when both its candidates were eliminated in the first ballot, to stimulate a renewed effort. At first, the creation of a new Parti Socialiste in July 1969 made little difference. Only after the election as its first secretary of Mitterrand at the Epinay congress in June 1971 were new initiatives apparent.

Mitterrand was an outsider who had not been identified with any of the party's warring factions. He had moved towards the left as a means of opposing Gaullism. His reputation as a leading figure in the wartime resistance reinforced his credentials and, until 1994, he carefully managed to conceal his pre-war leanings towards the neo-fascist Croix de feu, as well as his initial commitment to Pétain and the Vichy regime and long post-war friendship with René Bousquet, secretary-general of the Vichy police and a leading collaborator. Agreement was reached with the Communists on 7 June 1972 to present a common programme to the electorate. The Socialists agreed that the objective should be a 'break with capitalism' by means of the nationalisation of key sectors of the economy; the Communists conceded that an election victory would not be followed by a 'dictatorship of the proletariat' and adhered to a democratic electoral politics. The partnership was never going to be an easy one. The leaders of both parties were determined to assume the predominant role whilst at the same time preserving the autonomy of their own organisations. Even so, the results of the March 1973 legislative election seemed to confirm the value of the alliance. Although the performance of the left had improved only in comparison with its abysmal showing in 1969, the Socialists had managed to arrest their electoral decline and had attracted almost as great a share of the popular vote as the Communists.

In spite of the misgivings this caused them, the Communists agreed to support Mitterrand's candidature in the presidential election in

May 1974 and made a major contribution to his creditable result. From the end of the year, however, Communist Party spokesmen, and particularly its secretary-general, Marchais, made increasingly frequent attacks on their erstwhile allies. Finally, in September 1977, denouncing their partner's moderation and willingness to engage in class collaboration, the Communists renounced the union. Certainly, there were still substantial ideological differences between an increasingly pragmatic Socialist Party and a Communist Party committed to state socialism on the Soviet model. This change of tactics, and the mutual recriminations that followed, made little practical sense, however, at a time when opinion polls had suggested that the left stood a good chance of achieving a majority in the March 1978 legislative election.

The twists and turns of Communist Party policy reflected Marchais' opposition to those he described as the *liquidateurs* in his party – that is, the modernisers who favoured an unambiguous commitment to democracy – as well as his growing fear of the permanent decline of what had so recently been the strongest French political party. Already, from 28 per cent of the first ballot vote in 1946 and an average of 26 per cent throughout the Fourth Republic, the Communist Party's share of the vote had fallen to 20 per cent by 1978. This trend would continue, with a subsequent collapse of electoral support to 16 per cent in 1981, and to 9.8 per cent in 1986 (fewer than the Front national). Electoral failure was accompanied by a decline in membership and in militant activity, the falling circulation of the party's press, widespread demoralisation and its growing marginalisation even in the 'red belt' towns of the Paris region. In any case, it would have been difficult to resist a complex of mutually reinforcing pressures and, particularly, changes in social structure involving the decline of the traditional working class with its distinctive subculture; a lack of interest amongst young voters in Soviet-style communism; and more effective competition from the Socialists. The inability of the Communist hierarchy to develop a coherent and sustained response to these problems and its constant determination to weed out dissidents compounded the damage. The party consistently followed the Soviet line, supporting the Russian invasions of Hungary in 1956, Czechoslovakia in 1968 and Afghanistan in

1979. The leadership's feeble response to the events of May 1968 in France itself, and then the impact of the publication of Aleksandr Solzhenitsyn's *Gulag Archipelago* in 1974, threw further doubt on their moral as well as political credentials. Only Mikhail Gorbachev's efforts in the late 1980s to liberalise the Soviet system would eventually provoke Marchais into criticism of the Moscow leadership. This weakening of the Communist Party and the rise of a moderate Socialist alternative would combine to deradicalise the left and make it more electable.

More immediately, however, the effect of the Communists' abandonment of the electoral alliance in 1978 was only too clear. In the legislative election the left did well in the first ballot, and even strengthened its position in the run-off, but it failed to achieve an overall majority. This was largely because of the unwillingness of many of those who voted Socialist in the first round to support Communist candidates in the second – an outcome that led to a further deterioration in relations between the two parties. Once again, the left had revealed that it found it even more difficult than the right to respond to the bipolarising tendencies set in play by the political system of the Fifth Republic. If anything, these divisions were reinforced during the lengthy campaign that preceded the 1981 presidential election. The Communists seemed preoccupied with destroying the chances of a Socialist victory and presented Marchais as their own candidate. Initially, the Socialists themselves were divided between the supporters of Michel Rocard and those of another

Table 8.2 *Results of National Assembly election, 12 and 19 March 1978*

	First-ballot votes	Share (percentage of votes)	Seats after second ballot
Communists	5,791,125	20.61	86
Socialists	6,403,265	22.79	114
UDF	6,712,244	23.89	137
RPR	6,416,288	22.84	154

Plate 8.3 Presidential election: Valéry Giscard d'Estaing and François Mitterrand engage in a televised debate, 5 May 1981. Photo: AFP/Getty Images.

Mitterrand candidature. Fortunately for the left, these disagreements were offset by dissension on the right, as the RPR and its candidate, Chirac, constantly criticised the policies favoured by Giscard and a government in which it was actually represented, going so far as to delay the 1980 budget.

The surprise of the first ballot, in which Mitterrand and Giscard tied, with each of them gaining 26 per cent of the vote, whilst Chirac obtained 18 per cent and Marchais only 15 per cent, was the continued collapse of the Communist vote. Marchais was forced to desist in favour of Mitterrand. His failure weakened the validity of a major conservative criticism of Mitterrand, namely that his election would let in the Communists. Moreover, the left maintained better electoral discipline. Disappointed by his elimination in the first ballot, Chirac peevishly called on each voter to vote 'according to his conscience' in the second, leading the political commentator Raymond Aron to observe bitterly that 'it's not so much that the left won as the right committed suicide'. Giscard himself would accuse Chirac of 'premeditated treachery'.

Plate 8.4 Mitterrand's appeal as *la force tranquille*, making use of a calm rural background, combines the promise of change with reassurance. Poster by Séguéla.

Mitterrand's carefully planned campaign presented him as *la force tranquille*, the guardian of established values as well as the proponent of sensible and moderate reform. This was in marked contrast with the aggressive approach favoured by Marchais and Chirac and the studied ambiguities of Giscard. The policies presented by Mitterrand were indeed substantially less radical than the official programme of the Socialist Party. Nevertheless, his final victory, with 15,708,262 (51.76 per cent) of the votes cast, was due especially to support from a left made up of the proponents of social reform. It reflected growing concern about unemployment and the threat to living standards, for which the incumbent government was inevitably blamed. He was victorious in sixty-five of the ninety-six departments, and made unexpected progress in Catholic areas of the east and west, traditionally hostile to the left, as well as strengthening his position in the industrial north, the Paris region, Midi and Burgundy. Sociologically he did particularly well amongst manual and white-collar workers and the lower managerial groups.

New voting patterns were beginning to emerge to reflect socio-economic change and the decline of both the Catholic and Communist subcultures. The electorate was becoming more fluid. In any event, the politician who had first gained eminence as a resistance activist, who had been a leading light of the discredited Fourth Republic, a man dismissed by conservatives as 'the eternal loser', and even accused on the left of seeking the leadership of the Parti Socialiste out of opportunism rather than any deep sense of commitment, had come back to prove his political skill as a critic of conservative governments and as the leader of a rejuvenated Socialist Party. Finally, at the third attempt, he had achieved his goal of securing election to the presidency. A reflective individual variously described as aloof, arrogant and narcissistic, Mitterrand, like de Gaulle, was concerned about his place in history. He was similarly determined to secure France's status amongst the great powers and, in order to ensure this, to continue with the process of economic and social modernisation. Additionally, however, and although motivated by overweening ambition, Mitterrand also appeared to retain a vague humanitarian commitment to greater social justice. He would occupy the Elysée Palace for fourteen years, admired by many but also widely loathed. During these years, in spite of his previous condemnation of the regime's authoritarian character, Mitterrand would seek to exercise the authority of a *monarche républicaine*, making full use of the powers of the presidency, particularly those of appointment, to create a network of dependants and, at least during periods of Socialist administration, retaining control of decision making. Even during the awkward periods of *cohabitation* with conservative premiers Mitterrand was able to exert considerable influence, especially in what had come to be seen as the reserved areas of foreign and defence policy.

As he had promised, following his election Mitterrand immediately dissolved the National Assembly in an attempt to secure a parliamentary majority committed to his support. The election, held in June 1981, marked a profound shift in the balance of power. In large part this was due to the abstention of large numbers of habitual conservative voters, discouraged both by the election of a Socialist president and by the disarray of the right. It was not only the right that suffered, however. The effective working of the political system seemed to demand that the president and parliamentary majority be drawn from the same political milieu. As a result, the Communist Party lost over half its seats, leaving the Socialists with an absolute majority.

Table 8.3 *Results of National Assembly election, 14 and 21 June 1981*

	First-ballot votes	Share (percentage of votes)	Seats after second ballot	Share (percentage of votes)
Communists	4,003,025	16.13	44	9.0
Socialists	9,387,380	38.02	285	58.0
Union pour la nouvelle majorité (RPR and UDF)	10,649,476	42.9	—	—
RPR	—	—	88	17.9
UDF	—	—	62	12.6

The Socialists celebrated their presidential victory in a fashion that revealed a strong sense of history, with a massive demonstration on the Place de la Bastille and a ceremony at the Panthéon in which the new president placed roses on the tombs of Victor Schoelcher, who had played a leading role in the abolition of slavery in the colonies in 1848 and subsequently in the democratic-socialist opposition to the future Napoleon III; of Jean Jaurès, the humanitarian socialist assassinated by an extreme nationalist in 1914; and of Jean Moulin, the Resistance martyr. In power for the first time during the Fifth Republic, the left was in euphoric mood. A powerful sense of expectancy had been created, based on the radical programme of the Socialist Party, with its condemnation of the capitalist system, rather than the more cautious proposals presented by Mitterrand. This was further encouraged by the appointment to the premiership of Pierre Mauroy, history teacher, trades unionist and youth worker, representing the old working-class bastions of the north. The government itself was made up of thirty-six Socialists drawn from its various competing internal factions and including such luminaries as Delors (minister of economy and finance), Gaston Defferre (interior) and Alain Savary (education), together with two left radicals; but it was the presence of four Communists that attracted the most comment, both at home and abroad. Their uneasy participation in government, for the first time since 1947, represented a reward for electoral support, and on their part an attempt to reverse their party's declining popularity, though their obviously subordinate position made this a dangerous tactic. They were indeed to enjoy little influence, whilst the alarm bells that rang in Washington were soon stilled by Mitterrand's obvious desire to improve cooperation with the Western allies.

The measures introduced by the new government nevertheless heralded an unprecedented programme of reform, influenced by Keynsian economics, the experience of the Popular Front and a determination to reinforce the welfare state and to secure the 'break with capitalism' represented by the nationalisation of banks and major industrial enterprises. The introduction of a 'wealth' tax affecting the very rich, a rise of 10 per cent in the legal minimum wage and increased family allowances, as well as a project to create an immediate 55,000 public sector jobs, were also announced. The death penalty was abolished and a controversial plan to extend the military training areas at Larzac abandoned – a symbolic concession to peasants and ecologists. The law on decentralisation (3 March 1982), pushed through by Defferre, marked a major shift away from the centralising traditions of the French state. Over the following decades it would do much to revive local democracy. It provided the twenty-two regions, established in 1972 for the purpose of economic planning, with elected assemblies enjoying substantial power. At the same time executive authority at departmental level was transferred from the prefect to the president of the elected department council (*conseil général*), made responsible especially for health, social services and roads. The planning powers of the communes were also increased. This was an attempt to make local government more democratic and accountable, as well as more efficient.

Certainly, decentralisation did not become effective overnight. The problems of overlapping responsibilities had to be overcome. It took time for the rules of the political game to change. Moreover, dependence upon the financial support of the central state, its technical services and its decision-making power continued to obstruct the achievement of real autonomy. Nevertheless, a major step had been taken towards increasing the sensitivity of central government, big business and the media to local needs. The larger towns benefited, in particular. Economically depressed centres such as Lille and Saint-Etienne were better able to develop the social and cultural facilities needed to attract investors and tourists. On the negative side, as in the case of Lille – the fiefdom of Mauroy – the city's debt was increased substantially. Massive government investment also proved necessary to pay for the detour required to take the high-speed train (TGV) through Lille on its way from Paris to the Channel coast. Even more disturbing was the subsequent investigation by the Cour des comptes, which revealed grossly over-optimistic estimates of the traffic likely to be generated and, worse still, collusion between Société nationale de chemins de fer (SNCF) executives and civil engineering contractors to overestimate costs. Tenders were then rigged in order to avoid competitive bidding. Throughout the 1980s a rash of scandals revealed considerable confusion between, and corruption of, public and business life in cities as diverse as Paris, Lyon, Marseille, Nantes, Nice, Grenoble and Angoulême. This appears to have been the outcome of measures that gave planning powers and greater financial autonomy to the mayors of most communes; intense business competition for public works contracts; the growing cost of elections; human greed; and the contacts promoted through membership of social networks often associated with voluntary associations, such as Masonic lodges. Nevertheless, until the prosecution in 1996 of the Socialist deputy and former minister Henri Emmanuelli and of Alain Carignan, the RPR mayor of Grenoble and minister, it was extremely rare for leading government officials – or, indeed, the businessmen with whom they had dealings – to be held to account for trading on their influence, whether for personal gain or the benefit of their political parties.

Although only a minority of politicians were implicated, the problem of corruption at the very highest levels of the state nonetheless proved to be systemic, rather than simply a matter of individual greed. The magistrates' new-found determination to root out dishonesty itself emerged initially out of the settling of scores between rival political groups, but it also represented the growing reluctance of a new generation of magistrates, investigative journalists and policemen, encouraged by the successes of their Italian colleagues, to tolerate misdeeds to which their predecessors, as a result of political pressure or careerism, had been prepared to turn a blind eye. Concerned by the impact of accusations of a cover-up on public opinion, ministers were unable to prevent a series of damaging investigations. In 1992 the

Socialist prime minister, Pierre Bérégovoy, established several inves-
tigatory commissions, and succeeding conservative administrations
made their own contributions. This resulted in much stricter rules
for public procurement contracts and for political funding, with a
ban on corporate contributions and a substantial extension of the
public subsidy of political parties, first introduced in 1988.

The complex programme of economic and social reform engaged
in by the Socialist government inevitably aroused considerable internal and international criticism. Mauroy himself warned that, as in
1936, the outcome of an attempt to ignore the logic of the market
would be the rapid collapse of the administration. His desire for a
substantial reversal of policy generated a struggle for the soul of
the Socialist Party, in which the prime minister was supported by
Delors and Rocard, and opposed by Jean-Pierre Chevènement and
Bérégovoy, the proponents of a more radical socialism. The implementation of a new economic strategy would begin in the summer
and autumn of 1982, however, as Mitterrand accepted its necessity.
Defeat in the municipal elections in March 1983 seems to have
further convinced the president of the need for greater caution.
When, on 24 June 1984, Savary's attempt to make progress towards
achieving the old left-wing dream of creating a single secular educational system, by reducing subsidies to denominational schools,
provoked a demonstration involving as many as 1 million people in
support of the (heavily subsidised) independence of Catholic schools
and of an exclusive, élitist education, Mitterrand withdrew the policy
without consultation. Both Savary and Mauroy felt obliged to resign.
Chevènement, Savary's replacement, committed himself to adapting
education to the needs of a changing world by means of the restoration of standards. The core curriculum, with its emphasis on science
and technology, and also on basic literacy and numeracy, and its
concern with measurable results rather than individual fulfilment,
were features of the educational reforms proposed by French as well
as British governments of whatever political hue.

Further dramatic policy reversals were also in prospect. The president had himself encouraged the illusion that a break with capitalism
was possible. The main thrust of the policy of the government
headed by Mauroy had, however, been directed towards stimulating
economic activity in order to reduce unemployment and secure a more

widely shared prosperity. Initially, although committed to economic modernisation and particularly the development of information technology, the Socialist government poured resources into the declining coal, steel and shipbuilding industries as a response to the demands of its traditional constituents. To ensure that in future they would support the state's economic strategy, and in order to compensate for the apparent timidity of private and institutional investors, financial institutions such as Paribas and Suez were nationalised, as were the thirty-nine banks remaining in private hands. Other targets for state ownership were the major steel companies, all on the verge of bankruptcy, and, more significantly, manufacturing companies strategically placed in such sectors as aeronautics, electronics, chemicals and information technology. A controlling interest was also acquired in the leading armaments companies Dassault-Breguet and Matra and in another potential national champion, the struggling computing firm CII Honeywell Bull. These were to serve as growth poles, whose development would stimulate the entire economy. As a result, the state's share of industrial turnover increased from 16 per cent to 30 per cent. The proportion of industrial workers employed in the public sector rose from 11 per cent to 24.7 per cent. It was assumed that government control over a much larger proportion of economic activity than was the norm in the other advanced economies would permit the development of a coherent investment programme. In practice, though, existing managers were allowed to retain control. It had further been expected that increased investment and industrial restructuring would soak up unemployment and place French industry in a good position to take advantage of the expansion of the international economy so confidently – and incorrectly – predicted by the economic forecasters of the Organisation for Economic Co-operation and Development (OECD). Whilst these Socialist Party economic policies had surprisingly little impact on levels of unemployment, they certainly horrified the business and financial world and the wealthy in general, and generated almost unprecedented verbal violence.

Business confidence was further diminished by measures designed to secure greater social equity. These included the increase in the minimum wage and in welfare payments, together with the wealth tax. This essentially symbolic measure affected only the *Gros*, the 1 per cent of households whose fortunes exceeded F3 million.

Nevertheless, together with rhetorical attacks on the wealthy, it provoked a flight of capital, as in 1936. So too did efforts by the minister of labour, Jean Auroux, to improve workers' collective rights at the expense of managerial authority. To the *patronat* this seemed to represent an assault upon its essential prerogatives. There was grave concern also about the impact of the reduction in the working week (to thirty-nine hours) and the granting of a fifth week of paid holiday. These were measures that the government hoped would both improve the quality of life and, along with early retirement and retraining, contribute to the reduction of unemployment. The primary effect of efforts to stimulate demand, however, was to increase imports and cause a deterioration in the balance of payments, as well as rapidly rising inflation. Although not as damaging as Chirac's reflation in 1975, the attempt to stimulate the economy inevitably reduced the competitiveness of French enterprises, at a time when competitors were pursuing deflationary policies. It led to three devaluations of the franc in the space of eighteen months and revealed the narrow limits to national autonomy imposed by international economic constraints. Above all, the inflationary spiral forced the government to further reassess its strategy.

An initial wages and prices freeze (July–November 1982) was followed by the imposition of wage restraint in the public sector, whilst the private sector was able to take advantage of the fear of unemployment and the chronic weakness of the trades unions. Increased taxation and a squeeze on welfare expenditure reduced the government's budget deficit. High interest rates restricted consumer expenditure. Automatic wage indexation was ended to assist the fight against inflation – a measure the right had not dared to introduce. The wisdom of nationalisation was also questioned. Whatever the intentions, it had clearly reduced the commercial freedom, the discipline of the market place, and hence the competitiveness of major companies such as Thomson, Pechiney and Rhône-Poulenc, as well as resulting in the waste of resources poured into the coal and steel industries. It seemed clear that only the encouragement of business initiative would secure a return to higher rates of growth, and the effective reduction of unemployment.

In place of Mauroy, who resigned on 17 July 1984, the president appointed the youthful Laurent Fabius, formerly head of his private office, as both the symbol and agent of a major policy shift. The objectives of the new prime minister, an upper middle-class product of ENA, and a social democrat, were to promote economic recovery and to reconstruct the government's image in time for the 1986 legislative election. The change of policy would be much resented by the left wing of the Socialist Party, by trades unionists and by the Communists, who finally resigned from a government in which they had felt increasingly uncomfortable, hoping that this would reinforce their appeal to the left. Most Socialists seem to have accepted, and with surprising ease, that there were limits to what the state could achieve in terms of social reform, however. They participated in the general shift of opinion towards neoliberalism, perhaps concealing the truth from themselves with the assurance that the new policy was only a temporary adjustment. The reversal of policy had a profoundly negative impact on the government's popularity nevertheless.

Inevitably, the twists and turns of economic policy were damaging to Mitterrand's reputation. Many of those who had turned to him in hope of change were alienated. The government's recognition of the power of market forces, and its acceptance of the need for business rationalisation and modernisation, led to growing unemployment. The results of both the municipal elections in spring 1983 and the European election in June 1984 were decidedly unfavourable. According to an IFOP poll in November, only 26 per cent of the electorate were satisfied with Mitterrand's performance. The strategy of the Fabius government would be to encourage profitability as the means to finance investment rather than directing state funds into a limited number of 'key' sectors. Privatisation commenced. Investors were invited to bid for up to 25 per cent of the shares of nationalised companies, as well as for outright ownership of some of their subsidiaries. Substantial reductions in capacity were imposed on the coal, steel and shipbuilding industries. Public and private companies alike were encouraged to reduce costs by shedding labour. In May the government did nothing to prevent the bankruptcy of the leading engineering company Creusot-Loire, which employed 30,000 workers. It was coming to be recognised that rapid technological change and the intensification of international competition had established a pressing need for structural change in the economy. Higher levels of unemployment than had previously been regarded as acceptable were likely for the foreseeable future. By 1985 inflation had been reduced to 5 per cent, but unemployment remained stubbornly above 10 per cent. A gulf existed between the majority of the population, which continued to enjoy rising living standards, and an 'underclass' – made up of the unskilled and poorly paid, together with the unemployed – who were increasingly exposed to labour market 'flexibility' and all the insecurity and stress caused by short-term and part-time employment. Approximately 29 per cent of all families were officially classified as 'poor', and in spite of support provided by the welfare system many of them would experience considerable deprivation.

In sharp contrast, in the following decades the wealthy would gain from a massive growth in the value of property and in share income (from F452 billion to F5,390 billion between 1980 and 1995). At the same time the incomes of wage earners, which had risen by 62 per cent over the previous fifteen years, would rise by only 5 per cent. A new economic order had been inaugurated. The Socialists had been obliged to recognise the primacy of the market. Their failure would ensure a conservative victory in the 1986 legislative election and a period of *cohabitation* between President Mitterrand and Chirac, the prime minister imposed on him by the majority. The policies of this and subsequent administrations were to be characterised by substantial continuity as they adopted essentially neoliberal policies in an effort to come to terms with globalisation, as well as with the Single European Act of 1986. The latter was intended to eliminate non-tariff barriers to the flows of trade and capital, as well as the whole range of anti-competitive practices, including government subsidies, traditionally favoured by French governments. The policies of further periods of Socialist government following the 1988 and 1997 elections would confirm these options, in spite of the continuing search for a 'third way', between state *dirigisme* and liberal capitalism.

These reversals for the left gave renewed heart to conservatives, who had been absolutely stunned at first by their unexpected loss of power in 1981. They had faced considerable difficulty in making their opposition effective, partly because there were now three competing parties on the right with elections confirming the rise of the

Front national. Initially that party's militants had included members of previously marginalised extreme right-wing groups, including monarchists, former supporters of Vichy and of Algérie française, anti-Semites, student neo-Nazis and traditionalist Catholics. Increasingly it broadened its appeal to voters disillusioned with the existing parties. The Front national possessed an eloquent, energetic and rather menacing leader in Jean-Marie Le Pen, who constantly reiterated a relatively simple populist appeal to all those who disliked foreigners, were concerned about crime and unemployment and wanted to pay lower taxes and to reassert French sovereignty by leaving the European Community. Many of the questions Le Pen posed were related to matters of common concern; his answers were based upon profoundly punitive racialist and xenophobic assumptions, a visceral anti-Semitism and a determination to expel Muslims from France. Thus the weekly *National Hebdo* could be expected to condemn 'politically organised *judaisme*' as well as Muslim immigrants. The party's 1991 programme demanded the 'repatriation' of 3 million 'immigrants' and 'national preference' in the provision of employment, housing and welfare. The longer-term survival of the Front was ensured by the enthusiastic commitment of local activists, particularly in urban areas in which large numbers of immigrants had settled, and by the creation of a specific, all-embracing subculture. Moreover, the Front was lent credibility by media attention and the contorted efforts of a succession of mainstream conservative politicians to avoid condemning a party that might turn out to be a useful electoral ally. Only when they calculated that more votes might be gained from an anti-racist stance were conservative leaders likely to attempt to isolate the Front national, whilst at the same time adopting the substance of its position on law and order and new immigration.

The conservative challenge to the Socialist government was further weakened by persistent feuding between and within the Giscardian UDF and Chirac's RPR, reflecting the mutual loathing of the two party leaders as well as policy differences. The UDF tended to lay stress both on individual freedom and the state's responsibility as a guarantor of social justice, the RPR to be populist and authoritarian in the Bonapartist tradition. In the meantime, Barre attacked both. The right thus found it difficult to commit itself to a single leader and potential presidential candidate, although the balance of popular support certainly moved in favour of Chirac, whose more combative style assured him a higher profile. Giscard's defeat in the 1981 presidential election and loss of patronage power had weakened the UDF significantly. Moreover, it lacked the basic organisational strength of the RPR. In spite of bitter rivalry, self-interest promoted an alliance, however, and the publication of a joint programme for the 1986 legislative election. This promised the privatisation of nationalised companies, reductions in government expenditure and tax cuts that would unleash 'individual initiative in economic, social and cultural life'. In all, it represented a reaffirmation of nineteenth-century liberalism's commitment to possessive individualism.

Whatever the problems of the right, it was clear in the run-up to the elections that the Socialists were in a very weak position. In an effort to minimise the effects of declining electoral support, Mitterrand brought forward an extremely controversial proposal to change the electoral system. Single-member constituencies were to be replaced by a form of proportional representation on a departmental basis. The danger was that this return to the electoral system of the Fourth Republic might promote the re-establishment of the unstable multi-party system that had characterised that regime, and in particular promote the fortunes of the Front national. This too appears to have been part of Mitterrand's calculation, presuming as he did that it would result in a loss of votes for the main conservative parties and contribute to the fragmentation of right-wing representation in parliament.

The main themes of the campaign were unemployment and the insecurity caused by crime and terrorism. More than ever the style was American, with the conservatives in particular employing the latest marketing techniques. Even so, the UDF and RPR together gained an absolute parliamentary majority of only two. Whilst the Socialists' efforts to stress the success of their economic policy following the abandonment of reflation in 1982 were not entirely convincing, the obvious divisions between conservative leaders also reduced the credibility of their campaign. Nevertheless, and in spite of the surprising ability of the Socialists to retain some of their earlier gains, most notably in the west, the results could hardly conceal the severity of their defeat. Moreover, both extremes – the Communists

Table 8.4 *Results of National Assembly election, 16 March 1986*

	Votes	Share (percentage of votes)	Seats
Communists	2,663,259	9.7	35
Socialists	8,688,034	31.6	215
RPR–UDF	11,506,618	42.1	—
UDF	—	—	129
RPR	—	—	145
Front national	2,701,701	9.8	35

and, in particular, the Front national – improved their positions, with the latter gaining representation for the first time.

This was a situation in which the president, as an arbitrator, was left with considerable room for manoeuvre, although he assumed that the constitution required him to call on Chirac, as the leader of the largest party in the conservative alliance, to serve as prime minister. An unprecedented situation was thus created, with the president and the prime minister drawn from different and contending political constellations. Where would final authority rest?

It took some time for the situation to become clearer, but by the autumn of 1986 an uneasy line of demarcation had emerged, with Mitterrand assuming a prominent role in the spheres of international relations and defence, as indeed the constitution suggested he should. A broad policy consensus in these areas anyway reduced the possibility of conflict. There was only limited disagreement over the continuation of such basic tenets of Gaullist foreign policy as the maintenance of an assertive French presence on the world stage, backed by an independent nuclear deterrent. As well as reversing their previous hostility to this policy of *grandeur*, the Socialists also made evident their commitment to strengthening the European Community, partly to provide a continuing stimulus to modernisation and in recognition of the weakness of individual European states in an intensely competitive international economy, partly as a means of containing the single most powerful European power – Germany.

An active role in international affairs had the advantage of allowing Mitterrand to remain constantly in the public eye. Furthermore, he did not hesitate to give advice – public and private – on a whole range of domestic matters, and by refusing to sign administrative decrees could delay their implementation. In effect, Mitterrand was beginning to refine a pose he had already begun to adopt towards the end of the period of Socialist government: that of the president above party politics. Even though, as leader of the parliamentary majority, Chirac remained the dominant partner, he was handicapped by the unexpected recovery in the president's popularity, and by the public's obvious desire that *cohabitation* should work in order to avoid a potentially destabilising political crisis. With their eyes set on the presidential election due in 1988, neither Chirac nor Mitterrand was prepared to risk accepting responsibility for failure.

The RPR leader quickly established a government dominated by representatives of his own party, mainly politicians with previous ministerial experience. To many commentators, this re-establishment of the right in office seemed like a return to normal. Influenced by prevailing liberal intellectual fashion, however, Chirac was determined to break with the authoritarian, statist past of Gaullism. He proceeded with widespread privatisation and deregulation, although this was not to include traditional public sector monopolies such as gas, electricity and telecommunications or strategic industries such as aerospace. Disagreement on these matters was to be only one of the causes of friction within the government and conservative majority. Others were to include the perennial problem of financing the social security system, the reform of labour legislation to favour employers, the rewriting of the nationality laws to discriminate against immigrants and the correct response to the Soviet leader Gorbachev's disarmament proposals.

Chirac was also unlucky. The implementation of privatisation was hindered by the international stock market collapse in October 1987, although by then many of the banks and industrial enterprises previously nationalised by the Socialists, with some 400,000 employees, had already been transferred to the private sector. The almost inevitable student protest against higher education reform at the end of 1986 and strikes in the public services created an impression of weakness. Moreover, the government failed to produce the magical solution to the country's economic problems that many of its supporters seemed to expect. Indeed, by the end of 1987 the main economic indicators – growth rates, budget deficit, inflation, unemployment, the balance of trade and international competitiveness – all seemed to suggest failure. The decline in the government's popularity was closely linked to this. Opposition criticism was indeed rather muted, with the Socialists suffering a crisis of confidence and paralysed both by Mitterrand's determination to make *cohabitation* work and their reliance upon his standing as the vehicle for a return to power. At its 1987 congress the party's various factions were able to agree at least on the need to construct an image of unity, pragmatism and moderation.

During the April/May 1988 presidential campaign Mitterrand continued to distance himself from the Socialist Party and to broaden his appeal. The dominant theme of his campaign was national unity – *La France Unie*. His programme was vague but reassuring on such questions as the welfare state, the commitment to continued economic modernisation and assistance to businesses to prepare for the Single European Market, due to be established in 1992. By 1988 the Socialists had clearly accepted the 'enterprise' culture. Mitterrand could also present himself as the guardian of democracy and of a pluralistic society, against the threats posed by the Chirac government's heavy-handed emphasis on 'law and order' and the posturing of the extreme right. In the end, the only surprise was the size of his second-ballot majority.

Chirac had been placed on the defensive by the need to defend a mixed record in office. The promise of further privatisation and what easily appeared to be tax cuts for the rich had limited appeal. Moreover, for the first ballot, he had to devote a considerable effort to defeating his right-wing rivals, Barre and Le Pen. Whilst he could not afford to alienate their supporters, because he would depend on their votes in the run-off against Mitterrand, it was also clear that adopting a gentle approach towards the Front national might result in the defection of conservatives committed to democracy and a multiracial society. Before the election, with his reputation for efficient economic management, Barre had seemed likely to become the leading conservative candidate. A dull campaign, partly resulting from a commendable but unrealistic unwillingness to employ professional public relations experts, was to cost him this position. Increasingly, a vote for Barre appeared pointless. Chirac offered much the same policy, and in Mitterrand France already possessed a reassuring elder statesman. On the first ballot Barre gained 16.5 per cent of the vote compared with Chirac's 19.9 per cent. The sensation was Le Pen's 14.4 per cent, the votes of almost four and half million people. On the major issues of immigration and law and order, he had indeed set the agenda.

With Barre and Le Pen eliminated, Chirac abandoned the quiet, statesmanlike pose he had adopted previously. He threw his considerable energy into confrontation, using terms such as 'mediocre', 'incompetent' and 'unfit for public office' to describe the incumbent president. Nonetheless, even the theatricality of the closing days of the campaign, with Chirac's government able to announce the release of hostages held by Arab terrorists in Beirut, as well as a bloody assault on Kanak nationalists in the Pacific territory of New Caledonia, failed to attract sufficient support. Mitterrand secured 54.01 per cent of the vote, drawn particularly from the ranks of the unemployed, industrial workers, public employees and the young, with farmers, small businessmen, upper management, the elderly and practising Catholics tending to prefer Chirac. Although, politically, Mitterrand's supporters were a mixed bag from left and centre, overall, a clear political polarisation between left and right was still evident. The nomination of Rocard as prime minister on 9 May 1988 was followed by the dissolution of the National Assembly and an attempt to secure a supportive Socialist majority. The results were disappointing, with large-scale abstentions and a renewed sense of unity in the face of adversity on the right. This could not conceal Chirac's own failure, reflected in the shifting balance between the conservative parties, together with the appearance in the National Assembly of a reconstituted centre, made up of forty-one deputies alienated by the radical neoliberalism of the right and reassured by the collapse of the Communists and the moderation of the Socialists. These would prove willing to consider an alliance with the left. Thus, although the Socialists lacked an absolute majority in parliament, their position in government was secured by this emergent centre-left, together with the fact that they could be defeated only by the combined votes of the opposition including the Communists. The party's own internal discipline, which belied its past record of factionalism, was to prove another key factor.

Table 8.5 *Results of National Assembly election, 5 and 12 June 1988*

	Share of votes (in per cent)	Number of seats	Share of seats (in per cent)
Communists	11.3	27	4.7
Socialists	37.5	278	48.2
UDF	19.5	130	22.5
RPR	19.2	128	22.2
Other right-wingers	2.9	13	2.2
Front national	9.7	0[a]	—

Note: [a] One subsequent by-election victory.

The choice by Mitterrand of a political rival, the austere Protestant Rocard, as prime minister might have appeared rather surprising, but, as the leader of just one faction within the Socialist Party, Rocard remained dependent upon the president. Mitterrand also continued to distance himself from day-to-day matters of government and allowed his prime minister considerable autonomy in domestic matters, whilst again establishing his own mastery of defence, foreign and European affairs. This division of labour eased the problem of relationships between the two. Having proved his managerial competence, Rocard was probably fortunate to be pushed into resignation in May 1991, following the successful conclusion of the Gulf War and just as economic growth slowed. To succeed him, Mitterrand appointed Edith Cresson as France's first female prime minister, presumably in the hope that her robust socialist outlook would give new impetus to a rather lacklustre administration and divert attention from both the economic slowdown and rumours of political corruption. Lacking strong factional backing within the Socialist Party she was also particularly dependent on the president, and was quickly nicknamed 'Edith At-my-feet' by the satirical television programme *The Bébétte Show*. Cresson's outspokenness and general incompetence soon proved to be a disaster. Damaging public sector strikes plagued her government, and her interventionist and protectionist conception of 'Fortress Europe' proved unacceptable to most of her colleagues. The presence in her government of political heavyweights such as her eventual successor (in April 1992), the increasingly liberal finance minister Pierre Bérégovoy, also imposed a severe limit on her authority.

In economic policy the lessons of the early 1980s did not need to be relearnt. The discipline of the international market seemed inescapable. Bérégovoy reduced public expenditure and corporation tax. The partial privatisation of the major oil companies Elf-Aquitaine and Total and of the chemicals giant Rhône-Poulenc was authorised. Internal reforms were to be very modest during this second term of Socialist government. The fight against inflation was given priority. Additionally, the European dimension assumed a greater prominence as part of the struggle to maintain economic competitiveness, but also as France sought reassurance following the reunification of Germany in 1990. Efforts continued to improve education and increase investment in research and development. In marked contrast with the British Conservative government, the Socialist administration also supported the 'social dimension' of the Single Market project. Nevertheless, reports revealing that the average annual growth in real wages between 1983 and 1988 was virtually nil, as well as the widening gulf between rich and poor, caused considerable concern amongst those Socialist militants who believed that they should be aiming at more than becoming a party of government dedicated to the development of a 'tempered capitalism' (Rocard). Scandals caused by illicit political funding and outright corruption added to the sense of discouragement.

Undoubtedly, the right had been demoralised by its renewed exclusion from power, which had seemed so unlikely as recently as mid-1987. It faced important strategic questions on such matters as whether the RPR and UDF should fuse to form a single liberal-conservative party on the British model, and on what their attitude to the Front national should be. Looking for inspiration to the achievements of Napoleon III, described in his book *Louis-Napoléon le Grand*, the left-wing Gaullist Philippe Séguin was critical of a leadership that, he claimed, had moved too far to the right. Nevertheless, the potential for a conservative recovery was evident. The RPR, in particular, with its deputies, regional and municipal councillors, and efficient mass organisation, remained a potent force. Although far more fragmented, and seemingly under permanent threat of dissolution, the UDF also retained the allegiance of a substantial group of deputies. The two main parties of the right shared a commitment to essential conservative values and the support of a powerful complex of pressure group and media forces. As they began the long haul to the 1993 legislative and 1995 presidential elections, the joker in the pack, in spite of its poor showing in the 1988 legislative election – exaggerated by the return to single-constituency ballots – remained the continued ability of the Front national to attract voters who would otherwise have largely supported the other parties of the right. In these circumstances, Charles Pasqua reminded conservative deputies that their primary objective was to defeat the Socialists, and also of the values they shared with the Front national. Chirac remained silent. Only Simone Veil was willing to declare that, faced with a choice between the extreme right and the Socialists, she would vote for the latter.

The 1993 general election was to be catastrophic for the left. The representation of the Socialists and their allies was reduced from 282 deputies to sixty-seven and that of the Communists from twenty-seven to twenty-five, whilst on the right the UDF secured the election of 206 deputies in place of 129, and the RPR 242 instead of 127. Taking account of independents, 83 per cent of the seats in the National Assembly were filled by conservatives. In spite of the lip service paid to gender equality, the new parliament was also characterised by the lowest rate of female representation in the European Union (5 per cent). The Socialists' share of the vote, at 14.5 per cent, was the worst since the party's foundation in 1971. Harassed by Mitterrand's allies, Rocard felt bound to resign as party leader. On 1 May the former prime minister, Bérégovoy, committed suicide. He had been depressed by defeat and press speculation concerning the interest-free loan he had unwisely accepted from a shady businessman who also happened to be a close friend of Mitterrand. The Socialist Party seemed doomed to the electoral wilderness. Nevertheless, the result was less a declaration of support for the right than a vote against a president and government that the electorate felt had let them down. In the circumstances, Chirac, the obvious prime ministerial candidate, preferred to concentrate on preparations for the presidential election, leaving Mitterrand to enter into a period of quite amicable *cohabitation* with a prime minister, Edouard Balladur – a particularly suave product of

Sciences Po and ENA – who was a member of Chirac's RPR but who very soon emerged as a rival to its leader.

Blaming his Socialist predecessors for the parlous state of government finances, Balladur introduced an austerity budget with a freeze on public sector wages, increases in purchase tax and reductions in spending on healthcare. His air of apparent self-satisfaction soon led to him being portrayed in the satirical press as 'His Sufficiency', a bewigged and powdered Louis XVI carried by lackeys in a sedan chair. Even so, he was able to build on the public impression of competence previously established during his tenure of the Finance Ministry, and to gain support from the conservative press by means of substantial tax concessions to the wealthy. Furthermore, he seemed able to make *cohabitation* work. An attempt to reform the 1850 Falloux education law, in order to make it easier to subsidise Catholic schools, was criticised by the president, however, and even by Mgr Decourtray, the Archbishop of Lyon, as likely to reopen the 'school war'. Teachers in state schools went on strike, and on 13 January 1994 the Constitutional Council deemed that the proposals violated the principle of equality between citizens. A massive celebration brought some 900,000 people onto the streets of Paris. This was followed in March by more threatening demonstrations by teachers and students protesting about unemployment (which had reached 12.6 per cent) and proposals to reduce the minimum wage for young people. Mitterrand once again proved quite capable of taking advantage of divisions amongst conservatives, although he was suffering from the prostate cancer that would ultimately cause his death (on 8 January 1996) and was seriously damaged by revelations about his youthful right-wing leanings and Vichy past, as well as the shady financial dealings of some of his closest associates.

This is probably the place to offer an interim judgement of the Mitterrand years. In spite of his earlier tirades against de Gaulle, and his condemnation of the system of presidential government the general had inaugurated as 'a permanent coup d'état', Mitterrand made full use of the extensive powers of his office, and rejected constitutional reforms that might have weakened his authority. A president elected on a mandate for change, he rapidly and almost instinctively appreciated that politics is, or at least ought to be, the art of the possible. The Socialist experiment of 1981–3 was a failure, and Mitterrand quickly recognised that preserving international economic competitiveness in an era of globalisation required economic liberalisation and the reduction of state expenditure. The cost of this reversal of policy in terms of disappointed expectations and shattered ideals was heavy, nevertheless. Throughout the Western world neoliberalism increasingly reigned supreme, whilst the parties of the left failed to offer credible intellectual and practical alternatives. Mitterrand did nothing, neither more nor less, than share in this overwhelming failure.

During his long political life he had flirted with a wide variety of political credos. He has been criticised severely for this apparent lack of integrity. Certainly, there can be no doubting his intense personal ambition, or his determination to leave his mark on history. Towards the end of his second term in office his public image had become almost monarchical, that of a Machiavellian prince. In an interview with the historian François Bédarida, however, just forty-eight hours before handing over presidential office to Chirac, Mitterrand claimed that his Socialist convictions were unchanged. He had wanted to transform the relationships between the rich and powerful and the mass of the population but circumstances had rendered this impossible. Similarly, he spoke passionately about what had become the major objective of his second term, that of greater European integration as a means of securing the future of France in a world of competing regional power blocs and of containing the threat that might be posed by renewed nationalist tensions in a Europe dominated by a newly reunited Germany. Thus, in collaboration with the German chancellor Helmut Kohl, the French president had worked towards the completion of preparations for monetary union and the Maastricht Treaty (1992). Mitterrand had also successfully promoted the legitimacy of the institutions of the Fifth Republic and, in a potentially disastrous period of *cohabitation*, successfully defined the respective spheres of influence of the president and prime minister.

Persistence pays! In May 1995 Chirac finally achieved his long-standing ambition of securing the office of president. In a characteristically energetic campaign he presented himself as a strong leader, offering 'profound changes' and a 'break with the past', and simultaneously promised to reduce taxes and the government deficit.

Although deserted by Pasqua, the interior minister, as well by Sarkozy, the youthful budget minister – who would never be forgiven, both calculating that Balladur was the stronger of the two conservative candidates – Chirac had retained the loyalty of such Gaullist eminences as Alain Juppé, the foreign minister, and Séguin, president of the National Assembly, as well as control of the RPR party machine. He gained 20.8 per cent of the first-ballot vote, compared with 18.5 per cent for the rather stiff and uninspiring Balladur, 15 per cent for Le Pen and 23.3 per cent for Jospin, the Socialist candidate and a former education minister. Once his rival on the right had been eliminated, Chirac launched a populist appeal, focusing on the familiar right-wing issues of crime and immigration whilst seeking to outflank Jospin by addressing the issues of unemployment and poverty and the need to increase spending on education and welfare. He even called for wage increases to boost economic growth. As Mitterrand had warned, 'He runs fast, but he doesn't know where to.' This was not so much a political programme as an attempt to bribe the electorate, and it worked. With the exception of members of the Front national, conservatives of all shades rallied to his support. Although suffering from a certain lack of credibility, Chirac gained 52.6 per cent of the second-ballot votes (15,766,658), including a majority of the under-thirty-fives and 40 per cent of blue-collar workers. Jospin, selected by the Socialists only after the former president of the European Commission, Delors, had finally decided against standing, at least had the advantage of not being too closely associated with Mitterrand and the accusations of sleaze and lack of principle that had darkened the dying president's last years in office. Yet another graduate of ENA, he presented an imaginative programme with promises of a reduction in working hours, the imposition of taxes on 'speculative' capital movements and on industrial pollution, as well as a reduction in the presidential term from seven to five years. Just like Chirac, he too affirmed a commitment to European Monetary Union and the consequent need to reduce the budget deficit. In the circumstances, and considering the Socialists' feeble performance in the 1994 European election (with only 14.5 per cent of the vote), his 47.4 per cent share (14,191,019 votes) was quite an achievement – a reward for his apparent modesty and straightforwardness.

Plate 8.5 The investiture of Jacques Chirac as president of the Republic, 17 May 1995: the outgoing president takes his leave. Photo: Pascal Pavani/ AFP/Getty Images.

Once in power, Chirac immediately adopted a more relaxed style in comparison with the stately grandeur of his predecessors, abandoning the presidential fleet of aircraft and the motorcades with their escorts of police motorcyclists and blaring sirens. The warm-hearted, *sympathique* image he projected had wide appeal. Of much greater potential significance for the practice of government was the promise of longer parliamentary sessions and efforts to facilitate the more effective scrutiny of government activities, developments contrary, however, to both the authoritarian personality of the new president and the traditions of his office. The promise of less *dirigiste* government also ran counter to the opportunities presented to the right through its control of the presidency, of the National Assembly, of twenty of the twenty-two regional councils and four-fifths of the ninety-six departments. The appointment by the president of Juppé as his prime minister – yet another cultured and rather aloof technocrat educated at ENA – appeared to promise competence and continuity. In reality, the almost immediate collapse in the new government's popularity was to be the inevitable result of the president's inability to deliver rapidly, if at all, on the many, often contradictory, promises made during his electoral campaign.

It was widely accepted that the position of France as a leading economic power could be maintained only on the basis of high levels of capital investment, rising productivity and a reduction of costs. Economists and employers constantly insisted that the major obstacles were labour market rigidities, their impact exacerbated by the minimum wage and high social security costs, excessive taxation (41.1 per cent of GDP at the end of 1994, 47.5 per cent by 1996), budget deficits and the high cost of borrowing. The plan for 'modernising France' introduced by Juppé in November 1995 sought to implement long-discussed reductions in the cost of pensions and healthcare, to liberalise labour markets and to begin the reform of education and the civil service as well as the expensive railways (the SNCF). It was also intended to meet the criteria laid down in 1992 by the Maastricht Treaty providing for European Monetary Union, which required a reduction in government expenditure from 5 per cent to 3 per cent of GDP. These proposals and the arrogant fashion in which they were presented clearly threatened a powerful array of vested interests, and would largely be abandoned in the face of mass demonstrations and widespread and damaging strikes.

The government was also beset by widely reported scandals. Thus, in May 1996, Jean-Claude Méry, a property developer and unofficial treasurer of Chirac's RPR, began to divulge information about the widespread donations it, and to a lesser extent the Socialist and Communist Parties, had received from companies anxious to secure public contracts. In the case of the RPR, the practice had apparently been to cream off between 5 and 10 per cent of the value of contracts, via secret offshore bank accounts. Chirac, previously a long-time mayor of Paris (from 1977 to 1995), was amongst those implicated. His closest associate, Juppé, would eventually (on 30 January 2004) be found guilty of using Paris taxpayers' money to pay the salaries of full-time employees of the RPR whilst serving as city treasurer (and RPR secretary-general) between 1988 to 1995, and received an eighteen-month suspended jail sentence. That, immediately following his conviction, and posing as a victim, Juppé would receive an invitation to dinner from Chirac and be described by the president as an individual of 'exceptional quality, competence, humanity and honesty' represented an expression of the arrogance of power and of contempt for the law.

Certainly, there had been whisperings about some of Chirac's predecessors, and particularly Pompidou. De Gaulle, the patrician Giscard and the cynical and amoral Mitterrand had probably been guilty of vanity and arrogance rather than corruption. All had mis-used the secret service, however, to put pressure on newspapers and prevent the exposure of their associates. A nine-year investigation of the formerly state-owned Elf oil company – originally established to secure oil supplies in Africa – finally brought to trial in November 2003, threw up an amazing story of bribery, with gifts of money, jewellery and villas, and the siphoning off of around €350 million from company funds between 1989 and 1993. This had involved not only its senior managers but also arms dealers, the intelligence services and French and African politicians, together with their mis-tresses. It was also clear that President Mitterrand, through the agency of his son Jean-Christophe, had condoned these practices as means of exercising leverage in domestic matters and of preserving French influence in post-colonial Africa.

The failure of the government's economic reform plans was followed by a return to expensive, piecemeal and largely unsuccessful efforts to reduce unemployment. At the same time, accelerating technological innovation and heightened international competition encouraged mergers and 'downsizing' across the industrial and service sectors of the economy. The result was continuing job losses, the growth of part-time and short-term employment, increased insecurity, growing inequality and rising discontent. Increasingly, a two-tier labour market provided highly paid employment for skilled workers in some leading largely high-tech companies, or those offering luxury goods, whilst elsewhere work was transferred to eastern Europe or Asia and the young were excluded from employment by the high social costs imposed on potential employers.

Less than six months after taking office Chirac dismissed thirteen ministers in a desperate effort to counter criticism brought on by broken promises, rumours of corruption and hostile international reactions to the folly of a resumption of nuclear testing in the Pacific. The introduction of measures designed to reduce government spending by decree rather than through parliament and with virtually no preparation of public opinion was redolent of the worst practices of an autocratic presidential system. The faction-ridden Socialists appeared to be equally incapable of inspiring the electorate, however, and, apparently as a means of reinforcing his mandate, Chirac called a snap legislative election for 25 May and 1 June 1997, presumably assuming that the outcome was predictable. Much of the electorate appears to have been offended by what appeared to be a cynical political manoeuvre, however, and took the opportunity to punish the government. The conservative campaign was a fiasco, characterised by vicious infighting as ambitious politicians, with their eyes on the presidency, jockeyed for position. The usual calls in times of adversity for the creation of a single conservative party competed with the sound of disputes over European integration, economic management and strategy towards the Front national, which, in splitting the conservative vote, probably gave Jospin his victory. The Socialist leader had, moreover, promised to reduce the number of jobless by cutting the working week from thirty-nine to thirty-five hours without any reduction in pay, and by creating 350,000 public sector jobs; to reduce social inequality by increasing the wealth tax, and substantially expanding expenditure on health and on social benefits; and both to bring the privatisation programme to an end and reject the Eurozone's Stability and Growth Pact, which threatened to impose restrictions on government efforts to stimulate the economy. He also tried hard to enhance his dour image and, in alliance with the Communists and Greens, called on the electorate to 'Dare to return to the left'.

It was now the turn of a temporarily shell-shocked Chirac to *cohabit*, and with a Socialist leader, Jospin, who as prime minister was determined to use the powers of his office to the full. The scene was set for a bidding process, with victory in the 2002 presidential election as the prize.

Table 8.6 *Results of National Assembly election, 25 May and 1 June 1997*

Parties	Percentage share of votes cast in first round	Seats after two rounds
Mainstream left		
Socialists	25.5	258
Communists	9.9	37
Greens	3.6	8
Diverse	3.2	16
Total	42.1	319
Mainstream right		
RPR	16.8	140
UDF	14.7	109
DL[a]	2.8	1
Diverse	1.9	7
Total	36.2	257
Others		
Front national	14.9	1
Diverse	6.8	0
Total	21.7	1
Overall total	100	577

Note: [a] Démocratie libérale.
Source: Based on Economist Intelligence Unit, *Country Report: France*, third quarter 1997.

The global economic situation appeared propitious. As the dot-com boom enveloped the world economy, economic growth in France between 1998 and 2000 averaged 3.3 per cent per annum. Inflation, the public debt and the government's own deficit were all relatively low. The Socialists were anxious both to sustain growth and reduce unemployment. Jospin was also apparently more committed to a socialist agenda than were either New Labour in Britain or the German Social Democrats. Whilst accepting the reality of globalisation, he also insisted on the need to regulate capitalism. The formula he preferred was 'Yes to the market economy, no to the market society'. Thus the 'Law on social modernisation' made it more difficult for companies to shed labour, whilst the introduction between 2000 and 2002 of the thirty-five-hour working week by Jospin and Martine Aubry, the minister of social affairs, as a means of 'sharing' work and enhancing life was disruptive for employers, further increasing their costs and provoking a torrent of complaints. Employees were not obliged to accept a reduction of their working day; thus the main effect of the legislation was to extend their annual holidays and increase their overtime pay.

Due to this combination of factors, unemployment certainly fell, to 9 per cent of the labour force. Nevertheless, it remained substantially above British levels, and was especially high amongst the young. Furthermore, early retirement concealed the severity of the situation. Unemployment also remained stubbornly high amongst women, although the Socialists at least took a major step towards ensuring that they would enjoy fairer political representation. On 3 May 2000 the National Assembly, in which only 10.9 per cent of the seats in the lower house and 5.9 per cent in the Senate were occupied by women, voted to require parties to present an equal number of male and female candidates in all elections.

Chirac's counter-attack and the reassertion of his presidential authority were inevitable, and the prelude to an attempt to secure a more thoroughgoing reconquest of power at the next presidential and legislative elections, in 2002. Typically, he seized the opportunity provided by the traditional presidential broadcast to the nation on 14 July 1997 to commit himself to 'constructive cohabitation' with the Socialist administration whilst, in condescending tones, launching into a stinging criticism of most of the decisions taken by

A Concise History of France

the government. Called to order by Jospin two days later, Chirac insisted that he had a responsibility to express his views whenever he judged this to be 'useful'. Whilst formally pretending to respect each other's spheres of competence, the president and prime minister were in reality at daggers drawn, with each trying to reinterpret the constitution in his favour, and hoping that the other would experience a disastrous setback.

In government, Jospin would be more pragmatic than his programme had suggested. An attempt was thus made to combine egalitarian commitments to universal healthcare and a redistributive financial policy with efforts to reduce the deficit on government expenditure by cutting the cost of pensions and eliminating the waste in healthcare provision. Such features of the conservative credo as the fight against crime and illegal immigration were also taken up, whilst Dominique Strauss-Kahn, as finance minister, revealed a strong commitment to market liberalisation as the means of raising economic efficiency. At the same time as it developed policies designed to stimulate employment, the government indeed divested itself of some 2,000 businesses, worth F180 billion – far more than its conservative predecessors had achieved – although in 2002 the state retained a controlling interest in 1,500 companies, including such giants as the electricity and gas suppliers, the post office and the hugely expensive railways, all of which were sheltered from the full force of competition.

In many respects, the prime minister's tactical adjustments were impressive, but they resulted in a gradual weakening of trust in his judgement both amongst the general public and political colleagues. Serious dissension was evident within the governing coalition, particularly amongst its increasingly disgruntled Communist and Green members, but with some Socialists also accusing Jospin of seeking an accommodation with the liberal proponents of globalisation and the hegemonic projects of the American government. The loss of such key ministers as Strauss-Kahn as a result of unfounded allegations of corruption, of the education minister, Claude Allègre, because of his inability to persuade the obstreperous teaching unions to contemplate reform, of Aubry, the labour minister, to the desire to become mayor of Lille and of the even more self-indulgent interior minister, Chevènement, in protest against the reinforcement of

Corsican autonomy all contributed to the impression that this was a government in a state of decay. The weakness of trades unions, the lack of confidence in parliamentary democracy, and past experience of governments offering concessions in order to avoid confrontation furthermore encouraged direct action. In September 2000 lorry drivers protesting about high fuel prices blockaded oil refineries, taxi drivers went on strike and farmers used their tractors to block roads, adding to the sense of chaos. Petrol stations rapidly ran dry, whilst, unable to make deliveries or running out of spare parts, businesses laid off workers. This widespread dissent inevitably had serious political implications. The tax cuts offered by the new finance minister, Fabius, a former prime minister, appear to have been designed as much to restore the government's popularity as to reinforce the incentives to work and invest. Unfortunately, by 2001 economic conditions were less favourable. Unemployment began, once more, to rise. In spite of its reforms, the left had failed to generate popular enthusiasm. In the March 2001 municipal elections, although the right managed to lose control of both Paris and Lyon, elsewhere it made considerable gains.

The results of the first-round ballot in the presidential election, held on 21 April 2002, were a massive shock nevertheless. It had seemed likely to most political commentators that Jospin would defeat a president repeatedly besmirched by scandal. In the event he lost, because, in the personality contest, his austere personality, irritating air of self-confidence and rather wooden television performances failed to attract public sympathy. According to the satirical weekly *Charlie Hebdo*, the battle was between 'corruption' and 'constipation'. Moreover, in the competition to bribe the electorate, Chirac promised far more substantial tax cuts than Jospin, and even higher levels of expenditure on healthcare, education and fighting crime. Both candidates had appreciated the need to appeal to the centre, with Chirac stressing his commitment to social 'solidarity' and protection of the environment, and Jospin insisting that his programme was 'not socialist'. The propertied middle classes, Catholics and older voters had appeared more likely to be drawn to Chirac, and employees, particularly in the public sector, to Jospin. Opinion polls had predicted that Le Pen would obtain only 7 per cent of the votes cast in the first round, an error that suggests reluctance on the part of many sympathisers with the extreme right to admit this to pollsters.

It had been assumed that the candidates for the second round, following the elimination of the lesser figures, would be Chirac the conservative incumbent, strengthened by the creation of the Union pour la majorité présidentielle (subsequently populaire), uniting the three families of the republican right – the centre, liberal and Gaullist RPR – together with his Socialist challenger. Jospin, who to most impartial observers had proved himself to be an effective prime minister, received only 16.2 per cent of the votes cast in the first ballot, however, a smaller share than that gained by the neo-fascist Le Pen, who obtained 16.9 per cent. Chirac's total of 19.9 per cent hardly represented an affirmation of public devotion and was the smallest ever share of the vote gained by an incumbent president. Some 47 per cent of voters had dispersed their ballots in favour of thirteen other candidates, apparently in order to protest against the social and political systems. A record 28.4 per cent of registered voters did not bother to turn out at all. This all seemed to add up to a widespread sense of alienation. Many voters could see little to choose between a president and prime minister who had previously shared power.

Jospin suffered additionally because of the tendency for voters to blame the prime minister, rather than the president, for social problems such as crime and unemployment. Many left-wing voters supported a panoply of unelectable candidates, assuming that they could safely express particular preferences or exercise a protest vote in the first round and then rally to Jospin for the second. The alternative candidates on the left included Chevènement, the former interior minister, representing the Mouvement des citoyens, supposedly created to defend national sovereignty and republican values against the threat posed by the European Union. He gained 5.33 per cent, sufficient in itself to ensure that his ego trip deprived his former close colleague Jospin of a place in the second ballot. Arlette Laguillier, the perpetual representative of the authoritarian Trotskyite Lutte ouvrière, gained 5.72 per cent - better than the pitiful 3.37 per cent for the Communist representative Robert Hue, a figure apparently representing the final collapse of his once powerful party; whilst other Trotskyites – Olivier Besancenot of the Ligue communiste révolutionnaire, with 4.25 per cent, and Daniel Gluckstein of the Parti des travailleurs – added to the fragmentation of the left. Most of the share of the Green candidate, Noël Mamère, might also otherwise have gone to Jospin. Particularly disturbing for the Socialists was the decision of many workers to support Le Pen's Front national.

On 5 May, for the second round of voting, and on a turnout of over 80 per cent, Jacques Chirac obtained 82 per cent of the vote (21, 316, 647) as most of the electorate united around the proposition that Le Pen's political position was morally indefensible. Many habitual supporters of the left rallied to the slogan 'Vote for a thief, not for a fascist'. Nevertheless, the leader of the Front national received 18 per cent of the votes cast – presumably adding to his own first-ballot votes the 2.34 per cent originally cast for Bruno Mégret, his former lieutenant turned rival. Over five and a half million people voted for Le Pen, with regional concentrations in the Mediterranean south and economically depressed parts of the north-east. In the satirical television show *Les Guignols de l'Info*, the Le Pen puppet started making silent appearances and, when asked what he was doing replied, 'Nothing, just waiting' – presumably for the final catastrophic collapse of confidence in the mainstream parties.

The level of support for the extreme right, the evident commitment of local activists, a high degree of voter loyalty and Le Pen's ability to attract the young also raised the question of whether, at some time in the not too distant future, perhaps following the demise of its current leader, the Front national might not enter into a governing coalition with mainstream conservatives, on the Italian model, or informally, as in several French regions. Indeed, the split in the party, in 1998, had been caused partly by differences over strategy: Mégret, the more cerebral Polytechnique graduate, had come to reject a permanent and 'sterile' role in opposition, and was far more willing than his leader to contemplate electoral alliances. He despaired of the public image created by Le Pen's racist comments and his bullying demeanour and by such intemperate accusations as those recorded in an interview with *Le Monde* (2–3 March 1997), in which Le Pen maintained that Chirac was a 'kept man' (*tenu*), in thrall to international Jewish organisations such as Bnai Brith, which provided him with 'enormous sums of money'.

Plate 8.6 Poster supporting Jean-Marie Le Pen, presidential election, 30 April 2002. Photo: Getty Images.

In the meantime Chirac could enjoy the prospect of a further five years in office (reduced from seven by referendum in September 2000), protected from prosecution for corruption by a convenient ruling in 2001 by the Conseil constitutionnel that granted the president temporary immunity. As he had himself pointed out during a – typically respectful – television interview: 'We cannot allow media-inspired suspicion to prevent a president carrying out his proper duties.' The hallowed principle of equality before the law clearly did not extend to the president of the Republic.

His position was reinforced substantially by the outcome of the 2002 legislative election, which freed him from the constraints and frustrations of *cohabitation*. With the establishment of the UMP, Chirac had also come close to achieving the long-discussed goal of creating a single conservative party to fight the election in every constituency. The new grouping was based primarily on his own RPR but included most members of the other two main right-of-centre parties, Démocratie libérale and the Union pour la démocratie française, with only a rump of the latter, led by François Bayrou, holding out. Speaking with all the authority of the head of state, Chirac undoubtedly appeared to many voters as the man with the most to offer.

The first-past-the-post electoral system helped to maintain the primacy of the basic left–right divide and to ensure that extremist parties were not represented in the National Assembly. In any case, support for the extreme right fell to 12.5 per cent of the votes cast. The Socialist Party, led by its uninspiring first secretary, François Hollande, fought the election on a programme that promised an increase in the minimum wage, an end to privatisation and better protection of workers' rights. Utterly demoralised following Jospin's defeat and resignation, the left experienced a collapse in support, losing over 100 seats. Such luminaries as Aubry, author of the thirty-five-hour week, Hue, the Communist leader, and Dominique Voynet of the Greens were defeated. The Socialist Party was divided between 'modernisers' and 'traditionalists', the latter claiming that the party had moved too far towards the centre and, in the process, lost its distinctive identity. The former included Hollande and such ambitious eminences as Fabius and Strauss-Kahn, proponents of the market economy and determined to resist the temptations of what

Table 8.7 *Results of National Assembly election,*
9 and 16 June 2002

Parties	Percentage of votes cast	Seats after two rounds
Mainstream right		
UMP	33.4	369
UDF	4.8	22
Others	5.5	8
Mainstream left		
Socialists	23.8	141
Communists	4.9	21
Greens	4.4	3
Others	2.9	13
Extreme right		
Front national	11.1	0
MNR[a]	1.1	0
Others	0.3	0
Extreme left	2.7	0
Others	4.3	0

Note: [a] Mouvement national républicain.

the latter labelled *gaucho-populisme*, which would relegate the party to permanent opposition by losing the centre ground. Until it achieved a greater degree of unity and proved able to agree on a coherent set of policies, it seemed likely that representatives of the Socialist Party would opportunistically attack the government on every front. Longer-term recovery depended on widening its appeal, without losing part of its traditional constituency to the parties on its left, and on finding an electable presidential candidate.

Chirac's political position appeared unassailable, and his responsibilities immense – 'Five years to change France', according to the conservative newspaper *Le Figaro*. This would require skills greater, however, than those of a political manipulator anxious to avoid confrontation and with the habit of telling his audience what he assumed they would like to hear. Did the president of the Republic have the necessary vision and determination, and the ability to communicate the need for change to a population distrustful of politicians of all stripes?

Relations with the United States were one major cause for concern. In the aftermath of the 11 September 2001 terrorist attacks on New York and Washington, President Chirac expressed his sincere sympathy. At the same time, the former Socialist foreign minister, Hubert Védrine, warned the Americans against falling into 'the monstrous trap' set by the terrorists in which an extreme reaction would set off a 'clash of civilisations'. Following a similar line of thought, subsequently Chirac would feel it necessary to refuse to support the assault on Iraq in 2003, expressing concern – with good reason, as events would prove – about the untoward consequences of precipitate military action, and suggesting moreover that the invasion would itself provoke further acts of terrorism. There was also real concern that the invasion of an Arab state might exacerbate racial tensions within France itself. Chirac's despair at Tony Blair's efforts to reinforce Britain's so-called 'special relationship' with the United States and to exercise a moderating influence in Washington was clearly evident.

The dilemma posed by relative powerlessness was – and remains – considerable, however, particularly for politicians inspired by a latent sense of *grandeur*. The end of the Cold War had appeared to reduce dependence on American security guarantees. The new situation also required a fundamental rethinking of defence priorities. Although the initial temptation was simply to reduce expenditure, the growing threat from terrorism made the need to project French military power by means of the rapid deployment of highly mobile forces all the more apparent. In 1996 this had encouraged Chirac to announce the phased ending of conscription by the end of 2001, reducing the size of the army by one-third – a step of immense symbolic as well as practical significance. The need for greater professionalisation had become more important than the Jacobin ideal of the nation in arms. The decision to rejoin NATO's integrated military command structure, in 1995, also revealed a greater willingness to cooperate. The experience was not an entirely happy one. The 2003 assault on Iraq, which appeared to presage the implementation of a doctrine of preventative war, only confirmed French doubts about American leadership. The preferred alternative, pursued by successive French presidents since General de Gaulle, would be a 'multipolar world' in which the European Union, effectively dominated by an inner core led by France and Germany, would establish its own foreign policy objectives.

To achieve electoral success, Chirac had made all manner of incompatible promises – to reduce taxes, whilst at the same time spending more on defence, fighting crime and healthcare – and had justified the increased expenditure on the basis of exceptionally optimistic assessments of economic growth. One immediate result of these commitments would be to make it impossible to reduce government spending in line with the engagements previously entered into as part of the Eurozone's Stability and Growth Pact. Thus, plucked from relative obscurity to serve as prime minister, Jean-Pierre Raffarin faced a thankless task. Selected from outside the Parisian political élite, apparently affable and unassuming, it was hoped that he would contribute to the construction of an image of a government close to the people, as well as deflecting criticism from Chirac. Raffarin's political honeymoon would be brief, however. He found it difficult to impose discipline on his warring ministers. The rapid decline in his popularity was indicative of the extreme volatility of the electorate, further alienated from the political class when, during the summer of 2003, an estimated 15,000 mainly old people died in a heatwave, and ministers appeared unwilling to interrupt their holidays to deal with the crisis.

Raffarin moved cautiously to introduce greater 'flexibility' into the labour market by weakening the security enjoyed by employees. He also sought to provide for a gradual increase in the number of years' work required for pension entitlements. In the case of public employees, this would be increased from thirty-seven and a half to forty by 2008 and forty-two by 2020. It was clear, however, that public service workers were not going to give up retirement at fifty-five, job security and generous pensions without a fight. Neither the prospect of a longer working life nor reductions in the size of a 'bloated' and 'privileged' bureaucracy had much appeal for the employees of Electricité de France or the SNCF, or for teachers or civil servants. Although only 9 per cent of the labour force was unionised, and the number of days lost to strikes was relatively low, the proportion rose to 25 per cent in the public service, and most of the population had a vital interest in welfare provision and the health service. Faced with the threat of major demonstrations, Raffarin bravely maintained that 'the street can present its views, but the street doesn't govern' and faced down a month-long series of strikes and protests. This was just the first round, however. The regional elections fought in March 2004 were a disaster for the governing party: in spite of the continued weakness of the Socialists, it lost control of twenty of the twenty-two regions – all but Alsace and Corsica.

A further cause of concern for President Chirac was the likelihood that enlargement of the European Union from fifteen to twenty-five member states in May 2004 would increase considerably the difficulty of reaching workable policy agreements. It also threatened to diminish French influence. The Union had emerged from a desire to secure peace and stability in the aftermath of two catastrophic wars. Successive French governments sought to use integration to promote internal modernisation and, in close alliance with Germany, as a means of asserting French influence within and outside Europe. Nevertheless, the result of the gradual accretion of power by Community institutions, including the European Central Bank and the European Court of Justice, together with Community enlargement, was an inevitable loss of national sovereignty. Euroscepticism became increasingly popular and offered ministers a useful means of transferring blame for unpopular policies. Thus the stability pact that was introduced as the means of preventing fiscal irresponsibility on the part of member states committed to monetary union, and that restricted government deficits to a maximum of 3 per cent of GDP, was repeatedly breached by both France and Germany on the grounds that deficit spending and 'flexibility' were the essential means of countering economic recession. The European Commission tacitly accepted that there was little chance of France accepting the binding recommendations for fiscal policy that, in theory at least, it was legally bound to impose.

In 2005 a referendum, grudgingly conceded by Chirac, asked for approval of the proposals for yet greater European integration incorporated in a draft constitution prepared by a committee chaired by Giscard d'Estaing, the former French president. Although agreed upon in June 2004 by EU leaders meeting in Dublin, these proposals were humiliatingly rejected by 55 per cent of the French electorate. Conservatives and Socialists alike were bitterly divided. In spite of Chirac's insistence that the European Union offered the means of protecting the French social model from the threats posed by globalisation and Anglo-Saxon neoliberalism, there was widespread concern about the potential loss of national sovereignty and the prospect of being submerged within a federal system in which Germany, increasingly assertive since unification, would assume a leading role. The Socialists were particularly anxious about the prospect of the transfer of jobs to low-cost areas of central Europe. High levels of opposition were evident amongst industrial workers and the unemployed. Fabius claimed that the proposed constitution enshrined neoliberal principles at the expense of 'social issues'. The referendum also represented an opportunity to reject the leadership of an increasingly discredited political élite.

Chirac's response to this setback was to reshuffle the government, although he resisted the temptation to replace his embattled prime minister, partly because the obvious successor, Sarkozy, the hyperactive and publicity-obsessed interior minister – a figure reminiscent of the young Chirac – clearly harboured presidential ambitions. Chirac had no intention of becoming a lame-duck president. The 'promotion' of the former lawyer from the Interior Ministry to the politically more risky and lower-profile Finance Ministry, and of the foreign minister, Dominique de Villepin, to the Interior Ministry, probably represented an attempt to alter their relative

Plate 8.7 Jacques Chirac and Nicolas Sarkozy attend a ceremony to honour Lucie Aubrac, one of France's greatest wartime Resistance heroes, in the courtyard of the Invalides in Paris, 21 March 2007. Photo: Reuters/Charles Platiau.

status. Subsequently, Chirac would insist that Sarkozy's desire to succeed the disgraced Juppé as chairman of the UMP was incompatible with ministerial office, and force his resignation from the government. Nonetheless, the sacrifice left the young pretender with a powerful political base from which to pursue his ambitions. Indeed, *Les Guignols de l'Info* portrayed him burying a complacent Chirac alive. The scene was already being set for the 2007 presidential election.

In the run-up it was evident that attitudes amongst conservatives towards a further Chirac candidature had polarised. His personality, the appearance of *bonhomie*, proved attractive. His all-too-human peccadilloes even appeared to enhance his popularity amongst devotees. Many voters accepted his claim to be the hapless victim of scurrilous accusations and his lofty dismissal of them as *abracadabrantesque*. A serious crisis of confidence in the political élite and in the institutions of the Fifth Republic had nonetheless developed. An IFOP opinion poll in June 2006 registered a record 70 per cent level of dissatisfaction with the government. There was little surprise, therefore, when on 11 March, ageing and discredited, Chirac announced, without giving reasons, that he would not stand for a third term, leaving the way open for a Sarkozy candidature.

In his pre-election pamphlet, the new conservative contender described himself as committed to 'work, respect for authority, the family and individual responsibility' and as determined to solve the pressing problems of high unemployment, excessive public debt and rising crime. To burnish his right-wing credentials, in a speech at Metz he invoked the spirit of Joan of Arc and Maurice Barrès, two nationalist icons, as well as appealing to the 'heritage of two thousand years of Christian civilisation'. The prospect of electing a strong president firmly committed to reinforcing social order appealed to the many members of every social group, and especially the older generations, who felt threatened by the growing insecurity associated with globalisation. The promise of economic recovery as well as lower taxes was also very attractive.

On 21 April 2007, with a massive 83.8 per cent turnout, Sarkozy obtained 31 per cent of the first-round votes and the Socialist, Ségoléne Royal, 26 per cent. The candidate of 'Blairite' elements anxious to 'modernise' the Parti socialiste, Royal was weakened by divisions within the party, reflected in the half-hearted support from its secretary-general, Hollande – father of her children and supposed partner, although they had already separated. The results appeared to confirm that the epoch during which most members of the 'popular classes' voted for the left was over, with only 25 per cent of workers and *employés* voting for Royal. Support for the 'extreme' left had also declined. Bayrou's creditable 18.3 per cent indicated a reluctance to support the abrasive Sarkozy on the centre-left, whilst Le Pen's 11.1 per cent – a substantial decline compared with 2002 – revealed the success of conservative efforts to appeal to the extreme right. In the second round, on 5/6 May, Sarkozy's 53.06 per cent represented a clear margin of victory over Royal (with 46.94 per cent), based on his ability to win the support of the traditional conservative electorate and members of the managerial and liberal professions as well as to attract support from the popular classes. Nearly 70 per cent of first-round supporters for Le Pen also turned to him.

Many commentators subsequently judged Sarkozy to have committed two 'original sins' following his victory. These, it was maintained, would ultimately destroy his chances of re-election in 2012. The first was an ostentatious, triumphalist and much-publicised celebration with his wealthy associates in the exclusive Fouquet restaurant in Paris, seen as revealing the president-elect's love of money and luxury. The second was his general familiarity and lack of dignity, regarded as demeaning to the office to which he had been elected. The publicity accorded to his romance with the former supermodel Carla Bruni would only exacerbate the situation. By mid-2008 only 34 per cent of the respondents to opinion polls were willing to express confidence in their president.

Sarkozy had promised to inaugurate a 'new era in French politics', and made a vigorous start in spite of the serious difficulties caused by a deepening global financial crisis and the particular problems of the Eurozone. His style of government sustained an impression of dynamism. Whereas his predecessors had focused largely on foreign and defence policy, leaving domestic matters primarily to their prime ministers, Sarkozy intervened in every sphere of government, often relying for advice on his personal advisors – including, most notably, Claude Guéant, secretary-general at the Elysée, and Henri Guaino – and business leaders. Ministers were consulted less frequently than in the past. Cabinet meetings, as a result of the use of first names and *tutoiement*, became less formal but also less structured, and dominated by the president's rambling monologues. Ministers, including the prime minister, François Fillon, were frequently treated with bad-tempered contempt. The centrist politician Bayrou described the regime as an 'egocracy'.

Although the traditional weekly meetings with the defence and foreign ministers – the latter the former Socialist Bernard Kouchner, the high-minded co-founder of Médecins sans frontières – were regarded by the president as largely a waste of time, defence represented a major problem. The results of a policy review unveiled by Sarkozy in 2008 made clear the desperate need to modernise military equipment. Substantial investment was needed in surveillance satellites, drones, attack helicopters and heavy-lift aircraft – funded in part by reductions in orders for conventional aircraft. The construction of two nuclear submarines and a second aircraft carrier was also proposed, although the latter – a means of projecting power – would soon be postponed because of its cost. The central objectives were to create a 30,000-strong expeditionary force, with seventy aircraft and support from two naval groups; and to preserve the nuclear *force de frappe*, the ultimate symbol of *grandeur* – a 'life insurance policy' to which virtually the entire political élite was fully committed. Initially expected to retain a strength of 330,000, the armed forces were to be further reduced to 250,000 and the army to 100,000, provoking a warning in May 2011 from Admiral Guillaud, chief of the defence staff, that the 'fragile and weakened' armed forces would be unable to sustain traditional commitments such as the defence of former African colonies. This was confirmed by the experience of engagement in the overwhelmingly American NATO force in Afghanistan, from which the 4,000 French combat troops would finally be withdrawn at the end of 2012, following the development of a 'military impasse' and rising casualties.

Fillon had insisted on the urgent need to reduce government expenditure at a time when the accumulated public debt had reached 84 per cent of GDP, reflecting a consistent failure to balance the budget since 1974. This appeared to pose a threat to the sustainability of the country's much-vaunted social model. Furthermore, the substantial loss of competitiveness by French enterprises over the previous ten years seemed to urgently require reductions in taxation in order to reinforce incentives and competitive pressures within the market economy. A series of relatively modest initiatives designed to reduce the public deficit to 3 per cent by 2013 were based on extremely optimistic predictions of economic growth, however.

The 'law on the modernisation of the economy' introduced by the finance minister, Christine Lagarde, in April 2008 cut red tape for businesses, raised the retirement age from sixty to sixty-one, introduced more flexibility into the thirty-five-hour week and sought to penalise unemployed people who refused job offers – reviving the nineteenth-century liberal claim that, through laziness, the poor had brought poverty upon themselves. The mediocre and grossly overcrowded centrally controlled universities were shaken up by the prospect of greater autonomy in terms of appointments, salaries and competition for public and private funding. These measures fell far short of the structural reforms called for by the international rating agencies and the International Monetary Fund (IMF), however. Indeed, between 2007 and 2010 efforts to stimulate the economy in response to the financial crisis, as well as the impact of the crisis itself, pushed the budget deficit up from 2.7 per cent of GDP to 7.1 per cent, before it fell back to 5.7 per cent in 2011. Employers too were dissatisfied and demanded further deregulation, as well as reductions in payroll taxes, in order to stimulate economic activity.

Moreover, strikes and demonstrations, and the disastrous results of the March 2010 regional elections, in which support for the UMP plummeted to 35 per cent, leaving it in control of only one region, made it clear that the public was increasingly disenchanted with a president who appeared to be presiding ineffectually over a deepening economic crisis and rising unemployment. Characteristically, Sarkozy had continued to promise reforms designed to ensure greater economic competitiveness whilst simultaneously attacking the 'dictatorship of the market', and promising an industrial policy together with the protection of threatened jobs in the motor and steel industries. His much-publicised visits to factories threatened with closure and promises to prevent the transfer of work to eastern Europe were greeted with growing scepticism. A virulent anti-Sarkozyism was rapidly becoming a feature of the political scene. The president was increasingly perceived to be lacking in sincerity and identified as 'le président des riches'.

In the supposed interests of 'solidarity', powerful vested-interest groups, including not only the beleaguered health workers but also teachers and civil servants, protested about wage freezes and deteriorating conditions of employment in the public sector, as the government belatedly attempted to reduce the size and increase the efficiency of a 'bloated' bureaucracy. Although a surprisingly low proportion of French workers actually belonged to trades unions, and their influence depended on an official role in works councils and collective bargaining, as many as 3.5 million people in October 2010 were estimated to have participated in demonstrations against dilution of the thirty-five-hour week and pension reform. Whilst effective in securing the postponement of labour market reforms until after the 2012 elections, the potency of popular protest appeared to have been reduced, however, by legislation requiring the provision of a minimum level of service in schools and public transport during strikes as well as by a growing realisation that change had become necessary.

Populist appeals to anti-immigrant sentiment similarly had a mixed effect on the government's reputation. The establishment of a Ministry of Immigration and National Identity in 2007 was followed by efforts to link immigration to delinquency and vigorous efforts to expel illegal Roma immigrants from Romania and Bulgaria. These tactics might well attract potential supporters of the extreme right but they also risked legitimising the claims made by the Front national and dividing more moderate conservatives. Repeated scandals further discredited the president. Most notable was his attempt to secure the appointment of his student son Jean to the presidency of the administration of the La Défense business *quartier*. Just like his predecessor, Sarkozy and the UMP were also accused of illegal campaign financing, with the most-publicised case involving funds provided by Liliane Bettencourt, heiress to the L'Oréal cosmetics fortune. The murkiness of this affair was intensified by claims that, at the president's behest, the counter-intelligence authorities had engaged in telephone intercepts in an attempt to identify the sources of information leaked to *Le Monde*. Evidence of excessive and unwarranted expenses claims by ministers, together with the acceptance of luxurious holidays offered by the Egyptian and Tunisian governments to Fillon and the foreign minister, Michèle Alliot-Marie, and the open admission of the culture minister, Frédéric Mitterrand, that he paid for sex with 'boys' in Thailand, reinforced the public perception of élite arrogance, sleaze and greed. Nevertheless, Sarkozy's position did not appear to have been weakened by the trial of Chirac – in December 2011 – for the misappropriation of public funds when mayor of Paris. The former president was in poor health, suffering from severe memory lapses and had become a figure of public affection. He received a two-year suspended sentence.

Sarkozy also made considerable effort to improve his public image by adopting a less hyperactive and more presidential demeanour, both at home and whilst presiding over such international gatherings as the G8 at Deauville in May 2011 and the G20 held at Cannes in November. Successful French-led intervention in support of a rebellion against Colonel Gaddafi, the Libyan leader – to whom the government had previously sought to sell arms – represented a

dramatic foreign policy reversal, which surprised even Juppé, the new
foreign minister. Whether inspired by humanitarian convictions or
opportunism, this action enjoyed substantial public support. It also
contributed to Sarkozy's confident belief that, regardless of negative
opinion polls, which four months before the 2012 presidential election
revealed that support for him had fallen to a record low of 30 per cent,
anxious voters would favour a candidate who had previously adopted
a tough stance on crime and immigration and could now claim to
have provided effective leadership during the global and Eurozone
financial crises – a candidate with 'credibility'. The downgrading of
French debt by the credit-rating agency Standard and Poors in January
2012 would thus represent a severe blow.

This appeared all the more significant with opinion polls already
suggesting that the most likely Socialist candidate for the presidency,
Strauss-Kahn, an eminent former finance minister and current man-
aging director of the IMF, would be a runaway winner in competition with the sitting president. The accusations of rape directed at
Strauss-Kahn in New York in March 2011, however, forced the
ultimate 'champagne socialist', a legendary and utterly reckless
womaniser, to resign from the IMF, and ensured his withdrawal as
a potential candidate for the French presidency. He would be accused
subsequently of involvement in a prostitution ring in Lille. The case
highlighted the fact that an estimated 75,000 women are victims of
rape in France each year – usually by men well known to them – and
that only 1 to 2 per cent of those accused are eventually convicted.
What did this say concerning attitudes to women?

Undoubtedly, Sarkozy's position was reinforced by the disgrace of
an apparently unbeatable opponent, as well as by his replacement at
the IMF by Lagarde, the highly regarded French finance minister.
The Socialists were thrown into disarray, at least temporarily, as a
genuine competition for nomination as their presidential candidate
became possible. The contenders included Fabius, the urbane former
prime minister who had seriously divided the party by rejecting the
EU constitution in 2005; Bertrand Delanoë, the mayor of Paris; the
youthful Valls, insisting on the need to rethink an outdated socialist
ideology and thus accused of disloyalty; and Royal, determined to
repeat her 2007 challenge. Polls suggested, however, that the two
most likely victors over Sarkozy would be Aubry, the idealistic and

interventionist former labour minister and author of the thirty-five-hour law, mayor of Lille and leader of the Socialist Party since 2008, representing the left of the party, and Hollande, a social democrat and more moderate and less divisive former supporter of Strauss-Kahn, in spite of the fact that during eleven years as party secretary-general he had earned a reputation as a colourless hack, had presided over the disastrous presidential campaigns in 2002 and 2007 and, although close to Mitterrand, had failed to win ministerial appointment. A latex puppet in the satirical television show *Les Guignols de l'Info* had long represented him as an amiable incompetent.

When he had presented himself as a potential 'président normal' in March 2011, Hollande, like Chirac a deputy for the rural Corrèze, had not been taken seriously by his rivals. Indeed, Fabius dismissed his candidature as a joke. That was soon to change, as he developed a more authoritative and pragmatic air and reassuring moderate policies, and renewed his image by losing weight and wearing designer spectacles. Hollande promised a less authoritarian presidency by enhancing the role of the prime minister, and of ministers in general, and securing the autonomy of the judicial system and police. In a primary election open not only to members of the Socialist Party but to voters willing to pledge allegiance to 'the values of the left' and pay €1, Hollande would ultimately gain 2,800,000 (57 per cent) of the votes cast. Although they had lost three previous presidential campaigns and still bore the scars of Jospin's humiliation by Le Pen in 2002, the Socialists were strongly entrenched at local and regional level, had gained control of the Senate and expected to benefit from the hostility to Sarkozy revealed by a succession of opinion polls.

Fifteen candidates were declared for the first round of the election, on 22 April 2012. Four were regarded as having some chance of winning a place in the second round: Sarkozy, Hollande, Marine Le Pen (following the retirement of her father) and the centrist Bayrou. The president-candidate, posing as 'Captain Courageous', sought to appeal to such traditional values as 'work, responsibility, authority'. At Annecy on 16 February, whilst admitting to past errors, he insisted upon his honesty and sincerity. He maintained that the succession of crises since 2008 had marked the end of an era, but also represented an opportunity to create a new and better world. At the same time he rejected gay marriage and adoption by homosexual couples, as well as euthanasia, and furthermore promised to 'redonner la parole au peuple' through the increased use of referenda. The electorate was warned that it would be unwise to remove an experienced president at the height of the most dangerous crisis since the Second World War. Readers of the conservative press were reminded of the reckless policies pursued by Mitterrand following his election in 1981, which, through tax increases and higher spending, had destroyed French competitiveness and international financial credibility. Sarkozy predicted that in the era of globalisation the adoption of a similar approach by Hollande would have even more dire consequences. The German chancellor, Angela Merkel, concerned about Hollande's determination to press for growth-stimulating measures within the European Union, even took the unusual – and probably counterproductive – step of offering her support to Sarkozy.

In a typically pugnacious speech at Arras, Sarkozy also reminded voters who might be tempted to support Le Pen of his record on immigration, as well as his tough stance on crime. Together with his defence of *laïcité*, these policies were implicitly linked to the threat posed by Islam. It was suggested that a Socialist government would be weak on security, incompetent in dealing with terrorism and likely to offer too many concessions to Muslim fundamentalists. Such symbolic issues as the wearing of the burqa, the supply of halal meat, and prayers in the streets outside mosques were all employed – using inflammatory language – as campaign issues.

Although the influential British journal *The Economist* denounced the two leading candidates for engaging in 'an utterly frivolous campaign' and refusing to face up to the reality of a deteriorating economic situation, both of them accepted the urgent need to reduce government debt. Fillon, the prime minister, defending his government's record in increasing corporate and income tax, committed himself to further reductions in expenditure, increases in value added tax, taxes on major enterprises, pensions reform and penalties for unemployed workers who refused training and job offers. In contrast, Hollande proposed to introduce a 75 per cent tax rate for those earning over €1 million a year, and additionally to increase the annual wealth tax on assets over €1,3 million, together with a tax on dividends, as well as closing the tax exemptions that were so advantageous to the rich. He maintained that the increased revenue would allow the government to balance its books, and at the same time to increase the minimum wage, create 60,000 new teaching posts and re-establish the age of retirement at sixty, although only for those who had started work at eighteen. He promised that these measures would be funded by economies in government departments as well as fiscal reform, whilst a further economic stimulus would be provided through renegotiation of the Eurozone agreement to promote fiscal discipline.

The Socialist campaign really took off with a rally, attended by around 10,000 supporters, at Le Bourget, just outside Paris, on 22 January at which Hollande introduced his vision of a Republic based upon 'Redressement national, justice et espérance' and an urgent determination to 'overcome the crisis and free ourselves from the illegitimate power of finance'. This, he insisted, and not Sarkozy, was his real adversary. Adopting the Socialist Party programme, he called for a separation between the credit function and the more speculative investment activities of the banks, and for the abolition of 'toxic' financial products and tax havens. Small and medium-sized enterprises would be supported by a public investment bank, and a major effort would be made to ease the shortage of affordable housing through the construction of 1 million new dwellings. Hollande reiterated his promise to serve as a 'président normal' – in comparison with the man unflatteringly described by his spokesperson as 'a cross between Silvio Berlusconi and Vladimir Putin' – and his determination to engage in a 'social dialogue', and to serve all the people. He even insisted that he had not intended to attack wealth creators but only 'insolent wealth. . .the arrogance of the powerful, fortunes simply passed on by inheritance'.

Hollande's subsequent campaign represented an attack on both the personality and 'catastrophic' presidency of Sarkozy, described as representing only the interests of 'les puissants, les rentiers, les fortunés' and characterised not only by 'bling-bling' but also 'zig-zag'. In a multifaceted assault delivered at Besançon on 10 April he blamed Sarkozy for the loss of 400,000 jobs, for youth unemployment, for the decline of agriculture, for the collapse in living standards and for growing insecurity. In a statement of his political philosophy, published as 'Changer de destin', Hollande searched for inspiration from history – from the Revolution of 1848 and the Paris Commune, from the Dreyfusards and the Resistance, as well as the patriotism of General de Gaulle. Other inspirational figures included most notably the Socialist leaders Jaurès and Blum and, to a lesser degree, Mitterrand, his original mentor. An egalitarian redistribution appeared to interest him more than wealth creation. Hollande promised that taxes would be apportioned according to the same principles of republican justice that would inform his decisions in general. His commitment to the republican ideal of *laïcité* – toleration and the strict separation of state and religion – was also forcefully reaffirmed with a promise to add the key 1905 secularisation law to the constitution. In his long-awaited *Mémoires*, Chirac seized the opportunity to affirm that Hollande possessed the ability to become a 'true statesman' and to emphasise his contempt for the successor he had long despised. Followed by claims that the former president intended to vote for the Socialist candidate, this intervention was largely countered, however, by his wife Bernadette's enthusiastic campaigning for Sarkozy.

More threatening to Sarkozy's campaign for re-election were the ambitious efforts of the Front national to establish itself as the major party on the right. This involved an attempt to recast the image of the Front by engaging in a process of *dédiabolisation* – an attempt by Marine Le Pen to distance herself from the anti-Semitism that had led her father to dismiss the Holocaust as a mere 'detail' of history, his obsession with the 'loss' of Algeria, and thuggish chauvinism. Equally potent was her condemnation of the president's inability to maintain the authority of the state and of the political élites in general for ignoring the concerns of 'ordinary' people, the threats posed by rising unemployment, deteriorating living standards and the growing insecurity she associated with criminality. Le Pen called for tougher policing, restoration of the death penalty and curbs on immigration and 'Islamification', which she represented as posing a threat to the principles of *laïcité* and to the rights of women.

The Front national also offered protection against the threats associated with globalisation – 'un système économique sauvage' – and membership of the European Union. It was claimed that the affirmation of specifically French interests by means of the reintroduction of economic protectionism, together with devaluation, an inflationary monetary policy, a curbing of the 'financial feudalism' of the banks and reduced taxation of low-income families, would facilitate reindustrialisation and a return to economic growth. Pragmatic or principled, these policies represented an effort to maintain the allegiance of the traditional authoritarian extreme right and to widen support amongst women and, within the lower middle and working classes, amongst those afraid of unemployment and downward social mobility, as well as hostile towards people believed to be living idly off the welfare state. A lawyer and member of the European parliament, and an effective media performer, Le Pen sought to persuade voters that she represented a moderate, patriotic and respectable party. In depressed former mining centres such as Hénin-Beaumont in northern France – in competition with a regional Socialist Party weakened by accusations of nepotism and corruption – as well as in many rural communities, the Front established itself in local politics by holding small meetings in cafés and market places. By focusing on issues such as housing and the decline of services, Le Pen could establish a sustainable political base and present herself as the 'candidate of the forgotten'.

The continuities between Le Pen père and his daughter became all the more evident, however, when, during the electoral campaign, posing as the defender of 'l'ordre républicain', she warned about the 'breaking waves' of Muslim immigration and the threat of 'enslavement' through the imposition of sharia law. In a speech at Rouen on 15 January 2012, Le Pen condemned muticulturalism and insisted on the need for assimilation, pointing to the city's skyline as a reminder of the Christian roots of French civilisation. In March, in Marseille, she blamed the barely suppressed criminality of north Africans for drug trafficking and the city's endemic insecurity. The murders of three soldiers and four other people, including three Jewish children, by Mohamed Merah in Toulouse and Montauban, described as 'the tip of an iceberg', provided a further opportunity to demand stricter control of immigration, an end to the construction of mosques and a ban on radical imams. Le Pen was thus playing an important role in setting the political agenda.

Hollande was similarly weakened by forceful attacks from his left by Jean-Luc Mélenchon, a former Socialist senator representing a

Table 8.8 *Results of presidential election,*
first round, 22 April 2012

Candidate	Percentage share of vote
Hollande	28.63
Sarkozy	27.18
Le Pen	17.90
Mélenchon	11.10
Bayrou	9.13
Joly	2.31

Front de gauche backed by the enfeebled Communist Party together with various Trotskyist factions. At an enthusiastic rally in the Place de la Bastille on 18 March 2012 – the anniversary of the establishment of the Paris Commune in 1871 – that culminated in the singing of the *Internationale*, Mélenchon demanded pensions for all at sixty, an immediate 20 per cent increase in the minimum wage, a maximum salary of €360,000 and withdrawal from NATO. A protest vote in favour of the Front or the Greens and a divided left revived the nightmare prospect of the elimination of the Socialist candidate in the first round. On this occasion, however, and in spite of the relative success of the candidate of the Front de gauche, Hollande gained a narrow victory. The centrist and Green candidates (the latter the MEP Eva Joly) did particularly badly.

In the final run-off between Sarkozy and Hollande, on 6 May, success would depend on an ability to attract voters who in the previous round had supported the eliminated candidates. Whilst almost all Mélenchon's supporters would turn to Hollande (81 per cent, according to a subsequent poll), together with those who had supported Joly – attracted by the promise of a place in government and a scaling back of nuclear power - so too would much of the extreme right's electorate (14 per cent). Others would follow Le Pen's advice and cast a blank ballot paper or abstain (35 per cent) rather than vote for Sarkozy (although 51 per cent did). Clearly, his victory would threaten her aim of securing the Front national as the major force on the right. Her most vicious attacks were consistently focused on Sarkozy rather than Hollande. The centrist Bayrou, though extremely critical of Hollande's economic policy, decided to support him because of his greater humanity and support for Europe, although he would be followed by only around 29 per cent of his supporters.

Opinion polls suggested that the outcome was hardly in doubt, with the final Ipsos MORI poll claiming that support for Hollande was greater in the towns than rural areas, and amongst managers, members of the liberal and intermediary professions, clerical staff and workers, whilst Sarkozy led amongst artisans, shopkeepers, businessmen, the retired and higher household income groups. The president was nevertheless clearly determined to maintain his energetic and aggressive campaign. He continued to express his complete disdain for his Socialist rival, describing him as an indecisive lightweight, devoid of ideas, lacking charisma and energy – as 'l'énarque, le techno, le mou' – and, paradoxically, as the candidate

Table 8.9 *Results of presidential election, second round, 6 May 2012*

Candidate	Percentage share of vote
Hollande	51.63
Sarkozy	48.37

Plate 8.8 François Hollande and Nicolas Sarkozy during a televised debate at studios in La Plaine Saint-Denis, near Paris, 2 May 2012. Photo: Reuters/ France 2 Television/Handout.

of 'the system', a liar who would promise anything to win. Sarkozy's tactics were similar to those he had employed in destroying the image of Royal in 2007. His supporters were greatly encouraged by a televised debate on 27 April in which he appeared far more confident than a rather evasive Hollande, as well as by a carefully stage-managed mass rally at Villepinte during which he presented himself as a strong leader with a clear vision of 'la France forte'. His response to the murders at Toulouse and Montauban carried with it all the dignity and authority that might be expected from the president of the Republic. His essential problem was perceptions of his record in office – in comparison with the promises of 2007.

For the first time in a presidential election Paris supported the Socialist candidate, with 55.6 per cent of its votes. In spite of Hollande's apparent triumph, however, hints that all was not well were contained in a subsequent Ipsos MORI poll, which revealed that the dominant preoccupation of 55 per cent of Hollande's supporters was to remove Sarkozy, with only 45 per cent positively

Table 8.10 *Results of National Assembly election, second round, 17 June 2012[a]*

	Votes	Share (percentage of votes)	Seats
Socialists	9,420,889	40.9	280
UMP	8,740,628	38.0	194
Ecologist–Greens	829,036	3.6	17
Nouveau Centre	568,319	2.5	12
PRG[b]	538,331	2.3	12
Front de gauche	249,498	1.1	10
Parti radical	311,199	1.4	6
Front national	842,695	3.7	2
Alliance centriste	123,132	0.5	2
Centre pour la France	113,196	0.5	2
Other right-wing parties	417,940	1.8	15
Other left-wing parties	709,395	3.1	22
Others	165,050	0.7	3

Notes: [a] Results include thirty-six deputies elected in the first round, on 10 June.
[b] Parti radical de gauche.

inclined towards the Socialist candidate. In contrast, 54 per cent of Sarkozy's supporters had been absolutely determined to support him. Nevertheless, the initial Socialist victory was followed by success in the legislative election held in June.

The new Assembly would contain more women than its predecessor (25 per cent compared with 18), particularly amongst the Socialists. Although 40 per cent of deputies were newcomers, their average age was fifty-four. Moreover, 75 per cent of them would benefit from the controversial *cumul des mandats* by simultaneously holding local or regional mandates as well as national ones. The surprise of the second round was that it provided the Socialists with an absolute majority of their own and relieved them of the expected need to depend on the Greens and Front de gauche – the latter reduced from nineteen to ten seats (nine of them gained by the Communists). The Socialists also controlled the Senate, all but one of the twenty-two regions and much of local government. One discordant and slightly farcical note was sounded by the humiliating defeat in La Rochelle of an overconfident Royal – the 2007 presidential candidate, and former partner of Hollande – by a dissident socialist enjoying the tweeted support of the new president's current partner, the well-known journalist Valérie Trierweiler.

The erosion of support for the conservative UMP was particularly evident in the cities and their suburbs, and throughout the western half of the country (along the axis Le Havre–Perpignan). The party lost some of its leading figures, including Alliot-Marie, the former defence minister, and Claude Guéant, who had served as interior minister. Although Le Pen narrowly failed to win election in Hénin-Beaumont, where she had faced a deliberately symbolic challenge from Mélenchon and the Communist Party, as well as from an uninspiring – if ultimately successful – local representative of the Socialist Party, two members of her party – one of them her niece Marion Maréchal Le Pen – succeeded in the south. More significantly, and in spite of Fillon's warning about the fundamental incompatibility of their values, the perennial temptation amongst conservative candidates in difficulty of stressing the patriotic ideals they shared with the Front national was not always resisted. The continued collapse of the centre with the defeat of Bayrou was also evident,

Plate 8.9 Outgoing French president Nicolas Sarkozy and Carla Bruni-Sarkozy leave the Elysée Palace at the investiture of new French President François Hollande, 15 May 2012. Photo: © KeystoneUSA–ZUMA/Rex Features.

contributing to a process of political polarisation. More significantly, voter turnout in the second round was only 55.4 per cent, suggesting widespread scepticism concerning the political system and politicians in general, as well as indifference, particularly amongst the young.

In control, nevertheless, of the Chamber of Deputies and Senate, as well as, overwhelmingly, of regional and local government, the essential question was: what would the Socialists do with their victory?

CONCLUSION: AN INTERIM REPORT
ON THE SOCIALISTS IN POWER

The new president clearly realised that, following his inauguration on 15 May, his administration would face an unprecedented surge of problems. The situation in which the Socialist government found itself was extremely grave. The position of France as the world's fifth biggest economy was threatened by declining productivity, falling competitiveness, a growing deficit in international trade, rising state debt, high rates of long-term unemployment and the imminent danger of further job losses, together with the crisis in the Eurozone and the threat of global economic contraction, all pointing towards an urgent need for reforms of the kind promised by Sarkozy in 2007 but never effectively delivered. Failure to develop new economic and governmental models within France itself as well as in the wider European Union risked impoverishment, rising inequality and social tension. The viability of the much-vaunted French social model appeared to be threatened. The task appeared to be nothing less than the reinvention of social democracy.

A report presented on 5 November 2012 by Louis Gallois – the former chief executive of the EADS aerospace company – highlighted the rapid erosion of French competitiveness in a complex post-industrial and increasingly cut-throat globalised economy. In spite of the successes of major enterprises in aeronautics, food processing, nuclear power, communications and luxury goods, relative decline, as well as the accumulative process of deindustrialisation (with industrial output representing 22 per cent of value added in 1998 and 16 per cent by 2008), were particularly evident in comparison with Germany. The report blamed labour market inflexibility and the excessive costs imposed on enterprises by social charges; the low levels of labour productivity resulting from an excess of leisure and early retirement; insufficient investment in high technology and poor links between university research and development and business; the bureaucratic 'cult of regulation'; and the limited number and low capitalisation of small and medium-sized businesses. There was clearly an urgent need to stimulate a culture of innovation, and, rejecting a statist approach, Hollande promised to implement the report's proposals. Finally, a greater sense of urgency appeared to be developing. Once again, however, the key question was: would it be sustained?

In his inaugural speech the new president had committed himself to enhancing the effectiveness of government by re-establishing the Gaullist division of labour between the president, who determined priorities and appointed a prime minister and ministers, who were responsible for their implementation, and who would, he promised, enjoy much greater autonomy than his hyperactive predecessor had allowed. In making these appointments, and for the first time, a considerable effort was made to achieve gender parity amongst ministers – a difficult task given male dominance within the National Assembly. Following the peevish refusal of Aubry, disappointed at not becoming prime minister, to accept a lesser appointment, however, the only senior female minister would be Christine Taubira, a former Guyanese nationalist, to the Justice Ministry. Only four amongst the thirty-four ministers had previous experience of government. Their learning curve would be steep. Pressure from the financial markets and the political opposition, as well as the sense of expectancy evident amongst government supporters, ensured that the period of grace accorded to the new government would be extremely brief.

As prime minister, Hollande selected Jean-Marc Ayrault, a former teacher of German, who had served as the pragmatic, rather reserved and certainly uncharismatic leader of the Socialist parliamentary group since 1997, and as an effective mayor of Nantes. Other key figures included the more flashy former prime minister, Fabius, as foreign minister, committed to the complete withdrawal of combat troops from Afghanistan by the end of 2012 – two years sooner that previously agreed with the United States – and the equally ambitious Valls as an energetic interior minister reminiscent of a young Sarkozy. He too was an advocate of tough policing – convinced that even in the depressed 'quartiers oubliés de la République' there could be no excuse for delinquency and violence – as well as of more effective counter-terrorist legislation. The replacement of the director of counter-terrorist policing and of the Paris prefect of police, both judged to be too closely associated with Sarkozy, was indicative of the sensitivity of such issues and of an effort to avoid stigmatising Muslims and thereby encouraging the recruitment of home-grown terrorists – a matter of growing concern.

Pierre Moscovici, at the key Finance Ministry, would be responsible for increasing tax revenue and identifying economies. The government planned to reduce public expenditure from 56 per cent to 51 per cent of GDP by 2017, and to increase tax revenues by €72 billion – in addition to the €15 billion increase planned by the previous administration. This will undoubtedly administer a severe shock to a public ill-prepared by the populism and gesture politics favoured by both presidential candidates. The severity of the situation was further underlined by the discovery of a €10 billion shortfall in the accounts of the previous Fillon government, together with a report from the Inspection générale des Finances that suggested a need to realise economies of the order of €5 billion a year simply to achieve balance by 2017.

To reduce the impact on public services as well as on consumer confidence and economic growth, a 'redressement dans la justice' (rather than 'austerity') was proposed. This required an increased contribution by the 'rich' through higher taxes on wealth, inheritance and dividends, together with simplification of an extremely complex fiscal system in order to allow the closure of major tax loopholes. Increased taxation of the better off – with a rate of 45 per cent on earnings over €150,000, supplemented by an essentially symbolic temporary upper tax rate of 75 per cent to be imposed on the 3,000 individuals with incomes of over €1 million – was represented both as essential to fulfilling a commitment to the redistribution of wealth and as an equitable means of improving government funding. The 'indecent' remuneration of business leaders, who constantly demanded 'restraint' on the part of their employees, seemed unacceptable. The president and members of his government themselves accepted a 30 per cent reduction in their salaries.

Unsurprisingly, these measures provoked a storm of protest, combined with threats by those who saw themselves as the nation's major wealth creators to leave the country for the more welcoming climes of London, Geneva and Brussels. In the most-publicised case, the prime minister described the actor Gérard Depardieu's decision to seek Russian citizenship as 'pitiful'. The reactions of the foreign shareholders who held over 40 per cent of shares in the blue chip companies listed on the CAC 40 stock index were greater cause for concern. The man who at Le Bourget on 22 January had declared 'Mon adversaire, c'est la finance' also appeared determined to regulate the financial sector – which to be effective would require British and American as well as EU collaboration, in order to curb speculative activity and encourage more productive support for innovation, and particularly for small and medium-sized enterprises with the potential to create jobs. Hollande – a convinced European – was furthermore anxious to achieve a difficult renegotiation of the fiscal compact agreed by his predecessor with the German chancellor. Whilst accepting the urgent need for tighter financial discipline by means of a deflationary reduction in the government deficit to 3 per cent of GDP, the new president favoured a somewhat more gradual approach, in an effort to ensure that greater austerity did not tip the economy into an even more pronounced recession. He was also anxious to protect families on low incomes – although the increase in the minimum wage was limited to 2 per cent – as well as to accomplish his campaign commitment to create 65,000 new posts in the priority areas of education, justice and policing, with precedence accorded to the provision of nursery schools in deprived areas, to the better training of teachers and to equipping schools with information technology. Hollande had no intention of repeating the mistakes of previous Socialist administrations, however, which had, in 1981 at the beginning of the Mitterrand presidency, substantially increased expenditure or, during Jospin's and Fabius' *cohabitation* with President Chirac, sharply reduced taxes.

The proponents of austerity would nevertheless soon find themselves in conflict with Arnaud Montebourg, *ministre du redressement productif*, who was charged with ensuring an economic recovery but suspicious of the 'ultraliberal' advice given to the new administration by senior civil servants appointed by the Sarkozy government. As well as discussing the means of securing greater labour market flexibility with employers and trades unions, Montebourg would immediately attempt to prevent the planned lay-off of workers. In industries plagued by overproduction, however, including automobiles and steel, companies such as PSA Peugeot-Citroën and Arcelor Mittal were desperate to engage in restructuring in order to reduce costs. Although they were soon withdrawn, such gestures as the threat to nationalise a steel mill at Florange in Lorraine conveyed a sense of helplessness and did nothing to improve perceptions of the government amongst businessmen. The 'historic compromise' (Hollande) on 11 January 2013 between (some) unions and the employers' organisation (Medef), which should reduce labour market regulation, thus came as a surprise and provoked probably exaggerated optimism.

As could only be expected, aggressive attacks on the 'idiocy' of government policy poured from the conservative opposition. Fillon warned that its policies would result in 'social and economic catastrophe'. Hollande's support for gay marriage as a means of enhancing civil equality and of votes for foreigners (including many Muslims) in local elections, and his 'chasse des riches', further infuriated the 'peuple de droite' – including eminent Catholic spokesmen – and provoked a massive demonstration in Paris. Opposition was not without its own problems, however. As Sarkozy rapidly bowed out, recriminations began. Blame for defeat had to be apportioned, and a struggle over the succession commenced that threatened to fracture the unified conservative party once again into its centre-right and centrist elements. Sarkozy's focus on immigration, Islam and crime, and adoption of much of the discourse of the extreme right, together with the abandonment of the social Gaullism of the old RPR and of the social Christianity of the UDF, had already shifted the centre of gravity of conservatism to the right. Jean-François Copé, the UMP secretary-general and one of the two leading contenders for presidency of the party, rapidly adopted similar positions. Fillon, his rival – accused of having as prime minister weakly allowed himself to be manipulated by Sarkozy – risked being drawn to the right in a bitter and personal battle with Copé. The astringency of these divisions also encouraged some militants to look towards Juppé, the former foreign and prime minister, as a less divisive alternative, and, more seriously perhaps, to consider the prospect of a renewed Sarkozy candidature for the 2017 presidential election. Favoured at this stage in the proceedings by the opinion polls, a man who has lived for politics, who remains supremely self-confident and who is utterly contemptuous of the abilities of Hollande, as well as of his conservative rivals, might well be persuaded to dutifully abandon his comfortable retirement or at least to keep his options open and, with the support of the Association des Amis de Nicolas Sarkozy, make every effort not to be forgotten.

Public impatience and the apparent inaction of the Socialist government encouraged its critics. The completion of Hollande's first 100 days in power was marked on 12/13 August by two nights of violent protest in the popular *quartiers* of Amiens, which focused public attention on the scale of disaffection and the threats to social order posed by high and persistent unemployment, poor living conditions, educational failure, racial and social discrimination and police 'harassment'. Containing the threat posed by terrorism would

Plate 8.10 President Hollande reviews troops during a visit to a military base in Kapisa, Afghanistan, 25 May 2012. Photo: Joel Saget/AFP/Getty Images.

also absorb considerable energy and require a substantial investment of economic, police and military resources. The Commission sur la moralisation et la renovation de la vie politique, set up under the chairmanship of Jospin, might offer worthy suggestions on such important matters as ending the immunity from prosecution enjoyed by presidents whilst in office, on curbing the accumulation of local and national offices (the *cumul des mandats*), on election finance and on mediating conflicts of interest, but seemed unlikely to contribute much to restoring public confidence in politicians or interest in politics – in other words, to restoring the legitimacy of the state. Rapid and, at least initially, effective military action by the former colonial power in Mali, to stem a growing Islamist threat, briefly enhanced Hollande's reputation, but also reminded ministers of the constant risk of the unexpected.

France clearly faces major problems in preserving its prosperity, its social cohesion and its international status. There is a lack of consensus amongst politicians and economists on the solutions to current problems. The neoliberal answer to globalisation and to the increasing mobility of capital and labour has required business rationalisation, the privatisation of state assets, increased labour market flexibility and the reduction of non-wage (i.e. welfare) costs. Together with accelerating technological change – information technology, robotics, biotechnology – this has resulted in substantial gains in productivity and in national income and wealth, but at the same time in growing unemployment (expected to reach 11 per cent of the active population in 2013), insecurity, poverty and inequality, in a social divide between those with marketable skills and the unskilled, impoverished and excluded. Social legislation designed to protect the weak and to enhance social cohesion has come to be seen as an obstacle to the free working of the market. This is the new 'realism' so effectively promoted by international organisations such as the IMF and the OECD.

The *Etat-Providence*, the European social model developed after 1945, the product of a century of struggle, is under attack. Although, to a large degree, economic life remains embedded within national entities, the state's ability to manage the economy has been substantially weakened. Globalisation has massively enhanced the power of financial markets and of aggressive multi-national enterprises adept at avoiding taxation. National sovereignty, economic stability, cultural autonomy and even personal security are also threatened by the control over the diffusion of information exercised increasingly by Google, Amazon, Apple and Facebook. Internally, the main threat is posed by a coalition of conservative politicians and business interests enjoying the support of mass media owned by, or dependent for their advertising revenue on, major conglomerates and within which a small number of journalists/media personalities play a key role in 'informing' the public. The potential for profit is enormous. Substantial tax concessions – personal and corporate – have been presented as the essential incentives to enterprise, the necessary means of relaunching the economy. In the meantime the burden of taxation has been shifted more and more onto the lower-paid by the increasing use of indirect taxes to raise revenue. In the recent past privatisation offered state assets at attractive prices. The potential 'reinforcement' of social assistance by private insurance offers further lucrative possibilities. Symbolically, it would represent the growing commercialisation of every aspect of life.

Is there any alternative? In the immediate future much will depend on Hollande's ability and willingness to exercise his authority. Just like Chirac and Sarkozy, he has in the past proved reluctant to make difficult political decisions. Accusations of inaction and of a lack of coherence in government rapidly replaced the initial sense of expectancy. The Constitutional Council's unexpected rejection of the symbolic 75 per cent tax rate was an early blow to the president's self-esteem and the government's reputation. As it faces a complex of economic and social crises, it is too soon to judge the achievements of the Socialist administration elected in 2012, however. It will take time to implement the ambitious changes to which it appears to be committed. Effective intervention in the economy to increase productivity and competitiveness requires cooperation on the part of business leaders and employees, as well as a reduction in the scale, cost and sheer inertness of bureaucratic mechanisms. Nevertheless, collective guarantees of health and security ought to be defended on moral grounds and in the interests of democracy, or at the very least out of a self-interested concern to limit the growth of poverty and its companions – crime, social tension and conflict. There is substantial scope for the provision of socially useful employment in such areas as healthcare and education, which the market will never adequately provide. More generally, some degree of market regulation also needs to be reimposed to offset the insecurity caused by commercialisation and globalisation. The experience of the Socialist government in 1981, however, made it clear that no single state can hope to resist the pressures of the global market. Paradoxically, therefore, it is through the extension and strengthening of the European Union and of its social as well as economic dimensions – that is, through the further loss of national sovereignty – that the institutions and national identity of France can best be preserved and its further marginalisation on the world scene avoided.

In spite of the prosperity enjoyed by most of the population, a dangerous sense of malaise currently prevails. From this flows a perilous sense of alienation from the political system, with its constant internecine squabbles and the jockeying for position by leaders with presidential ambitions. Cocooned within comfortable surroundings and enjoying generous salaries and expense accounts, ministers, senators and deputies, as well as the newspaper and television journalists, and contributors to blogs and tweets, with whom they opportunistically interact, often appear out of touch to the wider public.

Public interest in politics, as a means of expressing moral values, and measured in terms of membership of political parties and trades unions or of social movements committed to ecology or feminism, or even by newspaper readership, has clearly declined. Disillusionment with the political system is widespread. The electorate remains volatile. The weakness of the National Assembly, the blurring of ideological differences and the shared liberal consensus on so many economic and social issues have left mass demonstrations or support for the political extremes as the only means available to many people of protesting against a system that appears to be letting them down. This sense of alienation applies in particular to the younger generations, faced with high levels of unemployment and diminishing prospects. French Muslims are also increasingly concerned by the official rejection of multiculturalism and demands for the assimilation of Muslims into the French 'mainstream' through the secular education system. Whilst it is necessary to encourage the development of a shared sense of community amongst all the ethnic groups occupying the same social space, greater emphasis might be placed on mutual tolerance, esteem for the individual, and respect for democratic processes.

In spite of these serious problems, the system of presidential government originally built upon the ruins of the Fourth Republic seems likely to survive, and with it the basic commitment to 'republican order', to a liberal-democratic political structure and to a welfare-orientated social model, within a fundamentally capitalistic, market-orientated economic system. A strong sense of national identity will continue to be expressed, whilst political leaders seek to influence the development of the European Union in the French interest. Short of a major international crisis – and there are potential causes aplenty – it seems likely that the French economy will continue to adapt to the opportunities and challenges of both the Single European Market and wider globalisation, and to changes in the international division of labour. In intensely competitive markets and in the face of the heightened competition for capital, oil and industrial raw materials induced by the rapid development of the Chinese and Indian economies, as well as the insatiable and predatory capitalism of the United States, this will not be without difficulty. Most of the population nevertheless seems destined to enjoy growing prosperity whilst, at the same time, adapting to greater insecurity and more stressful working conditions. There remains considerable potential for conflict, however, over unequal access to political power, to educational and employment opportunities and to wealth, whilst the hideous tensions caused by racial and cultural differences and terrorism retain their potency. There is thus nothing inevitable about rising prosperity. A previous period of globalisation in the nineteenth century was brought to an end eventually by protectionism and war. Every social system is subject to stress and to unpredictable pressures; we must earnestly hope that those who possess power, operating within an effective system of governance, will mitigate their impact.

A SHORT GUIDE TO FURTHER READING

This bibliography is designed essentially for English-language readers.

Readers of English might also usefully refer to the following journals: *French History*; *French Historical Studies*; *French Politics*; *French Politics, Culture and Society*; *Contemporary French Civilisation*; and *Modern and Contemporary France*. *H-France* is the most appropriate website.

GENERAL

Clout, H. D. (ed.), *Themes in the Historical Geography of France*. London, 1977.

Gildea, R., *The Past in French History*. London, 1994.

Jones, C., *Paris: Biography of a City*. London, 2006.

THE MIDDLE AGES

Allmand, C., *The Hundred Years War*. Cambridge, 1988

(ed.), *Power, Culture and Religion in France, 1350–1550*. Woodbridge, 1989.

Baldwin, J., *The Government of Philip Augustus*. Berkeley, CA, 1991.

Paris, 1200. Stanford, CA, 2010.

Bisson, T. (ed.), *Cultures of Power: Lordship, Status and Process in Twelfth-Century Europe*. Philadelphia, 1995.

Bouchard, C., *'Strong of Body, Brave and Noble': Chivalry and Society in Medieval France*. Ithaca, NY, 1998.

Bull, M. (ed.), *France in the Central Middle Ages*. Oxford, 2002.

Duby, G., *France in the Middle Ages 987–1460*. London, 1991.

Dunbabin, J., *France in the Making 843–1180*. Oxford, 2000.

Gaposchkin, M., *The Making of Saint Louis: Kingship, Sanctity, and Crusade in the Later Middle Ages*. Ithaca, NY, 2008.

Grant, L., *Abbot Suger of Saint-Denis: Church and State in Early Twelfth-Century France*. London, 1998.

Hallam, E., and Everard, J., *Capetian France 987–1328*. London, 2001.

Pegg, M., *A Most Holy War: The Albigensian Crusade and the Battle for Christendom*. Oxford, 2008.

Power, D., *The Norman Frontier in the 12th and Early 13th Centuries*. Cambridge, 2004.

Roux, S., *Fiefs and Vassals: The Medieval Evidence Reinterpreted*. Oxford, 1998.

Paris in the Middle Ages. Philadelphia, 2009.

Skoda, H., *Medieval Violence: Physical Brutality in Northern France, 1270–1330*. Oxford, 2013.

Sumption, J., *The Hundred Years War, 3 vols*. London, 1999–2009.

EARLY MODERN FRANCE

Beik, W., *A Social and Cultural History of Early Modern France*. Cambridge, 2009.

Bell, D., *Lawyers and Citizens: The Making of a Political Elite in Old Regime France*. Oxford, 1994.

Benedict, P., *Cities and Social Change in Early Modern France*. London, 1989.

Bergin, J., *The Rise of Richelieu*. London, 1991.

Church, Society and Religious Change in France, 1580–1730. London, 2009.

Briggs, R., *Communities of Belief: Cultural and Social Tensions in Early Modern France*. Oxford, 1989.

Burke, P., *The Fabrication of Louis XIV*. London, 1992.

Campbell, P., *Power and Politics in Old Regime France, 1720–45*. London, 1996.

Censer, J., *The French Press in the Age of the Enlightenment*. London, 1994.

Collins, J., *The State in Early Modern France*. Cambridge, 1995.

Darnton, R., *The Devil in the Holy Water, or the Art of Slander from Louis XIV to Napoleon*. Philadelphia, 2010.

Davis, N. Z., *Society and Culture in Early Modern France*. Stanford, CA, 1975.

Dee, D., *Expansion and Crisis in Louis XIV's France: Franche-Comté and Absolute Monarchy, 1674–1715*. Rochester, NY, 2009.

Dewald, J., *Aristocratic Experience and the Origins of Modern Culture*. Berkeley, CA, 1993.

Diefendorf, B., *Beneath the Cross: Catholics and Huguenots in Sixteenth-Century Paris*. New York, 1991.

Doyle, W., *Venality: The Sale of Offices in Eighteenth-Century France*. Oxford, 1996.

Greengrass, M., *Governing Passions: Peace and Reform in the French Kingdom, 1576–85*, Oxford, 2007.

Gruder, V., *The Notables and the Nation: The Political Schooling of the French, 1787–88*, Cambridge, MA, 2007.

Hardman, J., *Overture to Revolution: The 1787 Assembly of Notables and the Crisis of France's Old Regime*. Oxford, 2010.

Hoffman, P., *Growth in a Traditional Society: The French Countryside, 1450–1815*. Princeton, NJ, 1996.

Holt, M., *The French Wars of Religion, 1562–1629*. Cambridge, 1995.
(ed.), *Renaissance and Reformation France*. Oxford, 2002.

Hufton, O., *The Poor in Eighteenth-Century France*. Oxford, 1974.

Jones, C., *The Great Nation: France from Louis XV to Napoleon*. London, 2003.

Jones, P. *Reform and Revolution in France: The Politics of Transition*. Cambridge, 1995.

Knecht, R., *The French Civil Wars, 1562–1598*. London, 2000.
The French Renaissance Court. London, 2008.

Lynn, J., *The Wars of Louis XIV*. London, 1999.

Major, J. R., *From Renaissance Monarchy to Absolute Monarchy: French Kings, Nobles and Estates*. Baltimore, 1994.

McManners, J., *Church and Society in Eighteenth-Century France, 2 vols*. Oxford, 1998.

Parrott, D., *Richelieu's Army: War, Government and Society in France, 1624–42*. Cambridge, 2001.

Pitts, V., *Henri IV of France*, Baltimore, 2012.

Potter, D., *Renaissance France at War: Armies, Culture and Society, c.1480–1560*, Woodbridge, 2008.

Ranum, O., *The Fronde: A French Revolution, 1648–1652*. New York, 1993.

Riley, J., *The Seven Years War and the Old Regime in France: The Economic and Financial toll*. Princeton, NJ, 1996.

Roche, D., *A History of Everyday Things: The Birth of Consumption in France, 1600–1800*. Cambridge, 2000.

Stone, B., *The French Parlements and the Crisis of the Old Regime*. Chapel Hill, NC, 1986.

Swann, J., *Politics and the Parlement of Paris under Louis XV, 1754–74*. Cambridge, 1995.

Swann, J., and Félix, J. (eds.), *The Crisis of the Absolute Monarchy*. Oxford, 2013.

Wolfe, M., *The Conversion of Henri IV: Politics, Power, and Religious Belief in Early Modern France*. Cambridge, MA, 1993.

Wood, J., *The King's Army: Warfare, Soldiers and Society during the Wars of Religion in France, 1562–1576*. Cambridge, 1996.

REVOLUTIONARY AND NAPOLEONIC FRANCE

Alexander, R., *Napoleon*, London, 2001.

Andress, D., *The Terror: Civil War in the French Revolution*, London, 2006.

Aston, N., *Religion and Revolution in France, 1780–1804*. London, 2000.

Baczko, B., *Ending the Terror: The French Revolution after Robespierre*. Cambridge, 1994.

Brown, H., and Miller, J. (eds.), *Taking Liberties: Problems of a New Order from the French Revolution to Napoleon.* Manchester, 2002.

Campbell, P. (ed.), *The Origins of the French Revolution.* London, 2006.

Chickering, R., and Förster, S. (eds.), *War in an Age of Revolution, 1775–1815.* Cambridge, 2010.

Cobb, R., *The Police and the People: French Popular Protest 1789–1820.* Oxford, 1970.

Crook, M., *Elections in the French Revolution.* Cambridge, 1996.

(ed.), *Revolutionary France, 1788–1880.* Oxford, 2001.

Doyle, W., *The Oxford History of the French Revolution.* Oxford, 1989.

The Origins of the French Revolution. Oxford, 1999.

Aristocracy and Its Enemies in the Age of Revolution. Oxford, 2009.

Dwyer, P., and Forrest, A. (eds.), *Napoleon and His Empire, 1804–14.* London, 2007.

Fitzsimmons, M., *The Night the Old Regime Ended: August 4 1789.* Philadelphia, 2003.

Forrest, A., *The Soldiers of the French Revolution.* Durham, NC, 1990.

Paris, the Provinces and the French Revolution. London, 2004.

Garrioch, D., *The Making of Revolutionary Paris.* Berkeley, CA, 2002.

Gough, H., *The Terror in the French Revolution.* London, 1998.

Jennings, J., *Revolution and the Republic: A History of Political Thought in France since the 18th century.* Cambridge, 2011.

Jones, P., *The Peasantry in the French Revolution.* Cambridge, 1988.

Lewis, G., and Lucas, C. (eds.), *Beyond the Terror: Essays in French Regional and Social History, 1794–1815.* Cambridge, 1983.

Lyons, M., *France under the Directory.* Cambridge, 1975.

Markoff, J., *The Abolition of Feudalism: Peasants, Lords and Legislators in the French Revolution.* Philadelphia, 1996.

McPhee, P., *Living the French Revolution,* London, 2006.

Robespierre: A Revolutionary Life. London, 2012.

Popkin, J., *Revolutionary News: The Press in France, 1789–99.* Durham, NC, 1990.

Sutherland, D., *The French Revolution and Empire: The Quest for a Civic Order.* Oxford, 2003.

Tackett, T., *Religion, Revolution, and Regional Culture in Eighteenth-Century France: The Ecclesiastical Oath of 1791.* Princeton, NJ, 1986.

Becoming a Revolutionary: The Deputies of the French National Assembly and the Emergence of a Revolutionary Culture, 1789–90. Philadelphia, 1996.

When the King Took Flight. Cambridge, MA, 2004.

Woloch, I., *The New Regime: Transformations of the French Civic Order, 1789–1820s.* New York, 1994.

Napoleon and His Collaborators: The Making of a Dictatorship. New York, 2001.

THE NINETEENTH CENTURY

Agulhon, M., *The Republican Experiment, 1848–52.* Cambridge, 1983.
Collingham, H., *The July Monarchy.* London, 1988.
Gibson, R., *A Social History of French Catholicism.* London, 1989.
Harris, R., *The Man on Devil's Island: Alfred Dreyfus and the Affair that Divided France.* London, 2010.
Harvey, D., *Paris, Capital of modernity,* London, 2005.
Hazareesingh, S., *From Subject to Citizen: The Second Empire and the Emergence of French Democracy.* Princeton, NJ, 1998.
  (ed.), *The Jacobin Legacy in Modern France: Essays in Honour of Vincent Wright.* Oxford, 2002.
  The Legend of Napoleon. London, 2005.
Heywood, C., *The Development of the French Economy, 1750–1914.* Cambridge, 1992.
Lehning, J., *To Be a Citizen: The Political Culture of the Early Third Republic.* Ithaca, NY, 2001.
Magraw, R., *France 1815–1914: The Bourgeois Century.* London, 1992.
  A History of the French Working Class, 2 vols. Oxford, 1992.
McMillan, J., *France and Women 1789–1914: Gender, Society and Politics.* London, 2000.
  (ed.), *Modern France, 1880–2002.* Oxford, 2003.
Pilbeam, P., *Republicanism in Nineteenth-Century France.* London, 1999.
Pinkney, D., *The French Revolution of 1830.* Princeton, NJ, 1972.
Porch, D., *The March to the Marne: The French Army, 1871–1914.* Cambridge, 1981.
Price, R., *The French Second Republic: A Social History.* Ithaca, NY, 1972.
  The Modernization of Rural France. London, 1983.
  A Social History of Nineteenth-Century France. London, 1987.
  The French Second Empire: An Anatomy of Political Power. Cambridge, 2001.
  People and Politics in France, 1848–1870. Cambridge, 2004.
Tombs, R., *The War against Paris, 1871.* Cambridge, 1981.
  France, 1814–1914. London, 1996.
  The Paris Commune, 1871. London, 1999.
Wawro, G., *The Franco-Prussian War.* Cambridge, 2003.

A TIME OF CRISIS: 1914–1945

Adamthwaite, A., *Grandeur and Misery: France's Bid for Power in Europe 1914–40.* London, 1995.
Becker, J.-J., *The Great War and the French People.* Oxford, 1986.
Bernard, P., and Dubief, H., *The Decline of the Third Republic 1914–38.* Cambridge, 1985.

Boyce, R. (ed.), *French Foreign and Defence Policy 1918–40*. London, 1998.
Cobb, M., *The Resistance: The French Fight against the Nazis*. London, 2009.
Diamond, H., *Fleeing Hitler: France 1940*. Oxford, 2007.
Dombrowski, N., *France under Fire: German Invasion, Civilian Flight and Family Survival during World War II*. Cambridge, 2012.
Gildea, R., *Marianne in Chains: In Search of the German Occupation 1940–45*. London, 2002.
Graham, B., *Choice and Democratic Order: The French Socialist Party, 1937–50*. Cambridge, 1994.
Horne, J. (ed.), *State, Society and Mobilization during the First World War*. Cambridge, 1997.
Jackson, J., *The Popular Front in France: Defending Democracy, 1934–38*. Cambridge, 1988.
  France: The Dark Years. Oxford, 2001.
  The Fall of France: The Nazi Invasion of 1940. Oxford, 2003.
Jackson, P., *France and the Nazi Menace: Intelligence and Policy-Making 1933–39*. Oxford, 2000.
Keiger, J., *France and the Origins of the First World War*. London, 1983.
Kedward, R., *Resistance in Vichy France*. Oxford, 1978.
  In Search of the Maquis: Rural Resistance in France. Oxford, 1993.
Martin, B., *Years of Plenty, Years of Want: France and the Legacy of the Great War*. DeKalb, IL, 2013.
Nord, P., *France's New Deal: From the Thirties to the Postwar Era*. Princeton, NJ, 2010.
Passmore, K., *From Liberalism to Fascism: The Right in a French Province, 1928–39*. Cambridge, 1997.
Paxton, R., *Vichy France: Old Guard and New Order*. New York, 1982.
Prost, A., *In the Wake of War: 'Les Anciens Combattants' and French Society*. Oxford, 1992.
Rearick, C., *The French in Love and War: Popular Culture in the Era of the World Wars*. New Haven, CT, 1997.
Shennan, A., *The Fall of France*. London, 2000.
Sherman, D., *The Construction of Memory in Interwar France*. Chicago, 1999.
Smith, L., Audoin-Rouzeau, S., and Becker, A., *France and the Great War, 1914–18*. Cambridge, 2003.
Sweets, J., *Choices in Vichy France: The French under Nazi Occupation*. Oxford, 1986.
Vinen, R., *The Unfree French: Life under the Occupation*. London, 2006.
Wall, I., *French Communism in the Era of Stalin*. Westport, CT, 1983.

RECONSTRUCTION AND RENEWAL: THE TRENTE GLORIEUSES

Bell, D., *The French Communist Party in the Fifth Republic*. Oxford, 1994.
Berstein, S., *The Republic of de Gaulle, 1958–69*. Cambridge, 1993.

Evans, M., *Algeria: France's Undeclared War*. Oxford, 2011.

Fenby, J., *The General: Charles de Gaulle and the France He Saved*. London, 2010.

Gildea, R., *France since 1945*. Oxford, 1996.

Gordon, P., *A Certain Idea of France: French Security Policy and the Gaullist Legacy*. Princeton, NJ, 1993.

Gough, H., and Horne, J. (eds.), *De Gaulle and Twentieth-Century France*. London, 1994.

Hazareesingh, S., *In the Shadow of the General: Modern France and the Myth of de Gaulle*. Oxford, 2012.

Hewlett, N., *Modern French Politics: Analysing Conflict and Consensus since 1945*. Oxford, 1998.

Hitchcock, W., *France Restored: Cold War Diplomacy and the Quest for Leadership in Europe, 1944–54*. Chapel Hill, NC, 1998.

House, J., and Macmaster, N., *Paris 1961: Algerians, State Terror, and Memory*. Oxford, 2006.

Lorcin, P., *Imperial Identities: Stereotyping, Prejudice and Race in Colonial Algeria*. London, 1995.

Pulju, R., *Women and Mass Consumer Society in Postwar France*. Cambridge, 2011.

Rioux, J.-P., *The Fourth Republic 1944–58*. Cambridge, 1987.

Rioux, J-P., and Berstein, S., *The Pompidou Years, 1969–74*. Cambridge, 2000.

Talbot, J., *The War without a Name: France in Algeria, 1954–62*. New York, 1981.

Vinen, R., *France, 1934–1970*. London, 1996.

Wall, I., *American Influence in France 1944–54*. Cambridge, 1991.

A SOCIETY UNDER STRESS

Bell, D., and Criddle, B., *The French Socialist Party: Emergence of a Party of Government*. Oxford, 1987.

Cole, A., *François Mitterrand: A Study in Political Leadership*. London, 1994.

Daley, A. (ed.), *The Mitterrand Era: Policy Alternatives and Political Mobilization in France*. New York, 1996.

Drake, H., *Contemporary France*, London, 2011.

Elgie, R., *Political Institutions in Contemporary France*. Oxford, 2003.

Fenby, J., *On the Brink: The Trouble with France*. London, 2002.

Gaffney, J., *French Presidentialism and the Election of 1995*. Aldershot, 1997.

Gordon, P., and Meunier, S., *The French Challenge: Adapting to Globalization*. New York, 2001.

Jackson, J., Milne, A.-L., and Williams, J., *May 68. Rethinking France's Last Revolution*. London, 2011.

Laughland, J., *The Death of Politics: France under Mitterrand*. London, 1994.

Goodliffe, G., *The Resurgence of the Radical Right in France: From Boulangisme to the Front National.* Cambridge, 2012.

Gregory, A., and Todd, U. (eds.), *Women in Contemporary France.* Oxford, 2000.

Hanley, D., *Party, Society, Government: Republican Democracy in France.* Oxford, 2002.

Keeler, J., and Schain, M. (eds.), *Chirac's Challenge: Liberalization, Europeanization and Malaise in France.* London, 1996.

McMillan, J. (ed.), *Modern France.* Oxford, 2003.

Rosanvallon, P., *The New Social Question: Rethinking the Welfare State.* Princeton, NJ, 2000.

Ross, G., Hoffman, S., and Malzacher, S. (eds.), *The Mitterrand Experiment: Continuity and Change in Modern France.* Cambridge, 1987.

Sa'adah, A., *Contemporary France: A Democratic Education.* Oxford, 2003.

Simmons, H., *The French National Front.* Boulder, CO, 1996.

INDEX

CAMBRIDGE CONCISE HISTORIES

Titles in the series:

CPSIA information can be obtained
at www.ICGtesting.com
Printed in the USA
LVHW060111090723
751827LV00003B/38